A BUYER'S GUIDE TO THE

RARE COIN MARKET

Q. David Bowers

A BUYER'S GUIDE TO THE

RARE COIN MARKET

Q. David Bowers

Published by
Bowers and Merena Galleries, Inc.
Box 1224 Wolfeboro, NH 03894

About the Author

Q. David Bowers has been a rare coin dealer since 1953. A 1960 graduate of the Pennsylvania State University, he received that institution's Distinguished Alumnus Award in 1976.

Bowers has written over three dozen books and has been the recipient of more Book of the Year Award honors given by the Numismatic Literary Guild than any other author. Such works as *The History of U.S. Coinage* (written for The Johns Hopkins University), *Adventures With Rare Coins, Coins and Collectors, U.S. Gold Coins: An Illustrated History, High Profits From Rare Coin Investment, The Strange Career of Dr. Wilkins*, and a series of "Action Guides," among many other titles, have been widely acclaimed. He was commissioned by the ANA Board of Governors to write *The ANA Centennial History*, a work of over 1,000 pages in length to be published for the 1891-1991 anniversary of the ANA. His columns, "Numismatic Depth Study" in *Coin World* and "Coins and Collectors" in *The Numismatist*, appear regularly.

The author is the only person to have held the highest offices of both the American Numismatic Association (president 1983-1985) and the Professional Numismatists Guild (president 1977-1979). He is a recipient of the highest honor given by the PNG, the Founders' Award, and of the ANA Medal of Merit.

Bowers and Merena Galleries, Inc. and Auctions by Bowers and Merena, Inc., owned by Q. David Bowers and Raymond N. Merena, have handled many of the greatest collections to come on the market, including the most valuable collection ever auctioned, the $25 million Garrett Collection sold for The Johns Hopkins University, the second most valuable collection ever sold, the $20 million Norweb Collection, and many more, among which the Eliasberg Collection of U.S. Gold Coins, the Virgil Brand Estate sales, and others are an indelible part of numismatic history.

Contents

Acknowledgements 6

Introduction 7

CHAPTER 1.   Connoisseurship 11

CHAPTER 2.   Collectors and Investors 29

CHAPTER 3.   Have a Plan 43

CHAPTER 4.   Dealing With Dealers 57

CHAPTER 5.   Coins and Wall Street 73

CHAPTER 6.   Auctions and Mail Bid Sales 95

CHAPTER 7.   Mints and Minting 113

CHAPTER 8.   Determinants of Value 119

CHAPTER 9.   Grading 123

CHAPTER 10. Grades and Prices 149

CHAPTER 11. Purchase Recommendations 179

CHAPTER 12. Copper and Nickel Coins 185

CHAPTER 13. Silver Coins 209

CHAPTER 14. Gold Coins 253

CHAPTER 15. Commemoratives 273

CHAPTER 16. Other Collecting Areas 279

CHAPTER 17. Maximizing the Rewards 295

Notes 311

Glossary 329

Index 357

Acknowledgements

Many of my ideas and topics have been taken from conversations, correspondence, and transactions with clients over a long period of years. Additional material came from the All About Coins course I gave for a number of years at the American Numismatic Association Summer Seminars and from the Introduction to Numismatics course given by my business associate, Raymond N. Merena, not to overlook conversations with Dr. Richard A. Bagg, Jennifer Douglass, Michael Hodder, Mark Borckardt, Liz Arlin, Andrew W. Pollock III, Frank Van Valen, and other members of the Bowers and Merena organization. Other topics have been developed especially for inclusion in the present work, and still others have been adapted from my "Numismatic Depth Study" column in *Coin World* and my "Coins and Collectors" column in *The Numismatist*. Above all, the philosophies are based on much practical experience as a professional coin dealer and as an observer of the numismatic scene.

Mrs. Beth Deisher, editor of *Coin World*, gave permission to include data from the "Trends" section of that periodical, conducted by Keith Zaner, and other information, including items which appeared on the opinion and letters to the editor pages. A rereading of issues of *Coin World* printed in recent years reminded me that an entire shelf of books could be written by utilizing the wealth of information that has appeared in that publication alone.

Bob Wilhite, editor of *Numismatic News*, gave permission to include data from the "Coin Market" section of that paper and editorial comments. Appreciation is also expressed to Ron Downing, owner of the *Coin Dealer Newsletter* and the *Certified Coin Dealer Newsletter*, and to Dennis Baker and Robert Korver of the same publishing organization for numerous ideas gleaned from conversations and from reading their weekly market guides. David L. Ganz, Phoebe Morse, and Donn Pearlman made valuable suggestions. Thanks also to the various individuals quoted in the present text, including James L. Halperin, who gave permission to quote from his book, *How to Grade U.S. Coins*.

Raymond N. Merena made many valuable suggestions. Mark Borckardt shared his observations after reading page proofs of the work. Chris Karstedt reviewed the book in its draft stage and furnished ideas. Mary K. Valley, my secretary, assisted with correspondence and research notes during the preparation of the present volume.

Typography and layout of this book represent the work of the Bowers and Merena Graphic Arts Department, including Lee Lilljedahl, Roberta French, Judy Bouchard, William Winter, Linda Heilig, Jennifer Rose, John Maltzie, and Jennifer Meers.

Introduction

Recently I received a call from a gentleman in Connecticut. The owner of an international company, he had achieved great success in the business world. An advertisement in *The Wall Street Journal* offering a $20 gold coin for sale had caught his eye, and he was considering buying it. However, a friend who was a client of our firm suggested that he contact me first, which he did.

"Tell me about coins. I find coins to be incredibly interesting, but how do I get started? How do I know which ones to buy? What makes a coin valuable?"

Others have inquired about the same things. From such conversations a germ of an idea grew. Why not write a book for the person who is interested in rare coins for collecting or investment, but who is not familiar with the field? Why not write a buyer's guide to aid people unfamiliar with the seemingly complex market for rare coins?

This book, then, is for the gentleman in Connecticut and for others who have asked questions, as well as for anyone else who wants to learn more about how to advantageously buy coins which are choice, rare, and interesting to own. Get set to read some contrary opinions, for I will do my best to tell it like it is.

The coin market may be unique among areas of collectibles, antiques, and investments. More than any other field which I have ever studied (and I am familiar with quite a few), the coin market is characterized by much self-criticism. All one has to do is read the letters to the editor columns in *Coin World* and *Numismatic News* to see numerous complaints, suggestions for improvement, and other evidences that the market as presently constituted is not ideal to a large number of people. Similarly, the *Certified Coin Dealer Newsletter*, the *Rosen Numismatic Advisory*, and other well-respected newsletters and market reports often detail flaws in the coin trading system, such as the lack of support for bid levels, problems of grading, differences of opinion, etc. Of course, these journals print much good and uplifting news, too.

Contrast that with the field of art and antiques. Most of the leading publications concentrate on publishing news of museum exhibits, auction results, the contents of public and private collections, and the like, with very little space devoted to dealer practices, market ups and downs, investment profits and losses, grading and evaluation, margins of profit, fakes and forgeries, etc. (A notable exception is *The Maine Antique Digest*, edited by Samuel C. Pennington and published in Waldoboro, Maine; this monthly journal prints information which is incredibly realistic and useful.)

In the securities industry the vast majority of newsletters tell people what to buy and issue glowing reports on various companies, but devote a very small percentage of space to negative aspects such as bankruptcies, the over touting of stocks, etc. Few people buying stocks can get much in the way of truly candid information until it is too late to do anything about it.

In a way the "tell it like it is" philosophy in the coin market has benefits for the collector or investor entering the field, for numerous warning flags are there to be readily seen. On the other hand, it is easy to become discouraged when confronted with negative information.

Balancing the negative information are many positive philosophies which make their way into print, but often these are in the form of hype—encouragement to buy one particular coin variety or another, or to invest in this or that hot item. It is difficult to combat the almighty vested interest. More difficult to find is basic information about buying coins for the pure joy of owning them and the pleasures afforded by being involved in the numismatic hobby (or *industry*, as many have called it in recent years).[1]

I suggest that the problems in the coin market are sufficiently well defined that anyone reading this present book or reading leading numismatic periodicals such as *Coin World* and *Numismatic News* can learn of them readily, but that such problems are no worse than those in other fields, and are probably much less than the problems an uninformed buyer would find in such investment areas as art, the stock market (in particular), and real estate.

I encourage each reader of the present book to develop a positive attitude and to use the words I have to say, and the quotations of others, as a jumping off spot for a truly rewarding experience in numismatics. Having been a rare coin dealer since 1953, I can say without hesitation that dealing with countless thousands of collectors and dealers over the years has been very enjoyable. I doubt if anyone in any other profession is happier than I am in mine.

The basic premise of this book is that collecting or investing in coins can be a very enjoyable and financially rewarding pastime, but that for best results a buyer should obtain basic knowledge before making purchases. That knowledge is essential is a philosophy which has appeared in print numerous times since the last century, and is echoed by numerous people quoted in the pages to follow, many of whom are leaders in the field of numismatics. For years the emblem of the American Numismatic Association depicted the Lamp of Knowledge. The motto of the Professional Numismatists Guild is "Knowledge, Integrity, Responsibility." I didn't invent the idea.

This book contains no high-minded theories, nor is it intended to sell you anything. Whether your numismatic preferences are Franklin half dollars,

Introduction

twenty-cent pieces, large cents, or $20 gold coins is up to you. No matter where you buy coins, and no matter what series you would like to acquire, my hope is that this book will enable you to buy more intelligently and to obtain a better value for each dollar you spend.

United States and related coins provide the focus for this book. Currency notes, world coins, ancient coins, and other series are interesting and important parts of numismatics and are mentioned in passing but are not treated in detail in the present study.

The experiences related are my own or ones with which I am familiar. The opinions given are mine, and those of others may differ. The activities and policies of certain firms with which I am associated—notably Bowers and Merena Galleries, Inc., Auctions by Bowers and Merena Galleries, Inc. and our subsidiary, Kingswood Galleries—are discussed here and there throughout the book. I could have avoided this and could have created "composite" or theoretical examples, but I suspect that the average reader of the present work prefers me to share information on subjects of which I have specific knowledge. Such information is factual. It is real. It happened.

To satisfy the reader who seeks my opinions concerning how to buy coins and what coins and series I consider to be good values, I have included, beginning with an explanation in Chapter 11, recommendations for three classes of buyers for each major U.S. rare coin category:

• **Budget Recommendations:** Suggestions for the cost-conscious buyer.

• • **Recommendations for the Connoisseur:** Ideas for the individual who wants a combination of high quality and excellent value for the price paid.

• • • **Elite Recommendations:** Possibilities for the buyer for whom cost is not a major consideration.

While in the past it has been true that selected rare coins have been superb investments, the future is unknown, and no one has ever been able to accurately predict what will happen.

In my opinion there are many wonderful opportunities available to today's alert, well informed buyer. In this regard I believe you will really enjoy the last chapter in this book. It is my hope that by reading the following pages you will become one of the best informed people in the hobby (industry?) today.

— Q. David Bowers

CHAPTER ONE

Connoisseurship

Today's Coin Buyer

Why collect coins? Or, why *acquire* coins? (Some buyers do not *collect* coins; they simply buy or accumulate them.)

Ask a dozen different buyers this question, and you will receive a dozen different answers. Samples:

"I heard that coins are a good investment."

"I want something to do in my spare time, and I think collecting coins would be a good idea."

"I inherited a 1908 $5 gold piece from my grandfather, and I became interested in numismatics when I sought to learn its history and value."

"I received a telephone call at my office, and the person on the other end of the line told me that I would make a lot of money if I bought coins, so I sent him a check for $35,000, and I am expecting a package shortly."

"I have been looking for a high-grade 1846-O Liberty Seated dollar for over five years, and the MS-60 piece you quoted to me is just what I want."

Coins are the footprints of history, it has been said, and without question it is interesting to hold history in your hand. Whenever I see a Morgan silver dollar with a CC mintmark, minted in the 1880s, I can conjure up in my imagination a vision of Carson City, Nevada in the rough and ready days of the Wild West, of miners working underground to take precious silver ore from the Comstock Lode, and of the main street of nearby Virginia City, with its saloons, gambling parlors, red-light district, and perhaps even a shootout between the sheriff and an outlaw. I almost forgot to mention Mark Twain (Samuel Clemens), who early in his career in the 1860s was on the staff of the *Territorial Enterprise*, the local newspaper.[1]

However, even if coins are the stuff of which nostalgic and romantic dreams are made, the inescapable fact is that most buyers of coins are in the game for the money (no pun intended). While an 1882-CC Morgan dollar might for me stir up notions of a bygone era, the typical buyer of such a coin sees it as a store of value, an item to buy today with the hope that down the line it can be sold for a profit. Whether the coin will yield an investment return seems to be a more timely and important question than whether this very same silver dollar once figured in a Saturday night poker game in Virginia City. As a professional numismatist I realize that a basic precept of business success is that I must give my customers what they want. This thinking is sound, and doubtless most successful businessmen in any field become that way by responding to the desires of those who trade with them. So it is with rare coins. Collecting and investing trends change, markets and conditions change, and clients' requests change. Customers of the 1990s will seek different things from what buyers of the 1970s and 1980s wanted.

Slabs

Who would have dreamed as recently as five years ago that sonically sealed certified coins ("slabs") would occupy such a prominent position in the marketplace, and that many buyers (particularly those who are beginners) would believe that whatever is marked on a slab is gospel? It used to be that the dealer had some responsibility with his clients, but now it seems that the dealer can point to a slab and say, "Take it or leave it." Few customers complain about grading if the coin is in a slab.

A coin can be extremely ugly, but if it is in a slab marked MS-65, it finds a ready sale. In the early 1980s, before slabs were a factor in the marketplace, a dealer selling the very same coin unslabbed would probably be met with this comment: "The coin is ugly, and I don't want it." Now, coin buyers sometimes feel a sense of guilt if they *don't* like a slabbed coin! It is almost as if they are challenging the very precepts of what coin investment is all about, and few newcomers to the field are brave enough to do that! Of course, this is utter nonsense, and if someone doesn't like a coin, he should not buy it. I certainly wouldn't buy I coin if I didn't like it. Why should you?

I would be remiss if I didn't state at the outset that there are many beautiful coins mounted in slabs. However, among the petunias there are some onions as well. Slabs seem to legitimize overgrading and ugliness. However, for the dealer selling them, encapsulated coins can be a source of significant profits. Currently the regrading and resubmission of previously slabbed coins is all the rage. The letters to the editor and guest editorial pages of Coin World have contained many comments on grade inflation among slabbed coins.

Shouts of delight are not uncommon at conventions when this *dealer* or that finds that a coin he bought slabbed as MS-63 or MS-64 has just been reslabbed MS-65, or one he purchased "raw" as MS-65 all of the sudden became MS-67 once encapsulated. Rarely does one read of *customers* making such home runs. As the late Herbert Melnick asked, when contemplating rows of stockbrokers' boats docked in a harbor, "Where are the *customers*' yachts?"

Many coin sellers even go so far to say that all sales of slabbed coins are absolutely final, with no return privilege for any reason. Well-meaning coin buyers who are a bit cautious are apt to be ignored or told to take their business elsewhere. After all, there are other buyers who will buy such coins sight-unseen and won't complain, no matter what. At least this is what some dealers think.

Perhaps I should do nothing other than praise the practice of slabbing coins, for there is no doubt that for the professional numismatist encapsulated coins have made life much easier, have minimized complaints, and have made virtually any coin saleable. To many in the coin field, slabs are sacred cows which cannot be criticized or looked at objectively. Of course, there is a thread of illogic to all of this, but most coin buyers don't care.

This book is for buyers who *do* care. I suggest that buyers who do care—and I hope that includes *you*—will do a lot better in the market, both buying and selling, than those who invest before they investigate what they are doing.

An editorial in *Numismatic News*[2] suggested that now that slabs answered the grading question, the need to learn about coins is minimized, but that this lack of learning represents a loss for the hobby. Overlooked was an important aspect of coin buying: connoisseurship.

Beyond the Grade of a Coin

What is connoisseurship? The term has never been used in numismatics to my knowledge, except in a few of my articles, although it is heard often enough in fine art circles. John Marion, president of Sotheby's, refers to it often in connection with collecting art,[3] and I suspect that in the halls of the fine art auction house of Christie's the term is popular as well.

Connoisseurship in numismatics, to my way of thinking, is appreciating fully the ownership of coins. Anyone owning a coin wants to know its grade. But there is so much more to coins and coin ownership than simply knowing if a piece is Mint State-65, or About Uncirculated-50, or Extremely Fine-40—or, for that matter, Good-4.

Would anyone want to own a coin in G-4 grade? Yes! A connoisseur interested in collecting Vermont copper coins minted under authority of that state and bearing dates from 1785 to 1788 would consider G-4, nearly worn smooth and on the verge of indecipherability, to be a very desirable grade for the 1785-dated variety catalogued as Ryder-5,[4] for few higher grade pieces exist among a total population of fewer than 10 coins.

Of course, among later coins such as Morgan silver dollars, G-4 would not be an acceptable grade, and the discriminating buyer would want a specimen in MS-63, MS-64 or some other Mint State category. But for early colonial and state coins, half cents, large cents, and other series, some varieties are not known in Mint State or even close to it. One of the most famous of all American coin rarities, the 1793 Strawberry Leaf large cent, is known only in well-worn grades.

Anyone owning a coin also wants to know its market price. But there is so much more to coins and coin ownership than simply knowing if a piece is priced at $225,000, $6,000, or $575—or, for that matter, $13.

Could a coin priced at just $13 be desirable? Yes! Later, I will discuss an interesting Lincoln cent, in Uncirculated grade, which costs only $13 but which is something that any connoisseur would enjoy owning.

Then and Now

A few decades ago, in the 1950s, the typical coin buyer was a numismatist. According to the best tradition, a numismatist was and is a person who buys coins for the intellectual satisfaction they provide. To the numismatist, the 1882-CC silver dollar is indeed a footprint of history, a footprint stamped directly upon a pile of silver ore brought up from the earth beneath the Nevada sagebrush.

To the numismatist, a 1787 copper coin bearing the imprint AUCTORI CONNEC (which translates to "by the authority of Connecticut") bespeaks that time shortly after the American Revolution when individual states had the right to coin money, and Connecticut, Vermont, Massachusetts, and New Jersey did so.

In the case of Connecticut and certain other states, the job of minting was farmed out to independent contractors who at first produced coins struck from dies prepared with care, with many fine details, but who in the absence of legislative oversight later became careless and turned out poorly-struck pieces of light weight. As several hundred different dies were employed to produce Connecticut coins from 1785 to 1788, the numismatist can enjoy taking a magnifying glass to closely inspect the surfaces of this particular 1787 coin and to identify its specific variety according to a technical work on the series, *The State Coinages of New England*, written by Henry C. Miller and Hillyer C. Ryder and published in 1920 by the American Numismatic Society.

Connoisseurship

A few decades ago the average numismatist would eagerly pore through the pages of *The Numismatist* and *The Numismatic Scrapbook Magazine*, enjoying the research articles therein. The discovery of a new variety such as the 1955 Doubled Die cent was a cause for excitement, and it was hobby-wide news when a new overdate, die combination, or other variety was first publicized. Changes in pricing came slowly, usually on a yearly basis. Each summer a new edition of *A Guide Book of United States Coins* was released, and every summer the typical collector would go through his record book and mark up the price changes which had occurred during the preceding 12 months.[5]

Coin investment was popular then, as it had been for most of the preceding century. However, coin investment was considered as a side benefit to collecting. Forming a meaningful collection was most important, and investment benefits came naturally as part of the package.

It is no longer a few decades ago. It is now. And today is different. I suspect that the average reader of *Coin World* and *Numismatic News* today skims the research articles, of which there are numerous excellent ones, and concentrates on information about investment, changing market trends, and other topics having to do with making money. Investment is the name of the game, and without a doubt the vast majority of those entering the marketplace now do so with the idea of turning a quick investment dollar. There is nothing wrong with this desire. After all, everyone likes to turn a profit, and if it is an investment profit with no physical labor involved, so much the better. A number of publications, the *Coin Dealer Newsletter* and the *Certified Coin Dealer Newsletter* prominent among them, exist solely to provide investment and market information and are widely read.

To today's average buyer an otherwise romantic and historical 1882-CC silver dollar in Uncirculated grade most likely represents an item with a bid and ask price, a brilliant, lustrous round disc which, it is hoped, will prove to be a good investment. Assuming that an 1882-CC is bought at the current market price, and, as is the case with stocks and bonds, it is difficult to buy anything worthwhile for less than the market price, the overwhelming concern of today's buyer is this: Will my 1882-CC dollar increase in price? Who cares whether it was minted from Comstock Lode silver, or whether Miss Anna Williams, a young Philadelphia schoolteacher, modeled for George T. Morgan shortly after he arrived from England and secured a position in the engraving department of the Mint, and that her portrait was subsequently used on the coin?

As to the previously-mentioned 1787 Connecticut copper cent, no one

15

in his right mind would buy such an obscure coin for investment purposes, especially considering that a desirable grade for such a coin might be only Fine-15 or Very Fine-20 (more about grading and grading numbers later), rather than MS-65, or superb Uncirculated. So goes the prevailing philosophy of many investors.

Investors will buy 1882-CC dollars for investment purposes, and stay away from 1787 Connecticut cents. After all, the record demonstrates that in the past 1882-CC dollars have been excellent long-term investments. However, I suggest that in addition to whatever investment benefits an 1882-CC dollar may offer, it can provide the pleasure of ownership, the satisfaction of acquiring a piece needed as part of a collection of Morgan silver dollars of the 1878-1921 span, and the quintessential enjoyment of having a link with a romantic past. Besides, in the short term an Uncirculated 1882-CC silver dollar might go down in value, perish the thought! Coin prices do fluctuate.

As to the 1787 Connecticut cent, there is no need to persuade the intending buyer to appreciate its past, for most specialists in the state coinage series already have an excellent grounding in the subject. As strange as it may seem to the average coin buyer, as an investment area Connecticut cents can hold their own, as vividly demonstrated by record prices achieved when we sold the Frederick W. Taylor collection of Connecticut and other state coppers at auction a few years ago.

Connoisseurship

Coins are meant to be enjoyed, to be appreciated, to be owned with pleasure. This is connoisseurship.

Dorothy Parker, the celebrated writer and member of the Algonquin Roundtable, once said, "You can lead a horticulture but you can't make her think." (Dorothy is also remembered for this timeless advice: Candy is dandy but liquor is quicker.) Neither I nor anyone else can make you become a connoisseur if you don't want to become one.

Is connoisseurship *necessary* in order to buy coins advantageously? I believe this question will answer itself as you read this book.

"I have been looking for three years to find an 1877 Indian cent to match the color of the others in my set," a New Jersey client said to me recently.

"Now I have found it," he continued, pointing to a glittering Proof 1877 he was viewing just before one of our New York City auction sales. A day later when the sale took place, the coin was his. After three years of careful collecting his Indian cent set was now complete!

"I have read quite a bit about the Saint-Gaudens High Relief $20 gold piece of 1907 with the date in Roman numerals," a Colorado client mentioned to me at a Midwestern convention, "and I would like to begin collecting gold coins by getting one of these." It so happened that I had brought one with me to the show, and a few moments later a transaction was consummated. This man had done his homework, knew what he wanted, and now was set to experience the joy of connoisseurship, the pleasure of owning something which at once is beautiful, interesting, and rare.

What do you see when you contemplate a coin? Like the Sphinx, a coin keeps many secrets. We can learn the answers to some. Others will remain forever unknown, which perhaps is all for the best, for nothing makes something more interesting than having a certain mystique. Why does Mona Lisa smile?

When I view a coin, I consider the following aspects concerning it:

Denomination

What is the denomination or face value of the coin? In the American series denominations were produced from the half cent to the $50 gold piece, including such unusual values as the two-cent piece, three-cent piece, $2.50 gold piece, and $3 gold piece. In the year 1873 one could choose from three different styles within the dollar denomination alone: the standard silver dollar of the Liberty Seated design, the silver trade dollar minted for export purposes, and the tiny gold dollar. During the same year there were two types of five-cent pieces, the Shield nickel and the half dime. It is a wonder that more unusual denominations weren't created, for over the years Congress has considered many proposals, including a few decades ago a 15-cent coin to facilitate admission to motion picture theatres, and a revival of the two-cent piece to make it possible to use just a single coin to buy newspapers on the street.

Denominations wax and wane in popularity. Today we have the following: the cent, which is in everybody's purse or pocket and which facilitates the payment of odd amounts of sales taxes (although scarcely a year goes by without someone capturing headlines by claiming that the "penny" is obsolete); the nickel five-cent piece of the Jefferson design, which is also used in small transactions; the dime, tiny but useful; and the quarter dollar, which seems to be the main coin to use in vending machines and for most payments amounting to less than $1. Half dollars are currently minted, but they are seldom seen in pocket change. The government has on hand hundreds of millions of Susan B. Anthony dollars coined 1979-1981, and these could be considered a current denomination, but they are hardly ever used. In practice, we have four actively traded coins: the cent, nickel, dime, and quarter.

Years ago the situation was much more confusing. Consider that in 1875 a shopkeeper would have been familiar with Indian cents, two-cent pieces, three-cent pieces of two types (nickel alloy and silver), Shield nickels, half dimes, dimes, 20-cent pieces, quarter dollars, half dollars, silver dollars, trade dollars, and gold coins of the $1, $2.50, $3, $5, $10 and $20 denominations— a bewildering array! In practice there were certain denominations which were not popular. Twenty-cent pieces were used for just a short time and discontinued. In 1875 very few silver three-cent pieces were to be found in pocket change, trade dollars were elusive to the average citizen, silver dollars were apt to be circulated primarily in the American West, and gold coins were found primarily in banking circles, not in everyday commerce.

Forming a collection of one of every United States coin denomination minted can be an interesting challenge.

Date

What is the date on the coin? 1793? 1851? 1964? Normally the date serves to identify the time of mintage, but not always, as among early United States coins, for example, it was the practice of the Philadelphia Mint to keep dies on hand until they wore out. Although 19,570 silver dollars were coined in Philadelphia in the year 1804, these are believed to have been struck from dies dated 1803 and earlier. All 1794-dated half dimes were struck a year later in 1795, for although the dies had been prepared in 1794, the Mint didn't get around to coining half dimes from them until a leaf had turned on the calendar. However, for most coins the date represents the actual time of striking. All 1909 Indian cents were struck in 1909, and all 1951-S Franklin half dollars were struck in 1951.

I have always found it interesting to visualize events which occurred at the time of a coin's mintage. Although this drifts away from basic numismatics, I believe that it contributes to connoisseurship.

When I see a 1916 Standing Liberty quarter, or a Mercury dime of the first year of issue, I think of America prepared for the World War, up to date on the latest news from Europe, but hoping it would not be drawn into the conflict.

An 1854-S, 1857-S, or other early double eagle with an S mintmark instantly recalls the Gold Rush era and San Francisco, the commercial center of activity at the time.

Connoisseurship

1652-dated Pine Tree shillings of Massachusetts evoke feelings of colonial times, of a primitive way of life, of a time when America was largely unexplored.

No doubt a typical 1906-D $5 gold piece was coined from metal extracted from the Cripple Creek District, about 75 miles distant from the Denver Mint, an area once described as the richest gold camp on earth, a district which at one time had 50,000 inhabitants but which by the 1990s had fewer than a thousand.

The rare 1877 Indian cent—rare because of its low mintage—was produced in small quantities because there were financial hard times then, and the need for small change was lessened.

Zinc-coated steel cents of 1943, common and inexpensive today, are interesting as they represent a pivotal time in our nation's history, when copper went to war and had more important uses than making Lincoln pennies.

Mint

Where was the coin produced? For most pieces you are apt to encounter, the answer is that it is a product of one of the United States mints, but other coins in private collections and museums may have been stamped out in the Tower Mint in London, the Leningrad Mint in Russia, in John Higley's workshop in Granby, Connecticut, in one of over a dozen mints in Mexico, or perhaps by some unrecorded coiner in ancient Greece.

Among United States coins, the general rule of thumb years ago was that a coin without a mint letter was produced at Philadelphia, whereas pieces struck at any one of a half dozen other locations bore distinguishing mintmarks. Among the exceptions, remembered today only as numismatic footnotes, are some 1837-dated large cents said to have been struck at the New Orleans Mint to test the presses prior to the implementation of regular coinage in 1838, and the 1925 Fort Vancouver commemorative half dollars, struck at the San Francisco Mint, but for some unexplained reason lacking the S mintmark. Wartime silver-content Jefferson nickels minted from 1942 through 1945 bore the P mint letter for Philadelphia, an unprecedented use. In recent times the P mintmark has appeared on many coins, but back in 1942 it was a decided novelty.

Each mint was apt to have its own peculiarities. Morgan silver dollars struck at the Carson City Mint during the 1880s have a boldness of strike and a frostiness which is quite distinctive. Show me an 1885 silver dollar, face up, with the mintmark not evident, and chances are that I will be able to tell you if it is a Carson City piece, for the Philadelphia, New Orleans, and San Francisco varieties of the same year look ever so slightly different. Show me an 1861 gold dollar, face up, again with no obvious clue as to the mint of origin, and if it is irregularly struck with the U of UNITED nearly obliterated, I can identify it as a product of the Dahlonega Mint, even though the mintmark is unseen on the reverse.

It is interesting to contemplate the point of origin of coins. Large cents struck in Philadelphia in 1797 were there during the great yellow fever epidemic. At one point the ravages of the disease were so dreadful that the Mint closed its doors, and dies were transferred to a bank vault. An 1870-CC Liberty Seated dollar was on hand in rough and ready Nevada during the glory days of the Comstock Lode. Double eagles minted at New Orleans during the 1850s were produced right in the middle of a city which was thronging with prosperity and riverboat commerce.

Design Type

What is the basic design type of the piece? Who created it? Some coin dates exist in more than one type. For example, among 1795 silver dollars there are the earlier Flowing Hair style pieces and the later Draped Bust type coins. Some 1866 half dollars minted in San Francisco are of the type without motto, and others are of the later style with IN GOD WE TRUST. Among 1907 $10 and $20 pieces there are more types and varieties than you can shake a stick at, and the same is true of 1909 cents and 1883 nickels.

Some designs were created by famous artists, Augustus Saint-Gaudens, Victor David Brenner, James Earle Fraser, Hermon MacNeil, and Adolph A. Weinman among them. Coin motifs created by these people have an additional appeal if you learn about the artists themselves. Books have been written on the life of Saint-Gaudens, for example.

Forming a type set of United States coins is a popular way to collect. What is a type? From time to time United States coin designs have been changed. Whenever a major change was made, such as a new representation of Miss Liberty, the addition of a word to the inscription, a rearrangement of certain elements, etc., a new type was created.

Variety

Many coins, particularly older ones, are attributable as to die variety. Nowhere in American numismatics is this more evident than among large cents bearing the date 1794. Several dozen die varieties and combinations were created, some of them extremely distinctive. Dr. Edward Maris, a physician by profession and a 19th-century student of the series, assigned fanciful names to the portraits of Miss Liberty on cents of this date, including Coquette, Venus Marina, and Patagonian. Distinctive reverses found on 1794 cents include a variety in which the bar is missing in the fraction 1/100 and the famous Sheldon-48 variety with a circle of 94 five-pointed stars around the rim. John Weston Adams, a distinguished numismatist of our own time, whose collection I had the honor of presenting for sale in 1982, made a specialty of this particular date. He was not alone; over the years others have enjoyed the same challenge.

Reference books furnish the key to identifying varieties. The student of Capped Bust half dollars minted 1807-1836 will use Al C. Overton's book on the subject, which describes minute differences in the positions of stars, the motto E PLURIBUS UNUM, the numerals of the date, and other aspects, to differentiate one die from another. Sometimes die differences are obvious at quick glance to the unaided eye; other times detailed study is needed.

Among coins of an earlier era, such as the previously mentioned copper coins minted under the authority of the state of Connecticut 1785-1788, die varieties are the basic reason for collecting. Some Connecticut coins are sharply struck from expertly engraved dies, and are on full weight planchets, while others are poorly struck, from crudely prepared dies, on lightweight copper stock.

Among certain varieties of Vermont copper coins of the same era, poorly struck and crude pieces are the rule, not the exception. A variety known as the 1786 Baby Head, attributed as Ryder-9, nearly always comes on streaky, laminated copper planchets. Numerous other examples could be cited.

After 1836 the Philadelphia Mint produced coins by steam power, rather than horse power (in the literal sense of the word). New methods of making dies were adopted, and coins took on a stereotyped appearance. There is little difference among Liberty Seated silver coins of a given date in the 1840s, except for variations in the date numerals, which continued to be punched into the dies by hand. Repunched dates, overdates, and even silly errors can be found during this era. In the later category we have a variety of 1846 half dollar with the last digit of the date punched over an erroneous horizontal 6; the engraver, possibly James B. Longacre, first punched the 6 lying on its side!

One of the weirdest of all 19th century mint products was produced during the 1850s, when the date 1858 on a half dime die was punched in completely upside down, the error recognized, then repunched in the correct position. Under magnification the inverted date can still be seen.

Among 20th-century coins significant die varieties are few and far between, but those which have occurred are avidly collected, among them being the 1955 and 1972 Doubled Die cents and the 1937-D three-legged nickel. There are, however, a host of minor repunchings, die doublings, and the like which have attracted attention.

Grade

The grade of a coin is determined by the amount of wear it has received. As grade is a determinant of value, buyers are eager to verify the grades of the coins they have and to gain some reasonable assurance that the stated grades will remain the same in a buying and selling transaction. As grading is a matter of opinion, two people can look at the same coin and come up with different ideas.

Computer grading, the commercial debut of which was provided by the Professional Coin Grading Service in May 1990, may eventually reduce grading to a series of precise mathematical numbers. Even if this happens, two coins with the same number can have vastly different values, if one is aesthetically pleasing and the other is a dog.[6] During the past century no subject has spurred more heated debate than grading, and the more precise grading becomes, the more debate it seems to engender! If grading were to be abolished *Coin World*, for one, would have to figure out what to do with all of the empty space on its letters to the editor page! Unquestionably, what readers write to *Coin World* editor Beth Deisher reflects what is on a lot of people's minds, and now in the early 1990s slabbed coins are in the forefront.

Grading has an impact upon connoisseurship inasmuch as the discriminating buyer will usually endeavor to obtain the highest *reasonable* grade for each coin in his collection. What is reasonable and what isn't is apt to be a matter of opinion, and the concept of *value* enters the equation.

I can afford to pay $25 for an ordinary Hershey chocolate bar if I want to, but I won't, for I believe that it does not represent a good value at that level. Fifty cents or a dollar, yes, but $25, no. A 1936 Cincinnati commemorative half dollar certified as MS-68 recently changed hands, I was told, for $21,000. At the same time the market price for an MS-63 Cincinnati was $310. Even if I were John D. Rockefeller or Croesus and had all the money in the world, I would not buy an MS-68 Cincinnati half dollar for $21,000 if I could buy an MS-63 coin for $310. To me, the value just isn't there. However, for someone else the $21,000 coin might be just the ticket to numismatic happiness.

Connoisseurship

I suggest that one can be a connoisseur of commemorative half dollars and have a set which grades, say, MS-63, and be proud to display it. I mention this, for there is entirely too much pap in print these days telling coin buyers that the *only* way to have worthwhile coins is to buy them in the highest grades possible, regardless of cost.

John Albanese, who runs the Numismatic Guaranty Corporation certification service, announced a year or two ago that he would not encapsulate modern Proof coins, for there were too many abuses with telemarketers selling Proof-68 and other high graded common coins for uncommon prices, and he was not going to be a party to such deception. In one instance, an uninformed investor paid $200 for a Proof-68 1979-S Jefferson nickel, thinking that he had bought the bargain of the decade, not knowing that there are hundreds of thousands of other Proof 1979-S Jefferson nickels which are just as nice.

Do you remember my illustration of a rare 1785 Vermont copper coin, variety Ryder-5, in Good-4 grade? Here is a coin for the connoisseur. A Proof-68 1979-S Jefferson nickel is a coin for the connoisseur too, but it is so common that a connoisseur wouldn't give it more than a moment's attention, and, of course, he wouldn't be the slightest bit interested in paying anywhere close to $200 for it. In fact, one one-hundredth of that amount, or $2, would probably be about right!

In the same vein as the worn Vermont copper coin, let me mention that I own a very worn and somewhat decrepit-appearing 1787-dated Washington and Columbia medal made of copper and used as a souvenir when two ships named *Washington* and *Columbia* set sail from Boston and sought to explore the Pacific Northwest, trading medals like this to the native Indians. My specimen was once the property of well-known connoisseur T. Harrison Garrett, of Baltimore, Maryland, who acquired it in the 19th century. When the Garrett Collection was sold, John Weston Adams, certainly a person of numismatic taste and discrimination if there ever was one, was the successful bidder. When Adams secured a somewhat finer piece he sold the Garrett example to me. Probably someone who would pay $21,000 for an MS-68 1936 Cincinnati half dollar or $200 for a Proof-68 1979-S Jefferson nickel would not want the 1787 Washington and Columbia medal *free*, let alone for the several thousand dollars it might cost today.

Why did I want such a medal? Because, at the suggestion of John J. Ford, Jr., I spent a weekend reading a reprint of the log kept on the voyage in question, and could envision that owning one of these 1787-dated medals would truly be a link to what I was learning about.

This medal came to mind recently when Anne Bentley, keeper of the medals and coins in the collection of the Massachusetts Historical Society, visited our offices to have Cathy Dumont, our staff photographer, take pictures of the three specimens of the Washington and Columbia medal owned by the Society. These three pieces, none of which would be called "choice" or "gem" by investors or anyone else, were truly exciting for me to contemplate and are among the foremost numismatic treasures of that institution.

The higher the grade of a 1936 Cincinnati half dollar, or an 1979-S Proof Jefferson nickel, or a 1785 Ryder-5 Vermont copper, or a 1787 Washington and Columbia medal, the better, but don't believe that grading is everything.

Price

What is the price of the coin? How much does it cost? (Which may be a different question from: How much is it worth?) This question is apt to be the first to be asked by the beginning collector. The price of a coin is apt to vary over a period of time.

Often, a coin will seem more desirable if it has recently increased in price or seems to be scheduled to do so. In the 1950s and early 1960s I often refrained from listing 1909-S V.D.B. Lincoln cents in catalogues and price lists, for this key Lincoln cent variety was on just about everyone's want list, was rising steadily in value each year, and as I never had more than a few in stock, I did not want to send out dozens of "sold out" letters. The 1909-S V.D.B. was eminently desirable, and as a dealer I would have been delighted to have purchased as many as possible. Today in the early 1990s the same specimens of 1909-S V.D.B. cents are in various collections and dealers' stocks, but they are largely forgotten, for the market price has declined and they are no longer on the "most active" list. To be sure, the student of numismatic history and the specialist in Lincoln cents each know that the 1909-S V.D.B. is rare and important, but the typical newcomer to the hobby could care less. Thus, a 1909-S V.D.B. is now viewed by many as a stock in trade item, something to be bought and sold, but not a coin with a special aura as a guaranteed blue chip investment scheduled for a rise in price each year.

As these words are being written in the autumn of 1990, a MS-65 1881-S dollar is about half the price it was a couple years ago. Two years ago, at twice today's price, the coins sold more quickly than they do now—for they were on the way up. Now that they are available for half price, few people want them. Perhaps if the price triples, they will be in great demand once more!

In my opinion there is entirely too much emphasis on price, and not enough on all of the other considerations I have mentioned. As J.P. Morgan

Connoisseurship

said about stocks, coin prices will continue to fluctuate. The same coins all of us own now will still be in existence a century from now, and in the meantime they will have brought joys to their owners, and possibly sadnesses, the sadnesses coming from dips in market value, if such occur. The joys are always there–art, history, romance, and other considerations.

Pedigree

Often a coin will be accompanied by a pedigree stating who owned it earlier. In my company's catalogue of the John W. Adams Collection of 1794 large cents an effort was made to complete the pedigree of each coin as far back as possible, and many pieces were traced through a succession of owners back to the previous century. In my firm's sales of the famous Garrett, Eliasberg, Brand, Norweb, and Emery-Nichols collections, to mention just a few illustrious cabinets we have handled, pedigrees were stated when known. Many were the buyers who told me after each of these sales that the knowledge that this coin or that had been purchased from the Chapman brothers, or had been in the Parmelee Collection in the 1880s, or had some other interesting pedigree, added a special dimension of enjoyment to the piece. When I contemplate my previously-mentioned 1787 Washington and Columbia medal I think not only of the voyage of the *Washington* and *Columbia* sailing ships and the possibility that my medal may have been aboard one of the vessels, but also that the piece was once owned by T. Harrison Garrett, who kept it as part of his collection at Evergreen House, a beautiful 19th century Italianate mansion in Baltimore, recently restored by its current owner, The Johns Hopkins University. What a nice pedigree!

In the modern market pedigrees are often lost sight of, which is a shame, because they are part of a coin's history. One reason dealers don't include pedigrees with their coins is that they are afraid that someone might complain if they ask $20,000 for a coin they bought for $10,000. I say that dealers should charge what the coin is worth, and if a coin is worth $20,000, whether it cost $10,000, and the dealer is making a nice profit, or whether it cost $30,000, and the dealer is taking a substantial loss, is irrelevant. Recently, my company paid $50,000 for a coin and sold it for $32,000. On another occasion I bought a rare Liberty Seated quarter from a dealer who priced it for $1,000, and I sold it for $3,500 a few days later.

Rarity

Is a coin common or is it rare? This thought goes through the mind of most buyers when they consider a coin.

Among Liberty nickels, the rare 1885, 1886, and 1912-S issues are viewed as the highlights of any set, and they have a special desirability for this reason. Among large cents, such rare dates as 1793, and 1799 and 1804 are objects of affection and desire. For the specialist in small cents, the 1856 Flying Eagle cent, the 1877 Indian cent, and the 1909-S V.D.B. and 1914-D Lincoln cents are eagerly sought.

The double eagle specialist may search years for an example of the rare 1927-D in any grade, while the half dime specialist would mortgage his farm or sell the family jewels to buy a top grade 1802. These coins and others are the classics of American numismatics. Apart from their denomination, date, mintmark, variety, grade, and price, such issues have a special appeal—that of rarity.

Some coin varieties can be common in one grade and rare in another. For example, in such grades as Fine-20, VF-30, EF-45, and other circulated states, the 1817 large cent with 15 obverse stars instead of the usual 13 is readily available. However, in MS-65 grade the variety is a major rarity, so rare in fact, that I have never seen one! However, I have handled countless dozens of worn examples. Another example is the 1850 $20 gold piece, representing the first year of issue of this denomination. Specimens in circulated grades such as VF-20 to EF-40 are frequently encountered, but in Mint State the 1850 $20 is a rarity. Coins which are easily found in lower grades but which are rare in very high grades are called *condition rarities*. Later in this book I will tell about the 1892-S dollar, which is common and quite inexpensive in worn grades but which emerges as a major rarity in a grade such as MS-65.

For the sake of provoking a discussion, or at least some thought, I should also mention a type of coin for which no term has yet been devised, although perhaps *reverse condition rarity* might be appropriate: a coin which is common in high preservation but which is rare in worn grades. An example is provided by the 1950-D Jefferson nickel, a low-mintage variety which was widely hoarded shortly after the time of its mintage. Hundreds of thousands of Mint State coins exist, and these are much easier to find than are worn examples! The 1970-D Kennedy half dollar is known primarily in Mint State, for these were sold in mint sets to collectors. The only way you could ever find an EF-40 coin would be if you came across one which was inadvertently spent. As higher-grade coins are typically worth more than lower grade ones, no special desirability is attached to items such as a worn 1950-D nickel or a worn 1970-D half dollar.

Better Than a Museum

In an introduction to a section of one of our recent catalogues, Michael

Connoisseurship

Hodder stated that the personal possession of a collection of coins brought a far greater pleasure than viewing cold objects in a museum. Coins are history you can hold in your hand; the past comes to life. This is what connoisseurship is all about.

Connoisseurship requires some effort, but it is enjoyable pursuit. Once you buy coins and add them to your collection, it is rewarding to learn as much as possible about them. Perhaps this is putting the cart before the horse. Ideally, you should study about coins *before* you buy them—but not everyone does, particularly when a specialty is just begun. In fact, most coin buyers make some purchases in a specialty and then learn about the specialty in depth.

At one of our auction sales a few years ago, a gentleman bought a Proof gold coin, paying about $20,000 for it. After the sale he came to me and asked if he had made a good buy, and I queried him as to the reason for acquiring it. He had no particular explanation, except that he enjoyed the catalogue description, which pointed out that only a few dozen had been struck, and fewer still survived. As he seemed to know nothing at all about the market price, I gave him the assurance, correctly so, that he had not gone too far wrong, for also competing for the same coin were several dealers and collectors who did know their values, and his winning bid was just $1,000 over the next highest increment.

I suggested that he would add to his knowledge of this Civil War-era gold Proof rarity if he did some reading on the subject, and I recommended David Akers' books on gold coins as well as a copy of Walter Breen's *Encyclopedia*. He brushed me off, stating he had no time to read. His office was on Wall Street, and he was busy buying and selling securities. A few months later he telephoned me to say that he had decided to give up collecting, and that he would be consigning his recently acquired Proof gold rarity as well as a few other coins he had purchased to one of our auction sales, which he did. As it turned out, the market had risen in the meantime, and even after our selling commission was deducted, he registered a small profit. The point of this is that the gentleman entered numismatics, stayed for a short time, owned some very nice coins, but never took the time to appreciate them, so he never enjoyed what he had.

Contrast that man to Harry Bass, the well-known Texas connoisseur, who has spent countless hours over many years studying the die varieties of gold coinage, their early history, pedigrees, and other considerations, and who has made a number of significant numismatic discoveries. His collection, on view on a loan exhibit in the museum of the American Numismatic Society during the Coinage of the Americas Conference in 1989, attracted a wide circle of admirers, as well it should have, for it contained many formidable rarities[7] as well as numerous other pieces in the finest grades of preservation. Harry Bass has always appreciated the stories behind coins, and because of this his interest has endured for many years.

To such connoisseurs as Louis Eliasberg, Mrs. R. Henry Norweb, John Work Garrett, and Virgil Brand, coins were a way of life, and although price paid and grade were certainly considerations for each specimen, these in the long run were exceedingly minor aspects. The pure joy of possessing coins and studying them was first and foremost.

In a way the terms *collector* and *connoisseur* are interchangeable, except that when I envision a connoisseur I think of someone who is really involved in the field and who strives to acquire pieces in finer grade levels. However, the connoisseur balances grade, price, and value and does not blindly pay top prices for common coins in high numerical grade levels.

Donn Pearlman, a member of the American Numismatic Association Board of Governors, in recent correspondence[8] with the author indicated that connoisseurship was alive and well in Utah and possibly everywhere else:

"Interestingly, there seems to be a vein of connoisseurship running deep in many collectors who may not be aware of it. Richard and Alma Blaylock of Utah, who serve as regional coordinators for the ANA, recently took a survey of collectors in that state. Many of those questioned indicated they enjoy collecting coins for their art, their history, and their beauty. They also indicated they expand their collecting interests by sharing information with others and building numismatic friendships; certainly a strong indication of connoisseurship even though that particular word was not on the survey. I'll bet you'd get similar results from collectors' surveys in every state. Collectors appreciate items for what they *are*, not just for what they *might become* (more valuable)."

CHAPTER TWO

Collectors and Investors

Motivation

It is important to understand what motivates the collector and what motivates the investor.

In general the collector is confident, knows what he or she wants, and enjoys forming a meaningful collection over a long period of time. To become a collector (or connoisseur) you have to make an investment in the time needed to read a few books about coins and to study the subject. Don't think of studying as a dry, boring activity, because it isn't. Learning about coins can be a lot of fun. By doing this a new world of enjoyment will open for you, and the entire spectrum of numismatics will make sense. You will be able on your own to determine whether a coin is worth owning, whether it offers good investment potential, and whether it is a desirable specimen of its particular date and variety.

Illustrative of this, suppose that you were offered the following coins. Which ones represent great rarities in the grades listed, and which ones are easy to find? Which should you buy right away, even at a price higher than current market if necessary, and which should you ignore unless the price is right?

• **1859-S Liberty Seated silver dollar, MS-63.** My opinion: The 1859-S Liberty Seated dollar is a great rarity in MS-63 grade and ranks among the top half dozen finest known specimens. Offered at auction, it would probably sell for a record price as many numismatists competed to own it. Go for it!

• **1881-S Morgan silver dollar, MS-63.** My opinion: The 1881-S Morgan dollar in MS-63 grade is exceedingly common, and anyone caring to pay the price could accumulate thousands of specimens in a short time. No need to hurry on this one. If the price isn't right, there will be plenty around tomorrow, next week, and next month.

• **1876-S $5 gold, MS-65.** My opinion: The 1876-S $5 gold piece in MS-65 grade is an extreme rarity, and it is believed that only one specimen exists, the coin my firm sold at auction as part of the Garrett Collection. (In circulated grades the 1876-S $5 is available, though it is still scarce.) Here is a prime item for the numismatic connoisseur. The chance to buy this may truly be a once in a lifetime opportunity, literally!

• **1901-S $5 gold, MS-64.** My opinion: The 1901-S $5 gold piece in MS-64 grade is very common. Buy it only if the price is right.

• **1809 half cent, MS-60.** My opinion: The 1809 half cent in MS-60 grade is scarce. However, a dozen or more specimens come on the market each year. Consider it carefully, and if it is nice, buy it. Otherwise wait for the next one.

• **1808/7 overdate half cent, MS-60.** My opinion: The 1808/7 overdate half cent in MS-60 grade is a great rarity, and if you don't reach for it, even above current market levels, you may have to wait many years before having the opportunity to acquire another specimen.

• **1909 V.D.B. Lincoln cent, MS-65.** My opinion: The 1909 V.D.B. cent in MS-65 grade is common, as these were produced during the first year of the Lincoln cent design, and many were saved by the public. Here is a very historical and desirable coin, but wait for one which has the right price and aesthetic appeal.

• **1915-D Lincoln cent, MS-65.** My opinion: The 1915-D cent in MS-65 grade is quite elusive and although it catalogues for relatively little, several months of effort may be needed to acquire an example. Buy this one if it is nice.

• **1941-S Walking Liberty 50c, MS-65, sharply struck.** My opinion: A sharply struck 1941-S 50c piece in MS-65 grade is very hard to find, as 95% or more of this variety have weakly defined features at the obverse and reverse centers. Buy it.

• **1937 Walking Liberty 50c, MS-65, sharply struck.** My opinion: Most MS-65 1937 half dollars are sharply struck. Buy it only if the price is right.

Now, let's consider these same coins and their relevance to collectors and investors:

The advanced collector would give an eyetooth for any of the following: 1859-S Liberty Seated silver dollar, MS-63 grade; 1876-S $5 gold, MS-65 grade; 1808/7 overdate half cent, MS-60; 1915-D Lincoln cent, MS-65; and the 1941-S Walking Liberty 50c, MS-65, sharply struck. Of course, a collector would also need the commoner coins as well, as no silver dollar collection would be complete without a common 1881-S, etc., but it is the rarities which are the hardest to find and which create the most interest.

On the other hand, the typical uniformed investor would probably not know which coins were scarce and which were common, and in any event, if he didn't make his own investment decisions, he would be apt to accumulate in quantity such items as the 1881-S Morgan silver dollar, MS-63 grade; 1901-S $5 gold, MS-64 grade; 1909 V.D.B. Lincoln cent, MS-65; and so on.

An investor once told me that his entire holdings consisted of a quantity of bank-wrapped Uncirculated rolls of 1963 Washington quarters which he had purchased for $10,000 the group. After owning them for five years and not realizing a profit, he sold out and left the field of coins to become involved in investing in baseball cards, which he was told were "a real growth area." This was a shame for numismatics, for he was a professor of English literature at a well-known Eastern university, and undoubtedly he could have made some interesting contributions to the rare coin hobby.

The uninformed investor usually ends up buying coins which are desirable in high grades but which are not rare. I suggest that while owning one each of such coins is fine, as each is a necessary part of a specialized collection of its particular series, it is important to acquire rarities as well. On the other hand, anyone with a limited budget can form a truly interesting and numismatically important collection simply by acquiring inexpensive examples of coins with "stories."

Inexpensive, Interesting Coins

Coins do not have to be expensive to be interesting, and while in the American series we all enjoy reading about 1913 Liberty Head nickels, 1804 silver dollars, 1822 half eagles, 1787 Brasher doubloons, and other rarities priced at the best part of a million dollars each, such coins do not have a monopoly on historical and numismatic interest or desirability.

One nice thing about numismatics is that it offers a wide spectrum of price ranges. There are many pieces available in high grades for just a few dollars, or just a few hundred dollars, which have absolutely fascinating stories to tell and which are exciting and interesting to own. Consider the following examples. Prices are taken from the 1991 edition of *A Guide Book of United States Coins.*

• **1787 Connecticut cent, Draped Bust Left. Fine $125.** Struck from hand-prepared dies, the typical 1787 Connecticut cent is apt to be weakly defined in areas and quite crude in overall aspect, characteristics which impart a quaintness and charm.

• **1857 large cent. EF-40 $70.** Representing as it does the last year of the large-size cent, produced from 1793 onward, the 1857 large cent has a particular niche in numismatic history. By that year the large American copper cent had become cumbersome in the channels of commerce, and the Mint decided to replace it with a smaller version, the Flying Eagle cent. Just 333,456 large cents were minted in 1857, and it is quite probable that many of these were never released, but went to the melting pot. The entire series of United States large cents is one of the most popular in numismatics, and the acquisition of an 1857 provides the passport to learning more about this interesting field of specialty.

• **The cents of 1909, three major types in all.** As a trio the different varieties of 1909 Indian and Lincoln cents form an interesting chapter in numismatic history. **1909 Indian cent. MS-60 $45.** 1909 was a year of transition for the one-cent piece, and the Indian motif, in use since 1859, was discontinued after a relatively modest coinage. The 1909 Indian cent represents the last of the Mohicans, so to speak, and illustrates what to my eye is one of the most attractive motifs in 19th century numismatics. Although Indian cents are not high on the popularity charts with collectors today, at one time they were certainly among the top 10 most actively collected series. Curiously, the market values for many Indian cents are no higher today in 1990 than they were 10 or 15 years ago, perhaps indicating an opportunity. **1909 V.D.B. Lincoln cent. MS-60 $13.** In the summer of 1909 a new variety of cent appeared, the Lincoln motif, bearing the initials V.D.B. on the reverse. The public objected to the prominence of Victor David Brenner's initials on the reverse, and the Mint removed them. This was an illogical step, as there was ample precedent for the initials of designers and engravers on coinage. George T. Morgan's initial M had appeared on 1878 and later dollars, Charles E. Barber's initial B was on all dimes, quarters, and half dollars minted since 1892, and the elaborate ASG monogram of Augustus Saint-Gaudens was prominent on the obverse of double eagles made 1907 and later, to mention just three examples. The 1909 V.D.B. cent was thus isolated as a one-year type. **1909 Lincoln cent (without V.D.B.). MS-60 $12.** Soon after the release of the 1909 V.D.B. cents, the design was revised, as noted, and subsequent 1909 cents were made without the initials, creating a third variety.

• **The nickel five-cent pieces of 1883.** Again we have three coins of three different types minted in the same year: **1883 Shield nickel. MS-60 $110.** The 1883 Shield design typifies a motif used since 1866. Designed by James B. Longacre, the obverse shield is somewhat similar to that found on the two-cent piece of 1864, also by Longacre. The Shield nickel made its debut in 1866 at a time when silver coins were not seen in circulation (payment of same having been stopped by the Treasury Department in 1862, not to resume until 1873). The new nickel coin, actually containing more copper than nickel (three parts copper to one part nickel alloy), became immediately popular, and the denomination continues its popularity today. **1883 Liberty nickel without CENTS. MS-60 $40.** In 1883 Charles E. Barber, drawing on pattern designs made as early as 1881, redesigned the obverse of the nickel to the Liberty Head style. Now the nickel depicted Miss Liberty with a coronet, said to have been modeled after the goddess Diana, encircled by 13 stars and the date. The reverse of the first issue bore the denomination expressed as the Roman letter V, without any mention of the word CENTS, leading some unscrupulous individuals to gold plate the pieces and pass them as $5 coins of comparable diameter. **1883 Liberty nickel with CENTS. MS-60 $150.** Recognizing the mistake in design, the Mint quickly corrected the reverse of the Liberty Head nickel to add the word CENTS, thus creating the third major type of the year.

• **1942 Mercury dime. MS-63 $13.** I have selected this dime as an inexpensive example of the 1916-1945 Mercury motif. Other dates could be picked as well, including 1916, the first year of issue, which catalogues $60. In 1916 Adolph A. Weinman, a well-known sculptor, was commissioned to prepare designs, and he created the Winged Liberty Head dime and the Walking Liberty half dollar. Miss Liberty, with wings on her head, soon became known as "Mercury," although Mercury, the messenger of classical mythology, was *male* and had wings on his *feet!* The reverse is dominated by a fasces, or bundle of sticks, an ancient symbol of unity. Mercury dimes and the other new silver motifs of 1916 represented a new artistic era in American coinage and were widely heralded at the time of issue. From then until the style was discontinued in 1945, pieces were collected avidly, and they still are. Upon the passing of President Franklin Delano Roosevelt in 1945, it was determined to redesign the dime to include his portrait, for during his life he had been associated with the March of Dimes.

• **1917 Type I Standing Liberty quarter. MS-63 $500** (MS-60 is not priced in the *Guide Book*). This issue, designed by sculptor Hermon A. MacNeil, was first produced in 1916. Miss Liberty is portrayed as a goddess standing in an entryway, holding an olive branch for peace and a shield for preparedness. Her right breast is fully exposed, a situation which caused public comment and resulted in a change being made part way through 1917, with the later Type II quarters of 1917-1930 showing Miss Liberty with her upper body encased in a coat of armor—perhaps a classic case of overcompensation. The Standing Liberty quarter has always been a favorite with collectors and was coined until the design was replaced by the Washington quarter in 1932, to observe the 200th anniversary of our first president's birth.

• **1942 Liberty Walking half dollar. MS-60 $50.** I have selected this as an inexpensive example of the 1916-1947 design by Adolph A. Weinman, who also created the Mercury dime. Depicted on the obverse is Miss Liberty striding toward a sunset, wearing a star spangled cape. The reverse illustrates an eagle on a rocky crag with a pine branch. Perhaps no better testimonial to the beauty and endurance of this design can be given than by noting that in 1986 when the Treasury Department decided to issue silver bullion coins it could not find a better design than Weinman's old motif, and it was resurrected for further use. The Liberty Walking half dollar was produced during a very pivotal time in American history, an era which saw the entry of the United States into World War I, followed by the rollicking decade of twenties, the Depression of the 1930s, World War II, 1942-1945, and the post-war years.

• **1979 Anthony dollar. MS-60 $1.75** (but you can probably obtain one for the face value of $1 at your bank). The Anthony dollar represents an interesting coinage experiment of our own time—an experiment not far different from that of the short-lived 1875-1878 twenty-cent piece. From the outset the public confused the small-size Anthony dollars with quarters, as both seemed to be about the same diameter, especially if handled quickly in change. The Anthony dollar was a failure from the start. Hundreds of millions of them now are stored in Treasury vaults. Perhaps someday these will be avidly collected, as they deserve to be.

• **1907 Saint-Gaudens gold double eagle. MS-60 $1,000.** I have selected the style with Arabic numerals, which represents the first year of issue of the motif designed by one of America's most famous sculptors. There is something nice about owning a large, heavy, and impressive double eagle, and for my money the 1907 Arabic numerals Saint-Gaudens is a nice representative of the denomination. This coin is not inexpensive in the same sense that a 1942 Mercury dime or 1979 Anthony dollar is, but for an Uncirculated $20 double eagle it is among the cheaper varieties.

• **1892 Columbian commemorative half dollar. MS-60 $85.** Bearing the date 1892, this coin was minted for the World's Columbian Exposition, scheduled to open in that year, but postponed until 1893. Representing the first United States commemorative half dollar, it led the way for the creation of 47 additional major half dollar types through the year 1954. Charles E. Barber designed the obverse, featuring a stylized portrait of Columbus, while George T. Morgan prepared the reverse. These coins were offered for $1 each at the Exposition, but many remained unsold, and later vast quantities were released into circulation at face value.

There are 14 coins in the preceding list, most of which are Uncirculated. This group, which would make a fascinating display, is valued at $2,234.75, a figure within the range of most adult numismatists, even those who are just beginning their interest. If the 1907 $20 is subtracted, we have a group of 13 coins valued at $1,234.75. Further subtract the 1917 Type I quarter dollar and we have a group of 12 coins, still a fine exhibit and collection valued at just $734.25. I suggest that just about anyone with a serious interest in rare coins can afford $724.25.

I am not recommending that you rush out and buy this particular group of coins. They are given only as an illustration that coins to do not have to be expensive in order to be interesting and numismatically desirable. Make your own list.

Opportunities for the Collector-Investor

I believe that by reading this and other books, by keeping abreast of the numismatic market, by subscribing to periodicals, and by making your purchases carefully and with forethought, you can form a numismatically important collection which will bring you many years of enjoyment and, if present trends continue, may prove to be a potentially superb investment as well. If you want to invest a large sum of money you can acquire rarities along with commoner issues, but if you want to make only a modest investment, there are still many really interesting and desirable pieces available, as the preceding list of inexpensive coins with stories indicates.

It will take a few hours to read this book, and it will take several hundred dollars to build a basic numismatic library, to subscribe to numismatic periodicals, and to gain additional information. Knowledge is king, and the more you learn, the more enjoyment and profit you will realize. This fact is immutable. Anyone who tells you that you do not have to learn about coins wants to keep you uninformed so he can either sell you common coins or charge high prices or both. An investment of two or three hours of your time each week will make you a knowledgeable coin buyer, and within a year or two you will know more than 90% of the people in the field! I have seen it happen. You can become an astute buyer if you try.

Today's collector-investor has many exciting opportunities, probably more than anyone has had in the past quarter century. These include the following:

• **You can buy rare coins for reasonable prices:** In some series the opportunity exists to acquire many scarce and rare coins for little more than the price of common coins. This is because many buyers make purchases strictly for investment purposes and are satisfied with common coins. As they do not seek rarities, coins which are hard to find are often priced for less than they should be. Most buyers are not connoisseurs, which means that there are many opportunities for buyers who are. I am reminded of a French restaurant which priced a rather average quality wine at a high price, and bottles from a select vintage at a lower level. "My patrons who don't know any better will buy the average quality wine, and those who are connoisseurs will have the chance to buy the superb vintage wine for a very reasonable price," the owner told a magazine reporter.

• Slabbed coins offer advantages: Slabbed coins, while not solving the problem of grading as a precise determinant of market value, do offer the opportunity to acquire coins which have a reasonable assurance of being at or near the numerical grade levels indicated on them. The knowledgeable buyer can learn to separate the low-end and unappealing coins and leave those to other buyers, while purchasing those of premium quality. Years ago grading differences among sellers were much greater than they are today. Common and popular coins certified by the major grading services are very liquid, and a silver dollar described as, for example, 1885-CC MS-63 (PCGS) will readily trade sight-unseen[1] at a certain level. A hand-picked MS-63 coin with attractive lustre or toning or with a special aesthetic appeal will usually sell for considerably more than the sight-unseen bid price. Sight-unseen purchases are nearly always made by investors or dealers selling to investors, while most collectors insist on either seeing coins before they buy them, or having a return guarantee if the coin is unattractive. Since the late 1980s investors have held sway, and the sight-unseen market has been very active, although in recent times the number of sight-unseen bidders has been only a small fraction of the total dealer population. Most dealers indeed want to see coins before making a purchase commitment, except at a bargain-basement price. If the number of investors dwindles in the future, then a great price differential will develop within slabbed coins of the same numerical grade, for informed collectors will reject ugly coins and pay premiums for superb ones. Right now you can cherrypick[2] coins in slabs, ignore the ugly ducklings, and buy the nice pieces.

• **Information is readily available in print:** More good books and periodicals are available, and at reasonable prices, than ever before. As noted, for a few hundred dollars a good basic numismatic library can be formed. Krause Publications, Amos Press, Specialty Books, Whitman Coin Products (a division of Western Publishing Co.), Sanford Durst, and other numismatic publishers each produce many desirable titles, as does the Publications Department of Bowers and Merena Galleries. Out-of-print books, price lists, and auction catalogues are the specialities of a half dozen or more booksellers, most of whom issue informative catalogues. Apart from whatever valuable

Collectors and Investors

advice you may glean from books you buy, there is a great deal of enjoyment to be had by learning about coins, their designs and their history.

• **The market is very competitive:** There is great competition among dealers, which results in lower markups and provides the opportunity for you to buy or sell within a close margin. There are thousands of dealers who have coins for sale at fixed prices and a dozen or more auction houses which issue fine catalogues of important collections. The worldwide market assures you of a market for your coins when you sell.

• **You can enjoy numismatics:** The chance to have plain, old-fashioned fun is part of numismatics. Collecting coins is one of the world's most interesting, absorbing, most intellectually satisfying hobbies. Building a set of coins, reading about numismatics, attending coin shows, and becoming involved will add a new dimension of enjoyment to your life, as it has for thousands of others.

Collections vs. Accumulations

Times change, and the *collections* of yesterday are being increasingly replaced by the *accumulations* of today, miscellaneous groupings of coins assembled on the advice of one investment guru or another, and, more often than not, consisting of common coin varieties, although they may be in high grades. Of course, it is my hope that you will build a meaningful collection, not a miscellaneous accumulation.

At the outset, let me say that there is nothing wrong with amassing an accumulation of coins if this is what you wish. Cartoon character Scrooge McDuck reveled in his three acres of money, and novel character Silas Marner spent hours contemplating his hoard of golden guineas. I once had a client, Dr. Abraham Kaufmann, who would rather buy a roll of coins than a single specimen, and there is no doubt that he did well with the many rolls of Liberty Walking half dollars, early Washington quarters, Mercury dimes and other items he purchased in quantity from my company in the 1950s.

While accumulating coins can be profitable if you take the time to learn what you are doing, forming a collection is an even better way to acquire coins. You can buy coins for investment, and at the same time you can build a meaningful collection of true historical, numismatic, and financial significance. You can have your cake and eat it, too (more about this will be found in the last chapter).

What is the difference between a collection and an accumulation? Take, for example, the Morgan silver dollar series. The first Morgan silver dollar saw the light of day in 1878. From that point until 1904, silver dollars were produced at the Philadelphia, Carson City, New Orleans, and San Francisco mints. Not all mints produced silver dollars each year. In 1878, dollars were made at Philadelphia, Carson City, and San Francisco, but not at New Orleans. In 1894, dollars were produced at Philadelphia, New Orleans, and San Francisco, but not Carson City. After 1904 production was halted, and no more Morgan dollars were minted until 1921, during which year pieces were produced at the Philadelphia, Denver, and San Francisco mints.

A collector of Morgan silver dollars aspires to acquire one each of every date, mintmark, and major variety in the series. Thus, the collector builds a holding of nearly 100 different varieties dated from 1878 through 1921. A list of the collection might read like this: 1878 8 tail feathers, 1878 7 over 8 tail feathers, 1878 7 tail feathers, 1878-CC, 1878-S, 1879, 1879-CC, 1879-O, 1879-S, 1880, 1880-CC, 1880-O, 1880-S, and so on, to end with 1921, 1921-D, and 1921-S.

A complete collection of Morgan silver dollars contains common issues as well as rare ones, in effect creating a balanced "portfolio." Such varieties as 1881-S, 1884-O, and 1885-O are plentiful, even in MS-65 grade. Indeed, thousands, perhaps tens of thousands, of MS-65 1881-S dollars exist. There is nothing negative about this, for every collection must have one. In addition, anyone wanting an inexpensive 19th century silver dollar can own an example of the 1881-S. On the other hand there are a number of truly scarce and rare Morgan dollars. Such varieties as the 1879-CC, 1886-O, 1889-CC, 1892-S, 1893-S, 1895-O, 1895-S, 1896-S, 1901, 1903-S, and 1904-S, among others, are hard to find in Uncirculated grade. The 1895 is available only in Proof finish.

The 1895 Dollar Rarity

The 1895 Morgan silver dollar is worth mentioning in detail. In 1895 the Philadelphia Mint produced 12,000 silver dollars for regular purposes, with frosty, lustrous surfaces. These "business strikes," as ordinary coins are called, were put into 12 bags containing 1,000 coins each, with the intention of releasing them into the channels of commerce as needed. In addition just 880 silver dollars were made with a special mirrorlike Proof surface, for sale at a premium price to collectors. These 880 Proofs were sold, and, presumably, they went into 880 different collections, or at least 500 or 600 different, if you consider that some collectors may have stocked up on a few duplicates.

Years later, when coin collecting became popular on a wide scale, it was realized that 1895 dollars simply could not be found in circulation. Seemingly, they didn't exist. After a while, numismatists concluded that all 12,000 business strikes went to the melting pot and were destroyed under terms of the Pittman Act in 1918,[3] and that the only 1895 dollars available were survivors from the 880 Proofs made for collectors. So, that is how the 1895 became a rarity. The 1895, which has been called the "King of Morgan Dollars," is rare in any preservation, and even a scuffed, banged-up Proof would sell for thousands of dollars. The possession of a beautiful Proof 1895 dollar will be a source of pleasure to any specialist.

The 1892-S $1: Rare in Certain Grades

On the other hand the 1892-S dollar provides an example of a variety which is rare in some grades but not others. Of this coin 1,200,000 were minted. While some may have been melted under the provisions of the Pittman Act in 1918, there are enough worn pieces around to indicate that most were probably placed into the channels of circulation at the time of issue. Indeed, in worn grades such as VG-8, Fine-12, and Very Fine-20 the 1892-S is quite common. Uncirculated pieces are another thing entirely. In 1892, when the coins were minted, few collectors saved mintmark varieties. Most were concerned only with acquiring just one coin of a particular date, and it did not make any difference if the coin had no mintmark at all (as a Philadelphia issue) or if it had a CC, O, or S. Accordingly, no one bothered to save any 1892-S dollars. Nearly all slipped into the channels of commerce and over a period of years became worn.

Let's look at the prices of the 1892-S dollar in various grades, from well-worn (VG-8) to superb Uncirculated (MS-65). These figures are taken from the *Coin Dealer Newsletter*, issue of June 22, 1990, and indicate average prices dealers were willing to pay at the time: 1892-S $1: VG-8 $12.00, F-12 $13.50; VF-20 $32.00; EF-40 $100.00; AU-50 $600.00; MS-60 (Uncirculated, minimum quality) $5,500.00; MS-63 $18,500; MS-64 $31,000; and MS-65 $80,000.

Stated in a spectacular manner, an MS-65 1892-S dollar is worth 6,853 times the price of a VG-8 example. In other words, one can buy 6,853 specimens in VG-8 grade for the price of a single MS-65!

This study brings up another point, one which will be discussed later: sometimes a very small difference in grade can make a very big difference in price. An MS-65 1892-S silver dollar at $80,000 is more than two and one-half times more expensive than an MS-64 coin at $31,000. Obviously, it becomes quite important in a transaction of this magnitude to know if a coin offered as MS-65 is really in that grade; that is, if the same coin offered as MS-

65 today will be bought as MS-65 by someone else in the future.

As a comparison, let's look at prices for the 1881-S Morgan dollar, a coin which is very common in all grades, including Uncirculated: VG-8 $11; F-12 $12.50; VF-20 $15; EF-40 $16; AU-50 $18; MS-60 $20; MS-63 $25; MS-64 $62; and MS-65 $190.

Price is one thing and availability may be something else entirely. Recently I endeavored to buy an MS-65 1892-S Morgan silver dollar. Although I was quite willing to pay $80,000, the bid price, none was offered, and even if I had been willing to pay $100,000, I doubt if one could have been located. At the same time, by making a few telephone calls I could have bought a carload of MS-65 1881-S dollars.

Tail Feathers

When George T. Morgan produced his silver dollar design in 1878, the eagle on the reverse was given eight tail feathers. Objections were raised, possibly by some know-it-all birdwatcher, that an eagle has one central tail feather longer than the others. Thus an eagle must have an odd, not even, number of tail feathers, and eight could not possibly be correct. So, the design was modified slightly, and dollars minted later in 1878 as well as all other dollars through 1921 had seven tail feathers. Rather than waste a number of coining dies on hand with eight tail feathers, they were overpunched with the new master die with seven tail feathers. Coins minted from these overpunched dies show, under magnification, eight tail feathers protruding slightly below the new seven tail feathers design and are called the seven over eight tail feathers variety, sometimes abbreviated as 7/8 TF.

The dedicated collector of Morgan silver dollars, in addition to desiring one each of every common issue (such as 1881-S) and every scarce and rare issue (1879-CC, 1889-CC, 1892-S in higher grades, 1893-S, 1895, etc.), also desires to own a specimen of the 1878 with seven over eight tail feathers.

By now you can see that being a collector is no simple matter! Suppose that money were no object, and you could buy whatever you wanted. If you aspired to build a complete set of Morgan silver dollars in MS-65 grade, this would take planning in order to figure out which varieties you wanted to include, then it would take persistence in order to track down rarities. If you gave me a blank check it might take me months or even years to find superb MS-65 examples of such issues as 1892-S, 1893-S, 1896-O, and other varieties which are seldom seen in higher grade levels.

Being an accumulator poses no such problems. Tell me or any other dealer that you want to buy $100,000 worth of MS-65 dollars and that you don't care if you have any scarce varieties, and on your doorstep the next day can be a trunkful of 1881-S, 1884-O, 1885-O and other common issues. Actually, if you gave me such a purchase order, I would try to talk you out of the idea—and suggest that you start building a collection and buy rare dollars along with the common ones. But the point is that there is no lack of coins to buy if you are not particular about whether you acquire pieces which are scarce or rare, and are satisfied with common issues.

Common Coins: Advantages and Disadvantages

Common coins offer these advantages:

• They are easy to buy, for there are plenty of them around.

• They are often available in high grades such as MS-65.

• You can spend your money quickly, for countless dealers and investment advisors would be delighted to move these coins from their bank vaults to yours.

Common coins offer this disadvantage:

• No one will get excited when the time comes for you to sell. Yawn.

Rare Coins: Advantages and Disadvantages

Rare coins offer these advantages:

• When the time comes for you to sell, buyers will compete eagerly for them. Excitement!

• Rare coins are the centerpieces of any collection and ownership is a source of accomplishment and pride.

Rare coins offer these disadvantages:

• They can be expensive.

• They can be difficult to locate.

There you have it: collections vs. accumulations, rare coins vs. common ones. Take your pick.

CHAPTER THREE

Have a Plan

Quantity and Quality

Being somewhat of a numismatic purist and traditionalist, to say nothing of being an idealist, my quick answer to the question, "Should I buy a large quantity of common coins or a small quantity of rare ones?" is "form a collection and acquire one each of the pieces needed in the collection, some common and others rare."

If you were to ask, "If I don't want to form a collection, should I buy common coins or rare ones?" I would answer: "Buy the rare ones." If you enlisted Bowers and Merena Galleries in the search for rarities we would relish the challenge to put together a first-class holding, and at some later date hope to have the opportunity to showcase it in one of our auction sales, to the appreciation and delight of buyers from all over the world.

However, there may be more than one correct answer to each of these questions. Without a doubt, those who have carefully formed collections of high quality coins in the past have, in nearly all instances, done very well upon their sale. In an advertisement Stack's cited the instance of Harold Bareford, who formed a collection over a period of years—and this was long ago—and who paid approximately $12,700 for it. Upon its sale it realized about $1.2 million.

Then there is the Eliasberg Collection. Addressing an eager group of listeners at a gathering held in Baltimore in 1976, Louis Eliasberg related that his collection cost him slightly over $300,000 and had appreciated in value at a compounded rate of about 18% per year. In 1982 my company sold just *part* of his collection at auction, and that part brought $12,400,000!

In my book, *High Profits From Rare Coin Investment*, which was first published in 1974 and which has in the meantime gone through many editions and has become the best-selling volume ever written on the subject, I stated that over a long period of years I had purchased or had sold at auction numerous old-time collections, and in each and every instance anyone who had carefully formed a collection and who had held it for a period of years had realized a profit upon its sale. To this date I know of no exceptions to this statement. This is really remarkable, for in what other field—securities? real estate?—could a leading dealer make the statement that over the long term *all* of his clients who had purchased with care and forethought had made money?

While there are many success stories with collectors and collections, there are also stories of profits which involve hoarders and accumulators. One of the most famous of these is that of LaVere Redfield, a recluse who lived in Reno, Nevada, and who over a period of years stashed away over 400,000 Morgan and Peace silver dollars, paying face value or close to it for most of them. After his death his collection was sold in 1976 to the A-Mark Coin Company for $7.3 million in a transaction also involving Hugh Sconyers, a numismatic and financial genius who, years later, joined professional numismatist Kevin Lipton and the securities firm of Kidder, Peabody & Co. in the launching of the American Rare Coin Fund Limited Partnership.

Kenneth E. Bressett, editor of *A Guide Book of United States Coins*, tells the story of a friend who became interested in coin investment and wanted to buy two 40-coin rolls of Uncirculated 1950-D nickels a few years after they came out. He paid something like $20 each for the rolls, and then tossed them into his office desk drawer. In 1964, when the market for 1950-D nickels peaked, Ken called his friend, who had forgotten about the nickels, and persuaded him to sell for $1,200 per roll!

I know of several people who hoarded scarce and rare coins, ignoring common issues, and who did well. Don Corrado Romano, who for years operated the Worthy Coin Company in Boston, squirreled away as many 1795 half dollars and Proof 1878 trade dollars as he could find, and enjoyed watching the market price rise year by year. A Florida client thought that 1877 Proof Shield nickels were undervalued and formed a small corner on the market, eventually acquiring nearly 200 pieces, which he sold at an attractive profit. Michael Kolman, Jr., who operated the Federal Coin Exchange in Cleveland, decided that worn twenty-cent pieces of 1875 and 1876 were worth more than the market realized, and bought hundreds, perhaps thousands, of pieces, and upon their sale turned a nice profit. P.B. Trotter, Jr., a Memphis banker, hoarded hundreds of 1839-O half dollars. At the time of their issue Baltimore collector T. Harrison Garrett put away well over 2,000 gold dollars dated 1879, 1880, and 1881. One of our clients amassed all of the 1828 12-stars half cents he could find. Nat Schoen thought that Proof 1894 Barber dimes were undervalued and over a period of time bought nearly 100 of them, selling them later for a nice profit. The list could be expanded considerably.

A rising tide lifts all ships, and a rising coin market lifts the prices of all coins, common and rare. My own preference, and the advice I usually give, is to invest by building a meaningful numismatic collection: one of each

Morgan dollar variety, one of each different commemorative half dollar design, one of each major design type of U.S. gold coin, or some similar discipline. In this way a balanced holding is acquired, the common as well as the rare, and when your collection is sold there will be great enthusiasm among buyers. However, there is no question that accumulators have also done well in many instances.[1]

The Ultimate Consumer

Conventional wisdom has it that the ultimate "consumer" for a coin is an individual who desires an individual specimen for his or her collection.[2] Without this consideration, there is no reason why an MS-65 1892-S dollar, bid at $80,000, should be worth any more than an MS-65 1881-S dollar, bid at $190. For that matter, there is no reason that in the absence of a collector wanting to buy it, either coin should be worth more than its melt-down or silver bullion value of just a few dollars.

The concept of coins going up in value because investors are selling to other investors has always puzzled me, and I am just beginning to sort it out. Imagine a world without coin collectors, a world composed of many coin investors, but no collectors. Promotional hype would induce investors to acquire coins, and if prices were rising, the increase in prices would prompt still more buying and would cause further high prices. As long as new investors came into the market to replace those leaving, prices would remain stable or increase. Buyers without knowledge of coins, whose purchase desire was based solely on hopes of price increases, are, perhaps, subscribers to the so-called "greater fool theory," under which all is just dandy, providing that someone else comes along tomorrow to pay a higher price.

It may be irreverent to suggest the "greater fool theory," when the entire situation can be made to seem quite reasonable by comparing it to real estate, an investment arena which has attracted untold billions of dollars, far more money than has ever been placed in the coin market.

In real estate the ultimate "consumer" of a piece of property is someone who will *use* it to build a home, to situate a factory, to cultivate for the growing of corn, or to make a parking lot. However, the fact remains that many parcels of land have changed hands over a long period of years without being developed. Raw land was, is, and probably always will be a desirable commodity. In theory, all raw land will someday achieve its ultimate value when it is used by someone, but in the meantime nice profits can be made in anticipation of this time, even if the time is quite distant and beyond our lifetime.

Similarly, it may be reasonable to suggest that it is perfectly fine, and potentially quite profitable, for large numbers of investors to buy quantities of coins, including rarities, with nothing more in mind that holding them for future appreciation and selling them to another generation of investors. While it might be nice, at least in a theoretical way, if at some future time a collector were to own a particular coin, say one of those common 1881-S dollars, in the meantime it makes no difference in the market if today's buyer is a collector, an investor, or a combination of both. I can argue both sides of the question.

In recent times, particularly since 1989, much money from Wall Street has entered the coin business, which many now refer to as the coin *industry*. Kidder, Peabody; Merrill Lynch, and other highly respected securities firms have pumped millions into the marketplace with the expectation that a later generation of buyers, be they investors or collectors, will come along and pay higher prices. There is no doubt that Wall Street's acceptance of coins as a viable investment medium has greatly broadened the market. I will have more to say about this later.

Frank S. Robinson's Commentary

Frank S. Robinson, a coin dealer and veteran observer of the numismatic scene, contributed the following poignant and insightful article (here excerpted) to *Coin World* concerning the extreme importance of the role of the collector to sustain the basic foundation of numismatics:[3]

"Collecting enjoyment is a coin's only ultimate basis of value. The market, though, seems to suggest that coins also have some independent investment value. It is true that investment coins have done well while collector coin prices have stagnated due to a declining collector base. What happened was that, even though the coin hobby boom fizzled, it had meanwhile touched off an investment boom strong enough to outlive it (thus far).

"This investment boom is focused upon a very narrow segment of the coinage spectrum. Its watchword is quality. True enough, quality will always be a key criterion of value. But today's investors act as though they have finally latched onto the Great Truth that somehow eluded past benighted generations of numismatists. They forgot that fads within numismatics come and go. At one time, Washington medals were all the rage.[4] The past few decades have seen markets in which cents, then Proof sets, then rolls, then dollars, each in turn were kings. Today Quality is king; tomorrow it may be something else.

"American numismatics itself may be viewed as something of a fad. And if there is no law that coin collecting must always be popular,[5] there is certainly no law that the very highest grade coins must always be its holy grail.

"Further, a rule of reason must be applied. Value and quality must be reasonably proportionate. A coin that is greatly better than another should be worth greatly more; a coin only a teensy bit nicer should not. Yet in today's market, minute quality differentials make for huge price differentials.

"Some apparently consider this rational on the basis that a Mint State-65 may be several times rarer than an MS-64 and hence should be worth much more. And admittedly there is greater demand for the MS-65 too; this is what has pushed up the price, and demand is a valid factor. But consider: The extra grading point or two is being demanded not because the market values the added quality for quality's sake, but instead because it is betting that the future demand will be even greater still. And meantime, to the extent such grading increments can be differentiated at all—careful examination under magnification, perhaps under special lighting too, is required—and even then, experts cannot always agree (in fact, many people make their living out of this judgmental element).

"Collectors do desire quality and are willing to pay for it because a higher quality coin is prettier. But when prices reach four and five figures for otherwise non-rare coins based on minuscule quality increments not even apparent to the naked eye, it is unrealistic to imagine future collectors buying them out of love alone (and not investment).

"Actually, it could be argued that the market is making a huge mistake in focusing upon the high end coins for which the true collector market is exceedingly thin, and that it would be more rational to invest in those coins for which there is at least potentially a wide collector base—circulated Buffalo nickels and the like. But even this would be of dubious wisdom since all signs point to a declining rather than expanding collectorhood.

"At any rate, what the market has really done is to take a valid proposition—that quality will always be preferred—to an absurd extreme by seeing scarcely any limit to what collectors will pay for quality. It is somewhat ironic, too, that the market has decreed the primacy of quality, because this implicitly recognizes that a coin's value resides in the aesthetic collecting pleasure it provides. Yet the market at the same time imagines that investment buying can sustain prices regardless of collector involvement.

"This is of course a logical contradiction. But there is an even bigger problem: Nobody really imagines that the future buyers of investment grade coins will be financially disinterested collectors; the anticipated market is an investment-oriented one. And this precisely mirrors the classic Ponzi pyramid scam, in which people pay for the right to sell franchises in a business to other people, who are licensed to sell still more franchises. There may supposedly be some consumable product involved, but nobody's real expectations of profit are based on actually selling that product to the public—they are based on an expanding pyramid franchising—just as the coin investment market is based not on eventually selling coins to collectors for enjoyment, but rather upon a continuing pyramid of investing.

"The word 'pyramid' is used because an ever-expanding base is required—that is, each new tier of participants must be larger, or must spend more money. But the human population is infinite, and hence such pyramids (a chain letter is another example) must always collapse in the end.

"One might query how, if all this is true, the market has managed to flourish for as long as it has. The answer lies in the potent psychology of a speculative spiral. The track record is a siren song few can resist. The market's pervasive ethos says that because investment coins have gone up before, they must go up more. A great host of seemingly intelligent, knowledgeable, experienced professionals all play this same seductive tune.

"Of course, another powerful factor is the industry's own huge stake in the market. It has even been said that so much money is involved now that the market makers will never let it collapse; that investment coin trading has become so institutionalized, on such a giant scale, that its death is inconceivable.

"But history teaches that even the biggest, most powerful institutions can collapse when the conditions that sustained them end. Look at Communism! And the coin investment market is especially vulnerable because it requires a condition not of stasis but of continual advancement. Investment coin prices have to keep rising (faster than inflation) to keep up the crucial track record that stimulates more investment to expand the pyramid's base.

"Reason tells us this cannot go on forever, because coin prices would eventually outpace the financial ability of even the most avid and wealthy buyers. The pyramid cannot expand indefinitely; and when it stops, no amount of support and promotion by the numismatic industry will be able to keep the investment delusion alive. All the king's horses and all the king's men won't be able to put Humpty Dumpty together again.

"I wince to invoke that old chestnut, the Dutch tulip bulb mania, but the analogy to the coin investment market is so perfect. Centuries ago, tulip growing became very popular in Holland, and prices for rare and unusual bulbs naturally rose. Then a speculative frenzy ensued, and prices reached levels which made no sense in terms of planting bulbs to grow tulips. But of course people were not buying bulbs now to plan in gardens. Instead—bedazzled by that notorious old fooler, 'track record'—they expected to sell their investment-grade bulbs at a profit to buyers who would in turn expect the same thing. Predictably, the market ultimately collapsed, and bulbs fell back to being worth only what people would pay to plant them in their gardens.

"Today, people aren't buying investment coins to plant in their gardens— that is, to put in collections and enjoy them. They're buying to sell to investors. They're buying tulip bulbs. In the end, prices will inevitably fall back to levels that true collectors—buying for pleasure and not investment—are willing to pay. *If* any collectors are left."

While I suggest that if you become a collector, a connoisseur, you will derive many benefits, it is also the case, as implied by the preceding commentary by Mr. Robinson, that numismatics *needs* you. If you become a collector, then investors everywhere owe you a debt of gratitude!

Is the Collector Still King?

Under the above title, professional numismatists Julian Leidman and Mark Mendelson contributed an article to the "Monthly Summary" of the *Coin Dealer Newsletter.*[6] Many of the thoughts are similar to those just expressed by Frank S. Robinson. In addition, the writers exhorted their fellow dealers to sow seeds for the future of numismatics by encouraging clients to learn about coins, to become collectors. Excerpts:

"We, as dealers, are becoming increasingly concerned about the lack of enthusiasm our fellow dealers seem to show for dealing with the public. If dealers don't begin to 'fire-up' their customers' *collecting* desires, they might as well fire up the furnaces to melt all those 'rare' coins back into bullion— because that is what they will be worth.

"We feel that numismatics would prosper if dealers spent half as much time and energy on cultivating their customers as they do on slabbing, cracking [breaking coins out of slabs, to resubmit them in the hope of having them slabbed at higher grades], and short-term money-making.... What percentage of dealers' time and effort is dedicated to motivating the public to collect or invest in coins? How often do dealers use their knowledge to support the long-term growth of the industry?

"Part of our uneasy feelings come from our extensive participation at major coin shows, where we see fewer collectors and potential customers in attendance.... There must be a commitment of time to the customer, and specifically to helping him develop a sense of direction in his collecting. Most transactions are product-based; a customer wants a Morgan dollar, and a dealer sells him a Morgan dollar. This type of transaction is even more accentuated on the busy bourse floor where the customer is often a stranger. Regardless, every retail sale of numismatic property should be accompanied by an exchange of *information*, not just dollars....

"The dealer must examine to what degree the customer is a collector or an investor, what the customer reads, what his budget is, and his motivation behind his numismatic interests. The dealer should play a vital role in helping the neophyte collector discover what kind of collection he wants to put together....

"We certainly welcome the business of the investor, and recognize that he must share some of the traits of the collector if the industry is going to benefit in the long run. The cold investor who sells on a moment's notice, as soon as the market shows any sign of weakness, will find himself participating in a self-fulfilling prophecy. If all the collectors are driven out of the market and the only stimulus left for buying coins is the investor's need to have prices rise, then the market will collapse.

"Much has been made in the numismatic press about how dealers treat the young and beginning collectors who venture into their shops or onto the bourse floor. The young collector is the future of the hobby, and the neophyte collector or investor, getting ready to take his first real plunge into numismatic purchasing, needs to be treated a good deal like that youngster. Both are relatively new to numismatics, and they need a dealer's attention and experience to shape their activities. The amount of money spent by investors may be larger, but time spent in cultivation will be amply repaid in the long run. The loyal customer who spends years assembling a collection will use the services of the dealer in two ways—for buying and, ultimately, for selling. The investor may have the 'big bucks' necessary to buy the nicest coins, but if the purchase demonstrates no desire, then the dealer is likewise denied the opportunity to live through his clients' collections. Pleasure and pride of ownership are emotions shared in a trusting relationship between dealer and customer....[7]

"What can dealers do to support their collector and investor customers?...

"Participation in local coin clubs provides the opportunity to meet additional collectors and perhaps move some of that lower-priced material. Local numismatic events, with their slower pace, allow dealers more time to share their expertise with collectors. Making use of the educational facilities of large collector organizations like the American Numismatic Association and American Numismatic Society can also help dealers educate and guide their clients.

"The dealer can also provide service and education to the non-collecting public, making the joys of collecting more evident. Every community organization is looking for speakers; imagine how many Rotarians there are who know nothing about numismatics.[8] Find out about specialized community events—that two week display on Russia at the public library just might need a few coins! Sponsor a scholarship to the ANA Summer Seminar for a local youngster. Becoming more involved with the local community will spread a basic understanding of numismatics and possibly entice a few customers.

"While the mail-order numismatic houses may not have this opportunity for local involvement, they can also do much to advance knowledge and increase the sophistication of collectors. We can point to several examples of firms that have made this commitment. Dave Bowers stands tall among numismatists for demonstrating the extraordinary amount of education that can be packed into his sales publications, both in his retail lists and auction catalogs. Littleton Coin Company has certainly made its presence known among the collectors of lower-priced material, which is how many collectors start in numismatics. Stack's has long specialized in disseminating information over the counter.

"So what will be good for the long-term interests of numismatics? Making sure that the clients get the best coins (not necessarily the highest grade or closest to 'bid') for their goals and collecting plan. Giving the customer what he likes (as modified by your careful guidance, attention, and sharing of knowledge) will inspire additional demand. As all dealers know, there also seems to be a never-ending supply of interesting material to entice the sophisticated collector/investor. Maximizing the number and quality of collectors is the only way to provide the broad, firm foundation that price increases are built upon....

"The spark of coin collecting must be fanned into the flame of desire. In a supply/demand marketplace, nothing else can sustain higher prices...."

Sadly, Messrs. Leidman and Mendelson are in the distinct minority among dealers. At a meeting of Professional Numismatists Guild members a few years ago the president of that group asked for a show of hands from those who had given a public talk or program on coins within the past year. In the audience comprised of 100 or more hobby leaders, scarcely a dozen hands were raised.[9] Dealers in the "silent majority" delight in taking profits from the hobby (or industry) but apparently don't have the time or inclination to put something back into it.

A Veteran Dealer Speaks Out

In a feature article in *Dallas Life Magazine*[10] veteran Fort Worth, Texas dealer R.E. Wallace's comments on certain aspects of coin investment were quoted: "The standard of ethics between the [traditional] coin dealer and the nouveau coin dealer is the difference between light and dark. They'll lead a lamb to slaughter.... If you don't know what a Mint State-65 is, you've got no business buying a coin."

Wallace went on to say that coins can, indeed, be good investments, but not to investors: "If you want to make money in coins, you *collect* them. It's a lifetime proposition." He then mused: "The big question in my mind is all these investors buying all these coins—who the hell are they going to sell them to? They've got to feed back into the market, and the *collector* isn't going to buy them in these slabs. I will not buy slabbed coins, nor will I sell them."

Pleasure and Satisfaction

Unquestionably, the collector, apart from his being a largely unappreciated necessity for the strength of the very foundation of the rare coin business, derives a great measure of personal satisfaction and pleasure from coin ownership. Why? Here are some of my observations.

The American Numismatic Association was founded in 1891 by George F. Heath, a medical doctor who practiced in Monroe, Michigan, and who served several terms as mayor of that town. Heath was an intellectual giant, and to him coins were the passport to the streets of ancient Rome, the English court of Queen Anne, and to a ringside seat at the battles fought by Napoleon. His writings reveal that he could quote Greek and Latin at will, was familiar with classic literature, and was a philosopher. Coin collecting, Heath asserted, provided the possibility for a richer, fuller life, one filled with happiness and satisfaction.

For several years during the late 1980s I researched and wrote *The American Numismatic Association Centennial History*, a volume commissioned by the Board of Governors of the ANA. In the course of doing this I read through all issues of *The Numismatist*, the official publication of the ANA, from the earliest numbers down to the present time. Time and time again I read of the rewards of numismatics experienced by those who followed the hobby. While many contributors undoubtedly experienced great financial success, the memory of profits was fleeting. Such aspects as the pleasures of completing a collection, the enjoyment of meeting and knowing fellow hobbyists, the excitement in tracking down historical information pertaining to a newly acquired specimen, the reading of a truly interesting book or catalogue, and the satisfaction of accomplishing something worthwhile seemed to have the best and longest-lasting effect.

Have a Plan

American coins touch upon virtually every aspect of history. Crudely struck Massachusetts Pine Tree shillings dated 1652, if bent twice, are said to have been ideal for warding off witches; that piece in your collection may have been in Judge Samuel Sewall's pocket when he presided over the Salem witch trials. That Carson City silver dollar may indeed have been spent in a poker game in Virginia City. President Theodore Roosevelt may have flipped that 1891 Liberty nickel or 1907 Indian cent to settle a bet. The possibilities are endless.

Earlier, I touched upon the Carson City Mint, the Comstock Lode, and other considerations in connecting with the minting of Morgan silver dollars. Now I will discuss forming a complete collection of dollars of this design. The discipline is representative and simply illustrates a procedure. The illustration could have been of any other series as well. I will try to put myself in the shoes of a client, one who doesn't mind expending some effort. If I were forming a set of Morgan dollars 1878-1921, I would do the following, but I admit that I might be going overboard a bit, and that the typical reader of these words is apt to be more casual:

• **Gain knowledge:** I would read everything I could find about Morgan silver dollars, how they were designed, which mints produced them, the mintage figures for each variety, etc. I would read about the great Treasury release of dollars in 1962-1963 and the unexpected effect this had upon the market.

• **Devise a plan:** I would formulate a collecting plan. For example, I might set as a goal the obtaining of all of the more readily available issues in a high grade such as nicely matched MS-63 and MS-64, with some of the more plentiful varieties in MS-65 preservation. I would set my sights on obtaining the rarities in a lesser grade, such as MS-60. I would not propose to have everything in MS-65, even if I could afford it, for I would rather spend the extra amount on some other area of numismatics, perhaps building a set of Indian cents in addition to my Morgan dollars. It might be that certain really expensive coins such as the 1889-CC and 1893-S should be acquired in EF-40 or AU-50 grade.

• **Learn about varieties:** I would endeavor to learn something about the characteristics of each variety. I would find out which are usually found sharply struck, and which are usually have weakly defined features (especially on the on the hair strands of Miss Liberty at the center of the obverse and the eagle's breast feathers on the reverse). In this way I will know whether I should pay a premium for a coin with sharply struck features and excellent aesthetic appeal. For example, I would discover that nearly all 1881-S dollars are sharply struck and are attractive, so I would not have to pay a significant premium for a truly superb coin. On the other hand, I would learn that many New Orleans Mint dollars of the 1890s are flatly struck, and a needle-sharp coin may well be a great buy even at a premium price over market levels.

• **Determine market prices:** Once I have formulated a list of the varieties I want and the grades I want them in, I would consult the *Coin Dealer Newsletter*, the *Certified Coin Dealer Newsletter*, *Coin World* "Trends," *Numismatic News* "Coin Market," auction prices realized, dealer offerings, and other price guides in order to determine market levels and the frequency with which such pieces are offered. Sometimes price guides and bid prices are one thing and availability is another; an example is provided by a client who wanted to buy a high grade 1896-O dollar and who had spent over a year looking for one. Price was no object. He simply could not find one. Finally, he directed me: "Pay double or triple bid!" After a great deal of searching I finally found one that combined the numerical grade he wanted, with an aesthetically pleasing surface.

• **Formulate a buying strategy:** I would devise a buying plan. Should I acquire the rare ones first, or last? Should I send my want list to a single trusted dealer, or should I buy from several sources? Should I formulate a monthly budget for purchases? Should I only buy coins in slabs, or should I acquire other pieces as well? Do I want brilliant pieces or ones with light toning? Do I want to be fussy about aesthetic values, or should I be satisfied with any coin as long as the numerical grade is what I want?

• **Learn about the Morgan dollar era:** In my spare time I would read about the era of Morgan silver dollars, especially the years from 1878 to 1904, when the early series coins were made. I would learn about the "silver question," which was a key part of American politics, I would read about everyday life in the 1880s and 1890s, and I would try to acquire an "I am there" feeling and relationship with the time. How were silver dollars used? What was their purchasing power? Were they used all over America, or were they more popular in certain geographical areas?

I have every reason to expect that if I followed the procedure just outlined, the following would happen:

• Over a period of time I would build a first-class set of Morgan silver dollars of excellent quality and of good value for the price paid.

• I would enjoy my silver dollars, would experience a satisfaction each time a needed piece was added to the collection, and would have great appreciation for Morgan dollars, their place in numismatics and their position in American history.

• Years later, upon being sold, my collection would attract attention because of its completeness, the rarities it contains, and its quality, and I would realize a nice profit on my investment.

The Road More Often Travelled

The road more often travelled is not the one I would personally elect to follow, but, then, I have never taken the easy way out. The easy road to coin investment, but not necessarily to coin investment *success*, can be described as follows and is *not* recommended by me:

• Determine how much money you want to spend on coins, and determine to spend it as quickly and easily as possible. Don't determine on your own what you want to buy; leave it up to others to sell you what they have in stock.

• Learn a few "facts" about coins from promotional brochures, from salesmen, and from prediction sheets. The more profits a firm promises, the more you should believe what its representatives have to say. Come to the conclusion, for example, that just about anything shiny, round, and in MS-65 is a wonderful investment. Don't build a numismatic library, for books cost money and take precious time to read.

• Spend your money as soon as possible, preferably with the seller who offers either the best bargains or the most glowing promises and predictions of profit, or, better yet, offers both at the same time.[11]

I have every reason to expect that if you followed this procedure, the following would happen:

• You would spend your money quickly, and the dealers you patronized would be very grateful for your business and would no doubt assure you that you were doing the right thing. Of course, if you spent even more money than you planned to, that would be even better.

• You would gather accumulation of common coins. If you did buy some rarities, you would overpay, for you would not know on your own how rare the coins are, whether they are nice examples of their type, or whether the price charged was reasonable. If you buy slabbed coins, you will acquire low-end examples and pieces with little aesthetic appeal, for these are the pieces that dealers try hardest to sell.

• Years later, upon being sold, your accumulation would appeal mainly to the wholesale buyer who, of course, wants to pay wholesale prices. Experienced collectors, leading dealers, and others would not take particular notice of your coins, nor would your collection attract much attention with anyone else.

I fully realize that many people have a gambling instinct, and that logic isn't always important. If you head for the gaming tables in Las Vegas or Atlantic City, you don't want someone telling you that it is mathematically impossible in the long run to win at roulette or the slot machines. You want the fun of the play, you want action. In coins, many people want to spend their money right away; they want action. If this is your motivation, please be careful and do not invest more than you can comfortably afford to lose.

A Happy Medium

Not everyone wants to spend time learning about coins, but everyone wants to maximize the chances of making a profit. A compromise can be effected by learning something, not everything, about coins. Learning just the basic facts will help immeasurably. Indeed, reading this book will repay its cost many times over if you utilize its contents. It won't tell you everything you need to know, but it will go a long way in the right direction. Beyond this book, if you place your want list or business with a carefully-selected professional coin dealer, or perhaps two or three dealers, and at the same time keep abreast of market trends and prices, your chances for success will be improved measurably.

A little secret: A quick, enjoyable, and effective way to learn about coins— a shortcut to becoming a numismatist—is to read all you can on just one limited series such as Morgan dollars, commemoratives, large cents, or some other single area of interest. Learning just about Morgan dollars (for example) is easier than learning about everything from half cents to double eagles. Once you have familiarized yourself with all that you can find in print about Morgan dollars, you will be very knowledgeable. I guarantee it! Then, as time and inclination permit, go into another specialized series and learn about it. Soon, *all* of American numismatics will make sense.

CHAPTER FOUR

Dealing With Dealers

Ways to Buy

There are a number of different methods to buy coins advantageously, and I discuss the most important here. Most collectors acquire their holdings in several different ways, buying some pieces outright, bidding for others at auction, and acquiring still others at club meetings or conventions. At one time, from the 1930s through the 1950s, the main way millions of people became involved in numismatics was to build sets of Lincoln cents, Jefferson nickels, Mercury dimes, and other specialties by looking through pocket change. Today in the 1990s few older pieces are seen in everyday commerce, so this is no longer a viable option except for relatively modern issues.

There are two main ways to buy and sell coins: at fixed prices through dealers and at variable prices through mail bid sales and auctions. I will introduce some caveats, not to dissuade you from buying coins, for that is not my purpose (indeed, my professional career is that of a coin dealer and auctioneer). My intent is to demonstrate the value of education and knowledge. Knowledge is something to gain before you buy coins, not after you do.

Direct Purchases

Let me discuss the dealer method first. Individual professional numismatists and large companies acquire coins by buying private collections, by transacting with other dealers on electronic trading circuits, by bidding in auctions, and by attending conventions. Over a period of time an inventory is built. Some dealers maintain comprehensive stocks containing examples in all United States denominations from half cents to double eagles, as well as commemoratives. Others are specialized and build inventories in a particular area, such as United States large cents of the period 1793-1857, Morgan and Peace silver dollars, Civil War tokens, or gold coins.

Dealers buy for their stocks by grading and evaluating coins offered to them, then naming a price they will pay. In the case of coins sonically sealed by ANACS, Hallmark, the Numismatic Guaranty Corporation (NGC), or the Professional Coin Grading Service (PCGS), the grading work is done for the dealer, and the main element of negotiation is price, although it is to be remembered that not all coins technically graded MS-65, for example, are worth the same price. There are so-called "low end" coins which are worth less, "high end" coins which are worth more, and what Hallmark calls "Premium Quality" coins (sharply struck, etc.) which are also worth more. I have more to say about this in my chapter on grading.

Dealers sell coins from their inventories by running advertisements in leading coin periodicals such as *Numismatic News, Coin World, CoinAge,* and *Coins* magazine, by issuing printed catalogues and price lists, by sending approval shipments to clients who have submitted want lists, by sending electronic messages, by fax, and by telephone solicitation.

Prices and markups are apt to vary. Common items such as bulk silver dollars, bullion coins, etc. are apt to trade at low markups. A dealer may buy a quantity lot of bullion coins for, say, $20,000 and turn it over quickly for $21,000 or even less. On the other hand, for particularly scarce or rare items, or items which are in truly exceptional condition, the markup may be 10%, 20% or more. One of the great fallacies in the coin market is that rare coin dealers can operate their businesses, pay their advertising bills, pay rent, buy airplane tickets, purchase insurance coverage, hire employees and pay them benefits, and borrow money from the bank to use as operating capital, and then buy and sell coins profitably on a margin of just a few percent. It can't be done.

There are no hard and fast rules, and the best advice I can give is that you should know your dealer and also gain a familiarity with prices. Whether the dealer makes a 5% profit on a coin he sells you or whether he makes a 35% profit is immaterial. What matters is the actual price of the coin. I once paid $12,000 for a rare Vermont copper coin which the seller, a prominent dealer, had bought an hour before, paying $400 for it. I did not begrudge him the $11,600 profit he made, for I thought the piece to be a good value when I bought it. In fact, I sold it for $20,000 several months later, and the next owner turned it over quickly for an additional profit.

Before you buy anything, learn the following:

• What is its true grade?

• Considering its sharpness (or weakness) of strike, surface characteristics, and aesthetic appeal, is it an outstanding example of its type?

• What have comparable pieces sold for recently?

Learn these things, and you will be an informed buyer.

A Court Case

An example of what can go wrong if a buyer knows little or nothing about coins is provided by a court case which involved an outfit known as Rare Coin Galleries of America. Ms. Phoebe Morse of the Federal Trade Commission asked me to testify in a proceeding the agency was mounting against this firm.[1] In the course of examining the coins submitted as evidence, I saw numerous Liberty Walking half dollars of the 1930s and 1940s which were what I graded AU-50, and which were worth in some instances just $20 or $30, sold to unsuspecting clients as choice Uncirculated pieces for several hundred dollars apiece.

In his book, *The Investor's Guide to Coin Trading*, Scott Travers discussed this particular scam and noted that R.C.G.A. had sold a $250,000 group of coins to the parents of a retarded child, who had received the funds in a lawsuit settlement. The money had been intended to provide a lifetime income for the unfortunate youngster. Travers wrote that the coins which had been sold for $250,000 were worth approximately $5,000.[2]

Discussing certain other disreputable rare coin investment firms of the early 1980s, Travers noted that the typical company "provided their clientele with a 'value' of five or 10 cents on the dollar."[3] The same writer stated that investment firms had moderated their tactics somewhat since then, and by 1990 dealers who had previously purchased coins for one price (1X) and sold them for 12 times that amount (12X) were now buying coins for 1X and selling them for "only" 3X. He then hastened to add: "It's still unconscionable for someone to make a systematic 100% or 200% profit on coin sales to the public. But it isn't nearly as unconscionable as a 1,000% or 2,000% markup."[4]

Dr. Richard A. Bagg (director of auctions for Auctions by Bowers and Merena, Inc.) and I had the opportunity to talk with numerous clients of the Rare Coin Galleries of America when the Federal Trade Commission referred victims to us for appraisals and advice about recouping what they could. In response to the general inquiry, "Why did you buy these coins?" we heard such answers as:

"A telephone salesman told me that he had intended to call me last October and had picked out a group of coins for me at that time, priced at $4,000. Since then a half year had passed, and the salesman said the coins were now worth $6,000, but as they 'had my name on them' I could still buy them for just $4,000. How could I refuse?"

"They were so professional, so elegant in their presentation, and the profit return was so attractive—better than anything else I knew of—I decided to put my clients into coins. I figured if the profits were only half as great as they said they would be, my clients would still make windfall profits." (This comment was from a financial advisor who spent hundreds of thousands of dollars of his clients' money with the firm.)

"They said that they were one of the largest rare coin companies in America, and they sold only the highest quality, and that they would buy my coins back anytime I wanted to take a profit." (This case involved a woman who invested $14,000 and who received coins really worth about $1,100.)

So far as I could determine, not one of R.C.G.A.'s clients to whom I spoke had ever checked on the prices or grades of the coins they bought! Each invested blindly, lured by the promises of fantastic returns.

For every Rare Coin Galleries of America there are many other dealers who treat their customers fairly, who do their best to provide excellent values, and who give sincere advice. However, as a general rule (and there are exceptions), the glitzier the advertising is, the more persuasive the advertising messages are, and the more glowing the promises, the more you should watch out!

Whimsy

Dr. Joel Orosz, well-known numismatic author and researcher, studied advertisements in leading numismatic newspapers. Writing in *The Asylum*, quarterly journal of the Numismatic Bibliomania Society,[5] he shared some of his observations, including the following:

"In a culture that values excellence we have initiated awards for those whose performance merits honor, from Pulitzer prizes to Oscars, yet nowhere in numismatics do we celebrate the remarkable (I might almost say *awesome*) ability of those in the coin trade to employ hyperbole in the service of increasing sales. Now at last that oversight will be remedied. We herewith announce the first annual Shammy awards. The Shammies recognize those whose superb disregard of credulity goes beyond mere hype into the rarefied realm of wretched excess...."

Among the "awards" given were these:

The "Who is Buried in Grant's Tomb" award to an advertiser "whose pathbreaking research was summarized.... 'Do investors' demands cause gold prices to rise? Company believes link exists.'"

The "Best Public Service Announcement" award to a seller of modern Proof coins issued by the Isle of Man, "whose timely warning undoubtedly saved many a safe deposit box": "The coin could be ready to explode!"

Then there is the "Avoid the Rush, Buy a Portfolio That Has Already Crashed" award given to an investment firm which advertised: "Now you can buy a diversified, generic high quality portfolio for only $995. Last May it retailed for more than $1,995."

On the letters to the editor page of *Coin World*,[6] reader Hal Lutzky was prompted to write: "In your June 6 issue there is an ad with the banner headline 'WE SELL COINS–NOT HYPE.' Contained in the ad, however, are the following words and phrases: 'unimprovable,' 'phenomenal,' 'super,' 'superb,' 'fantastic,' 'truly remarkable,' 'monster,' 'perfect,' and 'breathtaking.' No hype? Gimme a break!"

The preceding is a good reminder not to take too seriously what you see in print, and also that rare coin advertisements provide the opportunity for some good, old-fashioned humor!

Check the Dealer's Reputation

How can you check on a dealer's reputation? If you are not sure, don't spend even a cent until you contact the following:

• The Federal Trade Commission, to see if the firm is the subject of present or past actions. (The FTC will only give information on cases which have been made public, not on current investigations.)

• The executive director of the Professional Numismatists Guild, to see if the dealer is in good standing and has a good reputation with that organization (there are many fine dealers who for one reason or another do not belong to the PNG, but most of the better, larger ones do).

• The Better Business Bureau in the city in which the firm operates.[7]

• *Coin World* and *Numismatic News*, to learn what you can.

Once you do this, go further and "ask around" to see what other collectors, particularly those who have been in numismatics for five years or more, have to say about the firm or individual. Sometimes organizations and publications are less than candid, as they fear to say anything negative or to impugn the reputation of someone who is financially important.[8]

If your investigation proves inconclusive, or if you detect hedging when you inquire about some firm's reputation, immediately take your business elsewhere. There is no lack of places where you can spend your money and receive a legitimate value.

Also, remember that there is no hurry to spend your money. Take all the time you need to check a seller's references carefully. With relatively few exceptions, coins available today will still be available at the same price next month. Don't buy in haste, and if you are just beginning your interest in rare coins, by all means don't buy anything on someone's investment recommendation unless you independently verify the price, grade, and market potential. Remember that anyone who cares to have a few business cards printed can call himself a professional numismatist; there are no rules against this.

On the plus side of the ledger, once you have found a firm with which you want to do business, you have the opportunity to build a fine relationship which will last many years.

Dealing With Dealers

In terms of the total volume of business transacted, the most popular way to acquire coins is by direct purchases from dealers. It has been estimated that there are over 6,000 people in the United States alone who designate themselves as dealers, or professional numismatists. Some individuals sell coins only on a part-time basis at club meetings, coin shows, and elsewhere, while others are part of large companies with an international clientele.

As I noted earlier, before you buy coins from any source it is a good idea to have some general idea of what to pay, and how rare the pieces are that you seek. Sources of pricing information are many and include the *Coin Dealer Newsletter* and the *Certified Coin Dealer Newsletter* (especially recommended for popularly traded items, Morgan dollars, commemoratives, common gold coins, and investment type material); the "Trends" section of *Coin World*, conducted by Keith Zaner,[9] which covers all series from half cents to double eagles; the "Coin Market" section of *Numismatic News* (which covers all federal series), updated weekly by Bob Wilhite; the *Guide Book of United States Coins*, issued yearly, which is useful for pricing rarities as well as items in more unusual series such as colonials and territorial gold; Teletype and other electronic transactions; dealer price lists (useful for making comparisons); and lists of prices realized at public auctions and mail bid sales. I will have more to say about sources of pricing information in a subsequent chapter.

Prices are not precise, and virtually all older coins trade within a range. For a given Morgan dollar, prices can often be found ranging from, say, $200 to $275. It will pay you to investigate this and other situations. Is the $200 coin unattractive, poorly struck, or otherwise not as desirable as one priced at $250 or $275? Is the $275 piece an aesthetically pleasing coin which stands as one of the finest of its issue, or is it simply overpriced? There are no hard and fast answers to these questions.

If a coin is common and is traded frequently, then there is no hurry to buy it, and you can investigate at leisure. In the Morgan silver dollar series about half of the different issues are readily obtainable, so you can pick and choose. Continuing the same example, among rarities in the Morgan dollar series, such as 1889-CC, 1892-S, and 1893-S, top grade specimens do not come along with frequency, and a purchase decision may have to be made quickly. Still, you want to be sure of paying somewhere within a reasonable price range.

Shop Around

When making purchases it will pay you to become acquainted with a number of different sellers. Among dealers in certified coins, some specialize in low-end or "generic" pieces which are sold to a price and appeal mainly to bargain hunters, particularly investors who are not discriminating. You will not be able to learn whether a coin is low-end by talking to certain dealers, for they do not want to do anything to discourage a sale. A former employee of a large telemarketing company told me that he was told that he was instructed to use the term "premium quality" whenever it would help to sell a coin, whether the coin merited that designation or not! In fact, this particular employee could not see the coins he was offering to his clients, as he worked only from listings which appeared on a computer screen.

An exception to this sort of salesmanship is provided by Silvano DiGenova, of Tangible Investments of America, who, telling it like it is, recently described a certified 1895-S Morgan dollar as a "pig," noting that it was very unattractive. Few sellers are this candid! This well-known and respected professional numismatist probably acquired it, as dealers often do, as part of a collection, and would not have selected it as a single purchase.

I recommend that you purchase hand-picked items and endeavor to secure premium quality pieces. It is obvious that the seller of generic bargains can offer coins cheaper than can a dealer who spends a great deal of time carefully looking at many coins before making even a single purchase.

One of America's most successful numismatic publishers recently told me that he was commissioned by his uncle to purchase some silver dollars, and looked through many hundreds of slabbed pieces but was able to find just six which he felt were sharply struck and with good aesthetic appeal. Of these six, just two were real beauties, and the other four were marginal.

At a recent convention I examined over 600 certified copper, silver, and gold coins, and purchased just three which I felt offered the proper combination of sharp strike, pleasing surfaces, and reasonable price. The seller, an East Coast firm, was an active trader on the electronic circuits and catered primarily to investors. He made no effort to acquire exceptional pieces. Whenever he did buy coins which had special appeal, they were quickly cherrypicked by dealers like me!

Writing in the field of stamps, Herman Herst, Jr., one of America's best known professional philatelists, made the statement that no great collection was ever formed by anyone who was a slave to published values. Stamps of special quality often sell for special prices, and scarce and rare stamps typically bring over market, he stated. So it is with coins. No great collection was ever formed by someone who tried to buy the most coins for the cheapest prices.

A Bargain-Seeker

Apropos of the way *not* to do things is this true story:

Several years ago a man who built a successful worldwide merchandising business and then retired, heard that coins were a really great investment. He also heard that certified coins were the way to go. He contacted our firm, and after establishing credit, purchased several thousand dollars' worth of commemorative gold and silver coins. The pieces were of hand-picked quality, and the prices asked were above those listed in the *Certified Coin Dealer Newsletter*. Had my client read the *Certified Coin Dealer Newsletter* carefully, he would have noted a front-page article in an issue which stated that hand-picked coins often sell for *considerably more* than coins which trade on a sight-unseen basis.

A few days later, taking advantage of our return guarantee, he sent each and every piece back, demanding an instant refund, which was duly given. The coins were not "bargains," he said. Several months later I came across this same gentleman at a convention, and eager to prove the point that our earlier offerings had been overpriced, he showed me several commemorative gold coins which he had purchased. In a slab marked "MS-65" was a 1904 Lewis and Clark gold dollar, a scarce issue, but one of the poorest I have ever seen at that grade level. I would have felt guilty had I graded it as high as MS-63! A 1926 Sesquicentennial half dollar marked in the same grade was another "low end" piece and, if removed from its slab, probably would have been regraded a point or two less. Then he showed me several of his bargain commemorative silver coins. A 1936 Long Island half dollar was an ugly brown color with yellow stains, technically an MS-65, a numerical grade with which I did not disagree, but aesthetically it was a disaster. An 1893 Columbian half dollar looked as if it had been heated in a frying pan, and a 1922 Grant was nearly as black as a lump of coal. These were good deals all right—good deals for the dealers who unloaded them.

Time went by, and the man decided to take a profit. If he couldn't buy from us, perhaps he could sell to us, he reasoned, so we were given the chance to make an offer, but we declined to bid any price, for although his holding amounted to several hundred thousand dollars, there were only a few pieces which we felt we desirable examples of their types. Apparently the coins were rejected by several other dealers as well, for they finally wound up in an auction, where they didn't do very well either.

A Connoisseur

On the other hand, Jimmy Hayes, a connoisseur from the word go, elected to buy coins only of hand-picked quality. Seeking to raise funds for what turned out to be a successful bid to be a delegate from Louisiana in the U.S. House of Representatives, Hayes consigned his coins to Stack's, where they did extremely well at auction. Certain of the pieces were purchased by Dennis Irving Long, another connoisseur. After Mr. Long, a respected financier and businessman from Louisville, Kentucky, passed away, his magnificent collection was consigned to us for auction, where further price records were established. One coin, a certified MS-65 1839 Liberty Seated half dollar without drapery at the elbow brought $99,000, or more than double the bid price at the time of $42,000, and was purchased by Kenneth Goldman, a dealer with a discerning eye who undoubtedly considered it to be a bargain even at that level. And, indeed it proved to be a good value, for by a few months later the bid price had jumped to $100,000. Today's auction record is often tomorrow's bargain. I have seen it happen many times.

The point of this is that quality is expensive, but is worth it. If you buy quality, when you sell your coins dealers and auction houses will beat a path to your door. As Ray Merena stated in a recent conversation on the subject, "Coins that are the hardest to buy are the easiest to sell." On the other hand, if you are a slave to published prices and want just bargains, you'll have no trouble buying coins, but selling them may be an entirely different manner.

Building a Relationship

Probably the most popular way to buy coins is by direct purchase from dealers, primarily through the mail. Often the details of a transaction are worked out on the telephone. There are two main types of rare coin dealers. Although some firms are in both areas, most go one way or the other:

• **The dealer who sells to knowledgeable collectors:** The dealer who sells to knowledgeable collectors usually does so by issuing printed catalogues, running advertisements listing individual rare coins in *Coin World, Numismatic News*, and elsewhere, or by servicing want lists. This type of dealer sells the specific coins his customers want to buy.

• **The dealer who sells to the general public:** The dealer who sells to the general public usually does so by running advertisements for common or generic coins (pieces available readily and in large quantities) in non-numismatic publications, including financial papers. His customers usually do not know what they want to buy, and have little knowledge of rare dates, grading, etc. This type of dealer tells his customers what they should buy, as the customers do not have sufficient knowledge to make their own decisions. Often, this type of dealer operates on a higher profit margin due to the expenses involved in advertising to the general public.

Often a person who becomes acquainted with coins through the second type of dealer will learn about numismatics and later become a good customer for the first type of dealer. Dealers of the second type perform a valuable function in that they serve to do missionary work for numismatics.

I consider it important for you to build a ongoing relationship with one or more dealers. In general, dealers have the coins that you want. If a dealer has two or three clients who need the same coin, the client who has established the best rapport often gets first chance. It will pay you to establish such a fine relationship.

It may strike you as unusual when I suggest that a buyer of coins such as you should make an effort to establish a relationship with a dealer, for many buyers take this attitude: I have the money, and the dealer can come to me and persuade me to buy something. Why should I go out of my way to be nice to a dealer? I have what he wants (money).

This may be true, and whether a dealer likes you or not, or whether you like the dealer or not, you can still make purchases. However, if a warm relationship of mutual trust and friendship is established, you will enjoy your transactions more, and chances are excellent that you will be given first pick of the dealer's new purchases or the better coins from his inventory. In my opinion, a close relationship with one or more trusted dealers is an absolute must.

Want Lists

As your interest in coins grows, you will find that certain coins needed to complete your collection or set will be difficult to locate. Try as you might, you may not be able to find an 1873-CC Liberty Seated dollar, 1895-O Morgan dollar, 1856 Flying Eagle cent, 1877 twenty-cent piece, or other coins in the condition and price range you want. An effective way to facilitate purchases of scarce and rare pieces is to make up a want list of the items you are seeking and send it to one or more dealers. I suggest that you accompany your want list with a personal letter, or introduce it by making a telephone call to the dealer. A Xerox or fax copy of a want list which looks as if it has been sent indiscriminately to a hundred dealers is less apt to produce results than a want list which looks personal and which is accompanied by a message directed specifically to the dealer recipient. A good compromise is to reproduce your want list on a copying machine and accompany it with a personal cover letter.

Many leading dealers make a specialty of servicing want lists. Liz Arlin, who manages the Want List Department here at Bowers and Merena Galleries, maintains a large and ever-changing file of clients' needs. Recently she has placed with our clients such rarities as a superb 1796 half dollar, the 1854-D $3 gold piece which we had sold earlier as part of the Eliasberg Collection, a 1794 silver dollar, an 1808 quarter eagle, and other rarities.

Often, Liz has to make a determination as to whom a newly-purchased coin should be offered, and she makes this decision based upon these factors:

• Does she know the client through earlier personal contact by telephone or letter? Is he a "nice guy"? Is he pleasant to do business with? To be frank, life is too short to do business with people who constantly complain, who don't like dealers (some buyers take an adversary position toward all dealers), or who want to buy the finest possible quality at prices below which we ourselves would pay.

• Will he appreciate the coin once he gets it? Someone who needs a coin to fill in the last item in a type set or collection, or who has been looking for a particular piece for a long time, will appreciate it more than someone who has just decided he wants to own a particular variety but who hasn't spent time searching for it.

• Will he pay for the coin promptly? Or, if the coin is not to his liking, will he return it promptly?

• Is he an established client of the firm?

Gail Watson, who manages the Collection Portfolio Program for Bowers and Merena Galleries, uses basically the same criteria when confronted with multiple clients for a single rarity.

Other Ways to Acquire Coins

While buying coins directly from dealers or by participating in auctions and mail bid sales (see subsequent chapters on the subject of bidding) represent the ways that most coin buyers add to their holdings, there are other methods as well. These include:

• **Mints and government agencies:** Buying directly from issuing mints and government authorities provides a way to update your collection with newly released issues. For example, each year the United States Mint offers Proof coins, mint sets, bullion pieces, and other current coins for sale.

• **Banks:** Buying current Uncirculated coins at face value from banks is a good way to acquire Lincoln cents, Jefferson nickels, etc. as they are issued. Some banks offer bullion-type coins and current commemoratives.

• **Pocket change:** Finding coins in circulation is the way that many people get started in the hobby. Today it is virtually impossible to find rare varieties in circulation, for most coins in the channels of commerce are apt to be dated this side of 1960. However, the possibility exists for finding 1972 Doubled Die cents and certain other scarce pieces of the present era.

Buying Advantageously

Here are the steps to follow in order to buy coins to your best advantage:

• **Determine what you want:** Decide which types or varieties of coins you want to buy and the grade ranges desired. This may sound silly, but as it is easier to buy coins than to sell them, it will pay you do determine what you want to buy before you place an order. For example, don't buy a rare 1877 Indian cent which looks appealing in a catalogue if you haven't determined that you want to collect Indian cents.

Formulate a collecting (or investing) plan. If you are not sure, then take your time and buy only when you are ready. Except for great rarities, most coins available today will still be available next week or next month. Typical buying plans might include these:

• A set of U.S. coins by design types, with coins dated from 1793 to about 1860 to be in Fine to VF grade, coins from about 1860 to 1900 to be in AU to MS-60 grade, coins from about 1900 to 1950 to be in MS-63 grade, and later coins to be MS-65.

• A collection of Indian cents 1859-1909, in nicely matched EF-40 to AU-50 grade.

• A collection of Morgan dollars 1878-1921 in MS-63 to MS-64 grade, except for rarities which can be EF to AU.

• A collection of nickel three-cent pieces 1865-1889 in Proof-65 grade.

• All of the coins minted in your birth year, in MS-65 and Proof-65 grade.

• A type set of late 19th and early 20th century gold coins in nicely matched MS-63 grade.

• A date and mintmark collection of Barber half dollars in MS-63 grade.

• A collection of 1787 and 1788 Massachusetts half cents and cents attributed by Ryder numbers, in VF-20 or better grade, except for rarities (which can be in any grade available).

• A date and major variety collection of later date large cents 1816-1857 in MS-60 grade, with brown surfaces.

• A type set of commemorative silver coins in MS-63 and MS-64 grade, with brilliant surfaces.

You get the idea. In this way, you can buy coins to fit in with the series you want to collect. There are many possibilities. Formulate your own objectives.

• **Figure prices:** Determine a reasonable price range to pay for the variety and grade of each coin. If you are offered a coin for $1,000, you should have some idea if it is worth $500, $1,000, or $1,500. It probably won't be worth $1,500, but it could be worth only $500. If you are in doubt, ask for advice from someone other than the seller.

• **Deal with the best:** Buy only from an individual or firm with an established reputation for integrity and fair dealing. Investigate *thoroughly*. Some of the phoniest outfits have the smoothest-talking salesmen and the fanciest brochures. Never (no exceptions!) buy coins over the telephone from someone you do not know.

• **Buying raw coins:** If you are buying a raw (unslabbed) coin, gain a general knowledge of grading first, or have the coin checked by a knowledge-able person after you buy it. Grading practices and interpretations do vary. Be sure that the coin is well-struck (if the issue is one that can be found well struck), on a good planchet, well centered, and is pleasing to your eye. Insist on a return guarantee. If you cannot get a money-back guarantee, then don't buy the coin.

• **Buying slabbed coins:** If you are buying a certified (slabbed) coin, use the technical grade only as the *starting point*. If the coin is ugly, poorly struck, stained, etc., don't buy it. Remember, there is no magic about a coin being in a slab. Be sure the coin also satisfies *your* standards for being well struck (unless it is a variety which is usually found only weakly struck, in which case you should learn about this), on a good planchet, well centered, and of pleasing appearance. Be sure you *like* it. If it is not attractive, don't buy it. Insist on a return guarantee, so you can see the coin before the sale is final. If you can not get a money-back guarantee, then don't buy the coin. This advice differs dramatically from that given by some sellers.

• **Document your purchases:** Insist upon a written receipt and a guarantee (with no time limit) of authenticity. If the seller won't issue a receipt, don't buy. Many fake coins have been sold to unsuspecting buyers who insist on "cash deals" without receipts. "If you pay me in cash and don't want a receipt, I can give you a bargain price," is a line as old as the pyramids. Many stolen, counterfeit, and overgraded coins are sold in this manner. The buyer-victim is often helpless, as these thoughts go through his mind: "I can't complain to anyone, for I paid cash using funds unreported to the Internal Revenue Service, so what can I do? Apparently nothing."

Advice From the FTC and the ANA

The Federal Trade Commission and the American Numismatic Association issued a pamphlet titled *Consumer Alert: Investing in Rare Coins*. The advice given, excerpted below, makes a lot of sense and, in fact, reflects much of what I have to say in the present book:

"If you intend to buy rare or bullion coins for investment, your best protection is to spend time learning about the coins you are being asked to buy. In the past, most investment gains have gone to collectors, often known as numismatists, who have taken the time to study carefully various aspects of coins, including rarity, grading, market availability, and price trends. Investment success over the years is the result of prudently acquiring coins of selected quality, proven rarity, and established numismatic desirability. Many careful buyers study coins for some time before buying even a single coin. Success can also be enhanced by researching dealers, as well as coins. If you receive any solicitation about investing in coins, keep these points in mind:

• **Use common sense when evaluating any investment claims** and do not rush into buying. Remember, anything that sounds too good to be true usually is not true.

• **Make sure that you know the dealer's reputation....** If you can, find out how long the company has been in business. Don't rely just on what a dealer's representative tells you on the phone....

• **Don't be taken in by promises** that the dealer will buy back your coins or that the grading is guaranteed unless you are confident that the dealer has the financial resources to stand behind these promises....

• **It is wise to get a second opinion** from another source about grade and value as soon as you receive your coins....

• Be cautious about grading certificates, especially those furnished by coin dealers. Have the grades of any coins you buy checked by an independent source.... *Grading is not an exact science,* and a certificate represents no more than the opinion of the certification service.... Because grading standards vary, coins certified by different services will be worth more or less than other coins of the same grade....

• **Comparison shop.** You need to be concerned not only with grades, but with prices as well....

• **Take possession of any coins you purchase** to ensure that they exist and to be sure they are properly stored....

• **As with any consumer purchase, be wary about giving your credit card number to strangers....**

"Fraudulent sellers frequently have elegant offices in the financial districts of major cities, employ 'account executives' or 'investment counselors,' and produce glossy, attractive brochures on coin investment strategy. They may claim to have leading coin experts on their staffs, or claim to be the largest or finest dealers in the business. Because fraudulent sellers often appear to be reputable, it is particularly important to check the information that you are given.... Be particularly careful about committing yourself to a purchase from an *unsolicited* caller...."

Advice from Kenneth E. Bressett

Kenneth E. Bressett, whose credentials include membership on the ANA Board of Governors, the conducting for many years of the "Consumer Alert" column in *The Numismatist,* and editorship of *A Guide Book of U.S. Coins,* devotes a page to coin investment in the current edition of the *Guide Book.*[10] Much of the information parallels that just quoted from the FTC and ANA. An excerpt:

"Investing in rare coins can be a rewarding experience for anyone who approaches the calling armed with the right attitude and background knowledge about this exciting field. It can just as easily become a costly mistake for anyone who attempts to profit from coins without giving serious thought to the idiosyncrasies of this unique market.

"The best advice that can be given to anyone considering investing in rare coins is to use common sense precautions that would apply to any contemplated purchase.... For hundreds of years rare coins and precious metals have proven themselves to be an excellent hedge against inflation, and source of ready money in times of disaster. There is no reason to think that this will change in the future. Gone are the days when coin collecting was only a passive hobby for those who would study the history and artistry of these enjoyable objects. It has now grown into an investment arena where speculation on the future demand for rare coins has made them a standard part of nearly every well rounded investment portfolio. With this change in attitude about collecting coins has come a measure of concern for those who purchase coins without the background or experience necessary to avoid costly mistakes in accepting overpriced or overgraded coins that simply are not worth what is paid for them. Extreme caution is advised for anyone considering an investment in rare coins...."

The same writer noted the potential of the field:

"The opportunities for successful collecting and investing in quality numismatic items are greater today than ever before." He went on to relate that grading services give buyers an assurance of safety, and that the dissemination of pricing information makes it possible to gain knowledge of market levels. Then he concluded with this suggestion, which coincides with my own feelings exactly:

"Collectors and investors alike can profit by investigating the background and history of the coins they buy. These are not just inanimate objects akin to stock certificates or gems. Coins are a mirror of history and art that tell the story of mankind over the past 2,600 years, reflecting economic struggles, wars, prosperity, and creativity of every major nation on earth. We are but the custodians of these historical relics, and must appreciate and care for them while they are in our possession. Those who treat rare coins with the consideration and respect they deserve will profit in many ways, not the least of which can be in the form of a sound financial return on one's investment of time and money."

CHAPTER FIVE

Coins and Wall Street

Limited Partnerships and Funds

Buying shares in a limited partnership or fund can be a way to invest in coins. In recent years a number of coin funds have been established, whereby those interested in investment play, but not in learning about coins or owning coins directly, can buy shares and participate in the rare coin market in this manner. The American Rare Coin Fund Limited Partnership, launched by Kidder, Peabody & Co. in 1989, Greg Holloway's Continental partnerships, and Bruce McNall's Athena funds are among many examples.

In recent times "Wall Street money" has caused a great deal of excitement in the rare coin field. Many articles, newsletter comments, and dealer advertisements have forecast that the advent of money from Wall Street will lift the coin market to new highs.

David L. Ganz's View

David L. Ganz, prominent attorney (specializing in numismatics), prolific author, and member of the ANA Board of Governors, gives this view of coins as an investment, as based upon what selected *rare coins* have done:[1]

"Salomon Brothers' annual survey of the collectibles industry, tangible assets and so-called 'financial' assets...shows that coins in the long run are a valid investment vehicle. In fourth place last year behind megabuck old master paintings and rebounding stock and bond prices, rare coins in the Salomon Brothers market basket once again demonstrate the validity of rare coins in an investment portfolio.... Grading on the coins was never Gem, but rather Choice collector coins.[2] Hence the importance of a 14.6% annual return even in a desultory market makes coin rarities and Gem material all the more interesting. Since Gem prices have risen even higher than MS-63 or Choice Uncirculated coinage, it is apparent that the rare coin market is actually moving along quite nicely, and offering a predictable rate of return that is quite tangible....

"Taking the Salomon Brothers survey over a 20 year period of time (the actual survey has gone on for half that time, but the survey has been extended back to prior years using auction and other records), rare coins are demonstrated to be a superior investment vehicle with a phenomenal rate of return that is not approached by any other financial or tangible asset.

"No wonder, then, that Wall Street is starting to dabble in the rare coin market, with 'funds' or limited partnerships (actually securities, any way you look at it) offering a 'mutual fund' type approach to take away from the investor the need to have any specific numismatic knowledge—and instead to allow the investor to rely on the purchasing manager's numismatic knowledge and the overall upward trend in the marketplace.

"Consequences of this have been significant movement within the marketplace—and perhaps the first evidence of what will most likely come from a genuine entry with serious Wall Street money—into the numismatic marketplace: the capacity and ability to manipulate prices (upward, as well as downward) for an ulterior purpose.

"Price manipulation has gone on in the coin field in a variety of capacities for many years, in a variety of ways. Few may now remember, but coin rolls were manipulated upward for investment purposes in the early 1960s; so were Proof sets, a decade earlier when tout boards at coin conventions showed their prices changing (upwardly) almost every hour.

"Telemarketing brought out new means for manipulation—is there any doubt that the Columbian Exposition half dollar is not a 'rare' coin, or that Uncirculated Morgan dollars are not exactly the best investment since Harold Corp.?

"There are those who view Wall Street's entry into the coin market as a panacea: new money, people ignorant of the rare coin field, companies likely to make extensive purchases, and progressively higher prices. They're wrong, and as the events will most likely bear out, the entrance of serious money into the numismatic field will have its pluses, and its minuses; but in the end, the coin market will never be the same."

A Key Word

The key word in David L. Ganz's commentary is *rare*. The Salomon Brothers index is based on *rare* coins. Apropos of the use and misuse of the Salomon Brothers study, the Federal Trade Commission and the American Numismatic Association warn:[3] "Dishonest dealers often mislead buyers by quoting appreciation rates for rare coins from an index compiled each year by Salomon Brothers, a New York investment banking firm. These quotes show appreciation of 12% to 25% a year. However, the Salomon index is based on a list of

20 very rare coins while the coins sold by dishonest dealers are more common coins that are not likely to appreciate at the same rate, if at all. However, almost all dealers, legitimate and dishonest alike, use the Salomon quotes.[4] Therefore, it is particularly important that you choose your dealer carefully. Remember, there is no guarantee that any coin will appreciate in value."

Details of the Salomon Report

Details of the latest Salomon Brothers report were given in an article in a recent issue of *Numismatic News*,[5] which reveals that the annual study comprises *rare* coins:

"U.S rare coins ranked fourth in one-year appreciation among 14 different investments in the annual investment survey conducted by Salomon Brothers. Thirteen tangible and financial assets and the government's Consumer Price Index are charted in the survey. Old Masters paintings were the biggest winner by far for 1989, as they posed a gain of 44.5%.... Chinese ceramics came in second with a one-year increase of 18%. Stocks took third place, appreciating 15.4% in the Salomon survey. U.S. coins gained 14.6%, and foreign exchange rounded out the top five with an annual return of 10.5%.

"Other investments in the survey are gold, diamonds, bonds, oil, three-month Treasury bills, housing. U.S. farmland, and silver. The metals were among the weakest performers in 1989, as gold gained 0.5% for a 12th place finish. Silver was last among the asset areas, as it fell 2.9%.

"Over the past 20 years, U.S. coins are ranked first, with a compound annual rate of return of 17.3%. Gold is in fifth place in the 20-year calculations, as it has a 12.3% average annual gain. Silver is in 13th place, appreciating at a 5.4% clip in the past two decades.

"Prices used in the most recent survey were based on certified coin values, according to Kelly Healey of Salomon Brothers. In the past, 'BU' coins were followed. Twenty coins are charted for price appreciation in the Salomon Brothers index. It is heavily weighted towards scarce and high-priced coins, according to Healey. Among the coins surveyed are the 1795 Draped Bust dollar, 1807 Draped Bust dime, 1873 Liberty Seated quarter with arrows, 1884-S Morgan dollar, and 1916 Standing Liberty quarter. The only copper coins in the annual investment rankings are the 1794 half cent and the 1873 two-cent piece. Type coins include an 1862 three-cent silver piece, a Liberty Seated half dime from the same year, 1866 Shield nickel with rays, an 1866 Liberty Seated dime (which had an original mintage of 8,725), and an 1886

Liberty Seated quarter. Four different half dollars are listed. They are Capped Bust halves dated 1815 and 1834, an 1855-O Liberty Seated, and a 1921 Liberty Walking. An 1847 Liberty Seated dollar and an 1881 trade dollar (a Proof-only issue) are also used in the survey. The only commemorative on the list is a 1928 Hawaiian half dollar. No U.S. gold coins are used in the index...."[6]

Dr. Gary North Views the Future

Dr. Gary North, in a letter to *Coin World*, gave an optimistic prediction of the future of Wall Street money influences in the coin market:[7]

"Having spent almost a decade on Wall Street before starting a more prudent reputable investment company in numismatics, I would like to point out that over 90% of the public that invests in the Wall Street futures market (I like to call it 'the not future market') lose money! Some even more than they invest! Many would also be surprised to know if they read the small print from the new issue stock they just bought at $5 was acquired by company executives at 50¢ and may also be owned by the brokerages for a discount.

"As the information age continues and the free world grows larger and smarter, rare coin prices will literally take off, being the only true supply demand investment medium. Everyone should have at least 5% of their assets in rare coins, and if this happens you will see million dollar Mint State-65 Washington-Carver commemorative half dollars. 'Americanism, freedom and opportunity for all.'[8] Invest today. There are billions on the way."

More about Wall Street

In a feature article in *Coin World*, staff writers Paul Gilkes and Keith M. Zaner, surveyed predictions for the 1990s:[9]

"PCGS founder David Hall says 'The direction of the coin market will be toward more efficient and accurate trading methods which will mean increased liquidity, an increased number of market participants, involvement of Wall Street and much higher prices. Wall Street is always hungry for new products. They are always looking for financial products that make sense. Because the grading problem in the rare coin industry has been solved and because the market is becoming sufficiently liquid and efficient, Wall Street can now play in our ball game.'[10]

"'Wall Street can only deal in certified coins,' Hall said. 'They cannot deal in raw coins. Second of all, I think that the certification business will gravitate to whichever business provides the best consistency of grading, the best service and the best liquidity. Speaking for PCGS, we intend to do everything we can to maintain our market leadership position.'

"The scream for consistency in grading fostered PCGS's creation in February 1986, followed by NGC some 16 months later. Not to be left at the back of the pack, the American Numismatic Association Certification Service began offering its own slab service, ANACS Cache, in February 1989. Even though the third-party grading services guarantee the grade of the coins in their respective holders, the grading controversy still rages because one service may be more or less strict in the grading than the others or employ a completely different grading philosophy.

"NGC founder and president John Albanese thinks 'a lot of people would like to tell you that the grading problem has been solved. We claim that we've solved the problem. Our competitors have claimed that they've solved the problem. I guess if we've all solved the problem, we wouldn't have this instability in dealers cracking coins out [of their holders] and resubmitting them.

"'Obviously, grading will always remain an area of controversy,' Albanese explained. 'Such as in Wall Street; even though they have Standard & Poor's and Moody's rating stocks and bonds, there is still controversy there, saying, 'Gee, why have they upped this rating and why have they lowered that rating?' I think grading is always going to be controversial. NGC's next big step, which is in the works now, is that NGC coins will be trading sight-unseen for the first time in 1990,' Albanese added. 'So that will be a major step for us. I think that will confirm we are the strictest grading service. I believe that you'll see our coins bringing nice premiums.'

"Numismatic consultant and writer Maurice Rosen said with the inflationary 1970s creating a bull market with thousands of new investors, and the loosening of grading standards amidst the fevered 1979-80 market peak, 'It's little wonder that the inevitable bust after 1980 resulted in tumultuous grading changes lasting throughout most of the 1980s.'

"Since there were also enormous abuses in the pricing of coins during the late 1970s and the 1983-87 'telemarketing blitz,' Rosen noted it could be expected that grading and its abuses would dominate the coin market.

"With the 'legitimate' industry's back to the wall, Rosen said a substantially better product in which the consumer and investor could have confidence had to be developed or the industry could be regulated away. PCGS and NGC provided that confidence, Rosen felt. 'Now, with the bulk of grading abuses behind us, the industry can turn its attention to expanding its market,' Rosen concluded.

"That's where Wall Street has come in.... 'Quite a few Wall Street firms seem to be watching the Kidder, Peabody deal very closely,' Albanese said. 'That's really the test case and seems to be doing very well. I'm sure one of the reasons for Wall Street getting involved, is, first of all, just reading the headlines lately—you can see with program trading and the volatile markets. I mean, I own some stocks that one day went to 180 points and believe me, it didn't feel good.

"'Wall Street has to get more in tune with Main Street,' Albanese continued. 'And really, Main Street says rare coins are a pretty good buy here, and I feel pretty comfortable buying rare coins. I think that is a reason I'll say though, with the amount of money they put in the market, they're just experimenting. The amount of money Wall Street has put in the coin business at this point is actually very small compared to what their potential is. I would say that they're just dabbling.'

"Hugh Sconyers, the California coin dealer serving as the manager for Kidder, Peabody's American Rare Coin Fund Limited Partnership, said other Wall Street investment firms are taking notice of the coin market, evidenced by the number of Wall Street firms who had representatives scouting the bourse floor of the American Numismatic Association's 98th Anniversary Convention in August in Pittsburgh.

"'There are other coin funds on the way from Wall Street, and you'll see a bigger interest from that financial community in the coin market,' Sconyers said. 'They've taken a look at it a number of times over the years but have gone away scratching their heads not being able to understand them [coins]. Now, it's not the most difficult thing for someone to understand [certified coins].'

"New York coin dealer and numismatic author Scott A. Travers says certified coins, to a great extent, are viewed as fungible items; items that are traded in similar units which tend to duplicate each other.

"'As a result of this fungible nature of rare coins we've known for a long time and have discussed this formally for a number of years that rare coins would be traded like stocks and bonds.' Travers said. 'What we didn't expect was that independent grading services, the likes of PCGS and NGC, to have such consistency and respectability so that the rare coin marketplace literally became 'commoditized' just about overnight as a result of independent, arm's-length consistent grading.

"'As long as independent, arm's-length consistent grading remains respectable and there are no major scandals surrounding PCGS or NGC, we should see eager growth in the field,' Travers stated. 'Further sound investments in rare coins through the traditional Wall Street investment

sources and general long-term price appreciation as a result of these investment dollars will occur.'

"There also seems to be a question over whether there is a difference
between the collector and investor.

"'It is a total and complete myth,' Hall said. 'There is no war between
collector and investor. I think 99% of collectors are doing it for investment
also, and well over half of the investors become collectors of some sort.[11] It's
a total myth that are two total opposite camps. There is no battle, there is no
debate.'

"NGC's Albanese says 1990 will be like any other year; the collector will
still be the foundation of the coin market. 'We're always going to have
investors coming in and out, buying coins and selling coins,' Albanese said.
'And again, investors do not really have the temperament or the patience the
collector does, and for that reason I feel the coin collector will be the
foundation. I'm happy to say that we have evidence that a lot of investors—
people not really caring about the history of coins or the theory of coins—many
of these investors we see turning into collectors.'

"Travers somewhat disagrees. 'We've seen an evolution in this marketplace away from the primary person who is the collector,' he noted. 'I don't
like the term collector being used with a certain mind set referring to an
individual sitting there with a 'penny' board who doesn't like slabs. The term
collector, as we have seen it being used in the past few years by certain
individuals, tends to pit the haves against the have-nots.

"'I don't believe that there is a great debate between the collector and the
investor, because there is a lot of room in between for people who are solidly
collectors or solidly investors,' Travers added. 'A lot of the people who are
solidly collectors are buying $10,000 and $20,000 coins, and they love these
coins. They are buying them because they want to complete their collections
and because they like looking at the coins. They basically don't ever want to
sell these coins, because they have a deep affinity for the historical and cultural
experience which these coins represent. I say we are seeing a new breed of
collector today.'

"Sconyers believes collectors and investors are one and the same. 'You
may call yourself different things at different times, but I don't think there's
anyone who spends the kind of money that they spend on either art or coins
without the hope that one day they'll make make money on what they've
acquired.' Sconyers said.[12] 'Rare gold and silver coin issues will still be the
mainstay of the marketplace, with the potential of many rarities to top the $1
million mark, trading at higher prices much like the art market.'

"Albanese notes that 'rarity has always been a concern, although it seems to me the new collectors coming in, since most of them have the background of coming in for investment, most of them seem more concerned with condition rather than rarity. You always have people looking for rarity. Again, with the new breed of collectors, in my opinion, since they have started as investors, they have had this ingrained that quality is probably the way to go.'"

Slabs and Wall Street

In August 1990 *The Wall Street Journal* ran a front-page article titled "Coin Industry Dealt a Blow by FTC Suit,"[13] which noted in part:

"The Federal Trade Commission accused the nation's major coin grading service—until now heralded as making the rare coin business safer for investors—of making numerous false and misleading claims. The lawsuit the FTC filed against the four-year-old independent coin grader, Professional Coin Grading Service, Inc. of Irvine, Calif., is potentially the biggest blow in years to the coin world's attempts to improve its image."

The story went on to say that the suit could set back the plans of Wall Street brokerage firms to sell investors rare coins and limited partnerships that invest in coins. The FTC charged in its suit that PCGS "engaged in numerous violations" of the FTC Act in its advertisements and promotional material and that PCGS hasn't provided the "objective or consistent grading" it claims, and that the firm misrepresented itself because "PCGS does not in all cases observe its 'strict anti-self interest policy.'"

PCGS entered into a consent decree with the FTC "in which it agreed to various restrictions, including prior FTC approval[14] of any advertisements it runs for the next five years. In settling, the company didn't admit liability for the alleged offenses."

In the same article, PCGS' chief executive officer, David Hall, was quoted as saying: "We see ourselves as good guys, doing our part to try and make sure coin buyers get a properly represented product. It seemed unbelievable that we could be the target of an FTC investigation. I'm convinced that PCGS runs the cleanest ship in the grading service business."[15] Hall went on to state that the FTC complaint "contains some obviously untrue allegations," but that PCGS settled the case to save court costs.

Phoebe Morse, representing the FTC, gave her view: "Probably the most significant thing about the case is that coin graders, dealers, and certifiers have to be very careful about the messages they give to the buying public. They haven't been careful enough."

A related article in *The Los Angeles Times*[16] treated the same subject and added: "FTC sources indicate the company was grading coins more favorably for preferred customers, something executives there strongly deny."

Barry J. Cutler of the FTC Speaks

Barry J. Cutler, director of the Bureau of Consumer Protection, the Federal Trade Commission, delivered the following remarks to a forum at the 1990 American Numismatic Association convention:[17]

"I want to start by thanking the ANA for extending this invitation for me to speak to you today. I have been a coin collector for more than 35 years; a litigator and counselor on numismatic matters for more than five years; and director of the FTC's Bureau of Consumer Protection for about six months. I therefore bring great enthusiasm and, I suspect, an unusual perspective (as FTC officials go), to my address today.

"The idea of my appearance today originated last autumn when I called the ANA's Jim Taylor[18] to say that I would be willing to give a presentation on the controversial legal issues of coin grading, which consumed a major part of the testimony in the Security Rare Coin trial in Minnesota last year. Although the ANA expressed some interest in that topic right from the start, I noticed a significant increase in interest during February of this year, shortly after it was announced that I would be appointed the FTC's new director of the Bureau of Consumer Protection. Not only as to numismatics, but as to advertising, credit, and other topics within the FTC's consumer protection jurisdiction, I began to feel a little like the working stiff who wins the state lottery. Everyone knows that he or she is still the same person—but they seem to pay more attention to what the person has to say. In fact, the standard FTC disclaimer[19] is particularly appropriate this week. Although some of my statements reflect where I believe the Bureau of Consumer Protection will be heading, other views are based on experience that I have had in your industry since long before my appointment at the FTC.

"A. Rare Coins: From the Corner Store to Wall Street

"During the 1950s, when I was growing up and getting interested in coin collecting, coins were basically either used or mint. The Sheldon system finally came along, primarily for collectors, and provided a systematic method to make objective descriptions of a coin's condition. By the 1970s the rare coin market had become attractive to individual investors as well as to collectors. A number of these investors were doubtless believers in hard assets, some of whom had a strong political distrust of banks and government generally. But others were more traditional investors who saw that rare coins, like bullion and other commodities, could appreciate in times of inflation. By then, the ANA had developed its Certification Service to create an appearance of objectivity about coin grading. New England Rare Coin Galleries, then headed by Jimmy Halperin, publicized a rare coin fund that capitalized nicely on the high inflation of the late 1970s.

"All of this background and other factors paved the way for the major boom in marketing during the 1980s. Telemarketing was starting to blossom as a marketing tool generally. Coin transactions were confidential and unregulated. Best of all, Salomon Brothers issued annual reports that made rare coins sound like the best investment around, eclipsing stocks, bonds, oil, and other commodities. All of the pieces were in place for the chaos that characterized coin investment in the early and mid-1980s. Even people unsophisticated about numismatics, who thought that 'whizzing,' 'sliders,' and 'toning' were terms that related to baseball and weightlifting, invested thousands of dollars in rare coins based on a telephone pitch or an ad in the newspaper.

"As we enter the 1990s, the landscape is changing even more dramatically. Wall Street has jumped into the rare coin market with both feet. Limited partnerships in the $50 million range are available. Major Wall Street brokerages, relying on both the rosy reports of Salomon Brothers and the claims by third party grading services about objectivity, liquidity, and the safety of rare coin investments, are making a major push into rare coins, just when the previously hot market for takeovers and junk bonds seems to be on hold for a while.

"It is too early, of course, to tell whether the bears or the bulls ultimately will dominate the thinking on Wall Street about rare coins. It is quite possible that rare coin funds and limited partnerships, managed by knowledgeable and honest dealers, will become a profitable staple in the Wall Street market basket of commodities and services. At the same time, some troublesome clouds raise concern and leave room for questions.

"One very thick cloud is the underlying premise that grading now is sufficiently objective to support a traditional sight-unseen market for rare coins. Coins typically trade sight unseen much better in soaring markets than in falling ones.

"Another big cloud is liquidity. It is hard enough for an individual investor to obtain a good price on a single coin that must be liquidated through a dealer. Do we really know what will happen when a Wall Street brokerage tries to sell off a $50 million portfolio in a relatively short time frame?

"Third, and most important, we know all too well that the temptations and opportunities to manipulate the rare coin market are still all too plentiful, notwithstanding optimistic and self-serving claims to the contrary. The FTC's lawsuit last week against Hannes Tulving suggests that even trading with an established dealer, rather than with a boiler room operator, provides no guarantee that an investment will be safe.

"So long as grading and pricing remain somewhat subjective and open to manipulation, and auctions are open to dealer and auction house practices that would mislead the average investor, the rare coin market will remain one of great upside potential and even greater downside risk. Add to the recipe the fact that Wall Street brokerages can lull into a false sense of confidence certain consumers who would not otherwise pay attention to the telephone calls of an unknown telemarketer, and the ingredients for major league trouble are all present.

"B. The Status of Grading in the Marketplace

"One of the keys to Wall Street's attraction to rare coins as an investment vehicle is its claimed reliance on new objective grading and certification techniques that purport to eliminate much of the investment risk previously associated with the telemarketing of 'raw' coins. Events in the last year or two, however, should be enough to convince knowledgeable numismatists that the 'promised land' of perfect grading standards has yet to be found. While there may be more of a consensus than there was 10 years ago, we all know that there is a certain inherent subjectivity between graders, and even between different grading services, whose grades for the same coin may result in very different price quotations in the *Certified Coin Dealer Newsletter* ('the Blue Sheet'). Just what is the state of the art?

"In the Security Rare Coin trial in Minnesota last summer, the FTC employed several experts on United States gold and silver coins. The defense used one expert and two suppliers who testified about grading standards and market practices generally. Both sides introduced deposition testimony of other dealers and experts.

"One expert for the FTC testified that knowledgeable dealers could routinely distinguish between an MS-62+ gold coin and a straight MS-63, even where the wholesale value for a particular coin might jump from $700 to $2,100 for that slight jump in grade. Others testified that a two-grade difference among experts would be very unusual. But when the FTC's experts were asked, without knowing about each other's testimony, to grade a common date Saint-Gaudens $20 gold piece, the opinions expressed in court ranged from AU-58 (with a wholesale value of about $400) to MS-64 (with a wholesale value of $1750).

"Thus, while some dealers may believe that there is extraordinary consistency in grading—and courts have made clear that overgrading can support a finding of fraud—the performance of graders in actual practice is not always as good as they would predict. Even the ANA *Grading Guide*, as you know, assumes that there will be a certain amount of honest subjectivity in coin grading.

"To solve the grading problem that was perceived in the early and mid-1980s, a number of coin grading services have sprung up in recent years. Although there are many lesser known services, the most prominent ones, including PCGS and NGC, have eclipsed your own ANACS both in reputation and acceptance in the commercial marketplace. Claiming to have resolved the 'grading problem,' as well as having added safety and liquidity to coin investments, these services have in a few short years made a dramatic impact in the marketplace. One can see this impact in the corner coin shop as well as on the bourse floor of a major coin convention. For some time, however, there has been some suspicion that some services, while undoubtedly benefitting the small investor who otherwise might have bought a 'raw' coin, have been making claims that were too good to be true.

"In the Security Rare Coin trial last summer, the testimony of more than one expert confirmed that there is an industry-wide practice of breaking coins out of PCGS's slabs and returning them for another certification, hopefully at a higher grade. One major dealer testified to resubmitting about one-third of his slabbed coins, and obtaining a higher grade for about half of the resubmitted coins. We are not talking about trifling differences. I doubt that there is anyone in this room who has not heard rumors of one dealer or another buying a coin at a show, flying it to a service for instant certification, and returning to the same show and reselling the coin for a substantial multiple of the acquisition cost. According to the trial testimony in Minnesota, at least one expert has been hired as a consultant by other coin dealers to travel to shows and pick out undergraded certified coins that could be bought at bargain prices for the purpose of breaking them out of their slabs and resubmitting them for a higher grade.

"The Federal Trade Commission has not been asleep at the switch as far as grading certificates and services are concerned. One of its first telemarketing fraud cases against a supplier involved Rare Coins of Georgia, which the FTC sued for allegedly furnishing bogus grading certificates that allowed Florida boiler rooms to sell as M5-65s large numbers of Morgan silver dollars that were originally acquired at MS-60 prices. Last year, the Commission settled with better known NCI, having alleged that the Dallas certification firm had misled the public about its grading standards in connection with sales by another Florida dealer. And just last week, the FTC brought what might be the most significant and far reaching complaint in the coin industry to date— a federal court complaint and simultaneous consent agreement with PCGS. I have a sense that the PCGS lawsuit has been the topic of one or two conversations at the convention this week.

"The FTC's complaint, which is now publicly available, makes some important allegations.[20] Specifically, the Commission alleged that PCGS had made a number of misrepresentations about its service in that (a) PCGS has not provided objective or consistent grading; (b) in numerous instances, PCGS coins can not be liquidated easily at reasonable, competitive prices; (c) investment in PCGS-certified coins does not eliminate all the risk associated with the grading of coins; and (d) PCGS does not in all cases observe its 'strict anti-self interest policy.'

"The attached consent decree, when it is approved by a federal judge in Washington, D.C., will prohibit PCGS from making any misrepresentation about the objectivity, consistency, or unbiased nature of its grading service. PCGS also will be prohibited from misrepresenting that PCGS-certified coins eliminate the risk associated with grading and that PCGS-certified coins are more liquid than they actually are. PCGS will also be prohibited from loosening or tightening its grading standards, allowing the grade of a coin to be based on the ownership of or financial interest in the coin, or deviating from its published policies regarding self-interest and fiduciary responsibility. In the future, PCGS will have to make certain affirmative disclosures about risk and, if it chooses to make liquidity claims, it will have to make certain disclosures about liquidity of PCGS-certified coins as well.

"C. The Future On Wall Street

"Major Wall Street brokerages, such as Merrill Lynch and Kidder Peabody, have already jumped into the rare coin market with large check-books. Rumors of other Wall Street entrants abound. Offering materials for these Wall Street partnerships claim reliance on the Salomon Brothers Report and on the certification services of PCGS and others.

"Revelations in the *Wall Street Journal* and in *Coin World* circa 1987 about the basis for the once highly secret Salomon Brothers Index did not seem to deter Wall Street brokerages from getting into the market. Even with the disclosures that the Salomon Brothers list of 20 rare coins comprised truly rare silver (no gold) coins that arguably had little relevance to the typical coin investment, and that the rate of appreciation touted by Salomon Brothers may have been grossly overstated by the failure to take into account either changes to grading standards or transaction costs, Wall Street brokerages cite the report to support the same bold claims of appreciation that boiler room operators have made for years. It remains to be seen whether the PCGS lawsuit and other enforcement efforts by the FTC will have any greater sobering effect on the emerging interest on Wall Street. I am sure that dealers, collectors, and government officials alike will all be watching with great interest as the situation unfolds in the coming months.

"There is no reason why rare coin funds and limited partnerships can not do very well as investment vehicles, particularly in times of inflation or growth for hard assets generally. At the same time, there are many troubling questions that need to be answered. How does one control the temptation and opportunity for manipulation of grading standards and market practices when a major brokerage opens a $50 million checkbook? How does one control the temptation and opportunity to manipulate auctions and selling practices when a $50 million collection must be sold in relatively short order? Who will constitute the market for these coins, other than dealers or other investment partnerships?

"Add to these questions the natural changes that will occur in grading and one adds further uncertainty to the investment equation. How will computer/laser grading compare to the grade certifications of PCGS and other services? Will grading by technology confirm the suspicion of some experts that the majority of slabbed U.S. gold coins have at least some rubbing and are not technically Uncirculated? How will computerized grading distinguish tiny amounts of rubbing that do not disqualify a coin from trading as Uncirculated from the slightly greater amounts of rubbing that lead us to classify the coin as a 'slider' that must be graded AU-58 or AU-59 [sic]? If grading by computer and other technologies becomes established and commercially successful in the next several years, how will the market treat the grading standards and certifications for the coins now held by Wall Street brokerages in their limited partnerships when the time for liquidation arrives?

"At this time, I confess to having more questions than answers. On the other hand, I have little doubt that these and other similar questions are the same ones that Wall Street lawyers should be asking when they approve a limited partnership prospectus for rare coins or otherwise engage in drafting documents that will come under the scrutiny of the SEC.

"In conclusion, this is an exciting time for the coin industry. Within the lifetime of many coin dealers and collectors who are here, we have seen the coin industry blossom from one of children looking for scarce dates in pocket change and visiting their corner hobby shops, to an investment industry that has captured the imagination of Wall Street. This trend in the marketing of rare coins, not to mention bullion products, will doubtless attract increased attention by the FTC, the SEC, and the CFTC. The ANA, together with umbrella organizations for dealers and others with numismatic interests, can play an important role in the development of a mature, legitimate, and lucrative rare coin investment climate. While industry self-regulation will not be enough,[21] as the PCGS lawsuit and other FTC enforcement efforts make clear, no one is better positioned to guard against abuses and manipulation of the rare coin market than you and other numismatic organizations, if you have the will to enforce the types of tough standards that $50 million partnerships warrant and demand.

"You and others like you have the knowledge needed for effective self-regulation. I hope that you have the courage to use it."

Harvey Stack Speaks

Harvey G. Stack, well-known rare coin dealer and president of the Professional Numismatists Guild, delivered the following remarks at the ANA convention forum in which Barry J. Cutler spoke:[22]

"The question of whether or not the coin business should be regulated needs careful examination. If regulations are needed we must try to determine what if anything needs regulation. Is it the professional dealer who needs regulation, or is it the telemarketer? Is it the 'Mom and Pop' coin shop who buys, and sells, and goes to a couple of local shows, and the ANA convention each year, or is it the firm whose chief 'coin trader' is a person who was selling last—week—copper futures or penny stocks?

"For example, looking at the Professional Numismatists Guild membership, I believe the application of independent, third party investigation of financial stability, character references and the 'Code of Ethics' of that organization, together with the standing facility of arbitration, has made the need for regulations a non-requirement. We at the PNG do self-regulate ourselves. To the best of my knowledge no investigation of complaint for action by a PNG dealer has ever been referred by an agency such as the FTC.

"I also believe that the small dealer who operates on a local market is self-regulating by normal economic pressure. Should he stray from fair dealing his business ethics are known quickly locally and if he does wrong, the word spreads like wild fire in the area he serves. The penalties are severe—he doesn't survive in the business.

"The marketing by non-numismatic firms or pseudo numismatic companies through the 'telemarketing' and 'get rich quick' promotions may need some control, but I believe that there is sufficient regulation today by the SEC, the FTC and the postal authorities which reduce the further need of more regulation.

"One of the basic reasons I oppose regulation is the individuals I've encountered who attempt to interpret and enforce the regulations that may be in use at a particular time. I have found that regulations administered by non numismatic agencies usually accomplish overkill and can damage an industry unintentionally. Let me reflect on the situation when a government agency did in fact regulate a portion of the coin business and almost caused the importation of rare coins from overseas to cease to exist.

"In 1960 it became evident to the U.S. Treasury that numerous counterfeit coins were being purchased by American travelers overseas as well as being shipped into the country. 'Protect the American citizen from this abuse' was told to Secretary of the Treasury Anderson, who whispered into the ear of President Kennedy about the abuse, and before long the Office of Gold and Silver Operations by presidential order became the regulatory agency to control this illicit import. Since the Treasury agents and Customs agents didn't have the skills to fully identify good from bad gold coins they relied on this office's regulations.

"Guidelines were established at the Office of Gold and Silver Operations but the officially published versions never set forth the basis for prohibitions. We as dealers had to apply for a license without ever knowing if we could get permission to import. The criteria were kept as deep government secrets. By 1965 the situation became so restrictive that many coins of great numismatic value were arbitrarily and capriciously denied an import license. It took two years of departmental hearings to get the restrictions reversed. I am proud to say that Stack's made the test case to get these unreasonable restrictions lifted.

"It was learned at these hearings that those who ran the office did not understand numismatics. Yet it took from 1962 to 1967 to learn the criteria in force. They took the gold value of a coin, multiplied it by four, and if the 1962 edition of Friedberg's *Gold Coins of the World* book valued the coin in excess of this formula it was admitted. If not, entry was denied. No licensing credit was given to grade or rarity even though Friedberg only listed value for types in average grade. The fact that the coin was a Proof or Specimen strike did not count. Only the four-times ruling prevailed. So a Proof Victoria sovereign was treated as a circulated Victoria sovereign and denied license. This is a perfect example of a non-numismatic decision by a government agency. The entire regulation was suspended as it was an arbitrarily and capricious action of a government agency.

"The same overkill could occur today should regulations try to set standards for the rare coin industry by those who don't fully comprehend collecting, collectors and numismatics. I don't envision qualified numismatists joining the FTC nor officials at the FTC training for two to five years to try to understand numismatics. This direct contact with the industry and its methodology for five years is one of the basic requirements for a full PNG member or two years for an associate membership.

"Another non-comprehending example occurs today with the 1099 requirements for certain coin dealings. If you talk to a government agent in the East, then the West, or if you ask a dozen government officials, you are sure to get more than a dozen different interpretations. No one at government understands the requirements, so enforcement differs from city to city, state to state. The trouble is no one understands the intent of the regulations as they would apply to the coin business, so there is a multitude of interpretation.

"I therefore believe that we at the PNG and of course the ANA can and should watch for abuses, offer services such as arbitration to the public, and not be involved in more regulations. In the end, without government regulation, we all can survive. With regulation, we will have a very different coin industry than we have today, and a very difficult if not impossible way to collect coins.

"Do investors need protection?

"Sure.

"But that protection should be in the form of disclosure requirements and prohibitions against misrepresentations—not police actions against everyone who buys and sells coins. Regulations surely will remove the fun and pleasure from collecting.

"In the 44 years that I have been an active coin dealer, I have found just about every collection of coins to be some form of investment. Although it starts as a hobby, it evolves to be an important store of value for the collection. Conversely, it is obvious that every investment in coins cannot be deemed a collection.

"It always amazes me that people without doing any study or investigation can fall prey to all the high pressure selling hype. Possibly if we must have regulation, we should try to regulate or control the greed of the buyer who falls for the 'get rich' promotions. Without a willing buyer, the promoter would have no one to sell to. It should be the obligation of the buyer to check the information given him and challenges the promoter sales pitch, rather than recklessly shower him with money. Further education by the ANA and other numismatic groups should provide this needed education.

"Speaking for myself, it is obvious that I feel the reckless investor needs the protection, but not the collector. I feel the inevitable price of arbitrary type regulations, if it comes, will he at the expense of the collector as the coins will be harder to sell by him or his estate. The inevitable confusion set up by regulation will make it harder for the next one to collect. With fewer collectors you get fewer buyers—hence coins will be more difficult to sell.

"I did not come here to proclaim the inevitable doomsday, but I surely believe that regulation, especially administrated by partially or completely uninformed regulators, will lead to the slow demise of the hobby and the industry I deeply love and have devoted my life to.

"In summary, I believe as does the PNG for whom I have served many years as an officer, that government regulation of coin dealers and coin buyers is inappropriate. There are no doubt abuses, but not at the *collecting* end. The problem is at the marketing end; better stated, with the telemarketing promotions which survive on hyping investment. And to this end I sincerely believe there is ample authority present and available to deal with that problem without burdening the entire industry with additional regulation."

Author's Commentary

Welcome to the world of Wall Street! Coin firms such as PCGS do not have large legal staffs and are used to operating in the somewhat casual atmosphere of coin buying and selling, where one does not have to look very far to find claims which are far more extravagant than any ever made by PCGS. My own feeling is that the FTC-PCGS matter could have been handled privately, without national publicity.

On balance, the certified grading services are seen as a boon by the majority of participants in the rare coin market. Old-time collectors may not need them, and certainly grading remains a matter of opinion and is subjective, but for the novice or unknowledgeable investor a coin marked "MS-65" in a PCGS, NGC, ANACS, or Hallmark slab is more apt to be in the MS-65 range than a typical coin purchased outside of a slab. As noted in the present text, the technical or numerical grade of a coin is just the starting point for determining a coin's value, and other factors such as sharpness of strike, toning, lustre, and aesthetic appeal are also very important (factors not addressed in most commentaries about the FTC, Wall Street, etc.). In my opinion, publicity for Wall Street funds, as well as any other type of investment solicitation for rare coins, would do well to include mention that, as Barry J. Cutler has observed, slabs are not the answer to everything, and that grading is still largely a matter of opinion. Of course, this is what I have been saying all along.

As a side comment, some readers may remember the situation in 1972 when Richard Nixon made a public statement that silver dollars being sold by the General Services Administration branch of the United States government were a great investment. As part of the same promotion a brochure[23] noted in part: "Uncirculated specimens—these coins are an extraordinary value...." "Excellent for investment...the value of these coins is high since the demand is great...." Prospective buyers were further told that this was a "unique opportunity" and were "sound investments"—in a pitch not much different from that used by telemarketers against whom so many complaints were later lodged!

Coin dealers, who were being cautioned by the government to be careful about unfounded investment claims, found it curious and somewhat contradictory that the president of the United States and the General Services Administration government agency were engaging in what coin dealers were forbidden to do!

The government continues to promote coins as an investment, now even as an *ideal investment*, per this statement released by the U.S. Treasury Department, U.S. Mint, in September 1990.[24] "Savvy investors are focusing their attention on commodities, such as gold," says U.S. Mint Director Donna Pope. "They're discovering American Eagle bullion coins as an ideal investment."

The Opinion of Philip Schuyler

Philip Schuyler, owner of Ellesmere Numismatics and publisher of *The Winning Edge*, one of the most respected rare coin market newsletters, recently commented[25] concerning Wall Street and its dependency upon collectors to furnish long-term strength and demand in the marketplace:

"For years I thought that Wall Street's entrance to our little world would fuel rare coin values, and perhaps it still will, but it has become apparent to me that because limited partnerships are trading funds, demand created by Wall Street is primarily speculative. The industry needs underlying demand, and that can only be created by creating numismatists. If coins are to increase in value long term, demand must come from people who want to hold coins long term, namely collectors and collector-investors. If you call any five rare coin investors, one or two of them will tell you that they are no longer interested in rare coins. I've never heard a numismatist make that statement."

Selecting a Fund or Partnership

When evaluating the desirability of a rare coin fund or partnership, I suggest that you keep the following points in mind:

• **Reputation of those involved:** What is the reputation of those who are *numismatically* involved in managing the fund? Do they have a good track record? Are they well thought of as rare coin dealers or professionals? What qualifications do they have for investing your money? The reputation of the securities firm underwriting the issue is important, but not nearly as important, in my opinion, as that of the reputation of the coin managers. Nearly every securities underwriter on Wall Street has its share of winners and its share of disasters. The association of a "big name" underwriter with a coin partnership or fund is no assurance whatsoever that the partnership or fund will do well. Check out the *coin* people!

• **Investment portfolio contents and operating strategy:** What kinds of coins will be bought with your money? Will they be *rare* coins, a la the Salomon Brothers index, or will they be common or generic coins, or will they be a mixture of both? Will the fund speculate in silver and gold bullion? Will the fund buy and hold, or will it engage in active short-term buying and selling, or will it do both?

• **Fees and expenses:** What is the load or commission charged to buy or sell fund shares? What are the annual fees paid to those who manage the fund, and what do those people do for the money? Are their fees based upon a performance incentive, or do they receive generous fees even if they do poorly?

• **What is the track record?** Coin funds are new, and relatively little information is available concerning their operating profits or losses. However, within the next year or two the performance records of several established funds will be available for study and will provide a basis for investment decisions.

• **Your motivations:** What are your motivations and objectives? What kind of return do you want or expect? Is it better to buy a fund than buy coins on your own directly? Why?

I pose questions rather than give recommendations. If I were asked to state what I thought the single most important factor is when choosing a coin fund it would be this: check the *numismatic* reputation and track record of the people involved in the fund (and as information becomes available, check the track record of the fund itself).

In a recent conversation[26] with Phoebe Morse of the Federal Trade Commission we both discovered that we each had a common experience: on different occasions Wall Street securities firms had telephoned us to ask about the validity of the rare coin market as an investment vehicle for funds and partnerships, and we both endeavored to give objective views, pointing out some things to watch for in the coin market, such as dealer hype, grading inconsistencies, etc., but those on the Wall Street end of the line didn't want to hear about such things!

I believe that Wall Street firms are in numismatics to stay, and that investment in a carefully selected fund may well offer the opportunity to share in any broad-based market movements of the rare coin field. However, there is no magic in a rare coin fund per se, any more than there is any magic in a random stock or a piece of miscellaneous real estate per se. It is *careful selection* on your part that will make the difference. The securities underwriters may *not* be careful on your behalf. This is something you have to do on your own. Be sure the fund is managed by good *coin people*.

The only rare coin fund of which I have any detailed knowledge is the American Rare Coin Fund Limited Partnership, founded by Hugh Sconyers and Kevin Lipton, and underwritten by Kidder, Peabody & Co. In a visit to their offices[27] I was impressed with the sincere effort the principals were making to study the coin market carefully, to acquire numerous truly rare coins in addition to common ones, and to turn a trading profit.[28]

Subsequently,[29] Hugh Sconyers supplied the author with a record of the fund's performance since March 1989, starting with a base asset value of $995. By July 1990, after 17 months of operating in a very uncertain market, one fraught with many declines, the fund showed an asset value of $1,168.15, equal to a gain of 17.40% for the period.

Since that time, additional funds and partnerships have been launched by others, but I have no knowledge of how they operate (but would be grateful for such information to include in any future edition of this book). It could be that on this subject the reader of this book would do better by consulting with someone else other than me—with someone having more knowledge of the securities market and its involvement with rare coins. Before long, the actual performance of multiple funds already in business will be published and can be studied, just as coin prices and coin market movements can be analyzed. When this happens, there will be important additional information available for the intending investor. In the meantime the data given for the American Rare Coin Fund L.P. shows that at least one fund has turned in a worthwhile performance.

CHAPTER SIX

Auctions and Mail Bid Sales

Public Auctions

A very important way to buy and sell is through public auctions. By this route a coin auction house, such as our own Auctions by Bowers and Merena, Inc., acquires coins on consignment from private collectors, dealers, government agencies, estates, museums, banks, and other sources, and presents them for sale in a catalogue. Bids are received by mail and in person, and the pieces are sold to the highest bidders.[1] Participating in an auction or mail bid sale can be a lot of fun—like going fishing or treasure hunting—and there is no doubt that most major collections have been formed, at least in part, by acquiring coins in this manner.

How an Auction is Conducted

I shall describe how a typical Bowers and Merena public auction is conducted, as it may be of interest for the reader to go behind the scenes. Held in New York City and other metropolitan areas, these events have created worldwide attention. Public auction sales are conducted in the same manner as mail bid sales (to be described later), except that the final determination is made in an auction conducted by licensed auctioneers on our staff, with floor bidders attending in person.

From the standpoint of the auction company, conducting a sale is a detailed, complex procedure involving many people over a long period of time—as part of a program beginning long before the sale is announced or the catalogue printed. A year or more before the auction occurs, planning begins for the event. Consignments are gathered, a process which takes many months, and much care, as we endeavor to have each sale contain a wide variety of material appealing to a large cross-section of buyers. Consignments continue to arrive up to two or three months before the sale date.

Ideally, the typical public auction contains a number of rarities to appeal to advanced buyers and to create publicity, backed up by thousands of "regular" coins in many different series, to fill the needs of specialists in nearly every numismatic area. While the emphasis in many our sales is on early American and United States coins, we handle significant amounts of currency as well, and over the years we have had many notable specialized sales in the fields of tokens and medals and foreign and ancient coins.

As auctioneer we represent both the seller (known as the consignor) and the buyer (the bidder). In the early stages of auction planning, emphasis is on the seller. What type of collection does he or she have? When should it be sold and where? The answers vary. One client, an Ohio gentleman, had a small hoard of nearly a dozen 1794 silver dollars, a classic American rarity of which only about 120 specimens are known to exist. It was left up to us how to present them for sale. Rather than include all of the pieces in a single sale, we spread them out, one or two per sale, over a period of time. Undoubtedly, the prices realized were higher that way.

On the other hand, when we sold coins from the Virgil Brand estate on behalf of the Morgan Guaranty Trust Company and the heirs of Jane Brand Allen, we decided to sell a remarkable hoard of superb Uncirculated Cuban one-peso gold coins in a group of lots in a single sale. This turned out to be the right thing to do, for anyone who had ever wanted to own one of these sparkling little coins made it a point to bid, and the prices set new records. Similarly, we once sold a client's holding of six MCMVII High Relief double eagles in a single sale, and the coming together in one catalogue of so many superb pieces drew a great deal of attention, and all agreed that the prices were higher for each piece than if just one or two had been offered.

Often a client will have preferences. One gentleman wanted his coins sold in New York City in June, because that time of year was ideal for him and his family to attend the sale and combine it with a vacation trip.

Another client had a group of scarce and rare coins, several of which would have attracted attention if offered singly, but he wanted them sold as one lot under the "Miscellaneous U.S. Coins" category, for he felt that they would bring more money that way, and that two or three pieces which were rather ordinary would go along with the tide and do better in the company of rarities. He was right, and the lot sold for significantly more than what we figured was the sum of its individual parts. In our auction of the Abe Kosoff Estate[2] we sold a huge group of late-date Mercury dimes of the 1934-1945 era in a single lot for $18,150, far more than observers felt the pieces would have brought if offered in smaller groups. Someone wanted to get a "corner" on a large supply!

Anonymity is requested by many of our consignors, particularly museums and other public collections, and we follow this direction carefully. Others enjoy having their biographies and collecting histories presented for bidders to enjoy and appreciate.

After all of the consignments for a given sale are in our vaults, our cataloguing begins. First the coins are graded, and if it is deemed desirable, certain coins are sent to one of the certification services. Scarce and rare pieces are earmarked for photography. The coins are assigned lot numbers, and then research begins leading to the creation of a catalogue. Die varieties have to be checked, pedigrees verified, and market information studied. Sometimes this research can lead to surprising results, as in the case of a consignor, a prominent Cleveland attorney, who paid $200 for what he thought was a common variety of 1800 large cent, only to have us attribute it as a rarity which brought the breathtaking price of $13,750 in our Sussex Collection sale!

At any given time a dozen or two people are busy working on the preparation of our future auctions, even though the given auction may be months away. The culmination of all this effort is the production of a Grand Format™ catalogue. I am very proud of the catalogues issued by our firm over the years, and I am especially pleased that the Numismatic Literary Guild, which reviews auction catalogues each year and presents awards, has given our catalogues more "Catalogue of the Year Award" honors than have been given the auction catalogues of all of our competitors combined. We never rest on our laurels, and during the preparation of each catalogue, our Graphics Department has many meetings and discussions concerning cover designs, layout, and other artistic and numismatic aspects.

We are fortunate to have a full in-house facility for the complete creation of auction catalogues from beginning to end. As time permits, the Graphics Department also designs and prepares reference books and other works. Our staff, under the direction of Lee Lilljedahl, never rests, for there are always more projects to do.

After they are printed, the auction catalogues are distributed worldwide to clients on our mailing list, as well as to others in the fields of numismatics, fine arts, finance, and elsewhere who have responded to our publicity and advertising. Before long bids start pouring into our office by telephone, fax, and mail. We are kept busy from morning until night answering questions, posting bids, and getting ready for the sale. As the auction date draws closer, lot viewing is set up in New York City (or wherever the sale is scheduled to be held). Clients personally inspect the pieces they wish to bid on, for sales to floor bidders are final, and it is important that they verify beforehand the grade, appearance, and other aspects of each piece. In the meantime, we check bidders' credit references and do our best to comply with special bidding or payment requests.

Then the sale itself takes place, usually consisting of several sessions, the first of which typically begins at 7:00 in the evening. The auctioneer greets the audience, gives a few words concerning the sale, and tells the terms by which it will be conducted.

Then the auction begins. Seated at the elevated front table are several members of our staff, flanking the auctioneer, who stands behind a podium at the center. To his left is a spokesperson who follows the mail bids entered beforehand in the bid book. As a lot comes up for sale, the spokesperson calls out the starting bid, which is typically an advance over the second highest mail bid. For example, if the two highest mail bids received on a lot are $2,000 and $2,500, the lot may be opened at, say, $2,200.[3]

To the auctioneer's right are two other staff members, who with the aid of a computer take care of the "One Lot Only" and "Maximum Expenditure" bids, whereby a bidder can enter figures for several of the same kind of coin but be sure of winning no more than one, or give us bids totaling up to eight times the amount he finally wants to spend.

After the spokesperson calls out the opening bid of $2,200, the auctioneer cries, "I have a $2,200 bid, do I hear $2,400?" If there is floor competition, hands will go up, the auctioneer will advance rapidly–$2,400, $2,600, to $2,800, $3,000–sold to bidder 323 for $3,000!

If no one in the audience bids higher than the opening call of $2,200, then it goes to the mail bidder for that amount, and the person who bid $2,500 acquires it for less than his top authorization. If a floor bidder bids the same amount as a mail bidder, the mail bidder, being the earlier bidder, takes preference.

At the sale bidding paddles with numbers are given to the participants. Most hold the paddles in the air, making it easy for the auctioneer and others to follow the action. However, some bidders wish to remain anonymous, and this is fine. By prearrangement systems are sometimes set up with the auctioneer. I recall one instance in which a well-known specialist desired to purchase a rare early American coin, but was afraid that if others in the audience saw him bid on it, they would bid slightly more and take it away from him–knowing that he had the best idea of anyone as to what it was truly worth. No comparable specimen had appeared on the market for years. And yet he did want to bid obviously, for he would be in the audience and others would expect him to bid. He set up this arrangement: Taking a prominent seat in the audience, he told the auctioneer that he would put his hand in the air and would be bidding up to a certain level. If the competing bidders forced him to exceed that level, then his hand would come down, but Herbert Melnick, a well-known dealer (since deceased), would be bidding on his behalf, but no one would know this. If Melnick bought the lot it was to be charged to our client's account. The coin opened at a modest figure, and my client put his hand in the air, at the same time looking around to see who else was bidding. Five or six other hands were in the air at the same time. The bidding progressed, level by level, until our client and just two or three others were bidding, when at which time the client lowered his hand. Everyone except the auctioneer thought he had dropped out. Then Herbert Melnick raised his hand, and our client, not being a shy type of person, said so that all in the audience could hear: "The price is getting ridiculous—it's not worth that!" He was endeavoring to dissuade anyone from bidding much more. However, the competition continued, and finally Melnick bought the lot for a world's record price.

In another instance a client told me that if he was seated and was holding his bidder paddle, then he was bidding, but if he was standing and not holding his bidder paddle he was also bidding. When a particular lot, a rare early $5 piece came up, he sat in the back row and bid until it reached the $11,000 level, at which time he put his paddle on the seat, ostensibly stopped bidding, and stood up—but really continued bidding past $20,000.

And then there is the "shock bidding" technique. John Jay Pittman, well-known numismatist and past president of the American Numismatic Association, once wanted to own a rare Cuban gold coin being offered at auction. During the bidding he walked to the front of the sale room, turned to face the other bidders, and held his hand straight up in the air in an attempt to indicate to everyone that he would not stop bidding, no matter how high the price. It worked.

Similarly, in one of our recent New York City sales a lot opened at $1,500, and a bidder who just had to have it shouted "Five thousand dollars!"—without waiting for the normal auctioneer's advance to $1,600, then to $1,700, etc. This technique worked, too, although I suspect that the new owner of the coin might have had second thoughts later, and wondered if he could have bought it for much less, for the coin had never sold at the $5,000 level before.

Sometimes bidding is so hectic that it is difficult to keep track of what is happening. In our sale of the Garrett Collection for The Johns Hopkins University, I recall that the father and son team of Art and Don Kagin was present, and in one instance Don and Art, seated apart from each other in the room, were bidding against each other on the same coin!

It is often the case that a bidder attending a sale in person does not want to bid from the audience, and gives us bids, which we enter in the bid book just before the sale, just as we would enter mail bids. Then when the lot crosses the block, if his "mail bid" is exceeded by floor competition he may step in and do some bidding in person or have an agent do it.

When all is said and done, and the last lot has been sold everyone breathes a sigh of relief. Many hours of planning, excitement, and anticipation are over! Now it is time for those attending the sale to pick up their new treasures, or to arrange to have us ship them. Now the coins are parts of new collections all over the world. Hopefully, we will get the chance to auction them again sometime in the future.

The Garrett Collection

As a professional numismatist I have catalogued and sold some of the most valuable collections ever formed. When The Johns Hopkins University decided to sell the Garrett Collection of United States coins my firm was selected to do the job. With lots of help from my staff, I immersed myself in the project, and in the process created a book, *The History of U.S. Coinage as Illustrated by the Garrett Collection*, four auction catalogues, and a lot of publicity, all of which added up to a realization of $25 million when the coins crossed the block in our sales held in New York City and Los Angeles. Top price honors went to a 1787 Brasher gold doubloon which was sold for more than any other coin had brought up to that time: $725,000, a world's record that stood for nearly a decade. A memorable thing about the collection was that just before it was consigned to us, another leading firm had appraised it for $9 million. When all was said and done, the coins realized nearly three times the pre-sale expectation!

The Garrett Collection was an old-time holding, begun in the 1860s by T. Harrison Garrett, whose father was the main figure in the operation of the Baltimore & Ohio Railroad, and continued into the 1930s by T. Harrison's son, John Work Garrett, who as a profession followed a distinguished diplomatic career. Time and time again bidders at the Garrett sale paid double, triple, or more in relation to current catalogue values.

In a front-page article in *Coin World*, David L. Ganz reported that "simply no superlatives are adequate" to describe the intense action, and that record after record was shattered. Not only were the bidders buying rare coins, but they were also buying *selected* specimens of rarities, for the Garretts were connoisseurs and purchased the best. One of my clients, a Georgia businessman, sent a letter of credit for $500,000 before the sale. "I don't know what I will be buying, but I want *something*," he commented. As it turned out, competition was so intense that he wasn't able to spend the full amount he had hoped to.

The success of the Garrett Collection sale was best summed up by a California client who attended and stated: "The coins were premium specimens from a premium collection described in a premium catalogue, so they brought premium prices."

The Eliasberg Collection

Louis Eliasberg is a name familiar to all students of American numismatic history. From the 1930s until 1950 this leading Baltimore banker and financier endeavored to accomplish what no one had ever done before: to build a collection containing an example of each and every major United States coin variety from the 1793 half cent to the 1933 double eagle, the alpha and omega of federal coinage. One by one such rarities as the 1913 Liberty Head nickel, 1873-CC No Arrows and 1894-S dimes, 1876-CC twenty-cent piece, 1827 and 1873-CC No Arrows quarter dollars, the 1838-O half dollar, silver dollars of 1804 and 1870-S, trade dollars of 1884 and 1885, the unique 1870-S $3 gold piece, the beautiful Flowing Hair and Coiled Hair $4 stellas of 1879 and 1880, the legendary 1822 $5, and other delicacies were acquired, until at long last the collection was complete!

In 1975, while I was attending the American Numismatic Association's annual convention, held that year in Los Angeles, I received a hurry-up call from Mr. Eliasberg, who bid me to come to Baltimore as soon as possible, right away in fact. I left the business of the convention to others, and I boarded the next plane for Baltimore, whereupon I spent the next week examining all of the coins and discussing their possible sale through our firm, something which he planned to have happen at an unspecified time in the future.

Soft-shell crabs, a Maryland delicacy, are among my favorite things to eat, and each day my host treated me to a generous serving at his private club. In the evenings we would "talk coins," and I learned first-hand of the challenges and joys experienced by Mr. Eliasberg as he narrowed his want list down to just a few dozen, then to just a few individual coins, then to just one, before he completed it in 1950.

Several years elapsed, and I was deeply saddened when I learned that Mr. Eliasberg had passed away, for I had lost not only a client but a fine friend. A year or two later his son, Louis Eliasberg, Jr., contacted me and consigned for public auction sale the gold portion of his father's collection, the only complete collection of United States gold coins ever formed. As per usual procedure, I drew up an auction contract. Upon presenting it to Mr. Eliasberg, he politely handed it back to me, shook my hand, and said, "I will not sign any contract, for if I didn't have faith in you and your company, I would not have given you the coins."

The Eliasberg Collection, billed as The U.S. Gold Coin Collection, made auction history. The unique 1870-S $3 brought $687,500, and the only 1822 $5 outside of the Smithsonian Institution also sold for $687,500, the two highest prices United States gold coins have ever sold for at auction. Numerous other world's record prices were achieved as well, adding up to a total of $12,400,000, making the Eliasberg sale second only to the Garrett Collection in total value for a coin collection sold up to that time. Thus, the world's second most valuable collection was sold on an agreement consisting only of a handshake!

A contrast to my relationship with the Eliasberg family were negotiations leading to our selling at auction a large estate which had passed to the owner's son, a prominent New York City attorney. I sent him our standard auction contract, he revised it, we revised his revisions, and he re-revised our revisions. Countless telephone conversations, fax messages, and Federal Express shipments were needed to put all of the details in the order that the consignor wanted. The customer is always right, and what the consignor wants is what the consignor gets, if we can possibly accommodate it. Some want just a handshake. Others want every possible contingency covered in writing, signed, sealed, and delivered.

The Norweb Collection

Let me mention another major collection which will always occupy a special place in my affections. For many years Ambassador and Mrs. R. Henry Norweb had been clients. Their collection, the foundation of which was formed by Mrs. Norweb's father, Albert Fairchild Holden, at the turn of the century, was legendary in its proportions. Like the Garrett family and Louis Eliasberg, the Norwebs sought the finest, and when the finest was offered they paid the going price to get it. Year by year they added to their holdings, so that by the 1970s they had just about one specimen of each variety in the areas in which they specialized, and that specimen was apt to be one of the finest of its kind.

My first sale to the Norwebs was an 1894-S dime, which I had purchased at auction in 1957 through the efforts of James F. Ruddy, a long-time friend and, later, business associate. The price paid was $4,750, a record price at the time. A year later the Norwebs purchased it from me, paying $6,000. We kept in close contact over the years, and as their collecting activities drew to a close, I assisted with a number of appraisals, including one when they donated their 1913 Liberty Head nickel to the National Numismatic Collection at the

Smithsonian Institution. When Ambassador and Mrs. R. Henry Norweb passed away, they left a rich legacy of memories, and of numismatic benefactions, the latter in the form of many rarities given to the Smithsonian Institution and the American Numismatic Society.

I was deeply touched when R. Henry Norweb, Jr. and his wife, Libby, selected me and my firm to auction the Norweb Collection. Against a pre-sale estimate of $10 million, our series of three sales yielded twice that amount, or $20 million. The star of the collection was a magnificent gem Uncirculated 1861 Philadelphia Mint double eagle with the Paquet reverse, which Gerald Bauman, representing the MTB Banking Corporation, won for $660,000, the third highest price any United States gold coin has ever realized at auction and the highest auction figure ever achieved for a $20 piece.[4]

The three Norweb sales made numismatic history, and the front pages of *Coin World* and *Numismatic News* told the whole collecting world of new price records. After all was completed, and after the Norweb family had received the net proceeds of the sale, Henry and Libby Norweb extended an invitation to all the staff members of my company, and their families, to visit their beautiful seaside summer home in Maine for a deluxe lobster dinner and outing. We all appreciated this nice touch.

An Interesting Occurrence

Not all collections are valued into the millions. In fact, few are. Of the more than 10,000 collections and properties consigned to our sales over the years the typical holding is apt to have been valued from about $10,000 to several hundred thousand dollars.

One particularly pleasant memory comes to mind concerning a small, or at least it was supposed to be small, collection owned by a retired, elderly lady of modest circumstances who spent her summer months on a New Hampshire lake not far from our offices. It seems that she read about our company in an article in *The New York Times* and had saved the clipping until her next trip northward. After making an appointment with Dr. Richard A. Bagg, our director of auctions, she brought to our office a small box of coins for which she had been offered several thousand dollars by a leading dealer. Immediately Rick Bagg recognized that the silver Liberty Seated Proof coins and other items added up to a much higher sum. Further, she indicated that she had additional items at home, and they were of the same quality. She left our offices with a signed receipt and an auction contract, and upon going home she shipped the remaining pieces.

Her collection was catalogued, photographed, and showcased in our next

New York City sale. After the last coin had been sold, her net realization amounted to a total of a quarter million dollars. When Rick Bagg sent her the settlement check, she said, "I was hoping to receive $25,000 at most. I don't know what to say!"

A Collection From the Midwest

In the same category was a collection sent to us by a Midwestern lady who had inherited the coins from a relative. The group consisted mainly of commemorative half dollars housed in brown paper envelopes bearing the imprint of B. Max Mehl, the famous Fort Worth, Texas coin dealer who was in business from 1903 to 1957 and who during the course of his career sold many memorable collections, including those of Ten Eyck, Dunham, Atwater, and Neil. Before contacting us, she had taken the coins to two local dealers and had experienced unsatisfactory results.

During the course of her conversations with Rick Bagg at our office she stated that she had hoped to use part of the auction proceeds to make a down payment on a $220,000 home. After the coins arrived, Rick glanced at them quickly, then telephoned the owner to state that she could without hesitation make an arrangement to purchase the house of her dreams, for her coins would bring much more than the $25,000 or so she needed to sign the home purchase contract.

The collection was duly catalogued and was found to contain a number of pieces in extraordinarily high grade, including a 1923-S Monroe half dollar in MS-67 preservation which, as it turned out, brought nearly $35,000 all by itself! After the sale ended, Dr. Richard A. Bagg telephoned the lady to tell her that the collection had netted her not the $25,000 or so she had hoped for, but a total of $302,000!

Then there are the collections we have auctioned of several past presidents of the American Numismatic Association, including Matt Rothert, M. Vernon Sheldon, Admiral Oscar H. Dodson, Arthur Sipe, and George Hatie. These distinguished gentlemen enjoyed owning their coins and currency, of course, but they added an extra dimension by becoming involved with people.

The New York City Public Library

When the New York City Public Library decided to auction its collection of rare coins it contacted us. The holding had been gathered over a period of many years, with numerous pieces bearing notations indicating their purchase or donation in the 19th century. I had visited the library often in the course of conducting historical research, and it was a dream come true when we were awarded the privilege to sell their world-class numismatic holdings. Particularly interesting to me were the tokens, medals, and other unusual items, including two 1861 Confederate States of America restrike half dollars which were given to the institution in the year they were restruck, 1879, by the person who restruck them, J.W. Scott.

The Brand Collection

Selling coins in 1983 and 1984 and again in 1989 and 1990 for the heirs of Virgil M. Brand was an experience that all of us involved will always remember. The reputation of Brand, who had passed away in 1926, remained larger than life in numismatics. Everyone had heard about Brand and his immense collection, which at one time numbered some 350,000 specimens, but little was available in the way of factual information. With the assistance of David and Susan Tripp[5] and the Brand family, I was able to write the biography of this remarkable man, a giant of a numismatist who ate, slept, and breathed coins.

When the Brand coins crossed the auction block, the entire numismatic world was thrilled to see rarities and other pieces which had been off the market for a generation or more. Interestingly, one of my favorite items in the Brand Collection was not a coin at all, but was a set of 1796 Seasons medals issued under the administration of President George Washington for distribution as peace medals to Indians. The gorgeous set of four silver Proof medals fetched $50,000, a record, but in terms of numismatic significance and American history, a bargain.

Selling coins at auction can be a profitable way to dispose of your holdings, and buying at auction can be exciting and fun. There is no doubt that just about every notable collection ever formed was acquired, at least in part, by auction purchases. In America there are a number of fine auction houses to choose from, and in addition to the well-known Auctions by Bowers and Merena events, sales held by firms such as Stack's, Heritage, Mid-American, Pacific Coast Auction Galleries, David Akers, Superior, and Rarcoa, among others, attract a wide clientele.

How to Buy at Auction

Buying at auctions can be a very enjoyable and profitable procedure if you follow certain steps. Certain procedures are similar to those you should follow in a mail bid sale (to be discussed subsequently). Here are some guidelines:

• **Read the terms of sale:** Read the terms of sale carefully, for once you bid you are legally bound to abide by the rules. If you have any questions about how to bid, or at what level to bid, ask the auction firm. It is also a good idea to ask others, perhaps collectors or investors who have done business there before. If some coins are sold "as is" (certified coins are sometimes sold on this basis, as are bullion-type coins and large lots of bulk coins), be aware of this. If you attend the sale personally and are a floor bidder, then you probably will not be able to return a coin after the sale if you later disagree with the grading or some other aspect, although most (but not all) auction houses will permit the return of a fake coin.

Most auction houses are careful to note in the terms of sale that consignors can bid on their own coins, the auction house may have an ownership interest in certain lots, and that certain coins may have reserves, a situation common in the art and antiques business as well. Because of these and other factors, an opening bid of, say, $10,000 for a coin might not necessarily represent a bid received from an intending buyer, but may be a reserve or starting price. The auction house must represent the interest of the seller as well as that of the buyer, and to use a facetious example, although the buyer would be delighted, I am sure, an auction house offering a $100 bill for sale would not sell it for just $75 because no higher bid had been received. I reiterate: read the terms of sale, for they vary from sale to sale and from auction house to auction house.

• **Become familiar with the auctioneer's descriptions:** When bidding in an auction sale you will use the catalogue descriptions, possibly modified by in-person viewing if you attend the sale. However, many bidders participate by mail and do not have the chance to see the coins in advance (unless they take advantage of the opportunity to view by mail, a service offered by some auction houses). By making inquiries and possibly even by some "test bidding" (start modestly in one sale, and if you are pleased, bid on more items or bid more aggressively in the next sale) determine if the coins offered actually match the catalogue descriptions.

In some instances, I have seen great rarities in slabs, catalogued simply in a manner like this (a fictitious example): "1893-CC MS-63 (PCGS)," without any mention of its surface characteristics. Is is toned or is it brilliant? A catalogue illustration may help, but many lots are not photographed. In such an instance, it may pay you to telephone the auctioneer and request a more detailed description. Once you become familiar with the auctioneer's cataloguing methods and build a confidence level, you can bid by mail with assurance that what you hope to get is what you will get.

• **Establish price ranges in advance:** Establish beforehand the price you want to pay for a given coin. If you feel that the most you wish to pay for a certain 1889-CC silver dollar is $17,500, set your limit beforehand, and if it crosses the $17,500 barrier let someone else buy it. Of course, if a coin you desire is a rarity and in nice condition, don't sent your limits at a bargain basement level or you will expend a lot of effort and won't buy it! If a coin is especially rare or desirable, don't be afraid to bid aggressively. However, base your bids on a foundation of knowledge. As an auctioneer, I have no quarrel with "auction fever," as it is always nice to see coins sell for very high levels. However, my more reasoned view is this: I believe that each buyer should feel that he or she has received a good value for the price paid. If a coin is common, then don't get carried away and bid too much. If the coin is a rarity, then an "auction fever" price might be merited, and next year may prove to have been the buy of your lifetime.

• **Be flexible:** Be adaptable, and if you have $5,000 to spend, prepare bids for $25,000 or more worth of coins. In this way you won't be out of the game if the first items you bid on go for more than you want to pay. Some firms help out by computerizing this procedure for mail bidders. For example, in our sales we have the "Maximum Expenditure Option" whereby clients can submit bids up to eight times the total amount they wish to spend, and our computer will track the bids until the desired amount is spent. For example, if you want to spend $10,000 you can submit $80,000 worth of bids, and the bids will be handled in order until your $10,000 limit is reached.

Mail Bid Sales

Under this general category fall offerings of coins published in numismatic periodicals and in catalogues, which invite prospective bidders to participate by telephone, fax, or mail, without floor participation. In the antiques trade these are known as "absentee auctions," but the term has not been used in the numismatic field. Many of the procedures in a mail bid sale are similar to those in a public auction. Bernard Rome's Teletrade, Mid-American Rare Coin Galleries' Numismatic Express offerings, certain Coin Galleries' sales, and our own Kingswood Galleries combined telephone, mail bid, and fax sales are among the many players in this category.

In effect, in a mail bid sale the auction gallery is in your own home or office, and you can bid from the comfort of your favorite armchair. Our Kingswood mail bid sales have been popular with many clients. Here is a view of how they work:

In the introduction to a recent Kingswood catalogue I wrote the following:

"Welcome to the Amherst Sale conducted by Kingswood Galleries. In the pages to follow you will find many choice, rare, and desirable numismatic items. Colonials, state coins, half cents and large cents, two-cent and three-cent pieces, important silver coinage, gold coins, commemoratives, and other series are presented for your bidding consideration... Devotees of slabbed coins have the opportunity to compete for numerous coins certified by Hallmark, ANACS, PCGS, and NGC....

"While scarce coins and rarities always get a lot of attention, and deservedly so, the backbone of numismatics is composed of coins which are affordable to the average buyer. In the present sale there are numerous lots which will probably sell in the $50 to $500 range. Included in that span are many early colonial and state coins, half cents and large cents, and other pieces which even the most advanced numismatist will enjoy owning. I know this, for I, Mike Hodder, Andy Pollock, Ray Merena, and Chris Karstedt have enjoyed cataloguing them. One of the nicest things about being a professional numismatist is the opportunity to 'own,' if only briefly, the many fine coins and paper money notes that pass through our hands.

"Let me now say a few words about Kingswood Galleries. As any reader of *Coin World, Numismatic News*, the *Coin Dealer Newsletter*, and other periodicals knows well, it is an era of big money. Scarcely a week goes by without this coin or that one selling for $50,000, $100,000 or even $200,000, or without this auction or that bringing well into seven figures. We are active participants in the arena and in fact have had more than our share of auction price records and major collections. Along the way we have tried our best to maintain a close personal contact with our clients.

"Personal service is the prime objective of Kingswood Galleries. Chris Karstedt and the Kingswood team have enjoyed gathering the consignments offered herewith and produced in the catalogue. When the sale itself takes place, Chris Karstedt, Jennifer Douglass, Barbara Anderson, and Diane MacArthur will personally enter the bids on your bid sheet or answer your questions for help with bidding via toll-free telephone.

"We are old-fashioned here. We believe that while our clients appreciate accurate, detailed descriptions of the coins we offer, and the prompt manner in which we invoice successful bidders after the sale, they also appreciate our friendship and enthusiasm. Coins are not a necessity of life. They are a pleasure, an extra something which adds a measure of enjoyment to one's everyday activities. We want you to have a pleasant, enjoyable transaction, and when all is said and done, have the feeling of complete satisfaction with every aspect of the transaction. If there is anything we can do to make your bidding and buying experience better, we'll do our best to do it!"

I went on to describe the Kingswood guarantee, which stated that all coins were sold subject to client approval, and any items not pleasing for any reason whatever—including the grade, surface appearance, aesthetic quality, and anything else—could be returned within a specified period for a refund. I went on to note that a situation of mutual trust must be created, and while our clients have the right to return a coin within the time stated, if the coins were returned for no apparent reason we reserve the right to decline participation in future sales. "However, if you like what you receive from us, and we like the way you do business with us, we are both set for a fine, lasting relationship with mutual benefit."

As the closing date of the Kingswood sale approached, bids came in from all over the world. During the last week things became hectic, as clients telephoned and write to adjust this bid or that, to check to see how they are doing, to make additional bids, and to otherwise do their best to win the lots in question. Chris Karstedt, Barbara Anderson, and Cynthia Lassiter were on the telephone constantly, with scarcely a break, even for a sandwich.

The fax machine, unknown a few years ago, has become a major way to bid, especially for overseas clients who can send us bids during their business hours, knowing they will be on hand when we open in the morning. Hundreds of bids arrive by fax, especially during the last days before each sale.

By the time that the actual closing of this Kingswood sale occurred, at 4:00 on a particular afternoon, thousands of bids had been received. The next day or so was spent entering these bids into our computers and determining the winner of each lot.

For the next day or two after that, successful bidders were sent invoices by mail, and coins were shipped on open account to those who had furnished satisfactory references. The entire Kingswood staff pitched in to send the invoices and coins out as soon as possible.

By the time that the Kingswood staff was mailing invoices and coins for the Amherst Sale, the next Kingswood event, the Barrington Sale, was already well underway, consignments were being processed, and major parts of the catalogue had been researched and written, as part of a virtually non-stop ongoing program.

Mail bid sales have a time-honored tradition, and in the past many important collections have been sold this way. B. Max Mehl, of Fort Worth, Texas, who was unquestionably America's most prominent dealer during the first half of the present century,[6] conducted mail bid sales only. In fact, he never had a sale with public participation. Some of the greatest collections ever sold were dispersed in this manner, including the Dunham Collection in 1941, which had both an 1804 dollar and an 1822 half eagle, and the Atwater, Neil, Olsen, Ten Eyck, Slack, and other holdings.

How to Buy in Mail Bid Sales

Buying by mail or telephone in a mail bid sale can be a very enjoyable and profitable procedure if you follow certain steps. Certain of the steps are similar to those discussed earlier for bidding in public auctions:

• **Read the terms of sale:** Read the terms of sale carefully, for once you bid you are legally bound to abide by the rules. If you have any questions about how to bid, or at what level to bid, ask the firm conducting the sale. It is also a good idea to get information and advice from others who have done business with the firm. If some coins are sold "as is" or on a "no returns allowed" basis be aware of this.[7] Some sellers permit returns only at the seller's option. Others permit no returns of certified coins but have provisions for the return of other (non-slabbed) coins within a specified time. Although it is possible to argue with a seller and possibly achieve satisfaction, it is far simpler and more pleasant to read the terms of sale carefully and don't bid unless you agree with what you see in print. Our own Kingswood sales allow returns within a specified time *for any reason the buyer chooses,* but most sellers are not that liberal. The terms of sale of many sellers note that the seller reserves the right to bid on any lot, that he may have an ownership in certain lots, and that he may set starting or reserve bids. With regard to starting or reserve bids, it is important to remember that the individual or firm conducting the mail bid sale has a dual obligation; he must endeavor to protect the owner or consignor as well as the buyer or bidder. I reiterate: read the terms of sale before bidding.

• **Become familiar with the seller's descriptions:** Before you participate in a mail bid sale, ask about the seller's reputation and the accuracy of his descriptions. Cataloguing methods vary, and while some descriptions are very informative, others are bare-bones listings. A description such as the following is helpful: "1848 Liberty Seated dollar. MS-63. Light iridescent toning is seen around the borders, while the centers are mostly brilliant. A few bagmarks, normal for the grade, are in evidence." With such a word picture in front of you, plus possibly an illustration of the coin itself in the catalogue, you can be an informed bidder. On the other hand, a description such as the following tells you nothing except the technical grade: "1848 Liberty Seated dollar. MS-63 (NGC)." Is it a high-end coin, or is it an unattractive low-end coin? Who knows?

If information in the catalogue is scant, it may pay you to telephone the auctioneer and request a more detailed description. Once you become familiar with the auctioneer's cataloguing methods and build a confidence level, you can bid by mail with assurance that what you hope to get is what you will get.

• **Read the catalogue carefully:** Read the catalogue carefully to determine which items are of interest. Check the catalogue from cover to cover, and consult the index to be sure you do not overlook listings of the same coins or series.

• **Be flexible:** Using market information in *Coin World, Numismatic News, A Guide Book of U.S. Coins*, the *Coin Dealer Newsletter*, or other sources, as well as auction records, determine how much you want to pay. If a coin is common or in ordinary condition, bid an ordinary price. However, if you have the chance to bid on a particularly fine example or a rarity, be flexible. You may have to bid more, sometimes substantially more, than current listings in order to acquire it. In each sale we conduct there are some record prices set and, of course, the coins go to those setting these records. I am reminded of a Maryland gentleman who wanted a gem example of an MCMVII (1907) High Relief $20. In 1955, when the market price was around $300, he wanted to pay $200. When the price rose to $1,000, he would have been a buyer at $800. At the $5,000 level he wanted one for $4,000. Now the same coin would cost about $25,000, and he still doesn't have one! It would have been cheaper in the long run if when the market price was $300, he had set a new record at $400 and became the owner of the gem he desired.

If you have $2,000 to spend, prepare bids for $10,000 or more worth of coins, if the company conducting the sale permits this. In this way you won't be out of the game if the first items you bid on go for more than you want to pay. Some firms help out by computerizing this procedure for mail bidders. For example, in our Kingswood mail bid sales and our Auctions by Bowers and Merena public sales we have the "Maximum Expenditure Option" whereby clients can submit bids up to eight times the total amount they wish to spend, and the computer will track the bids until the desired amount is spent.

• **Use the telephone:** Use the telephone to check on your bids, to raise your limits, and to ask any questions you may have. As our Kingswood sales near the closing time, the telephone lines are constantly busy. While it is the policy of our staff not to reveal the highest bid of another client, if you bid, for example, $1,000 on Lot 25, we will gladly let you know if your bid stands a chance for success. If it doesn't, then you may want to raise it, or you may want to cancel the bid and then bid on something else. Don't be shy! Use the telephone. Others do!

CHAPTER SEVEN

Mints and Minting

How Coins Are Made

Coins are struck from dies, which are two cylindrical pieces of metal, each bearing an incised design, date, and other information. These dies are mounted in a coining press. A blank disk, called a planchet, is inserted on top of the lower die, the top die is then squeezed or forced against the planchet with many tons of pressure, and a coin is created.

As the metal is squeezed by the dies, it flows outward into a collar or retaining device. Certain retaining devices have ornamentation such as vertical stripes, called reeding. In early years of the mint, the blank planchets themselves were put through a special lettering machine before the planchets were struck, and on the edge of the planchet was inscribed lettering such as FIFTY CENTS OR HALF A DOLLAR. Such pieces are known as "lettered edge" coins. Certain later coins, the $20 pieces of 1907-1933 for example, had the lettering, such as E PLURIBUS UNUM, applied by the collar.

The entire minting process involves refining metal to the correct proportion, rolling it into strips, cutting planchets from it, striking the coins, sorting and bagging them, and distributing them into the channels of banking and commerce.

In the early days dies were cut by hand. By means of an engraving tool the die cutter would create the figure of Miss Liberty, an eagle, or other motif. Letters and numerals would be added to the die individually by means of punches. Certain other punches were used for elements as leaves and berries. Each die was slightly different from all others. The collecting of coins made by different dies is a fascinating pursuit. Sometimes a die would last long enough to make tens of thousands of coins before it broke, and thus coins from such a die are easy to find today. In other instances a die would break shortly after it was first used, only a few pieces would be struck from it, and today that particular die variety is rare.

Beginning about the year 1836 the preparation of dies was mechanized, and the lettering, eagle, figure of Miss Liberty, and everything else but the date was stamped on the die from a master die or hub. The date figures were then added individually. Soon thereafter, logotypes consisting of an entire date, such as 1898, were made, and the date was then punched in all at once, rather than individual date punches.[1] Still later, the date was included in the master die, and all working dies were stamped with all information on them—including the date, design, and lettering. That is the way dies are produced today. Consequently, there are relatively few die variety differences among modern coins.

Early Issues

Prior to the establishment of the federal Mint in Philadelphia in 1792, coins in circulation in America were a wide mixture of types, including coins produced in Mexico, Holland, France, England, Germany, and other parts of the globe. Certain issues, such as Rosa Americana coins, were produced in England for circulation in the United States. Other coins used in everyday commerce were minted by various individuals and entities in America. The New England, Willow Tree, Oak Tree, and Pine Tree silver issues were struck beginning in 1652 when the colony of Massachusetts decided to mint its own coins.

During the 1785-1788 period, Vermont, New York, Connecticut, Massachusetts, and New Jersey produced copper coins at mints within those states, either by contract or, in the case of Massachusetts, by a state-owned mint.[2]

Fugio cents dated 1787 were produced by a contract awarded by the United States government and are considered by many to be the first official United States coins, although they were produced privately.[3] Tokens and medals associated with President George Washington, and bearing dates from about 1783 through 1795, are listed in the *Guide Book* and are widely collected.

Early American coins were produced from hand-engraved dies, often utilizing crude minting equipment, and many varieties seen today exhibit a rustic crudeness, which makes collecting them a fascinating pursuit for specialists.

Mints and Mintmarks

• **Philadelphia Mint (1792 to date):** In 1792 the government acquired a plot of land and several buildings in Philadelphia and set up the first federal facility for the production of coins. The Philadelphia Mint has been in operation continuously since then, although in different buildings, with moves to new and larger premises being made in 1830, 1901, and 1967. At present the Philadelphia Mint is located on Independence Square not far from

Independence Hall and the Liberty Bell and is a modern facility employing hundreds of people who engage in all aspects of coinage production. A warm welcome is extended to visitors, who are able to see coins being made and to view many interesting ehibits.°

Most coins produced at the Philadelphia Mint bear no distinguishing mint letter. However, on Jefferson nickels minted with a special silver alloy from 1942 through 1945 only, the mintmark P appears on the reverse over the dome of Monticello. In recent years the mintmark P has been used again and can be found on various coinage.

The Philadelphia Mint is the "mother mint" and is where dies for all branch mints are made. From the early 19th century until the mid-1960s Proof coins and sets were produced there; after that time Proof production was transferred to San Francisco.

Over the years the Philadelphia Mint has produced many rarities, among the best known of which are the 1793, 1799, and 1804 cents, the 1913 Liberty Head nickel, the 1802 half dime, the 1827 quarter dollar, the 1794 and 1804 silver dollars, the trade dollars of 1884 and 1885, the 1841 and 1863 quarter eagles, the 1875 and 1876 $3 gold pieces, the 1879 and 1880 pattern $4 stellas, the 1822 $5, the $20 pieces of 1883, 1884, and 1933, as well as numerous patterns, prominent among which are the 1849 and Extremely High Relief $20 pieces and two varieties of $50 pieces dated 1877.

• **New Orleans Mint (1838-1909):** In 1838, due to increasing commerce on the Mississippi River and in the Gulf of Mexico, a mint was opened at the foremost trading center in the area, New Orleans, Louisiana. Coins were produced at this facility from 1838 until the Civil War in 1861, and again from 1879 through 1909. In 1861 the mint was seized by the State of Louisiana and was later operated for a short time under the auspices of the Confederate States of America.

The mintmark O appears on coins struck there. Pieces produced at New Orleans were in silver and gold metals; no copper coins were struck. A coin struck at the New Orleans Mint is described as follows, for example: 1879-O.

Among rarities struck at New Orleans are the 1861 Confederate States of America pattern half dollar and the $20 pieces of 1854-O, 1856-O, and 1879-O.

• **Charlotte Mint (1838-1861):** In 1838 a branch mint was opened in Charlotte, North Carolina for the purpose of producing gold coins from metals extracted from mines and streams of the area. $1, $2.50, and $5 pieces were produced there from 1838 until the Civil War in 1861, at which time the mint closed. Charlotte coins are identified by the mintmark C, as, for example, 1843-C.

All coins struck at Charlotte are either scarce or rare today. Heading the list is the 1849-C gold dollar with open wreath on the reverse, of which fewer than a half dozen specimens are known.

• **Dahlonega Mint (1838-1861):** The history of the Dahlonega Mint is similar to that of Charlotte. Gold produced in the Dahlonega area of Georgia was converted into $1, $2.50, $3, and $5 pieces from the period 1838 through 1861. The mint closed at the advent of the Civil War. Dahlonega coins have the mintmark D, not to be confused with the same mintmark later used for Denver coins, for the Dahlonega Mint operated 1838-1861, decades before the Denver Mint did. All Dahlonega gold coins are either scarce or rare and as a class are more elusive than their Charlotte Mint counterparts.

• **San Francisco Mint (1854 to date):** During the gold rush era in California many banks and private individuals produced coins. In 1854 the federal government opened a mint there using a building and equipment purchased from a private firm. Known as the San Francisco Mint, the facility used the S mintmark on its pieces. Coins were produced at San Francisco from 1854 until 1955, and again from the late 1960s until the present time. Over a period of years the San Francisco Mint has produced pieces in all metals. From 1968 onward, Proof sets for collectors have been produced there.

Among rarities struck at the San Francisco Mint are such issues as the 1870-S half dime, 1894-S dime, 1870-S silver dollar, 1854-S $2.50, 1870-S $3, and 1854-S $5.

• **Carson City Mint (1870-1893):** In 1870 a mint was opened in Carson City, Nevada to take advantage of silver (and to a lesser extent gold) found in the Comstock Lode in Nevada. Bearing CC mintmarks (the only mintmark with more than one letter), Carson City coins were produced from 1870 through 1885 and again from 1889 until 1893. Today the mint building serves as the Nevada State Museum. Carson City coins were produced in silver and gold.

Among the rarities produced at this mint are the 1873-CC dime without arrows (which is unique), the 1873-CC quarter without arrows (only three or four are known), the 1876-CC twenty-cent piece, and the 1870-CC $20.

• **Denver Mint (1906 to date):** The Denver Mint opened in 1906 and has continued in operation until the present day. The distinguishing mintmark D characterizes the coinage, which has been accomplished in all metals. A modern facility, the Denver Mint produces coins in large quantities and is second only to the Philadelphia Mint in terms of production capabilities today.

While only a few landmark rarities were produced at the Denver Mint, a number of issues are scarce today, especially in higher grades. Among these are to be found such varieties as the 1914-D cent, 1916-D dime, and 1921-D half dollar. Perhaps the key Denver Mint rarity is the 1927-D $20 piece, of which only about a dozen are known to exist.

• **West Point Mint (1984 to date):** Beginning in 1984 a special minting facility at West Point, New York (home of the Military Academy), has been used to produce certain gold commemorative coins. The distinguishing mintmark W characterizes these coins. In the 1960s Lincoln cents without mintmarks were made there, to help ease a nationwide coin shortage.

CHAPTER EIGHT

Determinants of Value

What Determines a Coin's Value?

As an aid to making purchase decisions it is useful to be aware of factors which determine the value of a rare coin. Here are my thoughts on the subject:

• **Popularity:** The more people who desire a given coin, the more expensive it is apt to be. Pricing follows the law of supply and demand. Among United States coins such series as large cents 1793-1857, Flying Eagle and Indian cents 1856-1909, Lincoln cents from 1909 to date, Jefferson nickels 1938 to date, Mercury dimes 1916-1945, Washington quarters 1932 to date, Liberty Walking half dollars 1916-1947, Morgan silver dollars 1878-1921, Peace silver dollars 1921-1935, gold coins, and commemoratives have been high on the popularity list in recent decades. Today the single most popular series is probably Morgan dollars, with commemoratives coming in second. Preferences change, and Indian cents, avidly collected in the 1960s, are not as sought after today.

Less popular today are series such as half cents 1793-1857, two-cent pieces 1864-1873, silver three-cent pieces 1851-1873, nickel three-cent pieces 1865-1889, and trade dollars 1873-1885. Less popular does not mean less desirable, and if you show me a sharp and beautiful 1793 half cent in Extremely Fine-45 grade, I would be delighted to write a generous check for it. However, coin for coin, a rare half cent will not bring as much money as a Morgan silver dollar of comparable rarity, for more collectors desire Morgan dollars. In numismatics there are exceptions to just about every rule, and sometimes obscure coins can bring higher prices than well-publicized ones.

An 1892-S silver dollar in MS-65 grade is worth the best part of $100,000, even though several dozen examples may exist in this grade. On the other hand, a token issued by Steve's Coney Island, a chili parlor in Springfield, Ohio, in 1933, and of which just two or three are known in MS-65 grade, might not find a ready buyer at $25. The reason is obvious. Thousands of people collect Morgan silver dollars and desire a top-grade 1892-S, while no more than a handful of individuals care about tokens issued by Springfield, Ohio eateries.

A good example of a popular rarity is the 1909-S Lincoln cent with the designer's initials, V.D.B., on the reverse. In MS-65 grade a nice 1909-S V.D.B. cent is worth over $1,000, even though at least several thousand such coins exist. Everyone but everyone who has ever attempted to put together a top-grade of Lincoln cents aspires to own a choice example of this variety. In the 1950s and early 1960s this was probably *the* most popular of all U.S. coins. Today it is still popular, but much less so.

In the market the popularity of various series and areas changes from time to time. Twenty or 30 years ago Lincoln cents were the most popular series. Fifty years ago in the 1930s more collectors desired commemoratives than any other series. In the 1960s veteran dealer and *Coin World* columnist Abe Kosoff conducted a survey of which areas were in the greatest demand. The winner was the Buffalo nickel series, and Morgan silver dollars were not even in the top 10! Today Morgan dollars would probably be No. 1 at the top of the list.

Donn Pearlman, well-known broadcaster and numismatic writer, conducted a survey early in 1990 and found that silver commemoratives were the most popular issues, followed by Morgan dollars, 19th and 20th century type coins, and Buffalo nickels.[1] An informal survey of Bowers and Merena Galleries clients taken at the same time suggested that Morgan dollars and commemoratives were, in that order, the two most popular series.

As a series becomes more popular, its market activity increases and prices increase as well. As a series fades from popularity, its price and activity are apt to fade also. Popularity, then, is a prime determinant of a coin's value.

• **Grade:** Demand for a coin can vary with the grade, and a coin can be highly desired in one grade but not in another. An example of a common coin which is not in demand in low grades and which sells for a low price is a well-worn 1881-S dollar in Very Good-8 grade at $11. As MS-60 coins are bid at just the $20 level (using prices from the *Coin Dealer Newsletter*), few collectors will pay much for a worn coin when a Mint State piece costs just a few dollars more. Indeed the VG-8 specimen may be expensive at even its $11 listing. On the other hand an MS-65, or Gem Uncirculated, 1881-S dollar at $190 is an actively-traded coin.[2]

In some series, *collectors* desire coins in many different grades. Early coins such as half cents and large cents are perfectly acceptable to experienced numismatists and are desirable in Good, Very Good, and other low grades, as they are needed to complete collections. For late 19th and early 20th century issues, grades such as AU-55, MS-60, and MS-63 are often quite satisfactory.

In contrast, investors have been conditioned to desire only high level coins, so most desire pieces grading in higher Uncirculated or Proof ranges, such as MS-63, MS-64, and MS-65, or Proof-63, Proof-64, and Proof-65, with particular emphasis on MS-65, Proof-65 and higher grades. In instances in which coins are better than the 65 level, investor interest increases even further. As a result of this the prices of certain investor-type coins have been driven to high levels, making them unattractive to collectors (who are content to buy cheaper coins in lower grades).

The grade or condition of a coin is sufficiently important that I devote the next chapter to the subject. Related factors such as sharpness of strike and planchet quality are also discussed.

• **Face or metallic value:** The value of certain coins is determined by their metallic or intrinsic value, or their face value. For example, a 1904-S $20 piece contains approximately one ounce of gold and is not a rare date. If the price of gold moves up in the world market, then the price of this coin will move up as well. If the price of gold goes down, the price of this coin will drop. Coins minted by the federal government from 1793 to date are worth at least face value (the repudiated trade dollar being an exception[3]), and in some instances (such as gold and silver coins) are worth more, for the metallic or melt-down content is now worth more than face value.

• **Publicity and promotion:** The more publicity given to a certain series, the more popular it will become. If such publicity ends, the popularity may end too. Cases in point: When the Franklin Mint was promoting its limited-edition silver medals nationwide in the 1960s and 1970s a great demand was created for them. When the promotion was curtailed, the demand dropped sharply, and today many such medals are worth little more than the melt-down value. In the early 1960s the low-mintage 1950-D Jefferson nickel was promoted extensively, and the price rose to over $1,200 per roll of 40 coins. Then promotion of rolls as an investment slowed considerably, and the price dropped to below $300.

On the other hand, promotion of Morgan silver dollars seems to be continuous, with no abatement in sight. In 1990 the Professional Coin Grading Service mounted an exhibit of superb quality Morgan dollars and sent it on a nationwide tour. The National Silver Dollar Roundtable, a large group of dealers who specialize in the subject, has regular conventions. There are enough Morgan dollars around and enough dealers with a vested interest to keep advertising them, that it will probably be the case that they will continue to be popular for a long time.

• **Other determinants:** A number of other considerations can determine value. Included are the following: rare die varieties, unusual designs, beautiful artistry, an interesting story behind a coin, an interesting pedigree for a given specimen, an unusual denomination, etc.

CHAPTER NINE

Grading

The History of Grading

Until 1958, when Martin R. Brown and John W. Dunn published *A Guide to the Grading of United States Coins*, illustrated with sketches, there was no book devoted to the subject of coin grading, although ever since the late 19th century the subject had been debated to a fare-thee-well in pages of *The Numismatist*. The *Standard Catalogue of U.S. Coins*, published from the 1930s through the late 1950s, contained a relevant commentary, and a few other scattered references found their way into print. However, there was no standadization or specific system until the Brown and Dunn treatise. What one person called Extremely Fine another might call AU or Very Fine.

In 1970 *Photograde*, by James F. Ruddy, was published and became an immediate best seller, going through many later editions and printings. In 1977 the book, *Official ANA Grading Standards for U.S. Coins*, appeared, and represented the work of Kenneth E. Bressett and Abe Kosoff, drawing upon contributions from many collectors and dealers. I wrote the introduction to the volume.

Grading Systems

To buy coins advantageously, a basic knowledge of grading is important, and familiarity with the terms is essential. A small difference in grade can mean a large difference in price, and the buyer who can't tell the difference between MS-63 and MS-65 is at the mercy of those who can. At the outset knowledge of grading may seem to be an insurmountable obstacle, but like many problems, if it is approached gradually, one step at a time, it will make sense.

Grading can be adjectival or a combination of adjectives (or their abbreviations) and numbers. Years ago, adjectival grading was used throughout American numismatics. Today the numerical system takes precedence.

Adjectival Grading Systems

Various adjectival grading systems have been proposed over the years.

The adjectival grading system in widest use in the United States starts with the lowest or most worn coin, Poor, then goes in a succession of steps to Uncirculated. The terms are capitalized in order to avoid confusion. In order they are as follows:

- Poor
- Fair
- Good (abbreviated G)
- Very Good (VG)
- Fine (F)
- Very Fine (VF)
- Extremely Fine (EF)
- About Uncirculated (AU)
- Uncirculated (Unc.)
- Proof

When capitalized, Fine has a specific meaning to the numismatist. Not capitalized, fine simply means "nice." Additional adjectives such as Choice and Gem, usually capitalized, are sometimes used. Ordinary words can be used to further describe a coin and to indicate whether it has nicks, marks, toning, etc. Proof is a special method of manufacture, which will be discussed later.

There are many variations in the adjectival grading system. A coin which is better than Good but not quite Very Good may be described as G-VG, a particularly nice Very Fine specimen may be described as Choice Very Fine (or VF-EF), etc. In the Uncirculated category there are, in ascending order of desirability, such gradations as Uncirculated, Choice Uncirculated, and Gem Uncirculated.

Here are some examples of typical descriptions under the adjectival system:

1909-S V.D,B. Lincoln cent, Extremely Fine.

1874-S Liberty Seated quarter, Choice Uncirculated with iridescent toning around the rims.

1916-D Mercury dime, AU.

1817 large cent, Newcomb-16, F-VF.

1854-O $20 Very Fine with some nicks on the obverse.

1793 Chain AMERI. large cent, Sheldon-1, AU, lightly cleaned years ago and now retoned a brown color.

1912-S Liberty nickel, Gem Uncirculated with light iridescent toning.

Numerical Grading Systems

Although numerical systems for grading have been proposed several times over the years (an early plan, outlined in the pages of *The Numismatist* in the 1890s, suggested Roman numerals, such as I, II, III, IV, etc.), the system in use today is based upon that created by Dr. William H. Sheldon in 1949 for use in his book *Early American Cents.* The Sheldon scale is a combination of numbers and letters and was originally intended to be part of a formula for determining market prices.[1]

Important steps in the Sheldon numerical system, as it is used today, are these:

- Poor-1
- Fair-2
- About Good-3 (abbreviated as AG-3)
- Good-4 to 6 (G-4, G-6)
- Very Good-8 or 10 (VG-8, VG-10)
- Fine-12 or 15 (F-12, F-15)
- Very Fine-20, 25, 30, 35 (VF-20, etc.)
- Extremely Fine-40 or 45 (EF-40, EF-45)
- AU-50, 53, 55, or 58 (AU-50, etc.)
- MS-60 continuously through MS-70 (MS-60, MS-61, MS-62, etc.)
- Proofs are graded the same as Mint State coins, 60 through 70, and are as follows: Proof-60, Proof-61, etc. An impaired or rubbed Proof can be assigned a lower grade, such as Proof-50 or Proof-58.

To determine the value of a coin the numerical or technical grade must first be established. Beyond that there are other important considerations, including the sharpness of strike, the quality of the planchet, the presence or absence of adjustment marks, whether the piece has been cleaned or artificially toned, how attractive the surfaces are, the pedigree (if it has one), etc. More information about these other aspects will be given later.

Grading: A Matter of Opinion

The following paragraphs, which describe modern grading "precision" and encapsulated (slabbed) coins, are intended as a caveat. As a professional rare coin dealer I have to grade coins every day, and each day I see numerous coins graded by others. Grading has been, is presently, and probably always will be an art and a matter of opinion. To be sure, there are some elements of a science, such as the measurement of wear on a coin or the counting of nicks and scratches, but the final determination is a judgment call. A computer can also measure wear or count abrasions, and come up with a precise number such as 65.48, but there is no computer to let me or you know if one coin graded as MS-65 is a low-end piece, unattractive and unappealing, worth $500, and if another is an aesthetically satisfying coin worth $1,000.

I suggest that you take nothing for granted, but *be aware that even though numbers such as MS-61, MS-65, etc. have a scientific or mathematical ring to them, they are not precise determinants of market value.* I consider this statement to be one of the most important in this book.

Many grading services have been created during the past decade or so. These are businesses, run for a profit, which for a fee give an opinion as to the grade of a coin. Often there is a sliding fee schedule, with fast turnaround costing several times more than normal service (which in busy periods can take up to several months).

As noted, grading was, is, and probably always will be a matter of opinion. So far as I have been able to determine, grading services, computers, and wishful thinking will not change this seemingly immutable fact. As an example, I quote from a study conducted by Kevin Foley, editor of *The Centinel*, official journal of the Central States Numismatic Society. He sent 10 different coins to four different professional grading services. On not a single coin did the four services agree on the grade, and for one coin, a 1919 Standing Liberty quarter, professional opinions ranged all the way from AU-55 to MS-65.

In my office is a Morgan silver dollar which was sent to the same grading service on three different occasions and each time was returned with a different grade.

In one of our recent auction sales a $10 gold piece was offered. The purchaser later sent it to a grading service, and it was returned with the notation: "Damaged, cannot be certified." Neither the purchaser nor I could see any traces of damage, so the coin was re-sent to the same service. Apparently someone else at the service saw it the second time around, for it came back certified, in a slab, with no mention of any damage, and at a grade 10 points higher than it was listed in our auction catalogue!

Norman Stack, the well-known dealer, showed me a Liberty Head $20 piece which he sent four times to grading services and had it returned in slabs marked with grades of MS-61, MS-62, MS-63, and MS-64. Harvey Stack, Norman's cousin and a partner with him in the operation of Stack's, tells of sending a gold dollar to a grading service, having it certified as AU-50, then sending it back to the same service, after which resubmission it "improved" to MS-60. What was a worn coin the first time around now was Uncirculated!

In *Penny-Wise*, journal of the Early American Coppers Club, editor Harry E. Salyards, M.D., had the following to say:

"There's been a lot of brave talk lately about how the slabbing of coins has cured the perennial grading problem. It hasn't. Nor will it, no matter how good the intentions of its promoters, as long as it is used as a kind of fishing expedition for the highest conceivable grade. And that will remain the case as long as there is human greed. There is simply too much money to be made on the 'spread' between MS-64 and MS-65, for example, to not see the marginal gem submitted again and again in search of the elusive '65.' And contrary to assertions that the market for collector material remains insulated from such 'product marketing,' there are in fact a growing number of overgraded coins in slabs."

Dr. Salyards went on to give many specific instances in which half cents and large cents graded by "one Early American Coppers Club dealer, whose grading is widely known to be impeccable," had been slabbed later and were now certified in significantly higher grades.

The same writer also related the situation of About Uncirculated later-date cents worth $200 being slabbed as MS-62 and priced at the $1,200 level. Another cent, described in an auction years earlier as MS-63, "undoubtedly artificially colored," was recently sold in another auction as a *Proof* "struck on a poor planchet" for $1,760. The coin then went through a succession of *four* slabs in six months, finally emerging as an MS-63, with no mention of artificial toning, and priced at $7,500.

In correspondence with the author, Dr. Salyards commented:[2] "There was a time, almost certainly, when a slabbed MS-65 was a more strictly graded coin than an MS-65 sold by the average dealer, but it is precisely the use of the slabbing process to 'fish' for a higher grade than the coin would support on its own merits that guarantees that a greater and greater proportion of coins which remain in slabs will be overgraded. There's scant assurance in that for anyone."

Writing in *Numismatic News*,[3] F. Michael Fazzari, whose credentials in the field of coin evaluation include work with the American Numismatic Association and the International Numismatic Society and the presentation of numerous grading seminars, gave details of a conversation he had with a coin dealer friend who specialized in slabs and, apparently, did not care whether the coins in the slabs were graded correctly or incorrectly, or what they looked like. Mr. Fazzari, a purist of the traditional school, commented on a coin which was a cleaned MS-64 but which looked like an MS-66. Coins such as this should be studied closely, he suggested. "This is the reason I still examine slabs very carefully. I have seen polished AU gold coins in MS-67 slabs and have had to bite my tongue to keep from howling."

Michael Fazzari's friend replied that "no one cares" whether a coin in a slab is graded correctly, and that Fazzari "should stop being a crusader." Fazzari continued: "He knew that I always wanted 'natural, full Mint State coins, but today the plastic slab is more important than the coin inside."

Fazzari gave an example of this indifference: "My friend said that he bought an MS-63 $5 Indian gold piece because [it was cheap]. As I raised the Indian MS-63 slab from the box I saw a cloudy bluish haze on the high spots and on some parts of the field. The coin was chemically altered to hide the rubbing and some bagmarks. I couldn't believe that he had bought it. I told him what I thought about his purchase, but he just repeated that the bought the coin for the grade....

"He told me not to even look at the next slab. It was the ugliest Maryland commemorative half dollar I had ever seen. It was graded MS-64. I was begining to understand. He had bought the coin cheap.... I'll never play this game, I told him."

Apparently most other experienced collectors, dealers, and those who have been in numismatics for more than just a few years don't want to "play this game" either, as indicated by a survey conducted by *Numismatic News*.[4] Alan Herbert analyzed the findings and reported: "Feelings about certified coins run pretty high. As a group, the collectors who started before they were 18 and who have been in the hobby more than 20 years, including a significant number of dealers, don't own a single slabbed coin and have no intention of buying one. A small percentage of them 'might' buy slabbed coins at some future date."

Sol Taylor's Commentary

In a recent issue of *Coin World*,[5] this commentary was printed from Sol Taylor, a numismatist who has been in the field for many years and who is currently president of the Society of Lincoln Cent Collectors:

"As a Lincoln cent specialist, I tend to disagree with more and more slabbed Lincoln cents. At the recent Long Beach show I examined many dozen slabbed Lincoln cents and would not buy most of them at the certified grade. One 1927 slabbed cent graded MS-66 had average color, a scuff mark across the field, and was average die state. To serious collectors it would marginally make MS-64. I have a 1910 MS-65 with fingerprints, spots, and which is a late die state, meaning some of the wheat lines are not struck, Mint red with light toning. No one would pay MS-65 money for this—except an unknowing buyer paying 'sight-unseen' prices. When it comes to resale, the buyer has to see and evaluate the coin—regardless of the certificate, slab, hologram, or paperwork."

Ed Lee, of Lee Certified Coins, Ltd., who is known for buying and selling coins of quality, advertised: "We do not buy coins sight-unseen."[6]

A West Coast coin dealer who is well known for handling rarities recently told me: "Buying sight-unseen is for the birds. Selling coins sight-unseen is just a way of unloading undesirable coins on investors." Actually, the sentence should end as: *unsuspecting* investors.

The following words by Russell Kruzell appeared on the editorial page of *Coin World:*[7]

"I had an opportunity to observe graders at a major grading service. While there, one grader said out loud to another grader: 'I have here a coin that one grader called AU, another called MS-60, another grader called MS-64, and I'm going MS-61 on the coin.'"

Lawrence N. Rogak contributed the following thoughts as part of an article published in *Coin World:*[8]

"Before long, it will become apparent to everyone that grading services merely provide a false sense of security to coin buyers. The grade on a slab is nothing more than the opinion of three or four individuals on a particular day at a particular time. People with common sense realize (or will realize soon) that to pay multi-thousands of dollars in premium for a one-point difference in grade is sheer folly because that grade is not only subject to the opinion of potential buyers, but is subject to inevitable changes in grading standards. It is even subject to regrading at a lower grade under present standards, depending on the mood of the graders at the moment they look at the coin!"

Of course not everyone agrees with my contention that grading is not precise and that a numerical grade is *only one* of *several* determinants of market value. Many feel that trading sight-unseen is the key to achieving a truly active stock-exchange-like coin market, and they don't want to listen to anyone who doesn't agree. However, as of this writing, I have never met even one *collector* who has told me that he will buy a coin sight-unseen and, without question or complaint, will keep it if he doesn't like it. I and numerous other professionals believe that collectors are the foundation of the hobby, and how they feel is of paramount importance to the health and well-being of numismatics.

Grading Services

The first certification company was the Professional Coin Grading Service, launched in 1986 by David Hall, one of the most brilliant thinkers in numismatics, who had been prominent as a rare coin dealer for many years earlier.[9] His basic premise was that a coin, if encased in a sealed transparent holder and marked with a grade that represented the combined opinion of several experts, would be more likely to actually be in that grade than a coin graded by just one person, and that once encapsulated, the grade of the coin would remain fixed in time. For the investor, a sealed slab offered a security not possible with coins stored loosely in envelopes or ordinary plastic holders, as the latter could be easily switched. PCGS was a success from the very start, and within two years it announced that over one million coins had been certified. By 1990 the enterprise employed about 80 people.

Today, grading services include these, among others: Professional Coin Grading Service (PCGS), Numismatic Guaranty Corporation (NGC), ANACS, Hallmark Grading Service, International Numismatic Service (INS), Photo-Certified Coin Institute, and Numismatic Certification Institute (NCI).[10] Staffing certain of these organizations are some of the most experienced, most qualified coin graders in numismatics. These certification services sonically seal coins in plastic encasements called slabs. The slabs have a market all their own. Bid and ask prices for certain slabbed coins are quoted continuously on electronic exchanges and are printed weekly in the *Certified Coin Dealer Newsletter*.

Most slabbed coins give just the numerical or technical grade of a coin and nothing else. This can be frustrating. Recently in one of our auction catalogues Michael Hodder expressed disappointment that he could not determine the variety of a 1794 half cent in question, for the particular variety is known with small as well as large edge lettering, and housed in a slab, with the edge not visible, he could not tell what it was. In another instance he was not able to determine whether a slabbed 1858 Canadian Proof five-cent piece had a plain edge or a reeded edge, although one variety is much rarer than the other! In still another instance, an extremely rare "gold coin" was removed from a slab and found to be a gold-plated copper pattern worth about 20% as much as if it had been struck in gold.

Not mentioned on slabs are such considerations as sharpness of strike, quality of lustre, attractiveness of brilliance or toning, planchet surface, pedigree, or overall aesthetic appeal, even though these factors can also be extremely important in determining a coin's value.[11]

Let me cite some examples: A buyer for our firm was offered two 1889-

CC Morgan dollars, each in a slab marked with the same numerical grade. One was a dingy yellow-gray color with dull surfaces and the other was brilliant with a hint of light toning. The ugly coin was priced at $10,000 and the attractive one at $14,500. We bought the $14,500 one and quickly resold it for a profit. Even if the $10,000 one had been priced at $6,000 we would have kept our checkbook in our pocket.

In another instance, a numismatist on our staff wanted to buy an *attractive* Proof 1856 Flying Eagle cent in any grade from Proof-63 to Proof-65. After looking at eight pieces he still could not find one which had any claims to being aesthetically appealing. Finally, the ninth coin, a Proof-63 coin, fit the bill— and was nicer than the several Proof-64 and Proof-65 coins examined earlier.

Generic Coins

I liken the "generic coin" situation to that of real estate. To assume that all MS-65 coins are worth the same amount of money, no matter if they differ in aesthetic appeal and other characteristics, is wishful thinking. Imagine, by way of analogy, a developer offering building lots of one acre in size, each priced at $50,000, all located in the same city. To the uninformed, the lots are all the same: one acre in size, priced at $50,000, and located in the same area. Similarly, the uninformed coin buyer might think that a given silver dollar listed as MS-65 with a bid price of $50,000 is just the same as another MS-65 silver dollar of the same variety with the same bid.

However, the knowledgeable buyer decides to examine the building lots in person. He then discovers that some lots are located next to a garbage dump, that others are swampy, that others are hilly and offer a nice view, and still others have frontage on a beautiful lake. Obviously, as all lots are priced at $50,000, he would snap up a few lots on the lake, or lots with a panoramic view, and would ignore the lots next to the garbage heap. This makes sense; so much so, in fact, that it almost seems silly to write about it.

It's a funny and perplexing situation that the same common sense has not extended to coin investors. They seem to care not whether a coin is beautiful or ugly; all they care about is the technical grade marked on the slab. To investors one MS-65 $50,000 silver dollar is just the same as another. Someday a lot of coin buyers will wake up to the fact that they own "garbage coins" rather than "lakeside coins."

It is probably contrary to good business sense to write about this, for, obviously, if buyers will gobble up all sorts of coins—good, bad, or indifferent— as long as they have a technical grade of MS-65 (or whatever), why not just sell them what they want? After all, it is a lot easier for a dealer to buy generic coins on the electronic circuits sight-unseen than it is to examine a whole pile of slabs and reject most of them for aesthetic considerations. Looking through lots of slabs is tiring, hard work.

The answer takes care of itself: The investors who are concerned with technical grade only, and who want only "good buys," will end up with low-end, ugly coins. They will not get beautiful coins with a high degree of aesthetic appeal, for those coins often cost more and are not "good buys." The *Certified Coin Dealer Newsletter* recently[12] stated in a front-page article that the prices listed in that sheet were for sight-unseen (generic) coins, and that prices for sight-seen (aesthetically appealing) coins were *substantially higher*. Those wanting hand-selected specimens have to pay more for truly beautiful pieces. Of course, when time comes to sell, these fussy buyers will get top prices.

Coin Grades Vary

I do not wish to convey the wrong impression, for I believe that on balance the grading services have done a great deal of good, particularly in the field of coin investment. While Kevin Foley found that the same 1919 quarter dollar could be expertly graded AU-55 and also expertly graded MS-65, such wide variations are the exception, not the rule. If you were to take a coin in a PCGS, NGC, ANACS, or Hallmark slab, mask the printed grade on the slab, and pass it around knowledgeable numismatists at a convention, the chances are excellent that if the coin has a brilliant or lightly toned surface (thus enabling it to be examined closely), opinions as to the *numerical or technical grade* would be within a narrow range. Opinions as to the aesthetic appeal would probably be in a much wider range, especially among coins dated prior to the 20th century.

I conducted a test of this nature, and showed several expert dealers a nicely struck San Francisco Mint silver dollar slabbed as MS-65, but with a sticker placed over the grade. The coin generated the following opinions: MS-64, MS-64, MS-65, MS-65, MS-65, MS-66.

Another silver dollar, this one a Carson City issue, was slabbed as MS-65 and earned these opinions: MS-64, MS-65, MS-65, MS-65, MS-65, and MS-65. Here was a coin which nearly everyone could agree on!

An Indian $10 piece slabbed as MS-63 drew these grades when offered: AU-58, MS-60, MS-62, MS-62, MS-63. Obviously, this was a "low end" coin.

An 1848 CAL. $2.50 piece slabbed as MS-62 drew these grading opinions: EF-45, AU-50, AU-50, AU-50, AU-50, and AU-55. This coin would seem to have been overgraded in the slab.

For deeply toned coins, the variations can be extreme. A somewhat stained and deeply toned 1936 Long Island commemorative half dollar slabbed as MS-66 drew these comments: MS-60, MS-63, MS-63, MS-63, and MS-64. One observer commented: "I wouldn't buy this coin for *any* price."

While this "precision" will not satisfy the purist, it is a lot better than the situation observed in the Federal Trade Commission's prosecution of the Coin Galleries of America case, in which certain coins, not slabbed, were sold as MS-65, but which expert witnesses, including the present writer, found were no better than EF-40 or 45.

Recall the earlier-quoted testimony from Barry J. Cutler, head of the Bureau of Consumer Protection, the Federal Trade Commission:

"One expert for the FTC testified that knowledgeable dealers could routinely distinguish between a MS-62+ gold coin and a straight MS-63, even where the wholesale value for a particular coin might jump from $700 to $2,100 for that slight jump in grade. Others testified that a two-grade difference among experts would be very unusual. But when the FTC's experts were asked, without knowing about each other's testimony, to grade a common date Saint-Gaudens $20 gold piece, the opinions expressed in court ranged from AU-58 (with a wholesale value of about $400) to MS-64 (with a wholesale value of $1750)."

This unbiased test (which was conducted by Barry J. Cutler when he was a defense attorney prior to joining the Federal Trade Commission) agrees exactly with my own belief: grading is an art more than a science, and expert opinions can and do differ, often widely.

If you want to conduct a test on your own, borrow a dozen slabbed coins in the following numerical categories, mask the grade, and ask several experts what the grades are: Buffalo nickel MS-63; deeply toned commemorative half dollar MS-64; *any* coin in MS-67 grade; Standing Liberty quarter MS-63, MS-64, or MS-65; Indian $2.50 MS-63 or MS-64; and Indian $5 MS-63 or MS-64. If you can find anyone who will agree in all instances with the grades marked on the slabs, then you will have done something which I believe no one has ever done before. Write to me about it, for I would like to congratulate you!

Note: I do not intend to be facetious here; but like the old story of the emperor without his clothes, in today's market few people care to tell it like it is, at least on the record in print. Based upon pressure being applied by Federal Trade Commission case decisions and settlements, I believe that more sellers will indeed in the future tell it like it is.

Assurance for the Investor

For the *investor* interested in buying quantities of Uncirculated Morgan dollars, or Saint-Gaudens $20 pieces, or other popular series, slabs offer the assurance that many if not most other buyers and sellers will agree at least approximately with the numerical or technical grade, and that slabbed coins are readily salable at a generic or sight-unseen price. In a market in which investors dominate the market for Uncirculated and Proof coins in higher grade levels, slabs would seem to be a blessing for the uninformed buyer; not the ultimate answer, and not the be all and end all, but an extremely valuable service nevertheless. In general, low-end and unattractive slabbed coins tend to be sold to investors and unknowing buyers, who are more interested in "good buys" than in quality, as I noted earlier. Many investors don't even know about quality, for they have been conditioned to believe that one coin graded MS-65 is just as good as any other coin graded MS-65.

Sight-Seen Coins Worth More

To illustrate the imprecise nature of the sight-unseen market I quote from cover stories in recent issues of the *Certified Coin Dealer Newsletter*. These commentaries provide a nice lead-in and understanding for subjects I will discuss in later paragraphs:

"The greatest asset belonging to the sight-unseen marketplace is instant liquidity. Of course, this could only be accomplished by the acceptance of third party grading. And now that the main grading services (PCGS, NGC, and ANACS) are firmly entrenched throughout the industry (other, newer services are trying to get a foothold: PCI and Hallmark), it is clear that possibly just one ingredient is still missing. The one missing ingredient is consistency. There is a lack of consistent bidding which causes the volatility that is seen almost on a weekly basis. While instant liquidity is most encouraging to the ultimate buyers of certified coins, it is dramatically bewildering to those very same buyers when they see the high bids of instant liquidity disappear overnight (or sooner).... One week a bid may be $1,000 and the following week only $700.... If something is not done to help alleviate the dramatic swings, the coin business will lose more potential customers to other methods of investments or collectibles."[13]

"Most coins of this quality [MS-66 and MS-67 grades are being discussed] usually command a strong price *over* any sight-unseen bid, and most buyers of these rare specimens would rather view the coin before putting their money on the table."[14]

"The market is steady to rising; but if you insist upon selling your coins today to the highest visible sight-unseen bidder, then yes, unfortunately, the price has really dropped that much. And, please remember that the purpose of the *Certified Coin Dealer Newsletter* is to report the highest sight-unseen bids; *sight-seen sales really do command a substantial premium.*"[15]

"Certified coin bids were generally firm to higher during the [Long Beach] show, but, of course, transactions on *rare* coins continued well above bid levels as sight-seen trading dominated dealer activity."[16]

"For dealers who don't participate on the electronic exchanges, there are substantial questions regarding the level of influence of sight-unseen electronic bids on the traditional sight-seen trading of the bourse floor. Most buyers, whether dealers, collectors, or [knowledgeable][17] investors, prefer to purchase their material sight-seen—that is certainly one of the main attractions of conventions. To accommodate the advantages of both methods of buying, a dual pricing structure often has dealers publishing one bid for a coin sight-unseen (usually at a level that would insure their happiness even if the coin was the worst possible example of that grade) and a higher bid level for sight-seen purchases (where personal examination could assuage all uncertainty)."[18]

"Dealers who have a strong client base seem to be having much better success in the current market over those who are committed to strictly wholesale or a primary dealer base. Those dealers with clients who understand the fundamentals of market cycles probably have customers beating down their doors so they can buy coins at these levels. In fact, this last point was brought to our attention by numerous dealers at the Long Beach show. The stronger your client base, the less you have to rely on the sight-unseen marketplace. The more educated the customer, the longer he will remain a valued customer."[19]

In summary, the *Certified Coin Dealer Newsletter,* one of America's most respected numismatic authorities, has stated the following:

• Most knowledgeable buyers prefer to see coins before buying them.

• Those buying sight-unseen run the risk of getting "the worst possible example" of a particular grade.

• The best client is an educated client.

James L. Halperin Writes

In the following introduction to his book, *How to Grade U.S. Coins,* James L. Halperin discusses varying standards of grading:[20]

"The grading standards described in this book are not the only ones in use today. They are not necessarily the 'correct' standards. I don't mean to assign any particular value to coins graded by these standards. There is presently a great deal of controversy surrounding the 'true' definition of Mint State-65 and Proof-65 as well as other Mint State coin grades.

"The standards outlined in this book are the approximate ones currently (as of June 1990) employed by the Professional Coin Grading Service (PCGS) and the Numismatic Guaranty Corporation (NGC).[21] They represent what I believe are the most accepted standards on today's market. They should not be confused with the more technical standards currently employed by ANACS or the more liberal standard currently employed by the Numismatic Certification Institute (NCI).

"In the words of noted numismatist and former American Numismatic Association president, Q. David Bowers, 'The interpretation of published grading standards is a moving target. The ANA Grading Service itself has changed its interpretations for many coins over the years.' Thus, grading standards are constantly changing as the nature of the coin market changes.

"Grading is fundamentally subjective, and the methods used to set a grade still often vary from dealer to dealer and from grading service to grading service. And the grading services themselves will sometimes grade a coin differently when it is submitted more than once. However, the methods outlined in this book are the product of a great deal of research. I have discussed even the most trivial components of grading with many dealers, particularly those recognized as the most competent wholesale coin traders. Great effort has been made to reach as objective a consensus as possible. Even so, some will certainly disagree with these conclusions. One of the goals of this book is to help improve consistency within the numismatic industry. However, total agreement throughout this industry will never come about because human subjectivity will always be a factor. Only the market itself can be the final arbiter of what ultimately determines the 'true' grade of a coin (if there is such a thing as the 'true' grade)."

In the same book, James L. Halperin observed that (even though certified coins exist) people who don't learn on their own about grading are apt to be at a disadvantage:[22]

"The next obvious question is: What if I don't have time to learn coin grading? The answer is that if you don't learn how to grade, then you will lose a certain edge in your coin purchasing efforts. You might still find coins to be a very profitable investment, just as a very knowledgeable investor can still lose money due to bad timing or bad luck. However, the more time you are willing to devote to your education, the more successful you are likely to be. No matter how competent and honest your coin dealer is, he is not going to be able to help you maximize value for your money the way you could yourself if you knew how to grade coins.[23]

"Grading is at least partially subjective. Every dealer has purchased and sold both undergraded and overgraded coins. Even if you buy only certified coins, you are better off knowing how to grade coins. How else can you tell whether or not a coin is really PQ (Premium Quality)[24] for the grade? Let's face facts. It is human nature for a dealer to give his own coin the 'benefit of the doubt.' Sure, you could get lucky and buy a coin that's been slightly undergraded. But that's going to happen less often than the other way around. The best coins are the ones that are most likely to sell before you ever have a chance to buy them.

"Don't be discouraged if you don't think you can ever become an expert. Nobody alive knows everything there is to know about coin grading (or gold, or practically anything else). Just remember: In the long run, the more you know the better you are likely to do financially with coins."

The same writer discussed the importance of being a *collector:*[25]

"One last bit of wisdom: As long as you're going to this much trouble, please don't forget to enjoy coins. Not only will enjoyment make the learning easier, but it also should become an end in itself. People collect because coins are interesting and fun!

"The best way to understand the collector mentality is to become a collector yourself. Even if you don't make a profit, at least you will have received something for your trouble. It's a funny thing though. As you learn more about coins, and start to buy the coins that appeal most to you, your judgments will start to coincide with the future of the coin market. *Collectors often seem to be one step ahead of the investor. They usually have a better instinct for value.*

"Collectors are the underlying basis of the coin market, a fact of which investors so often lose sight. To improve their chances of success, investors should try to predict which coins will be the most sought after by *collectors* ten or twenty years from now. Therefore, it really isn't so surprising that the most committed, passionate collectors often realize a better financial return when they sell their coins than many serious investors do."

The same writer discussed resubmitting coins to certification services:[26]

"Only a very tiny percentage of all coins in PCGS, NGC or other similar holders are likely to be graded higher by those services if broken out and resubmitted. A larger (though still relatively small) percentage, if broken out and resubmitted, are likely to be graded lower. This is because most of the coins on the market which the experts consider undergraded have already been resubmitted. Obviously, the more valuable a coin is, the more likely it is to have been resubmitted the optimal number of times to receive its ultimate grade.

"To illustrate, let's imagine a coin which three graders out of ten would consider MS-65. The other seven would grade it MS-64. Based on probability statistics there is approximately a one in five chance that a random selection of 3 graders from this mix will result in at least 2 of the 3 graders grading the coin MS-65, thus insuring an MS-65 rating by PCGS or NGC. If the coin is worth $50 in MS-64 and $150 in MS-65, most dealers would just sell it in the MS-64 holder—possibly as a PQ. But, if the coin is worth $300 in MS-64 and $1,000 in MS-65, chances are the dealer will resubmit it until the grading service *finally* grades it MS-65.

"Needless to say, given the cost in time and fees of resubmissions, a dealer's ability to predict how other experts would grade a particular coin is very important to the bust-out game. Since the vast majority of coins would grade the same and some coins would grade lower, only a few dealers can consistently make this a profitable venture. As an example, consider for a moment the above example. If one more person out of the 10 had graded the coin MS-64, this would have changed the odds to about one in eighteen, rendering most bust-out scenarios unprofitable.

"Note: The consumer is probably not harmed by this, because the market takes this bust-out activity into account. Obviously, if a coin could never be broken out of a holder once sealed, MS-65s would be considerably rarer than they are now. The prices bid on the ANE [American Numismatic Exchange] system[27] would be much higher as a result. Therefore, if a buyer purchases a coin based on the prices reported today on ANE (or any other sight-unseen bidding system), suffice it to say that he (or she) is only paying for a 'low-end' coin that has most likely achieved its ultimate grade."

There you have it. One of America's leading rare coin dealers has stated the following:

• "Grading is fundamentally subjective, and the methods used to set a grade still often vary from dealer to dealer and from grading service to grading service. And the grading services themselves will sometimes grade a coin differently when it is submitted more than once."

• "Passionate *collectors* often realize a better financial return when they sell their coins than many serious investors do."

• Those who buy coins at sight-unseen bid prices are buying low-end coins.

Dr. Richard Hayes on Third-Party Grading

The following commentary by Richard A. Hayes, Ph.D. appeared in *Coin World*[28] and gives one long-time collector's view of grading and grading services:

"In 1940 I began collecting coins after finding a brilliant About Uncirculated 1916 quarter in the cash register of my parents' diner in Lewiston, Maine. My interest in coins was encouraged by teachers and other adults who not only helped me to assemble complete sets of nickels and Lincoln cents but also fostered my development by taking me to coin clubs and shows.

"I always will remember viewing the very rare 1793 Strawberry Leaf, Wreath cent exhibited at a local show, because it sparked my interest in the study of numismatics. Thereafter, some fine numismatists, such as Toivo Johnson, shared their knowledge with me while others—William H. Sheldon, Al C. Overton, Roger S. Cohen, Jr. and Walter Breen—shared information via their excellent publications.

"Those were the salad days of a budding student of numismatics—in sharp contrast to my recent visit to a major coin show in Scottsdale, Ariz., where I sought a Mint State 1796 quarter and where I was ignored completely by every coin dealer (except one who specialized in foreign coins).

"In the early 1960s I became a part-time coin dealer and investor. Now, I have retired to devote my time to the management of my diverse investment portfolio which includes some rare coins. As an investor and student of numismatics, I now write my first letter to a coin publication—to share my views on the issue of third-party grading.

"The most generous thing that can be said about third-party grading is that it is a mixed blessing. On the one hand, it offers the advantage of authentication and the important advantage of encapsulation in inert 'slabs,' excellent for storage and preservation. Another advantage, cited primarily by coin dealers, is that slabs can be sold on a 'sight-unseen' basis but this is not a real advantage because coin dealer bid prices on sight-unseen coins are very low—often lower than 'sight-seen' bids on uncertified coins.

"Another advantage, also cited primarily by coin dealers, is the publication of 'population reports' by the Professional Coin Grading Service and Numismatic Guaranty Corporation of America, but these reports leave much to be desired because they overstate some coin populations to the extent that many valuable coins have been resubmitted countless times in the hope (sometimes successful) of obtaining a higher grade. On the other hand some coin populations are understated—not only because people like me have hundreds of scarce and rare coins which rest unslabbed in a safe deposit box, but also because it doesn't make much sense to pay $35 to slab coins in the $50-$100 price range.

"Third-party grading may be advantageous to people having little or no interest in or knowledge of coin grading; however, it is not an advantage to people like me who have learned how to grade coins over a period of years. Moreover, the hype and focus of coin dealers on slabbed coins will tend to make it more difficult for me to sell my unslabbed coins one of these days.

"There are distinct disadvantages to third-party grading by some of the grading companies. Here are a few of them:

"An oligopoly situation wherein a handful of grading companies require that coins be submitted through designated coin dealers—rather than being open for submission by the general public. Here's how it works: You buy an unslabbed coin from a dealer who makes a healthy profit on your purchase. Then, he will submit this coin to a grading company so that he can later receive a kick-back (or royalty) of a portion of the high fee you paid to have the coin graded.

"High fees for grading, ranging up to $35 or more for a few minutes of service. Such exorbitant fees are unjustified by the small amount of time spent on grading, and they result in enormous profit margins for the grading company cliques —including the generous kickbacks to the chosen circle of coin dealers who possess exclusive rights to submit coins. In view of the fact that a healthy sales revenue of $200,000 monthly would be generated by grading 20,000 coins at a price of $10 per coin, it is mind-blowing to imagine the outrageous profits now being generated by fees of $35 or more per coin.

"Grading inconsistencies among and within some of the grading companies appear to be commonplace. The result: undergraded coins are often broken out of their slabs and either sold as 'raw' coins at the correct grade or else resubmitted in order to obtain a higher grade. On the other hand, overgraded coins are being unloaded on unsuspecting investors who are not numismatists or on novice collectors.

"Turnaround time for grading is not guaranteed by the major third-party grading companies unless an even more exorbitant fee is paid. I understand that it can take up to three months for a coin to be graded and returned. Considering the long turnaround time and the minuscule amount of time spent in the grading process, one could conclude that either the grading services are very understaffed or that the inordinate delay is merely a ploy to persuade customers to spend up to $59 to obtain two-week grading.

"Cleanliness leaves something to be desired. There have been reports of

Mint State coins coming back not only with a grade, but also with fingerprints. Personally I have seen valuable coins encapsulated with what appeared to be dandruff flakes in the slabs.

"In summary, there are advantages to third-party grading, but they are outweighed by disadvantages. Having already reaped unconscionable profits during recent years, the time has come for one of the major grading companies to step forward and begin to treat us fairly. Sooner or later, I predict that the following will happen: direct submissions by the general public rather than the dealer clique; a reasonable fee for grading ($10 or less); a guaranteed turnaround time of two weeks, without the necessity of paying an extra ransom fee for prompt return; and cleanliness by graders.

"Moreover, the time has come for one of the major grading companies to recognize the debt owed to the numismatic hobby—and to allocate a portion of its fat profit to the betterment of the hobby, as well as to the encouragement of young numismatists (without whom this hobby may disappear one day). Also, this grading service which sooner or later will step out in front of the rest of the pack hopefully will foster research and the development of new numismatic giants who might one day fill the shoes of such numismatists as Walter Breen and the late Roger Cohen.

"Which one of the grading services will step forward and leave the others behind?"

The Importance of Knowledge

Peter A. Barone, a frequent contributor to numismatic periodicals, expressed his views on slabbed coins and the importance of gaining knowledge about coin grading, in a recent letter:[29]

"I recently received my copy of the *Rare Coin Review* and must congratulate you on an excellent magazine. It has provided me with additional knowledge and hours of enjoyment. I not only liked looking at, and reading about, the coins, I also enjoyed the many articles.

"One article in particular stuck out to me. It was by Mr. Dan Vandervort. I expressed similar sentiments in an article that appeared in the December 13, 1989 issue of *Coin World* under the 'Striking the Issues' column. Back then I wrote: 'However, slabbing has a natural product life. Items that are undergraded or high-end, are usually broken out and resubmitted or sold raw. The end result of this product is that only overgraded or low-end coins will remain in holders. Obviously, prices will reflect this change. (This is a subtle way of saying grading standards have changed.)'

"A point I did not mention at that time is that this process runs contrary to today's popular investment theory of holding coins for a long period of time (five years or more). The smart investor will sell now while an MS-65 coin may still bring an MS-65 price. Since we are fast approaching the saturation point with slabs, this process is quickly reaching the maturity stage.

"It should be noted that some slabbed coins are accurately graded or even undergraded; however, I am certain that once the collecting public 'agrees' that slabbed coins are 'optimistically' graded, dealers will use this opportunity to purchase these items at lower prices. It is identical to the old ANACS certified coins. While many of these ANACS coins were overgraded, others were not. The smart or knowledgeable collectors should use this time to obtain nice items for their collections at reasonable prices.

"I guess my point with all this is, to learn to grade coins yourself. Make use of the many books, reference materials and grading guides available today. As with most things in life, there is no substitute for knowledge."

The following letter from the same writer, Peter Barone, to *Coin World* gives additonal opinions concerning certified coins:[30]

"I would like to ask the third-party grading firms one simple question: 'What good is a slab anyway?' Now before everyone writes, I know all the stock answers. Two or more qualified, independent graders assign a grade and an additional person verifies this grade. I also know that a slabbed coin supposedly has a ready market with sight-unseen bids posted on the ANE [American Numismatic Exchange] and all that, but why then do other dealers not believe you? And why should I?

"Why is it that when a firm's 'buy prices' for certified coins are listed in *Coin World*, they are always on a sight-seen basis? (Has anyone else noticed this?) If a fellow dealer, someone who theoretically has the same amount of knowledge and expertise as you, does not trust your grading enough to buy it sight unseen, then why should I?

"Why do dealers who specialize in certified coins advertise that they only buy sight-seen coins? They did that before certified coins existed, so what has changed? What are they telling me when they say they buy and sell sight-seen only? Are they telling me that overgraded coins exist?

"Of course they are, so if I never learn to grade coins properly, how does buying a slab help me? If I cannot grade the coin out of a slab, what makes me able to grade it in one?

"Now you'll tell me that these agencies have no financial interest in the coin. That's not entirely true either. Some agencies encourage their graders to 'keep a sharp eye' by dealing in coins, which seems to make sense. Another firm just decided that not allowing graders to deal in coins was a good idea after years of doing something else. Isn't that like closing the barn door after the cows have left?

"You may not have a financial interest in a particular coin, but you do have one in the business. By not allowing graders to deal in coins are you not in fact saying to them, you can make more money grading coins than by dealing in them? Why else would an experienced grader do it?

"Slabbing coins must be a very profitable business since everyone wants to do it. If you are an expert grader, how long does it take to grade a coin: 10 seconds? At that rate (and a $25 fee) you earn $9,000 an hour. Not bad. I bet heart surgeons don't make that much. Even George Bush makes less than $100 an hour (if he worked only a 40-hour week). Seems like a good business to get into. Even if three graders look at a coin (at 10 seconds each) you still make $3,000 an hour. That is almost as much as baseball players make. I will not even try to figure out the amount you make on 24-hour service.

"Before you pass this letter off as just another complaining collector writing to *Coin World*, think a minute. This is an honest question and deserves an honest reply. I hope you can respond positively without labeling what I wrote as 'simply untrue' or 'totally inaccurate' or other such things dealers write when they respond to letters in *Coin World*. Other readers may have the same question.

"The theory behind certified coins is great and if I felt it worked, I would collect certified coins. But money clearly talks and it's saying, 'I must see you before I buy you,' thus it appears that smart thing to do is to learn to grade myself. Now if and when I do that, what do I need you for? So in ending, 'What good is a slab anyway?' "

A Veteran Numismatist Writes

Veteran numismatist George Caswell sent the following letter to *Coin World*:[31]

"In all my 65 years of coin collecting, I have never heard of such vocabulary on coins as I have at present. Since I started in coins long before most present day dealers wore diapers, I am amazed at our present dilemma in grading and slabbing of coins.... What in the world are we coming to? I remember many officers in the last war who were 90-day wonders. The same term could apply to many so-called graders in the grading services of today. How else would you explain a coin that was graded Mint State-60 the first time,

MS-65 the second time and AU-55 the third time. In the September 2 issue of *Coin World*, Mr. [Phil] Schuyler stated a buyer he knew sent a coin 11 different times to the American Numismatic Association Certification Service and, behold, he received 11 different grades for the same coin.

"It appears that we have a whole mess of 90-day wonders in coin grading. Mr. Schuyler stated that coin grading is a business and no one is the authority, and I agree. The grading service of today only benefits the dealer, and I will argue this until the cows come home. I predict that the day soon will come when there will be wailing and gnashing of teeth when the investors go to sell their slabbed coins. Thank heaven I will not be one of them.

"Some 30 years ago a 2-by-2 plastic three-part product came out for individual coins. I predicted then that they would in time fall by the wayside, and I was right. I now predict that slabbed coins will also 'peter out' as well as our so-called grading service. Many collectors are not buying slabbed coins as an investment for the future.

"What many dealers are doing is to buy one and break it apart and resubmit it in hopes of getting a higher grade. This practice is being repeated over and over at all coin shows, and I was amazed to see so many broken slabs on the floor. What has happened to our hobby? Lest we forget, it is the collector who keeps our hobby going."

Similar thoughts were the focus of a letter from L. Ruggles submitted to *Coin World:*[32]

"Having returned from another coin show and seeing hundreds of slabs may I add some advice to my fellow numismatists: Wake up. I've seen hundreds of slabbed coins and the grading is so inconsistent that its ridiculous. I saw Morgans graded Mint State-63 that looked like they were run over by a truck and others graded MS-60 that were close to blemish free with great luster. No wonder coins are broken out of their slabs and resubmitted.... Wake up fellow collectors. Take advantage of the knowledge that's out there and grade your own coins so you don't have to pay to have a third party tell you what grade your coins are."

A proposal to help eliminate the uncertainty of the quality of slabbed coins was recently submitted to the present writer by a New England dealer:

"If someone who has handled large quantities of premium quality coins, such as you have in connection with major collections, could set up a service to review slabbed coins and issue certificates stating that coins were of premium quality, this would enable buyers to avoid low-end coins. The certificates would bear the serial numbers of the slabs, to prevent switching. You could be an omsbudsman for the rare coin industry."

This suggestion is interesting, but as beauty is often in the eye of the beholder, what if I (or someone else) considered a coin to be exceptional, and others did not?

Satisfactory Experiences

Many people, undoubtedly the majority of investors and a goodly number of collectors as well, have had thoroughly satisfactory experiences with the leading certification services. Writing in *Coin World*, Maurice Rosen, a grader for NGC and publisher of *The Rosen Numismatic Advisory*, defended the certification services against criticisms made earlier in the same publication by others. Excerpts:

"'Not a change for the better in our human housekeeping has ever taken place that wise and good men have not opposed it—have not prophesied that the world would wake up to find its throat cut.'—James Russell Lowell....

"Rather than being subject to hyperbole, the buyer has been unburdened of confusion and danger by the PCGS and by NGC. Rather than suffering losses, the high-end 'slab' buyer has been cleaning up profits while the buyers of low-end coins may have been gaining hours of enjoyment but little or no profits. Rather than buying coins before a soon-to-become more conservative grading standard, the buyer has seen a consistent standard in effect for four years, backed by hundreds of dealers and rock-solid guarantees.

"While I won't dispute the claim that variations exist within a single-point grade, and one might disagree with how PCGS or NGC grades a particular coin, please don't hold either service to a standard of perfection which doesn't exist on this earth, nor for that matter exists in any other field of endeavor which attempts to grade, rate, measure or otherwise render expert opinions as to quality.

"Who is qualified to 'grade' the movies? Some critics rave about one flick, which you might see and wonder if the critic lost his marbles. Then again, some critic might pan a movie which you loved. This morning I read about a riff between colleges and universities and those folks who write books rating them....

"The point of all this is that people are entitled to their own opinion. Yet, for those who seek professional opinion, realize that even there it is not always a perfect one, universally accepted. With respect to the grading of rare coins, the 'slabbing' experience is but four years old, but remarkably strong, remarkably accepted and remarkably functional. The market—the great judger of these things—is saying it works. One wonders how worse off many consumers would be had neither PCGS nor NGC come into existence...."

On the editorial page of *Coin World*, Andrew Woodruff contributed these positive thoughts about slabbed coins:[33]

"In response to those opposed to certified grading, I say, stop knocking the grading services. No one says you have to buy certified coins or send yours in to be graded. But face it, no matter how keen one's grading skills are, whether one collects for fun or profit, with short- or long-term perspectives, nobody enjoys being taken to the cleaners on their coins. In my youth I purchased many Brilliant Uncirculated coins that turned out to be sliders. It is not a pleasant experience to sell coins at a loss.

"When it comes to selling, certified coins are much easier to sell than those which are not. This is because dealers know what certified coins are easily resold. Although certified coins make up a small part of my collection, I would not hesitate to have graded any premium coins I wished to sell. As yet, I have only had a few of my coins certified. The results were interesting.

"I sent a Lafayette dollar to the American Numismatic Association Certification Service that I had bought as a Mint State-63. It came back as an About Uncirculated-58. Oh, well. I sent off to the Professional Coin Grading Service a Walking Liberty half dollar I purchased as an MS-65. It came back MS-63. I also sent off a 1928-D nickel I had bought as an MS-64 after being told by some dealers that it was a nice MS-63 and being offered less than half of what I paid for it. This coin came back MS-65, and perhaps so as to placate my ego over the Lafayette and the Walker, I promptly sold it for five times what I paid for it.

"Recently, a friend of mine decided to sell her 1941 Proof set. Wisely, she sent off the half dollar for certification. Eventually returned as a Proof 66, she was then able to sell all five coins for almost double the 'Gray Sheet [*Coin Dealer Newsletter*] bid for the entire set. Perhaps it's simply the idea of putting a coin in plastic that bothers some? I learned early the folly of poor coin holders, and slabs offer a safe means of preserving coins in the condition in which they were certified.

"Therefore, I truly believe the grading services are good for the hobby. Of course, if you want MS-65 silver dollars, you'll pay top dollar; but you'll know that if you must sell, you won't be offered 50% less than the normal bid price because the dealer thinks he'll have a hard time moving a common-date Morgan for $300.

"But not if it's in a slab. The difference then between buy and sell is usually quite minimal and reasonable. Moreover, slabbing is beneficial to the lower income collector as well. While much of the high end material has reached rarefied levels, there are bargains to be had in grades of MS-63 and lower."

In the same vein are the comments submitted in a letter to the editor of *Coin World* by Robert Lehmann:[34]

"I think the advent and maturation of both PCGS and NGC provides an invaluable service to all parties concerned with numismatics. When I entered this hobby back in 1968, I only wish I had enough insight to culminate an idea of this magnitude—hats off to John Albanese and David Hall.

"First of all, let's look at these services from a collector's standpoint. PCGS and NGC offer the collector unbiased third-party grading and guaranteed authenticity. When and if the collector desires to sell his coins, liquidity is assured. As far as the slab is concerned, there is no law that says a coin bought in a slab must be kept in a slab. If albums are your niche, break the coins out but with the assurance that the Mint State-61 coin you bought is really an MS-61 and not an overgraded byproduct of some unscrupulous dealer.

"Yes, I know.... We always hear about the inconsistencies of PCGS and NGC. We hear about resubmissions with two-point differences and coins submitted 15-20 times with hope of achieving a grade one point higher and eventually getting to the right grader at the right time. I don't question the validity of these isolated horror stories but they are the exception, not the rule. Come on, folks.... These are human beings performing a subjective function. Obviously there is a slight margin for error! I do believe, from a collector's standpoint, that these third-party coins present a better value with a more minimal risk than raw coins which are almost always overgraded and overpriced. Don't have slab fear. Buy the coin for what it is. If you don't like the coin, don't buy it. Rejecting a coin merely for the fact that it's encased in a hermetically sealed plastic holder is ludicrous!

"Having bought and sold hundreds of PCGS and NGC coins over the last several years, I can honestly say the consistency is better than any single dealer I've ever dealt with. The coins are usually conservatively graded and priced so that I can make a few dollars on resale. I, for one, advocate third-party grading. I only hope that the up-and-coming Hallmark Grading Service develops into as fine a service as the aforementioned two. NGC and PCGS are here to stay. Live and grow with them in the years to come."

Start Your Own Grading Service

Time out for some humor: Donn Pearlman, a governor of the American

Numismatic Association and a long-time observer of the numismatic scene, included the following tongue-in-cheek commentary in his "Pearlman's People" column in *The Numismatist*:[35]

"At last count there were nearly 59,000 rare coin grading services. Perhaps not quite *that* many, but it sure seems like it. Remember when you'd happily browse through *Coin World* or *Numismatic News* for page after page of advertisements offering delightful coins for sale? Now you're also confronted with page after page of ads from establishments offering to grade those coins.

"The names of grading companies often include reassuring words such as Guaranty, Professional, Accurate, or Loves-His-Mother. Grading fees usually range from as little as $10 up to $125 per coin. The $125 fee gets coins returned in about a day; the $10 service is roughly equal to the time it takes to get an IRS refund....

"Every now and then—not very often, I'm told—an owner actually disagrees with the grade rendered by one of the consulting services. So, the owner removes the coin from the slab by using a ballpeen hammer, pliers, jagged tooth saw, acetylene torch, jackhammer, blasting caps, and other handy tools commonly found in most home workshops. The easily removed coin then is resubmitted to the same or a different grading service for a second opinion.

"Most grading services keep track of the grades they've assigned and regularly issue 'population reports' listing the number of specific coins encountered in specific grades. However, when owners resubmit the same coins several times, it can create oh-so-slight statistical errors. For example, only about 9.1 million 1879-S Morgan dollars were struck by the mint, but according to the aggregate population reports, there now are roughly 134 million of them graded MS-64.

"Most grading services were formed by coalitions of dealers with years of numismatic experience and lots of financial backing, pooling millions of dollars in start-up funds. But now, a New York-area merchant is offering assistance for launching do-it-yourself grading businesses.... His grading service advertisement suggests that anyone can get into the business. He'll provide personalized slabs imprinted with your name and even lease a sonic welding machine—all for as little as $9,500 (batteries not included).

"So, watch your favorite hobby publications for the forthcoming announcement of my own slab service. It will begin as soon as I come up with a catchy, reassuring name. How about 'Pearlman's Coin Grading Service.' Too long? Maybe I'll just use the initials...."

CHAPTER TEN

Grades and Prices

Grade vs. Price

Of the various considerations which help to determine the value of a coin, the grade of the piece is one of the most important factors. For many in the coin field, particularly investors and buyers without knowledge, the grade of a given piece seems to be the only factor.

I quote bid prices from recent copies of the *Coin Dealer Newsletter* and the *Certified Coin Dealer Newsletter*[1] to show the vast differences in price a coin can have, depending upon its grade:

• **1896-O Morgan dollar,** raw (unslabbed), sight-seen bid prices from the *Coin Dealer Newsletter*: VG-8 $10, F-12 $11.75, VF-20 $13.00, EF-40 $18, AU-50 $75, MS-60 $500, MS-63 $3,700, MS-64 $7,000,[2] MS-65 $45,000.

1896-O Morgan dollar, PCGS sight-unseen bid prices from the *Certified Coin Dealer Newsletter*: MS-61 $735, MS-62 $1,550, MS-63 $3,350, MS-64 $5,200, MS-65 $46,000, MS-66 $57,500, MS-67 $62,500.

An 1896-O dollar can be worth $10 in VG-8 grade and $62,500 in MS-67 preservation. An MS-67 coin sells for 6,250 times as much as a VG-8. In the higher echelons, a small difference in grade can mean a lot of money. If an MS-64 PCGS-slabbed coin is worth $5,200 and an MS-65 coin is worth $46,000, you can see if someone buys a high-end MS-64 and can have it reslabbed as an MS-65, this is a better way to make money than by printing it!

• **1923-S Monroe commemorative half dollar,** raw (unslabbed), sight-seen bid prices from the *Coin Dealer Newsletter*: EF-AU (EF-45 to AU-50) $21, MS-60 $40, MS-63 $190, MS-64 $800, MS-65 $7,000.

1923-S Monroe commemorative half dollar, NGC sight-unseen bid prices from the *Certified Coin Dealer Newsletter*: MS-61 $35, MS-62 $50, MS-63 $160, MS-64 $675, MS-65 $6,000, MS-66 $11,500, MS-67 $21,500.

To vary the discussion from that given for the 1896-O silver dollar (for the same points could be made), let me suggest that as the market for high level Monroe half dollars—coins in MS-65 to MS-67 grades—lies almost exclusively with investors, the lesser grades are very attractively priced, by default. Very few experts, including those employed by grading services, can consistently grade coins with precision sufficient that a group of 100 MS-64 Monroe halves, if broken out of their holders, would all be assigned the MS-64 grade again. Many, perhaps the majority, of the coins would, but some others would be called MS-63 or MS-65.

For the astute buyer, you, an MS-64 Monroe half dollar represents a much better buy at $675 than an MS-65 at $6,000. For my money, I would rather invest in nine specimens of MS-64 coins, for a total expenditure of $6,075 than a single MS-65 for $6,000. I challenge any reader to dispute the logic of my statement. If money is absolutely no object, and you have your mind set on outdoing everyone else, then by all means buy an MS-65 for $6,000 (or an MS-66 for $11,500 or an MS-67 for $21,500). However, few readers of this book will be in this category.[3]

Typical Proof Morgan silver dollar, raw (unslabbed), sight-seen bid prices from the *Coin Dealer Newsletter*: Proof-60 $935, Proof-63 $2,300, Proof-64 $3,250, Proof-65 $7,200.

Typical Proof Morgan silver dollar, PCGS sight-unseen bid prices from the *Certified Coin Dealer Newsletter*: Proof-61 $900, Proof-62 $1,300, Proof-63 $2,350, Proof-64 $3,350, Proof-65 $7,250, Proof-66 $12,200, Proof-67 $27,000.

Let me mention a Proof Morgan dollar offered in one of our recent auction sales. The buyer, a dealer, bid it up to $14,000, then cancelled his bid, stating that sometime between the time he viewed it at the sale and the time of our delivery, it somehow had become "artificially toned." This was a ridiculous assertion, of course, and Ray Merena, who handled the situation from our end, suspected that either the dealer ran out of money before he could pay for it, or he was bidding for a customer who changed his mind. As the coin had not been paid for, and as our integrity had been questioned, we sent it to a slabbing service, and were pleased when it came back one point higher than described in our auction sale. We put it in our next following auction sale, and the second time around it brought $24,000. Of course, the person who had consigned the Proof dollar to our sale was delighted!

Quite a few astute collectors have consigned high-end slabbed coins to our auction sales, realizing that if dealers attending the sale feel that they can be broken out of the slabs and sold for more, they will bring far over current standard market prices in the auction. The same coins if offered directly to a dealer (without going through an auction) are likely to bring no more than the bid price for a sight-unseen coin, for dealers often do not want to give away their secrets.

Obviously, a tiny difference in grade can mean a tremendous difference in value. Even within a numerical category, low-end unattractive coins can be worth less than quoted figures, and high-end pieces with aesthetic appeal can be worth considerably more. However, the prices just quoted illustrate the basic concept that the higher the coin grade, the higher the price.

When I wrote the introduction to the book, *Official ANA Grading Standards for U.S. Coins*, I inserted this paragraph:

"A note concerning market values: it is important to know that grade is *only a part* of market valuation. Two silver dollars can each be in MS-65 grade but can differ widely in value. The average specimen of a certain date might be worth, for example, $800, while a weakly struck piece with an unappealing surface, but still MS-65, might be worth $400, and a sharply struck coin with beautiful toning might worth $1,000 or more. It is important not to rely on grading alone to determine the value of a coin, for the stated grade of a coin—even if determined by experienced professionals or by grading services—is only part of the story."

Even if they read grading books from cover to cover and have received lots of advice, some people will never master the techniques of grading coins. There are many professional numismatists who do not know how to grade coins. A few years ago a leading marketer of coins to the public was taken to task for selling coins which were believed to be overgraded in many instances. His defense was that he bought coins at stated grades from well-known dealers, and how was he to know that they were overgraded?

Often people try to become professionals without knowledge of grading, authenticity, or anything else. Mike Gumpel, advertising manager of *CoinAge* magazine, wrote in 1990 that he had attended a convention and had seen a dealer who apparently knew *nothing at all* about coins, didn't even have a magnifying glass, and was equipped only with a computer! This "professional" traded over 100 coins valued in excess of $50,000. Is this the blind leading the blind? One cannot help but feel sorry for this dealer's customers, for if the dealer knows nothing about such questions as authenticity, toning, cleaning, sharpness or weakness in strike, etc., he and his clients are all buying pigs in pokes.

My advice about high-grade Mint State and Proof examples of coins which are not rarities: Let investors pay today's high prices for common coins. You, as an astute collector, can get a much better value with MS-64 and Proof-64 coins or pieces in even lower grades.

Sources of Pricing Information

Today's coin buyer has more pricing information available than anyone has ever had before. Indeed, there is so much information at hand that sometimes it is difficult to understand and digest it all. There is no single source that infallibly points the way to what price to pay. In all instances it is to be remembered that coins of hand-selected quality often sell for more than the prices listed. For some pricing sources, the values listed are for the *worst* examples of the grades indicated, meaning that coins are worth at least those values, and often even more.

The Direct Sales Department of Bowers and Merena Galleries uses the following sources, among others, but these are the primary ones (listed in alphabetical order):

• **American Numismatic Exchange:** Abbreviated as ANE and familiarly known as "Annie," the American Numismatic Exchange is an electronic trading system which posts sight-unseen bid and ask prices on popularly traded certified coins. ANE quotations are particularly useful for current trading information on common-date Morgan dollars, gold coins, etc., although some rarer issues are also listed. Dealers who post sight-unseen bids and stand by them are known as market makers.

• **American Teleprocessing Corporation.** This electronic exchange, similar in concept to ANE, posts sight-unseen bid and ask prices on certain certified coins.

• **Auction prices realized:** Results of actual sales at recent auctions are particularly useful in determining the value of scarce and rare coins of selected quality (assuming that the auction catalogues in question describe the surfaces, etc. of the pieces). Krause Publications issues a yearly study of coin auction prices, which is valuable not only for price levels but for the frequency of appearance of certain coins.[4] In order to study auction prices effectively you must maintain a file of catalogues issued by various dealers and also gain knowledge of which firms have a practice of buying-in a significant percentage of the items listed.

• **Certified Coin Dealer Newsletter:** This weekly newsletter lists bid prices for PCGS, NGC and, occasionally, ANACS and NCI coins in higher grades, primarily MS-61 to MS-67 (but not all grade ranges for all series). Prices given are for the lowest-quality examples traded on a sight-unseen basis. "Client or sight-seen sales may command a substantial premium," a notice in each issue states. The front page of the CCDN contains much valuable information concerning the current state of the market.[5] Nickname: *Bluesheet.*

• **Coin Dealer Newsletter:** This weekly newsletter, first published in 1963, gives market levels for non-slabbed (raw) coins in many different series, and in grades from Good to MS-65 or Proof-65 (but not all grade ranges for all series). Listed each week are popularly traded series such as commemoratives and silver dollars.

Specialized series dating back to the late 19th century are detailed in the *Monthly Summary*, issued each month. The *Monthly Summary* contains many superb in-depth articles about the rare coin market, collector and investor psychology, etc. Nickname: *Graysheet*.

• **Coin World:** The "Trends" section is carefully researched and contains realistic pricing information on all series from 1793 to date.

Keith Zaner, editor of the "Trends" section of *Coin World*, posed these questions:[6] 1. Just what do the values listed each week in "Trends" mean? 2. What do they indicate? His answers: "For better understanding, it may be easier to state what the 'Trends' section is not. 'Trends' values are not bid or ask prices. They are not the final price or one which is inflexible. 'Trends' values do represent 'ballpark' estimates or ranges of current retail values for rare coins. A single 'Trends' value is an established point from which a dealer, collector or investor can, if he chooses, deviate from to arrive at a market transaction price.

"For example, if a 'Trends' value of $5,000 is listed for a particular coin, it is reasonable to assume that a seller (dealer, investor or collector) may request a price above, at, or below that dollar amount. The same holds true for the buyer. Price is contingent upon many variables which interact with one another. The weighted variables are pertinent to determining price.

"If the seller wants $5,500, then that is well within the ballpark. Even at $6,000, availability and demand may dictate this greater increase.

"'Trends' values are all listed at the lowest grade level within each grading category, with the exception of the Mint State and Proof listings. When the Very Fine-20 values are listed, the 'Trends' value is for a VF-20 coin. Coins which grade VF-25, VF-30, and VF-35 are worth more than the VF-20, but less than an Extremely Fine-40 coin. A VF-30 coin may or may not be worth a value which is the midpoint of EF-40 and VF-20. This is because of the many variables which affect and are integral in establishing the price of a rare coin. Perhaps most important, the market establishes 'Trends' values, not the 'Trends' editor.

"'Trends' values are listed for coins which totally and by strict market standards meet the requirements at each grade level. Coins which are so-called borderline usually are and fall back to the next lowest grade level. The coin values in 'Trends' are for coins which do not exhibit any one of the many problems which may be a part of the coin's history. Problems such as harsh cleaning, heavy scratches, whizzing, rim or other surface damage can lower substantially the value of a coin, even though technically it is in a grade which may carry a much higher value.

"Color and eye appeal are important. If a coin has attractive color or better than average eye appeal, then it is reasonable to assume its market value may be greater than the 'Trends' value listed in that grade. Demand for top quality coins is increasing today. If the coin is dull for the grade, then the value will probably be less and so will the demand."

• **Dealers' fixed prices:** Catalogues and advertisements of dealers provide a guide to what certain coins can actually be bought for in the marketplace. Of course, some prices may be unrealistically high, and listed prices which seem to be too low may be for undesirable coins, but by and large a great deal of information is available from these listings.

• **Experience:** This may be the single most important factor used here at Bowers and Merena Galleries. Experience covers a wide variety of factors, including knowledge of market demand, the availability of other items of comparable quality (not only grade, but overall quality), etc. Experience is what makes a professional numismatist valuable to his clients.

• **Guide Book:** A *Guide Book of U.S. Coins*, published annually, is a very valuable source of information concerning mintage figures, which varieties exist for which series, historical information, etc. Pricing data is very valuable for all except the most actively traded series. The book is prepared a year in advance, and the 1991-dated edition was released in July 1990. The *Guide Book* reports prices, it does not create them, so it can lag behind the market. Nickname: *Redbook*.

• **Numismatic News:** The weekly "Coin Market" feature, edited by Bob Wilhite, is a valuable source of information, much like the *Coin World* "Trends." For many series, "Coin Market" lists three prices, explained as follows:

"BUY: What dealers pay to purchase coins for inventory or to wholesale to other dealers."

"BID: What dealers pay for coins, generally through other dealers on Teletype, which will sell immediately."

"SELL: Average price realized for a coin sold at retail."

A recent listing contained the following spreads, as examples:[7]

1893 Columbian 50c, MS-63: Buy $437, Bid $485, Sell $545.
1923-S Monroe 50c, MS-64: Buy $675, Bid $750, Sell $850.
1881-CC $1, MS-65: Buy $545, Bid $605, Sell $750.
1895-S $1, MS-60: Buy $665, Bid $740, Sell $950.
1922-S $1, MS-64: Buy $380, Bid $420, Sell $530.

Liberty Head type 5c, MS-63: Buy $125, Bid $140, Sell $175.
Barber type 25c, Proof-65: Buy $4,320, Bid $4,700, Sell $5,900.
Indian type $10, MS-63: Buy $1,200, Bid $1,300, Sell $1,450.

These are guidelines, and actual transactions may vary. For example, If I had a ready sale for a Proof Barber 25c at $5,900, and someone offered me one for $5,500, I wouldn't turn it down, to wait for the chance, which might never come, to obtain one for listed the "buy" price of $4,320 or the "bid" price of $4,700. On the other hand, if I had several dozen such coins in stock and envisioned no ready sale for them, I might not want to pay the "bid" price of $4,320, but would be a buyer only at some lower level. Further, if a coin was not aesthetically pleasing to me, I might not want it at any price.

The "Coin Market" feature offers excellent guidelines, and anyone wanting to know what an average Proof-65 Barber quarter is worth can certainly gain some ideas from the preceding spread.

• **Population reports:** Issued at regular intervals by PCGS and NGC, these reports show how many coins have been certified in various grades. They are not at all representative of the total population in existence of a certain issue, for few coins below MS-60 are submitted for common varieties, as it costs $20 to $25 or so to have a coin certified. As more and more coins are certified in the future, the populations will increase.

The popular practice of resubmitting coins has these two effects:

1. The same coin can appear twice (or more) and give the impression that an variety is more common than it actually is (one dealer I know submitted an MCMVII High Relief $20 four times before he was able to get the grade he wanted; this coin appears in the population report as four different listings, whereas in reality only one specimen is represented).

2. Proportionally, there are more higher-graded slabbed coins in existence that the data show, for many lower-grade listings which swell the report numbers do not exist, as they have been reslabbed at higher levels.

Population reports are quite valuable in determining the *relative rarity* of certain coins in higher grade levels. For example, if in a hypothetical situation the PCGS report lists 754 MS-65 examples, 63 MS-66 pieces, and 8 MS-67 specimens of a particular variety, if you own an MS-66 or MS-67 example, you have an item which will sell for a sharp premium above the MS-65 level.

Sample Prices: A Study

In July 1990, Mark Borckardt, senior numismatist at Bowers and Merena Galleries, studied the prices in print of selected coins, for inclusion in the present book. The prices listed are a mixture of bid prices and market prices, depending upon the source. Used in the study were the following:[8]

Certified Coin Dealer Newsletter, ANACS (bid prices). Abbreviated C-ANA.

Certified Coin Dealer Newsletter, Numismatic Certification Institute (bid prices). Abbreviated C-NCI.[9]

Certified Coin Dealer Newsletter, NGC (bid prices). Abbreviated C-NGC.

Certified Coin Dealer Newsletter, PCGS (bid prices). Abbreviated C-PCGS.

Coin Dealer Newsletter (bid prices). Abbreviated CDN.

Coin World "Trends." Abbreviated CW.

A Guide Book of U.S. Coins (market prices; the only prices listed by that authority). Abbreviated GB.

Numismatic News "Coin Market." Abbreviated NN.

In instances in which a source did not report on a given issue, that source is not listed. Listings which are ask (retail) rather than bid (wholesale), per the preceding explanation, are marked with an asterisk (*). For comparative purposes, these retail listings (*Coin World* and *A Guide Book of U.S. Coins*) should be discounted slightly. The study included the following coins:

• **1877 1c, EF-40:** CDN $775, CW $925*, GB $750*, NN $795.

• **1909-S V.D.B. 1c, MS-65 red:** C-ANA $1,400, CDN $1,600, CW $1,750*, NN $1,400.

• **Liberty Head type 5c, MS-65:** C-ANA $1,000, C-NGC $1,125, C-PCGS $1,250, CDN $1,150, CW $1,250*, GB $1,500*, NN $1,250.

• **Barber type 10c, MS-65:** C-ANA $2,250, C-NGC $2,650, C-PCGS $2,700, CDN $2,600, CW $3,100*, GB $2,300*, NN $2,650.

• **1917 Type I 25c, MS-63:** C-ANA $210, C-NGC $240, C-PCGS $260, CDN $250, CW $285*, GB $500*, NN $280.

• **1917 Type I 25c, MS-65:** C-ANA $1,400, C-NGC $1,600, C-PCGS $1,750, CDN $1,800, CW $1,800*, GB $2,500, NN $1,750.

• **1881-CC $1, MS-63:** C-ANA $140, C-NGC $150, C-PCGS $153, CDN $150, CW $170*, GB $235*, NN $150.

• **1883-S $1, MS-65:** C-NGC $17,500, C-PCGS $21,000, CDN $22,500, CW $26,500*, NN $23,500.

• **1886-O $1, MS-65:** C-NGC $33,500, C-PCGS $35,000, CDN $50,000, CW $45,000*, NN $40,000.

• **1898-O $1, MS-65:** C-ANA $160, C-NCI $80, C-NGC $180, C-

PCGS $200, CDN $190, CW $260*, NN $215.

• **Type II Gold $1, MS-63:** C-ANA $10,000, C-NCI $3,800, C-NGC $11,000, C-PCGS $11,750, CDN $12,000, CW $13,000*, GB $15,000*, NN $11,750.

• **Indian type $5, MS-63:** C-ANA $2,650, C-NCI $650, C-NGC $2,850, C-PCGS $3,000, CDN $3,000, CW $3,150*, GB $4,200*, NN $3,050.

• **MCMVII High Relief $20, MS-63:** C-ANA $11,000, C-NCI $8,500, C-NGC $11,000, C-PCGS $12,000, CDN $13,000, CW $15,500*, GB $16,000*, NN $16,500.

• **1936 Long Island commemorative 50c, MS-63:** C-ANA $70, C-NGC $75, C-PCGS $80, CDN $85, CW $115*, GB $135*, NN $100.

The preceding price quotations indicate that only rarely do two authorities precisely agree on the value of a coin in a given grade, but taken as a whole, the various sources indicate an approximate market level.

The wholesale price of an EF-40 1877 Indian cent is seen to be in the $750 to $800 range. For my money, I would pay that for a nice example. For a lightly porous or low-end coin I would pay $600 or less, and for a really nice EF-40 I might part with the sum of $900, but certainly $750 to $800 is a good average.

An MS-65 1886-O dollar is seen to be worth in the $30,000 to $50,000 range, quite a spread. In this instance, the study of recent auction records might furnish additional insights as would dealers' price lists (if you could find such a rarity listed).

Prices will always be a moving target, and even on the same day or at the same minute of the same day, different sources will furnish different numbers.

Surface Characteristics

As I noted when I wrote the introduction to the *Official ANA Grading Standards for United States Coins* book, there are specific factors which establish the characteristics of a coin's surface. These can affect a coin's value, sometimes significantly. What appear as imperfections or marks on a coin can occur because of the following:

• **Characteristics of the die used to strike the coin.** Before 1836, most dies were prepared by hand. The engraver, using a matrix or hub, punched in the portrait of Miss Liberty, the wreath or other device, and individual letters and numerals. Sometimes a tool would slip or an accident would occur, and unintended marks would appear on the die and be transferred to all coins struck from that die. A variety of 1795 silver dollar has a prominent "bar" behind the head, the result of an accident to the die. The die for a certain variety of 1804 half cent was apparently injured when a bolt from the coining press became loose, fell upon the lower die on the press, and was then forced against the bottom die when the top die came down. Many other examples can be given.

Clash marks are seen on many varieties of early coins and were caused by two dies coming together without an intervening planchet. An impression of the obverse die was made upon the reverse, and vice versa, so that any coin struck later from this die pair showed evidence of this accident. Clashed dies seem to be particularly common in the silver three-cent piece series, perhaps because the tiny planchets often slipped and were not easy to handle, but other series display them as well. Recently a correspondent sent me a fine photograph of a modern Kennedy half dollar with prominent clash marks on the obverse, showing traces of the heraldic eagle design transferred from the reverse.

After a die was used for a period of time it was apt to become worn or to develop cracks. Such cracks were filled with metal from the planchets when coins were struck, causing raised ridges or irregular lines known as die breaks. These are typically irregular in outline and extend inward from the border, although particularly severe cracks can extend all the way across a coin from rim to rim. Breaks caused by metal chipping away from the edge of the die produced blobs of metal at the rim and are sometimes called "cud" breaks. Most die breaks do not affect the value of a coin either positively or negatively, although among certain early issues in which breaks are severe and an entire section of the die shows injury, resultant coins display partial or missing inscriptions and are often worth less than fully struck examples.

As dies became worn, sometimes they were resurfaced by grinding, thus removing certain details. The 1937-D Buffalo nickel with three legs is believed to have been the result of one leg being partially rubbed away in the die by the use of a file or, as some texts say, an emery board. Liberty Seated half dollars such as 1845-O, 1846-O, and 1877-S are often seen with prooflike surfaces and with part of the drapery absent from Miss Liberty's elbow. When these dies were resurfaced, the drapery, being one of the lower relief features, was ground away. The grinding and resurfacing marks were covered up by polishing the dies, giving the coins prooflike surfaces.

Sometimes dies were stored in damp circumstances, with the result that coins struck from them show evidence of rust pits on the die. Certain 1833 quarters, 1876-CC dimes, and other issues were struck from heavily rusted or even corroded dies. The so-called "restrike" 1804 large cent was struck from dies which had been left to the ravages of the elements for many years.

In general, die characteristics such as rust spots, breaks, accidental marks in the die, etc., are not specifically mentioned in coin descriptions, unless they are felt to affect the value. Certain varieties are especially popular due to their having been struck from problem dies. Among these are the 1795 half cent without pole to cap (the pole to the liberty cap on the obverse was ground away during die resurfacing, thus creating this distinctive variety), the 1801 AMERICAI silver dollar (a die mark, possibly a break, exists after the last letter in AMERICA and has the fanciful appearance of an "I"), and the 1796 LIKERTY half dime (a rather silly variety, for the "K" is simply a defective R). Often a die defect of years ago can translate into a highly prized collectors' item today!

• **Characteristics of the planchet.** Marks seen on the surface of a coin can be due to the quality of the original planchet used to produce the piece. During the process of preparing planchets, metal is rolled into long strips. Sometimes bubbles, laminations, and streaks occur which can be transferred to coins. It is not uncommon among early silver coins to see black or gray streaks, the result of carbon and other imperfections in the metal, such imperfections having been distended into streaks by the rolling process. Particularly notable laminations and streaks should be mentioned when a coin is described.

Adjustment marks are common on silver and gold coins of the late 17th and early 18th centuries and are a result of the legal requirement that such pieces be of a precise weight and value. It was not possible to produce planchet of precisely the authorized weight, for such technology was not in place. It was realized that if the pieces were made too light, metal could not effectively be added, and such planchets would have to be remelted. The course pursued was to make the planchets slightly heavier than intended. Once this was done, the pieces were sent to ladies who worked at the Mint adjusting each piece. Each planchet was put on a scale, weighed, and then a file was drawn across the surface to remove any excess amount of metal. If the first filing did not suffice, then another pass with a file was used, perhaps in a different direction. The resultant planchet had parallel file grooves, ranging from light to heavy, on the surface. After this planchet was used for coinage, sometimes the file marks would not be obliterated, particularly toward the edge of the coin or on the higher parts of the coin's surface. Some adjustment marks are par for the course among silver and gold issues, particularly gold issues, of the 1790s and early 1800s, and are not usually mentioned in connection with the grade, although particularly extensive adjustment marks should be noted.

The metal from which planchets were made often had different characteristics. Collectors of early large cents know that issues of 1799, for example, almost always come with very dark brown or black coloration, due to the metal used, which came from various commercial sources. Cents of 1814 are often black, while cents dated 1836 are usually a pleasing chocolate brown color. Early Mint records indicate that freshly minted copper cents and half cents in some instances were dark, not brilliant, as they left the press. Among later coins, bronze Indian cents and Lincoln cents made at the San Francisco Mint in 1909 were struck on planchets made from an alloy giving the pieces a light yellow or straw color, rather than the normal red or orange surface, after striking.

During the preparation process, blank planchets are subjected to all kinds of rough treatment, and in this way acquire numerous abrasions, tiny nicks, etc. When the planchet is used to make a coin, if certain areas of the planchet are not fully impressed into the deepest recesses of the die so as to make the planchet metal flow against the die surfaces, it is the case the the original marks on the planchet can still be seen on the coin. This is a fine point of distinction, and most collectors and dealers are not aware of it. For this reason a softly struck Liberty Walking half dollar, for example, can have virtually flawless, frosty, lustrous fields but on the higher parts of the coin show nicks and marks from the original planchet.

Marks Acquired After a Coin is Struck

I have just described how marks, die breaks, evidence of die clashes, laminations, adjustment marks, and other attributes of dies and planchets can affect the appearance of a coin and are characteristic of a piece at the moment of striking. Now I address the grade or condition of a coin, which is determined by marks, abrasions, friction, and other evidences of contact which occur after a coin is struck. A explanation of the striking process is in order:

The typical minting procedure for a coin produced for circulation, known as a *business strike*, is as follows:

After the planchets are prepared they are put into a bin or hopper, from which they are jostled or, in early times, hand placed into a feeding tube on the coin press, which positions each planchet between the dies (certain types of modern coining presses have multiple dies and use more than one planchet at a time). The coin is struck when the top die, being movable, is forced down on to the planchet, which is resting on the bottom die. The metal is squeezed upward and downward into the recesses of the obverse and reverse dies and outward into a restraining device, called a collar (which imparts to the coin the characteristics of the collar, typically plain or reeded in modern times). No care is taken to strike coins with needle-sharp detail, as the object is to produce coins as rapidly as possible. As a result, some coins are carelessly or weakly struck (more about this later).

After a typical coin is struck it is mechanically ejected from the dies, and slides down a chute or tube into a metal box, where other coins are heaped on top of it. By this time the coin, if viewed under magnification, is apt to have a number of nicks and abrasions. From this point the coin is dumped from the metal box into a large storage bin, during which process the piece comes into contact with numerous other coins. As each bin becomes full it is taken to another area of the mint where it is unloaded, and the pieces are fed into a mechanical counting machine, which jostles the coins even more and imparts additional abrasions. The coins are then run at high speed through a mechanical counter, after which they go through a chute and are dumped into cloth bags and stored. The cloth bags are not handled with care and are piled upon each other. The bags are put into a safe storage place, until they are called for to be shipped to Federal Reserve banks or other locations, to which places they are typically shipped by motor freight.

• **Coin storage and distribution.** The Federal Reserve system distributes bags of coins to member banks, which often place them into circulation either as loose change or by running them through mechanical devices which count and wrap them (creating bank-wrapped rolls). To this point the typical coin has not been in circulation, nor has it been touched by human hands. However, it may have acquired enough nicks, scratches, and abrasions that it would barely make the grade MS-60! I remember seeing a bank-wrapped roll of 1958 Philadelphia Mint Jefferson nickels in which there wasn't a single coin I would grade better than AU-58, and yet the coins had never been in circulation! Perhaps from a technical viewpoint they were indeed Uncirculated, but no knowing buyer would have bought them as such.

The larger and heavier a coin is, the more susceptible it is to receiving abrasions and other handling marks. When in the 1970s the General Services Administration distributed Treasury-stored Morgan dollars, which had been kept by the government since the 1870s and 1880s in many instances, purchasers often found that the coins were heavily nicked, scratched, and abraded, although the pieces had never been out of government hands and had not circulated. Such issues as 1893-CC and 1895-S in particular are usually seen with extensive contact marks.[10]

In general, a Morgan silver dollar, a Saint-Gaudens double eagle, a Liberty

Seated half dollar, or some other large and relatively heavy coin will have more bagmarks and abrasions than a small, light coin such as a silver three-cent piece, half dime, dime, or gold dollar.

Mint State Coins

The presence or absence of handling marks is what determines various levels within the Mint State category. A coin with no handling or bagmarks visible under magnification is a candidate to be graded MS-70. A heavily nicked, abraded, and rubbed coin which has never been in general circulation but which shows extensive handling is a contender for the MS-60 category. In between there are divisions such as MS-61, 62, etc.

Among early coins, particularly those dated prior to the 1940s, the highest generally available Uncirculated grade category is MS-65, although for particularly common pieces (1879-S, 1881-S, 1882-S, 1884-O, and 1885-O silver dollars are examples) there are enough Uncirculated pieces around that a goodly number have been graded in higher categories such as MS-66 and MS-67. It seems to me that in the past year or two the certification services have been grading proportionately more coins at levels above MS-65, but I have never verified this. I do know that a few years ago slabbed silver dollars, commemoratives, and other popular issues were not often seen in MS-66, MS-67, or other higher grades, but now they seem to come on the market with frequency. Some of this is due no doubt to the resubmission of MS-65 coins to the services in the hope of securing higher numbers.

Little in the way of subjective information has ever been printed concerning guidelines for determining different Mint State categories. What may be MS-65 to one buyer may be MS-64 to another and MS-66 to another. Jack Ehrmantraut, Jr. related in a letter published in *Coin World* that a 1901-S Barber quarter was graded by PCGS as MS-66 and sold for $140,000, but on second examination the grade jumped two points to MS-68. Subsequently it was auctioned for $550,000!

The point of this is that there are no fixed standards that everyone agrees on, and one should be cautious when paying a great deal of money for a higher grade coin, particularly in grades above MS-65. While purchasing a coin as MS-66 and having it regraded as MS-68 is a pleasant experience, the opposite is not true.

Proof Coins

The grading of Proof coins in higher levels is similar to that of Mint State coins. An absolutely perfect coin can be judged as Proof-70. A few years ago my company sent several dozen 1953 Proof sets in their original mint packages, never opened, to a leading grading service. The typical grade the experts on their staff assigned to the individual Proof coins was Proof-63. Only a few were designated Proof-65. And yet these coins had never been handled by anyone outside of the mint! During a visit to the San Francisco Mint to watch the preparation of Proof coins there in 1975, I noticed that it was standard procedure for a press operator to stack Proof half dollars on top of each other after they were coined!

Then there is the situation of Matte Proof Lincoln cents of the 1909-1916 era. The Mint stored and sold them in so-called tarnish-proof tissue, which was anything but. The cents soon turned a deep brown or purple-brown color. For this reason any Matte Proof cent of this era with full *original* red surfaces is a rarity!

A few years ago *Numismatic News* ran a story about the Royal Canadian Mint and that institution's packaging of prooflike[11] sets for collectors. It seems that employees at the facility handled the pieces carelessly, and with their fingers pushed bronze one-cent pieces into holders, a situation which months or years later resulted in brown fingerprints on the coins' surfaces.

The following front-page comment in *Numismatic News*[12] addressed a somewhat related problem at the U.S. Mint:

"After months of testing and analysis, good old moisture appears to be the primary cause of corrosion and mold in damage occurring to coins on some 1984-1985 Proof sets, according to a report from the U.S. Mint."

A spokesman for the Mint, Andrew Cosgarea, Jr., was quoted as saying:

"Our inquiry into this unusual damage to Proof coins is not yet complete. However, preliminary findings point to excessive humidity as the primary cause of the coin corrosion. Moisture can also cause the growth of mold which enhances the corrosion. While our Proofs are sonically sealed, they are not hermetically sealed and very high levels of humidity for extended periods can be detrimental to the coins. As a general rule, coin sets should be stored in a dry place."

However, mishandling of a Proof coin after the point of striking is not usually done at the Mint itself but, rather, by purchasers and subsequent owners. Repeated dipping of a Proof coin to make it brilliant will over a period of time produce a cloudy, grainy surface which cannot be restored. Rubbing a Proof coin, even lightly, with a cloth can produce minute hairlines, and cleaning with a paste or substance which is even slightly abrasive can cause severe hairlines. Careless handling of a Proof coin can cause nicks or marks.[13]

Beginning in the 1920s it was popular for collectors to house coins in cardboard album pages with the openings covered with clear slides made of celluloid or other transparent material. Such slides, if brushed against a coin, caused minute parallel scratches, and numerous Barber dimes, quarters, and half dollars, Morgan dollars, and other issues in which the cheek of Miss Liberty is prominent show evidence of such slide marks. A Proof which has numerous hairlines, is cloudy, or which shows abrasions may be a candidate for the Proof-60 designation or even lower.

Terms such as Proof-50 and Proof-55 describe coins originally struck with Proof finish but which later were subjected to friction or even circulation. Proof-60, Proof-61, Proof-62, through Proof-70 describe ascending grades of finer quality Proof issues. An outstanding condition for a 19th-century specimen is apt to be Proof-65, and there are many nice Proof-63 and Proof-64 coins which are highly prized by their owners.

Opinion is divided as to whether manufacturing flaws in Proof coins should be mentioned or whether the grade of a Proof coin should be dropped to compensate for this. For example, I recently saw an 1858 Proof Liberty Seated quarter dollar, which, like numerous other small-denomination Proof silver coins of the period, had a myriad of lint marks in the fields. These lint marks consisted of lines, curliques, and other depressions in the coin's surface and were made by threads adhering to the die used to strike the piece, residue from an oily rag used to wipe the die. I suggested that an appropriate description would be "Proof-65 with mint-caused lint marks in the field," but the owner of the coin decided to offer it as Proof-63 with no further comment, believing that the coin was worth a Proof-63 price, which it undoubtedly was.

As is the case with Mint State coins, even the experts and the grading services are apt to disagree on their findings. What is Proof-65 to one person may be Proof-66 to another, or vice versa. As an example of this I mention the situation in which the purchasers of two important sets decided to have the pieces encapsulated by NGC, and this was done, after which it was decided to send the sets to PCGS. *Numismatic News* reported the following:[14]

"The King of Siam Proof set and a unique 1872 'Amazonian' set of gold patterns have been regraded by the Professional Coin Grading Service. Both sets had been graded by the Numismatic Guaranty Corporation. Several coins in each set received a higher grade from PCGS. The NGC Proof-65 brown 1834 large cent was certified as Proof-66 brown by PCGS, while the NGC Proof-66 1834 Bust dime was designated Proof-67 by PCGS.

"Other King of Siam coins that were regraded are the 1834 Bust quarter and the 1834 quarter eagle. NGC certified the quarter as a Proof-64, while

PCGS graded it Proof-65. The gold piece was an NGC Proof-63 cameo, while PCGS certified it as Proof-64. The two major grading services agreed on the grades assigned to the other five King of Siam coins. An 1834 half cent was certified as Proof-66 red and brown by both firms, and an 1834 Bust half dollar remained a Proof-65 after being cracked out of the NGC holder.

"Other coins that did not change grades are an 1804 dollar, an 1834 half eagle and an 1804 $10 piece. PCGS and NGC graded the coins as Proof-65, Proof-64 and Proof-63, respectively. The gold pieces were designated as cameos by NGC, a term not used for gold coins by PCGS. The three smallest coins in designer William Barber's Amazonian set were assigned higher grades by PCGS. The gold dollar and the quarter eagle were originally certified as Proof-65 by NGC, while the $3 pattern was graded Proof-66. All three coins were graded one point higher by PCGS.

"Both services assigned the same grades to the $5, $10 and $20 Amazonian patterns. The half eagle now resides in a PCGS Proof-65 holder, as does the $10 piece, while the double eagle is a Proof-64. The sets are owned in partnership by the Rarities Group, Inc., of Marlboro, MA and the Continental Investment Group of Wayne, PA...."

Prooflike Coins

Certain business strike coins were made with prooflike surfaces at the various mints, particularly in the 19th century in Philadelphia, Carson City, New Orleans, and San Francisco. These were not made for collectors, but were produced during the ordinary course of business. Such surfaces were caused by striking the pieces from polished dies. In some instances, a new die was given a mirrorlike finish as part of the die manufacturing process. In other instances, dies which had been used extensively were resurfaced by light grinding and then, to eliminate the grinding marks, by polishing.

Coins which exhibit a mixture of frosty mint lustre and prooflike finish are called prooflike (abbreviated PL). Coins which are so prooflike that they almost resemble Philadelphia Mint Proofs are called deep prooflike (abbreviated DPL), or, in a term popularized by Bruce Amspacher,[15] deep mirror prooflike (abbreviated DMPL).

Prooflike coins are especially popular in the Morgan silver dollar series, where separate listings for higher prooflike grade levels can be found in the *Coin Dealer Newsletter* and the *Certified Coin Dealer Newsletter*.

Two caveats:

• As prooflike surfaces tend to accent and make more prominent any nicks or marks a coin has received, in general an MS-63 or MS-64 coin with prooflike surface is unappealing from an aesthetic viewpoint. This is especially true in the Morgan dollar series.

• There has been an "inflation" in the grading of prooflike coins, and while years ago a coin described as DMPL would be virtually indistinguishable from a Philadelphia Mint Proof, this is no longer the case. Many slabbed DMPL coins are only partially prooflike. Never buy a DMPL coin sight-unseen.

Circulated Grades

As we leave the MS-60 to MS-70 Uncirculated category and Proof category, we encounter grade ranges for coins which show wear and other attrition. Business strikes were meant to be used, and used hard. This was their purpose in the scheme of things. As a cent, half dollar, or other coin passed from hand to hand it encountered friction, which caused wear, gradually reducing it to the AU-58 (just below Mint State) level, then to AU-55, then with most of the original mint lustre gone, down to AU-53, then to AU-50. To qualify as AU-50 the typical dime, quarter, half dollar, or other piece of a popular denomination probably circulated for up to several years. A silver dollar or gold coin, which was more apt to be stored in a bank and not handled except at infrequent intervals, may not have reached this state until after several decades of use.

As a coin acquires more evidence of circulation and wear, it becomes lower in grade, EF-45, EF-40, through the VF numbers to VF-20, in stages to Fine-12, then Very Good-8, Good-4, About Good-3, Fair-2, and finally, Poor-1. There are few coins which are Poor-1, for the Treasury Department redeems most pieces before this state of wear is achieved, but occasionally in numismatics one encounters an early coin which has been worn nearly smooth. I have had several 1793 Chain large cents which were worn so much that the date, letters, and nearly everything else was gone, with just a vestige of the Chain motif visible in order to identify them.

The more wear a coin receives the more it is apt to acquire other evidences of contact, such as nicks, edge bumps, and scratches. Such additional defects, if serious or especially prominent in nature, should always be mentioned in a coin description. There are different schools of thought about this. Some feel that a coin should be described, for example, as "EF-40, but with several edge bumps." Such a coin may be worth, say, a VF-20 price. Some feel that it is just as expedient to simply describe the coin as VF-20 and say nothing else, for this equates to the market price level.

Coins which have been polished, soldered, holed and repaired, used as jewelry, re-engraved or burnished, or which have other problems should always be specifically described as such, no matter what their grade level.

Sharpness or Weakness of Strike

The sharpness or lightness of strike can affect a coin's value and, in recent times (for views have changed on this), a coin's grade. Consider as an example the 1941-S Liberty Walking half dollar. Nearly all known specimens, probably 95% or more, have the details on the skirt of Miss Liberty and on the central part of her figure weakly defined. Had you or I been present at the San Francisco Mint in 1941, and at the moment of striking had we taken with a gloved hand a typical 1941-S half dollar from the dies, it would have exhibited a flatness not unlike that observed on a coin which had spent several years in circulation. And yet the coin would have received no nicks, scratches, abrasions, or handling marks, for the newly minted specimen had yet to come into contact with anything else except a gloved hand. From a technical viewpoint, I suggest that a proper numismatic description of this coin, if offered in an auction catalogue, should be something like this:

"1941-S Liberty Walking half dollar. MS-70 from the standpoint of handling and contact marks; there is absolutely no evidence of such. However, in keeping with nearly all other known specimens of the variety, the details of Miss Liberty are lightly defined on the higher areas, giving the coin a flat appearance at the center. This coin is worth an MS-63 price."

However, this view would not be at all in step with prevailing numismatic philosophy. Instead, the piece would be downgraded to, say, MS-63 to reflect its market level, with nothing said about the weakness of strike.

Let me take another 1941-S half dollar. This second coin is one that is among the very few examples that were sharply struck at the time of issue. This particularly coin was produced at the San Francisco Mint in 1941, was ejected from the dies, slid down a chute into a box, was dumped in a hopper, bagged, run through a counting machine, passed through the Federal Reserve system, sent to a bank, put in a paper-wrapped roll, and, finally, was acquired by a collector. The piece never circulated, but yet there were sufficient nicks, abrasions, and other evidences of handling to merit the piece being called MS-63 by today's grading standards. Thus we have a second MS-63 half dollar, this one sharply struck. From my viewpoint, the ideal description for the second piece would be as follows:

"1941-S Liberty Walking half dollar. MS-63. Sharply struck, and one of

167

relatively few known specimens to exhibit needle-sharp details on the higher areas."

If you were a bidder in one of my firm's auction sales, and these two 1941-S half dollars were listed, even though both might be worth MS-63 money, in your mind's eye you would be able to differentiate the two coins and determine which one you wanted. For the price of an MS-63 coin, would you prefer an MS-70 coin with virtually perfect surfaces, but which is flatly struck, or would you prefer a sharply struck piece with abrasions? This is up to you. However, you would have the opportunity to make an informed choice.

Today, in the world of slabbed coins, both pieces would simply be slabbed as MS-63, with no further distinction made. So few people seem to care about such distinctions as sharpness of strike, that it may be a waste of print to give the elaborate descriptions of 1941-S half dollars just cited.

Interestingly, when a coin is weakly defined on the higher parts, such as the 1941-S half dollar, or numerous Buffalo nickels struck at branch mints during the 1920s, or Standing Liberty quarters of the 1920s, 1921 Peace silver dollars, or other issues which are often seen flatly struck, this had nothing to do with the wear of the dies. Uninformed cataloguers have often said that such pieces have been struck from "worn dies," but this is not the case. When dies wear, they do so in areas which are subjected to the greatest amount of lateral metal flow on the planchet—areas such as the fields and near the rims. The deepest recesses of the dies receive the least amount of wear.

The weakness just described in the 1941-S half dollar was due to inadequate die spacing. During the production process, technicians at the Mint endeavored to space the dies closely enough together that the coins would strike up properly, but wide enough apart that excessive die wear and breakage would not occur. If the dies were spaced too closely together, after the metal filled the deepest recesses in the dies and filled the reeding or other areas of the collar, it had to have some place to go, and would either create a wire rim around the coin (a knifelike edge caused by metal extruding between the die and collar) or would cause die breakage. The simple solution was (and still is at the various mints) to space the dies slightly further apart than the optimum. In that way if a planchet was slightly overweight it would not cause breakage, nor would a wire rim be created.

Technicians were more careless than usual at the San Francisco Mint in 1941, and the half dollar dies were spaced too far apart. Another outstanding case is the 1926-D Buffalo nickel. Probably 99 out of 100 known specimens are flatly struck. Except for their lustrous surfaces, such coins give every indication that they have been in circulation for years! Similarly, nearly all known 1926-D Standing Liberty quarters have Miss Liberty's head weakly struck.

Apropos of grading in recent times, I have heard it said that unless a coin is sharply struck, it cannot be graded any higher than MS-65. This rule seems to be in general use at the present time. Thus, an 1892-O silver dollar, to mention an issue which is often lightly struck, cannot be graded higher than MS-65 even if it has virtually perfect fields. An extremely sharply struck 1892-O is a candidate for any and all higher grades, depending on the amount of nicks and abrasions it has received.

In other instances of weak striking, dies were created with the designs in low relief. Certain 1793 half cents have the words HALF CENT lightly impressed on the reverse, for these words were shallowly impressed into the dies. Sesquicentennial commemorative half dollars dated 1926 are often indistinct, simply because the design was executed in shallow relief without bold features. In other instances, particularly among issues of the 1790s, improperly hardened dies tended to sink in certain areas, resulting in evident weakness on coins struck from these dies.

In still other instances, the obverse and reverse dies were not completely parallel to each other, with the result that the coins of a particular variety can be weak on one side and sharp on the other. The 1794 large cent known as the "Shielded Hair" variety is very deeply impressed on the left side of the obverse and lightly impressed on the right side. United States silver dollars of the same year, 1794, are typically seen lightly impressed at the lower left of the obverse (and corresponding part of the reverse) and sharp at the opposite area of the coin—at the upper right.

"Market Grade"

Increasingly there has been a tendency to assign just a single number to describe a coin's grade, and to use no additional adjectives at all. Bumps, scratches, hairlines, etc. are factored into the grade, and, as noted, an EF-40 coin with problems can be slabbed simply as a VF-20, or a Proof-65 coin with lint marks can be encapsulated as a Proof-63 or some lesser grade. Do you remember my theoretical MS-70 1941-S half dollar, weakly struck, being called MS-63? Unquestionably, using just a single number simplifies things, as it makes prices easier to compute.

Under this philosophy, a coin is assigned a single grade number which reflects its market price, not necessarily its technical grade. This is a departure from the grading systems outlined in the 1970s and 1980s in *Photograde* and the *Official ANA Grading Standards for United States Coins* books.

To expand on the subject, I give three illustrations:

• **1895-S silver dollar.** Obverse heavily bagmarked, numerical grade for the obverse alone: MS-60. Reverse lightly bagmarked (fewer bagmarks than on the obverse, due to the protective nature of the letters and eagle design), numerical grade for the reverse alone: MS-63.

Old grading system: 1895-S $1. MS-60/63. Obverse heavily bagmarked (information a collector might want to know).

New grading system: 1895-S $1. MS-60.

In both instances the coins have the same market value. Only the descriptions are different.

• **1872 Proof Liberty Seated half dollar.** Cleaned long ago, and now with a few light hairlines in the fields. Deep gray, almost black, toning in blotches (information a collector might want to know). Numerical grade: Proof-64.

Old grading system: 1872 Liberty Seated half dollar. Proof-64. Deep gray, almost black, toning in blotches.

New grading system: 1872 50c. Proof-63. (Some would still call it Proof-64 and not mention the blotches, etc.; a low-end 64.)

In both instances the coins have the same market value. Only the descriptions are different.

• **1926-D Buffalo nickel.** MS-65 from the standpoint of wear, but very weakly struck, as usual for this variety.

Old grading system: 1926-D 5c. MS-65, weakly struck, as usual for this variety.

New grading system: 1926-D 5c. MS-63.

In both instances the coins have the same market value. Only the descriptions are different.

In today's market coin buyers are often confronted with just numbers, with little in the way of adjectival descriptions to indicate what a coin looks like. I suggest that you, as an astute buyer, determine in advance what any coins you want to purchase do indeed look like, for once you own them, you may have to look at them for many years! If, as extensively mentioned by the *Certified Coin Dealer Newsletter*, alert *dealers* pay higher prices for coins they can see before making a commitment, perhaps you should also!

Brilliant vs. Toned

In the 1950s and 1960s, the term "Brilliant Uncirculated," abbreviated as BU, was used to describe Mint State coins, particularly those in the silver and copper series. The philosophy was "brilliant is best," and numerous advertisements in *The Numismatist, The Numismatic Scrapbook Magazine,* and other periodicals of the time offered dips, lotions, pastes, and other substances to brighten otherwise dull or toned pieces. Collectors became conditioned to brilliance, and coins with iridescent toning or other attractive hues were apt to be rejected as unacceptable.

I was part of this syndrome. In the early 1950s I visited a leading metropolitan dealer and sought to add the two or three pieces I needed to complete my collection of Proof Barber half dollars 1892-1915, all of which were brilliant. I was shown a 1913 Proof with attractive toning around the borders.

"I don't want it," I said naively, "as I only have brilliant coins in my collection."

"There is no problem," the dealer replied. "I will dip it and it will look as bright as the day it was minted."

"I don't want any dipped or cleaned coins," I remonstrated.

"Dipping won't hurt the coin, and if you don't like it after I dip it, you don't have to buy it."

The coin was dipped, it emerged as brilliant as the day it was minted, and I saw that it was as nice or nicer than the other pieces already in my collection. The same dealer told me that toning was a natural process, and that probably every Proof Barber half dollar in existence was either toned, or if it was bright, had been dipped. It was chemically impossible for a Barber half dollar to be completely brilliant after all these years and not have been dipped, he related.

I subsequently learned that the same was true of commemorative half dollars, Liberty Seated coins, Liberty Walking half dollars, and every other type of older silver coin that has been stored *singly* over the years. Coins stored in bank-wrapped rolls tend to tone only on the edges, and retain their naturally brilliant surfaces. Morgan silver dollars and other pieces stored in bags often remained brilliant over a long period of years.

Professional numismatists have made a distinction between dipping and "cleaning." Today, in the 1990s, dipping is practiced infrequently, but, as noted, years ago it was a popular procedure.

A lightly toned silver coin, if emerged in a clear liquid silver dip, carefully rinsed, neutralized in a solution of baking soda and water (without the application of any friction or rubbing), and then carefully dried by patting, will have its original mint brilliance restored. If a Proof coin is dipped once or twice, chances are that there will be no problem. If a Proof coin is dipped multiple times, gradually the mirror surface will become hazy and cloudy, and the value will be impaired. James F. Ruddy's *Photograde* book discusses this and other considerations in detail.

Uncirculated business strike coins possessing lustrous surfaces can be dipped multiple times without apparent adverse effects, for the microscopic ridges which cause mint lustre tend to mask the effects of the clouding, but if a piece is dipped too many times, it will become dull and unattractive.

In my opinion dipping of a silver coin should be done only if the piece is toned in blotches, is spotted, or is unattractive. If a coin possesses attractive patination it should not be dipped. Dipping of a copper and bronze coin almost always results in lessening the value of the piece.

I recall that a California dealer showed me an attractively toned 1864 Small Motto bronze two-cent piece in what today would be called Proof-64 or 65 grade, toned a beautiful chestnut brown. The coin, a major rarity of which fewer than 20 Proof specimens exist, was very appealing and would have sold readily to any experienced buyer. I wanted to buy it, but it wasn't for sale—not just yet. Before pricing it, the dealer decided to dip the two-cent piece to make it brilliant and, presumably, to increase its worth. The dipping didn't go well, and he found himself the owner of a pale orange coin with dark stains in areas. He then tried retoning the piece by subjecting it to heat. Now he had a blotchy purple and brown coin, so it dipped it again. The last time I saw it the coin was a mess and was probably not worth the price of even a Proof-60 example, a far cry from its grade when I viewed it the first time around.

Whether a piece should be dipped or not is a matter of opinion, and there are arguments on both sides of the fence. In rare instances dipping a coin can dramatically increase its value. James L. Halperin relates[16] that he purchased a 1795 Draped Bust silver dollar for $33,500 from Steve Ivy (who later became his business partner) in February 1980. In Halperin's words "the toning was positively hideous; the coin simply lacked eye appeal" and was a "turkey." Then here is what he did:

"I suppose I had some reservations about dipping the coin. Even for an expert, dipping a coin is a risky undertaking. (And I would never recommend that a novice ever dip a coin.) What if the toning hid some unpardonable flaw? Or what if the lustre became dull as a result of the dipping? Still; no guts, no glory!

"A quick dip in Jeweluster produced the most stunning, blazing white semi-prooflike gem early U.S. silver coin I had ever seen! Really, nothing had changed except the eye-appeal factor. The coin was transformed from a 'technical MS-65' with no eye appeal, to a wonder coin, a coin that had it all. The coin that Steve couldn't sell now had suitors waiting in line. There were literally half a dozen knowledgeable buyers begging me to give them first shot at the coin. I sold it to a dealer in the Boston area for $137,500."

Less in question is the procedure of removing dirt, oil, grease, and other contaminants from a coin's surface by using plain soap and water, acetone (obtainable at drugstores; acetone is inflammable and must be used with great caution under well ventilated circumstances), ammonia (which may discolor copper coins but not silver and gold issues), or other solvents. In general, my advice is not to use a solvent or any other substance on a valuable coin unless you have experimented with inexpensive pieces first.

In the negative category are various processes which can be described as "cleaning." This term is normally not used to describe pieces which have been dipped or which have had dirt removed by the use of solvents. Rather, "cleaning" refers to the use of jewelers' pastes, polishes, pastes made of baking soda and water, and other methods which use friction or a combination of friction and chemicals to remove metal from a coin's surface. Shortly after the turn of the century Farran Zerbe visited the National Coin Collection on view at the Philadelphia Mint and reported to readers of *The Numismatist* that the silver coins had been cleaned multiple times with jewelers' paste, thus considerably lessening their value.

Apropos of cleaning coins, Jed Stevenson had the following to say in *The New York Times*:[17]

"Coins, like people show the effects of age. When roughly handled, coins pick up scars. Exposure to the elements causes tarnishing and even mild acids will pit and erode a coin's surface. Beware! Any attempt to improve a coin's features, perhaps with a little scrubbing or buffing, can do more damage than benign neglect. Cleaning a coin with household cleansers or metal polishers will bring out the original sheen, but at the expense of scratching the coin or rubbing away raised points. Because coins are valued by how closely they approximate their original condition, any changes in the surface of the coin since the day it popped out of the dies at the mint cause a loss of value. In the rarer types of coins, a small scratch can mean the loss of hundreds of dollars...."

It may be appropriate to relate an experience I had many years ago. I purchased a collection in which there was a sharply struck and very beautiful 1857 Flying Eagle cent, a desirable coin in every respect except that sometime in its past it had been lightly gold plated. This ruined its resale value, so I sought to remove the plating. Upon consulting with several people I finally determined that the only way to dissolve the gold covering was to immerse the piece in aqua regia, a potent acid. Acquiring same and pouring a small quantity into a glass dish, I then dropped the golden cent into the liquid. I watched it for a minute or two, and nothing happened. Then I was distracted by a telephone call or something else, and I forgot about the coin. Several days later I remembered it, rushed to see what had happened, and was greeted by the sight of a gray-colored sludge—all that remained of the cent—in the bottom of the dish!

Excellent commentaries on the subject of cleaning can be found, as noted, in *Photograde,* and also, relative to copper coins, in Dr. William H. Sheldon's *Penny Whimsy* book. In the latter reference, Sheldon tells how to judiciously retone copper coins which have been cleaned.

Attractive toning can often add to a coin's desirability. In the silver series, halo-like toning of iridescent hues is particularly desirable and is usually caused by the storage of coins in cardboard album pages of the old-style, such as those marketed under the National, Raymond, Meghrig names. These pages contained sulphur as an impurity in the cardboard, and over a period of time the sulphur tended to act on the coin, from the rims toward the center. The rims would tone first, and gradually toning would go toward the middle.

Silver coins stored loosely, or in paper envelopes, or casually in bureau drawers, etc., tend to acquire golden or gray toning over a period of time and can be quite attractive. Last year I inadvertently left a Bowers and Merena one-ounce silver medal exposed on the surface of an oak desk drawer. I had put the piece there and had forgotten about it. Several months later I lifted it from its position, and the reverse was toned the most gorgeous electric blue and iridescent hues I had ever seen!

Dr. Sheldon suggests that copper cents, if stored in earth in a flower pot, or left on a windowsill exposed to the weather, will tone attractively. This brings up the question: when is a coin naturally toned, and when is it artificially toned? In the strictest sense, coins stored in National and other album pages are artificially toned, but numismatists view them otherwise.

Although I haven't seen a definition for "artificial toning" in print, it seems to refer to a type of toning produced by heat, chemicals, or other substances and applied to a coin over a short period of time. Natural toning tends to be irregular. The rims or edges of a coin are apt to be darker than the centers, or at least differently toned. Artificial toning is often more uniform.

Those with patience and a knack for experimentation can come up with some interesting toning procedures. If I were to take a Morgan silver dollar and put it in the oak desk drawer in which I had put the silver Bowers and

Merena medal earlier, and left it there for two months, and if it acquired beautiful iridescent toning, would the toning be natural or artificial? This is a point to ponder. A dealer who has made a specialty of toning coins artificially pointed with great pride to a common date Morgan silver dollar illustrated in full color in one of my competitor's auction catalogues. "That's *my* color!" he exclaimed, "Didn't I do a good job when I retoned the coin?"

When we sold the Norweb Collection it included some of the finest silver dollars ever to cross the auction block. One of America's leading specialists in Liberty Seated coins acquired three beautiful Proof dollars, pieces which had been in the Norweb Collection for decades and which had been originally acquired shortly after the turn of the century. The three pieces each displayed beautiful iridescent toning. The buyer sent these to a leading grading service, which returned two of them stating that they were artificially toned and could not be slabbed! Frustrated, he sent them to another grading service which cheerfully slabbed them, both at a grade higher than we assigned in the auction catalogue.

On the other hand, there are many coins in numismatic circulation which are artificially toned, and unattractively so. Grayish-purple coins toned by using Clorox are often seen, as are brownish-gray coins toned by procedures not known to me.

My general advice is this: if a coin appears to be attractively toned and is pleasing to you, then it is probably worth buying, but if the toning appears to be artificial (an intuitive situation, one not particularly well defined) or is unattractive, then stay away from it or buy it at a lower price. Consulting with an established professional can be of help in this regard, but be aware that even the most expert of experts can differ in their opinions, as was evidenced by two of the Liberty Seated dollars in the Norweb Collection.

Coins which have been polished, whizzed (treated with a wire brush to produce artificial mint lustre), or which have otherwise been subject to processes involving brushing, etching, acid treatment, and the like should be described as such when sold, and when purchased should be acquired at a reduction from the regular price level. I recommend that you don't buy such coins at all. Your best protection against these practices is to buy from an established dealer who guarantees his merchandise, or to buy slabbed coins (only rarely does a whizzed, burnished, altered, or processed coin make its way into a slab).

Storage, Display, and Handling

As the owner of a coin you are charged with keeping it safe for future generations. The only reason that we can enjoy beautiful Proof and Uncirculated coins today is that earlier generations of numismatists took care to handle them properly. Of course, many numismatists abused the privilege, as attested by the numerous cleaned and unattractive pieces in existence now.

When examining a coin you should hold it by the edges and over a soft surface such as a piece of cloth. Avoid directly breathing on a coin, for breath contains small amounts of moisture which will later develop into tiny flyspecks or spots, particularly on copper and nickel alloy coins. Never allow your fingers to come in contact with a coin's surface, or a fingerprint will gradually appear in the form of discoloration.

Coins should be kept in dry circumstances, away from industrial or other harmful fumes, particularly those containing sulfur. Homes heated by coal-fired or oil-fired furnaces often have sulfur in the air which does not seem to affect copper coins much, but which will turn silver coins light yellow or yellow-brown. Gold coins in nearly all instances will not tone but will remain brilliant, due to the inert nature of gold metal.

Dampness is harmful to coins. Copper pieces exposed to dampness will often exhibit oxidation and corrosion. Silver coins are also adversely affected by dampness. If it is impossible to keep coins in a dry location, then keep them in a tightly-sealed box in which packets of silica gel (available at a photographic supply store) are kept, to absorb the moisture. These packets can be refreshed at regular intervals.

If coins are stored in inert hard plastic holders this will be of great help, as these are usually airtight. However, Carl W. Carlson studied certain copper coins which had been placed in slabs, apparently at a seaside convention or some location in which there were traces of salt or moisture, and within a matter of weeks brilliant copper coins had toned to a dull surface. As slabs are relatively new on the market (having first appeared in 1986), their long-term use for coin storage has not been fully evaluated. On balance, technical grading considerations aside, it is my view that slabs seem to be performing a wonderful service for collectors of future generations, in that coins in slabs cannot be cleaned, "improved," or otherwise mishandled by their owners.

For many years flexible vinyl envelopes known as "flips" were used to store coins. They were easy to handle, and the coins could be seen clearly. It later developed that polyvinyl chloride (PVC) used to make these flexible envelopes leached out over a period of time and adhered to the surfaces of coins, causing bright copper coins to tone a dull hue, nickel coins to corrode, and silver coins to acquire a greenish slime. Although color cannot be restored to damaged copper coins, the effects of PVC can be largely neutralized by rinsing the pieces with acetone, ammonia, or a commercial product known as Dissolve. In all instances, adequate ventilation must be used, and the instructions on the container must be followed carefully.

Flexible vinyl envelopes are used by auction houses for the storage of coins, as during the pre-sale viewing process many people may wish to view the pieces, and the auction houses do not want the surfaces of the coins to be touched. However, once the sale takes place the new owners should remove coins from these envelopes immediately and transfer them to hard plastic or other containers. Clear Capital (brand) and similar lucite holders, on the market for several decades, have proven to be excellent for storage of coins and will protect them against the elements. KoinTains, made of pieces of plastic which snap together to cover a coin, have likewise stood the test of time. Certain other commercial products are similarly useful. Before committing your collection to a one particular type of storage mode, check with a professional numismatist or a long-term collector and get an opinion or two. It is better to be careful than sorry.

Even when coins are carefully housed in slabs, clear lucite holders, or KoinTains, they should be kept away from light and, especially, heat, as both can cause discoloration over a period of time.

The handling and storage of coins is a simple matter, and one not to become worried about. If a few basic precautions are followed, you can enjoy your coins with the assurance that as long as you own them they will be preserved in the same grade in which they were acquired.

CHAPTER ELEVEN

Purchase Recommendations

General Introduction

Now that I have covered the topics of buying and selling strategies, grading, market information, and other elements entering into commercial transactions, I devote the next several chapters to specific recommendations.

What should I collect or invest in? American numismatics covers a wonderfully diverse panorama of denominations and designs. In following chapters I give brief sketches of most of the standard issues, beginning with what used to be called "minor" coins years ago; pieces struck in copper and various related alloys, including bronze and nickel.

Subsequent chapters treat silver (and later clad issues) and gold series as well as other disciplines. What I have to say is just the tip of the iceberg. Books have been written on many series, and I refer you to those if a particular denomination or type is of special interest.

Recommended Purchases

After each series I give three sets of purchase recommendations. These represent my own ideas for three types of coin buyers. These are not *investment* recommendations, but are suggestions to aid in formulating a *collecting* plan. I suggest that you study my ideas carefully, then refer to the appropriate listings in *A Guide Book of U.S. Coins* to determine the place of each series in numismatics, mintage figures of various coins, and the varieties included in each series.

Where you buy the coins I recommend, or even if you buy them at all, is up to you. As noted in the introduction to this book, I am not trying to sell you anything. However, today's market offers what I consider to be some truly exceptional values, and you may wish to take advantage of them.

For three classes of buyers I have listed recommendations in three categories:

• **Budget Recommendations:** For each series I give suggestions for a buying strategy for the collector who is on a budget or who wants to get as many coins as possible for the money spent. In general, coins under this heading are in circulated grades and are much more common than those in the next two categories, and in the past have not performed as well as investments as have higher grade coins (such as Mint State and Proof pieces). I have not listed the lowest possible grades available, for in some series, Morgan silver dollars for example, it seems to me that even the budget-minded collector would rather have an MS-60 1881-S $1 for $20 than a well-worn VG-8 example for $11.

It is important to remember that coins in the Budget Recommendations category often have all of the historical, romantic, and artistic (save for wear) appeal of higher-grade pieces and can be very interesting and desirable to own.

• •**Recommendations for the Connoisseur:** After each series I list issues in generally high grades which I consider to be especially good values for the money at today's prices. If your bank account has limitless resources, you may want to go beyond what I say and endeavor in the federal series to acquire MS-65 to 67, Proof-65 to 67, etc. coins, which can be extremely beautiful and desirable to own (see the Elite Recommendations category), but for the most part I consider slightly lower grade coins, such as MS-63 and MS-64 pieces, to represent better values now. This situation may change in the future, depending upon how strong an influence investors have on market demand and prices.[1] Under the Recommendations for the Connoisseur category are my suggestions for the discriminating, knowledgeable buyer who at once appreciates high quality and outstanding *value* for the price paid.

My feeling that in certain areas of the present market coins graded less than MS-65 represent an excellent value for the discriminating buyer, in relation to MS-65 pieces, is echoed by this letter from J. David Purvis, printed in *Numismatic News:*[2]

"Al Doyle's[3] observations on the tremendous price differential in many cases between coins graded MS-64 and MS-65 are right on target, and very important for investors. We find in most cases that coins in MS-65 are overpriced relative to MS-63s and MS-64s based on actual rarity as represented by the published population statistics. Though sometimes the difference in rarity justifies this price difference, it usually is not the case. Our theory is that many dealers and investors have been conditioned to believe that MS-65 is the 'minimum' quality grade appropriate for investment purposes, and because of the expense associated with these higher-grade coins, investors buy the MS-65s under the impression that they are getting the least expensive 'investment-quality' coins available. This causes an illogical increase in demand for MS-65s relative to their rarity.... Our research has uncovered a virtual 'across-the-board' overvaluation of MS-65 coins in this market. If you define 'investment-quality' as the 'potential for highest appreciation based on rarity' we find that MS-64s and MS-63s usually represent a better value for your money than MS-65s. The bottom line is that as investor dollars push up the prices for the higher-grade coins, these dollars will begin to flow into the lower 'underpriced' grades...."

The concept of value to be found among coins of grades other than those sought by investors is also found in the following commentary under the title of "Collector Market Strong," by Keith Zaner, market-watcher par excellence, in the "Trends" section of *Coin World:*[4]

"As many in the numismatic press concentrate on the state of the investment rare coin market, specifically the weak generic[5] market, it is easy to overlook the strong demand taking place in the collector market. The collector of rare coins is the ultimate consumer of coins. The collector is also the one who totally enjoys the study of numismatics and experiences the satisfaction and excitement of adding an individual scarce or rare variety to his or her collection. A collector is not stuck in the Mint State-64 or higher grade rut. A pleasing circulated example will serve very nicely at a fraction of the gem quality price.

"This is not to say that collector coins are all inexpensive or that they make a bad investment. On the contrary, collector type coins, the scarce or rare dates of each series, often perform adequately investment-wise. During an Auctions by Bowers and Merena sale conducted June 11 in New York City, a Very Fine-20 1800 Draped Bust cent, a Sheldon-201 variety, considered tied for the finest known, sold for $13,750.[6]

"Presently, collector clubs are enjoying increasing membership and showing greater interest in many series of rare coins. Of note, demand is strong for the Barber dime, quarter dollar and half dollar. It is becoming more and more difficult to locate a pleasing Very Fine or Extremely Fine key or semi-key date in the Barber series. The supply is inadequate to accommodate the demand. Many former common-date Barber coins are scarce today in part due to the great silver melt which took place during the late 1970s and early 1980s. Many Barber as well as other type coins were melted for their silver bullion value.

"Coins bearing the Liberty Seated design continue to attract many collectors. This popular design was struck in many denominations from half dime through the dollar.... There are many scarce varieties and mints to collect in the Liberty Seated series and the challenge of completing one of these series is certainly formidable. Other popular collector series include Draped Bust coinage, half cents, large cents, Flying Eagle cents, Indian Head cents, scarce

Lincoln cents, Buffalo nickels, Mercury dimes, Standing Liberty quarter dollars, scarce Washington quarter dollars, and Walking Liberty half dollars."

• • • **Elite Recommendations:** Listed under this category are suggestions for the buyer who is not primarily concerned with value for the price paid, but who wants to obtain, within reason, coins in high numerical grade categories, coins which are often among the very finest of their kind in existence.

I have limited my discussions to coins grading no higher than MS-65 (and Proof-65), as beyond this I believe that the market has quite a bit of sorting out to do. Right now the market for MS-66, MS-67, and higher coins of earlier dates seems to be mainly with investors or dealers selling to investors. If I perceive that this situation changes in the future, then some future edition of this book (if there is one) may recommend such pieces. MS-66, MS-67, and higher grade coins of modern issues are common and can be included, if you wish, in sets of recent coinage, such as commemoratives issued since 1982. High grade Proofs of recent years, especially 1968 to date, are likewise common.

It would be easy, and certainly a shortcut to having to do research, if I were to state that, for example, for Liberty Head $2.50 pieces of the 1840-1907 year span that a goal of MS-65 is the way to go for the listing under the Elite Recommendations category, but I would be wasting your time. Even if you were the Sultan of Brunei, with a limitless bank account, many issues either do not exist or probably will not be available in MS-65 grade within the next 10 years.

In general, the coins listed under Elite Recommendations are those which a buyer will stand a *reasonable* chance of buying over the next decade. Many of these recommendations would have been put in the Recommendations for the Connoisseur category had this book been written 15 years ago, before the investment emphasis in MS-65 coins, which had its beginning in a large way in the late 1970s.

Even so, now in the early 1990s the formation of high grade collections of certain early series such as colonials, half cents, large cents, early silver, Liberty Seated coins, etc. may well be an astute thing to do, for investors tend to concern themselves with the commoner later issues in the American series and overlook late 18th and early 19th century issues.

In summary, coins listed under Elite Recommendations are wonderful to own, but in certain instances (particularly in series which are very popular with investors) I believe that pieces included under Recommendations for the Connoisseur represent better values for the money. However, especially among the earlier series, if you can afford the tab, the formation of a high grade collection can be a worthwhile pursuit. And, it could be that value for the money spent might not be a consideration for you, any more than someone staying in a $3,000 per night hotel suite may not be concerned with value. There is something to be said for the satisfaction, value considerations aside, of owning the best (or for staying in the most luxurious hotel accommodations, to continue the analogy). If you are in the multimillionaire category, then perhaps recommendations under this category may be just what you want.

I fully realize that many others disagree with my statement that certain MS-65 and finer examples of otherwise common coins are overpriced in the present market. I respect that everyone is entitled to his or her own opinion. It is further to be considered that market conditions will continue to change, and it may be the case that in the future MS-65 and Proof-65 coins will be more reasonably priced than they are now.

I would be remiss if I didn't mention that among early coins choice pieces in really high grades are sufficiently rare that if more than a handful of people tried to put together sets, the result would be extreme frustration for everyone else! For example, if 10 readers of this book were to decide to follow my Elite Recommendations for United States large cents 1793-1857, the result would be gridlock; no one would stand a chance of completing a set within a decade, and each of the 10 buyers would have to be content with obtaining certain of the issues in lower grades than hoped for. If just two (that's right, just two) readers of this book were to decide to put together a set of top-grade Proof gold coins of the 1858-1915 years, of all denominations from the gold dollar to the double eagle, likewise there would not be enough coins to go around.

A Few Words About Investment

The following information is not presented as a series of investment recommendations, but, rather, is given as a synopsis of my ideas as to how to go about intelligently forming a meaningful collection of coins. In the past, selected rare coin collections, particularly those containing pieces in higher grade levels, have been good investments, but there is no guarantee that the trend will continue in the future. What will happen next month or next year or 10 years from now is unknown.

The following considerations are among those which will affect the investment performance of what you buy:

• **Price Paid:** In any given market, it is important to be aware of current values and, with due respect for quality and rarity, to pay reasonable prices.

• **Grades Selected:** In the past, coins in higher grade levels have performed better than well-worn, low-grade coins. However, in any given market, some grade levels, even among high grades, may be overpriced (or underpriced). It is important to study the market before buying.

• **Quality:** I am a stickler for quality, and I suggest that you would to well to follow my footsteps. Use the technical grade of a coin, including coins in slabs, simply as the *starting point* to evaluate a coin. Is it well struck? Is it on a good planchet? Is it lustrous or is it dull? Is it brilliant or is it toned (and if it is toned, is the toning attractive)? Most of all, is the coin aesthetically pleasing? If it is pleasing to you, chances are good that it will be pleasing to someone else in the future. If the coin appears ugly or unattractive to you, then others will probably feel the same way when you later offer it for sale. Quality usually costs a bit more but it is worth it!

• **Coin Market Performance:** If the coin market, or a segment of the coin market, is rising, then coins within that area will probably rise also. If the market is in decline, then even the finest coins may decline (hopefully, temporarily!) also.

• **Popularity:** As the collector is the ultimate consumer for a given coin, the more collectors interested in a given coin or series, the better it will do as an investment. If the popularity of a particular series increases, chances are good that quality coins within that series will increase in value. If the popularity declines, prices may decline also.

• **Outside Considerations:** The national or worldwide economy, the cost of borrowed money, rises and falls in gold and silver prices, political conditions, government regulations, etc. may affect coin values, and it is important to be aware of this.

• **The Key:** The key to all of the above is *knowledge*. The more you study about coins and the coin market, the better you will do in the numismatic marketplace.

CHAPTER TWELVE

Copper and Nickel Coins

Colonial and Early American Coins

The field of colonial and early American coins comprises issues produced in America by various individuals, states, and others prior to the adoption of federal coinage in 1792, coins struck in foreign countries and imported for use in America, and tokens and medals honoring President George Washington. Most of these were struck in copper, but some were produced in silver, pewter, brass, and other metals.

Among pieces struck in the United States, no series is more famous than that of Massachusetts silver, which commenced with the NE (for New England) coinage of 1652 and continued through the Willow Tree, Oak Tree and Pine Tree types made as late as 1682 (but nearly all were dated 1652, for the British crown did not want the colonists to produce coins, thus the fiction was maintained that no pieces were coined after 1652). Struck from hand-engraved dies and using crude equipment, Massachusetts pieces are fascinating to collect.

Higley threepence copper coins were produced by Dr. Samuel Higley and his brother John circa 1737-1739 using native ore taken from a mine near Granby, Connecticut. All Higley pieces are rarities today.

During the period 1785-1788 various states produced copper coins, usually by private contract with various individuals, although Massachusetts operated its own mint (and discontinued it when an audit revealed it cost two cents to produce each one-cent piece!). Issues of Vermont, Connecticut, Massachusetts, New Jersey, and New York are eagerly collected and exist in many die varieties.

Fugio copper cents, minted in 1787, were produced under a contract let by Congress and thus may be the first official United States coins made for general circulation, although the 1776 Continental Currency "dollar," usually seen in pewter but also known in brass and silver, may have been an official government issue, but no documentation has ever been located.

Pieces struck abroad for use in the American colonies include the Rosa Americana issues of 1722-1724, struck by William Wood, acting under a

185

patent from King George I; the 1773 Virginia halfpenny bearing the portrait of George III; circa 1796 Kentucky tokens; and numerous others, including the 1783 and 1785 Nova Constellatio coppers made in Birmingham, England, on the order of Gouverneur Morris, who undertook the distribution as a business venture.

Coins and tokens honoring George Washington have always been popular with collectors. Most bear dates from 1783 to 1795 and were made in England, although several varieties were produced in America.

Sources for information: *The Colonial Newsletter*, published by the Colonial Newsletter Foundation, provides a forum for new discoveries, historical information, and other aspects of early American coins. Books describing die varieties and giving other information include *The State Coinages of New England*, by Henry C. Miller and Hillyer Ryder, which describes Vermont and Massachusetts copper coins by Ryder numbers and Connecticut coppers by Miller numbers; a series of books by Sydney P. Noe describing silver coinage of Massachusetts; *The Fugio Cents*, by Alan Kessler, an expansion of an earlier work by Eric P. Newman; Dr. Edward Maris' *A Historic Sketch of the Coins of New Jersey*; W.S. Baker's *Medallic Portraits of Washington*, originally published in 1885, and recently vastly expanded and updated by Russell Rulau; and one of the finest reference works ever produced for any area of coinage, *The Early Coins of America*, by Sylvester S. Crosby, 1875.

• Budget Recommendations: Build a basic type set of colonial and state coins, beginning with the copper state coins of 1795-1788, to gain familiarity with the discipline of collecting. Select coins in G-4 to F-12 grades.

• • **Recommendations for the Connoisseur:** Build a basic type set of colonial and state coins, beginning with the copper state coins of 1795-1788, to gain familiarity with the discipline of collecting. F-12 to EF-40 grades represent a worthwhile goal. In a few areas, such as the 1722-1724 Wood's Hibernia coinage, the 1773 Virginia halfpenny, etc., MS-60 is attainable.

• • • **Elite Recommendations:** Form a basic type set in the highest grades generally available. These grades will vary from series, so I can make no across-the-board statement. A few examples of realistically obtainable high grades: 1652 Massachusetts Pine tree shilling, AU-55; 1737 Higley threepence, VG-8 to F-12; 1785-6 Vermont "landscape type" copper, EF-40 or better; 1788 Massachusetts 1c, MS-60; 1787 Fugio cent, MS-63. Such a high grade collection is recommended, for investors have not significantly skewed the market for early colonial and state coins, and a high-grade collection put together with care will undoubtedly reward its owner well.

Copper and Nickel Coins

Half Cents (1793-1857)

Early types: Half cents represent the smallest denomination ever produced by the United States government. First struck in 1793, these small copper coins were minted through 1857, but not continuously. Many gaps exist in the series.

The first half cents made their appearance in 1793. These coins, rare today, are of the Liberty Cap type and feature Miss Liberty facing to the observer's left, with a cap on pole behind her head. The motif is taken from the famous Libertas Americana medal struck in France, and was also used on one-cent pieces of the 1793-1796 period (but with Miss Liberty facing right). The denomination is expressed two ways on early half cents; as a fraction, 1/200, and as lettering on the edge: TWO HUNDRED FOR A DOLLAR.

In 1794 the Liberty Cap design was modified, with Miss Liberty facing to the right. The head on 1794 half cents is quite large in proportion to the surrounding field.

This design was continued through 1797, although pieces dated from 1795 onward have Miss Liberty's portrait proportionately smaller than in 1794. Two major rarities were produced during this time, the 1796 with pole to cap and a curious and even rarer 1796 variety in which, due to an engraving error, the pole was omitted.

Half cents of the early years are typically seen in well worn grades. Specimens in preservation from G-4 through F-12 are considered to be quite desirable. Even the advanced numismatist would be pleased with coins grading from VF-20 through AU-50. Uncirculated coins exist for certain issues, but are seen so seldom and are so expensive that collecting them in this level of preservation is not a realistic goal.

Half cents of the 19th century: No half cents were struck bearing the dates 1798 and 1799. In 1800 a new motif, the Draped Bust style, made its appearance and was continued through the year 1808. Particularly scarce is the 1802 half cent. For some reason, nearly all 1802 cents known to exist are in worn grades. A coin in EF-40 preservation would be a major rarity, and no Mint State examples with original color are known to exist. Numerous die varieties were produced in the year 1804, and include such variations as plain 4 (in the final date numeral) and stems to the reverse wreath; plain 4, stemless wreath; crosslet 4, stems to wreath; crosslet 4, stemless wreath; and *Spiked Chin*.

Desirable grades for Draped Bust half cents of the 1800-1808 style are VF-20 upward. Particularly in demand are coins with attractive, glossy surfaces. Uncirculated coins appear on the market from time to time, particularly bearing the dates 1800 and 1804, remnants of hoards which came to light years ago.

In 1809 the Classic Head half cent was introduced, a motif continued through 1836, but with many gaps. One of the most common of all half cent dates, perhaps the single most plentiful issue of the entire denomination, is the 1809. The 1811 is scarce, and the 1831 and 1836 are great rarities. No half cents were produced bearing the dates 1812 through 1824, as there was little demand for them in the channels of commerce, nor were any struck with the dates 1827 or 1830. A curious and readily available variety is the 1828 with just 12 stars on the obverse instead of the correct 13. Apparently an engraver at the Mint was daydreaming and lost track of what he was doing.

Half cents of the 1809-1836 Classic Head type are collectible in all grades, but the advanced collector and investor is apt to prefer EF-40 or better. MS-60 and MS-63 specimens are readily available for certain issues, especially 1828 with 13 obverse stars.

No half cents were struck from 1837 through 1839. In the former year an economic depression later known as the Panic of 1837 swept America, and on May 10th the government stopped paying out coins, and small change was hoarded by the public. Eventually many private businesses, banks, and other enterprises went out of business. Filling the need for circulating coins, numerous merchants and die sinkers distributed countless thousands of tokens. One of these privately minted issues bears on the obverse an eagle, with the date 1837 below. The reverse bears the inscription HALF CENT WORTH OF PURE COPPER. In the 1930s Wayte Raymond, a New York coin dealer and distributor of albums, decided that this half-cent size token would be ideal for inclusion in a half cent album, as it would give collectors the opportunity to add a date which was not represented in the regular half cent series. Thus, the 1837 token was adopted into the series. Today it is one of the few non-federal issues listed in the *Guide Book of United States Coins* among the regular series.

Braided Hair half cents: In 1840 a new motif, the Braided Hair or Coronet type, was introduced. Half cents were not struck for general circulation during most of this decade, and production from 1840 through the first part of 1849 was limited to Proofs made for collectors and for presentation purposes. Today, Proofs of the 1840s are highly prized rarities and sell from several thousand dollars each upward. Around 1858-1860 certain employees of the Mint realized that half cents of the 1840s, and certain earlier dates such as 1831 and 1836, were rarities and could be sold at a premium to collectors, so examples were restruck. A later generation of numismatists was able to differentiate originals from restrikes, noting, for example, that among half cents of the 1840s, originals have larger berries in the reverse wreath than do restrikes.

Beginning in 1849, half cents were again struck for general circulation. Production continued through 1857, with the exception of 1852, when only Proofs were made. Half cents of the Braided Hair type, dated from 1849 through 1857, are usually seen in grades from VF-20 upward. The denomination did not circulate for many years after its discontinuance in 1857, so coins of the Braided Hair style did not have the opportunity to become worn smooth. From the standpoint of the collector and investor, grades from EF-40 through Mint State are quite desirable. As is true with contemporary large cents (1793-1857) as well, condition for half cents often is not as important as surface quality and aesthetic appeal. Most advanced numismatists would prefer a lustrous, glossy AU-50 half cent with sharp design detail, to an MS-63 coin with spotted or blotchy surfaces.

Half cents have attracted the attention of many numismatists over the years. I consider it relevant to mention that James F. Ruddy, a true connoisseur and student of American numismatics (and my business partner for many years, until his retirement in 1977), began his interest in specialized coinage by putting together a date set of half cents. This was in the 1950s, and a highlight of his display was a beautiful 1796 from the King Farouk Collection.

Sources for information: Today, die varieties are classified by two primary references: *Walter Breen's Encyclopedia of United States Half Cents 1793-1857*, written by Walter Breen and published by Jack Collins in 1983; and *American Half Cents—The "Little Half Sisters,"* the second edition of which was published by Roger S. Cohen, Jr. in 1982. Varieties listed by these references are described as B-1, B-2, etc., or C-1, C-2, etc. The Breen book is an immense volume giving a great amount of technical detail, both as to half cent production and to die variety characteristics, while the Cohen reference is written in a more concise and popular style.

The Early American Coppers Club welcomes anyone interested in half cents, large cents, and other early copper series. *Penny Wise*, the magazine of the club, edited by Dr. Harry Salyards, is published several times a year.

• **Budget Recommendations:** Build a type set or date set in the following grade categories: 1793 to 1808, G-4 to VG-8; 1809-1857, F-12 to VF-20. Omit rarities (such as 1796, and possibly even 1793) and Proof-only issues. Select pieces with pleasing surfaces.

• • **Recommendations for the Connoisseur:** Start by building a type set of the various half cent designs. Issues from 1793 to 1797 are good buys in

F-12 to E-45 grades. Later issues from 1800 to 1857 are recommended in EF-40 to MS-60 grades. Proof-only issues are good buys in Proof-63 and Proof-64 categories. In all instances pick pieces with glossy, smooth surfaces.

• • • **Elite Recommendations:** Build a type set or date set in the following grade categories: 1793-1797, AU-50 to MS-60; 1800-1808, MS-63 or better; 1809-1857 MS-63 to MS-65; all of the preceding subject to availability (for example, 1802 is not available in even MS-60 grade, let alone MS-63!); Proof-only issues, Proof-64 or better. Such a high grade collection is recommended, for investors have not significantly skewed the market for early copper coins (indeed, the typical investor would probably be frightened if anyone recommended half cents as an investment!), and a high-grade collection put together with care will undoubtedly reward its owner well.

Large Cents (1793-1857)

An overview: Large copper cents of the 1793-1857 years have attracted a sizable following of enthusiasts ever since coin collecting became popular in the mid-19th century. Today, thousands of collectors pursue this specialty. Many belong to the Early American Coppers Club and attribute the die varieties of their coins to the two major references on the series: *Penny Whimsy*, by Dr. William H. Sheldon, which describes in detail the issues of 1793-1814, and *United States Copper Coins 1816-1857*, by Howard R. Newcomb, which details the later issues.

Among early cents, an outstanding grade for certain varieties might be VF-20 or VF-30. A 1793 cent in either one of these grades is highly desirable and will attract many bids if offered at auction. The charm of worn early cents is difficult to describe to investment oriented readers who are accustomed to buying bright Uncirculated coins in MS-63, MS-65, or some other high level in other series. However, as the popularity of later "investment grade" MS-65 coins in other series fluctuates over a period of time, the popularity of large cents has remained constant. In up markets and down markets there has always been a strong demand whenever a choice collection has been offered for sale. Perhaps one reason for this is that few collectors of large cents buy for investment's sake alone. Thus the pieces are spread over a wide population of serious numismatists, who are not apt to sell them quickly during an economic turndown or if some investment writer reports that they have lost favor.

Dr. Sheldon's commentary: In *Penny Whimsy* Dr. William H. Sheldon discussed the appeal of early cents. His words have been quoted many times, but they bear repeating here:

Copper and Nickel Coins

"One of the remarkable features of American life has been the sustained and almost universal affection shown for the humble copper cent. When the Mint started operations in 1793, cents were the first United States coins struck for circulation. This was at the old Mint building on Seventh Street in Philadelphia, and cents have been issued every year ever since, except during 1815 when an acute scarcity of copper resulted from the second war with England. No other coin was issued with comparable regularity during the early years of the nation, but it is necessary to look beyond mere occurrence of dates to account for the traditional vogue and charm of the 'old coppers.'

"At least three other factors must have contributed:

"First, a relatively great number of cents found their way into circulation. Almost everybody could afford to keep a few, especially bright, new ones. Being too big to swallow, they were safe as well as frugal gifts for infants and young children, and so they have been among the first familiar memories of childhood. Hundreds of thousands of them have been hidden away and forgotten, to be rediscovered and resurrected by rummaging offspring or descendants. Even now, occasional new discoveries of early cents enter the arteries of numismatic distribution. Viewed as a numismatic commodity, cents of early dates are sufficiently numerous to have prevented any individual or group from being able to corner the market and control prices. Early coppers have long been looked upon by coin dealers as the bellwethers of the market, and for a century and a half now they have been the backbone of American numismatics. They are less influenced by depressions and booms than are other coins, are less subject to speculative buying, and in the lower grades of condition, at least, can be obtained in decent numbers by people of slender means. For generations American schoolboys bought, sold, swapped, or swiped old coppers. Some of these boys, especially in old age, have returned to the early enchantment, there to forget or condone the singular incompatibility between human dreams and fulfillments.

"Second, the early coppers are rich in die varieties, cracked dies, imperfect and unusual planchets, misstruck coins, and other minor variations. If one possesses even a rudimentary flair for classification, these coins present a challenge which easily becomes a fascination. Among the cents from 1793 through 1803, the first 11 years of the series, 301 different true varieties are now known.[1] That is to say, coins of these dates are in existence which were struck from 301 different pairs or combinations of obverse and reverse dies. Dates mean but little to the advanced student of cents. It is the die variety that largely determines the rarity and value of the coin.

"In the early days at the Mint the dies were all cut by hand, and a good deal of the personality of the die cutter was likely to find its way into the new die. Moreover the method for hardening steel then in use was ineffective. The new die soon cracked or deteriorated, sometimes in many places, and the resulting coins showed these developing imperfections as ridges, irregular lines, and extra masses of metal on their surfaces. Often coins are found with cracks on both obverse and reverse—both dies were cracked. Die crack variations are not counted as different die varieties, but they are of great interest to collectors, who sometimes are able by means of them to trace the history of a die from the first few coins struck by it, through the whole progression of increasingly severe breaks, until at last it shattered and broke down altogether. Specialists on early cents have a keen eye for die breaks and have made great use of them in establishing, among other things, the probable order of issue of the known varieties of a date. Thus what the lovers of old coins like to call a science of numismatics is gradually built up.

"Third, old copper, like beauty, appears to possess a certain intrinsic quality or charm which for many people is irresistible. An experienced dealer in American numismatic materials recently wrote as follows: 'Sooner or later, if a collector stays at the business long enough, it is three to one his interest in all the other series will flag and he will focus his attention on the early cents.'

"Gold, silver, and even bronze appear to be very much the same wherever you see them. Coins made of these metals become 'old money' and 'interesting,' like the stuff seen in museums, but copper seems to possess an almost living warmth and a personality not encountered in any other metal. The big cent is something more than old money. Look at a handful of the cents dated before 1815, when they contained relatively pure copper. You see rich shades of green, red, brown, yellow, and even deep ebony; together with blendings of these not elsewhere matched in nature save perhaps in autumn leaves. If the light is good (direct sunlight is preferable) you will possibly observe that no two of the coins are of quite the same color.

"Copper oxidizes differently in different atmospheres, and the way it colors and weathers depends also upon the impurities and traces of other metals which it may contain. The copper that went into the early cents must have been of highly variable assay, recruited as it was from almost every possible source. Some came from Sweden, some from England, some was obtained by melting up copper nails, spikes, and copper finishings from wrecked ships (including both British and American men-of-war). Some of it came from kitchen and other household utensils donated or sold to the Mint in response to urgent appeals. George Washington is said to have donated 'an excellent copper tea-kettle as well as two pairs of tongs early in 1793 for the first cents. It is not surprising, therefore, that to some extent the different early die varieties are recognizable by characteristic color and surface texture, as well as by die breaks, peculiarities of the planchets, and so on. Every early cent has a character of its own.

"These three factors—plentifulness of the coins, nearly inexhaustible variation both in number and in condition of the dies, and the intrinsic beauty and variability of old copper—account in part at least for the unique regard in which early copper cents have been held."

Cents and collectors: While large cents have not appealed primarily to the investor, but to the collector, there is no doubt that tremendous investment profits have gone to those who have carefully built up cabinets of large cents and who have held them for a period of years. When Lester Merkin sold the Louis Helfenstein collection at auction in the 1960s, dealers and collectors alike scrambled to pay record prices for large cents, and many pieces which had been held for just a year or two brought more than double or triple the price the owner had paid. Similarly, when Superior Galleries sold the Robinson S. Brown, Jr., collection in 1988, large cents attracted as much attention when they crossed the block as any Morgan silver dollars or other investment series ever did.

Early large cent types and varieties: The first large cents made their appearance in early 1793 and were of the Chain type, so called from a circle of links on the reverse, enclosing the denomination ONE CENT and the fraction 1/100. On what are believed to be the very first issues, the name of our country was abbreviated as UNITED STATES OF AMERI. The obverse depicted Miss Liberty, with flowing hair, facing right. A contemporary newspaper account described the chain device as an ill omen for a country proclaiming its liberty. Perhaps because of this and related sentiments the reverse design was soon changed to a wreath and Miss Liberty's portrait was modified, creating another type. Toward the end of the year 1793 the Liberty Cap device was introduced, a style which was continued through early 1796.

Among early large cents there are numerous die varieties. The year 1794 alone comprises dozens of different variations, some major and some minor. Among the major variations is that described as Sheldon-48, the Starred Reverse, which displays around the reverse rim a series of 94 minute five-pointed stars, placed on the die for reasons unknown today. Another variety of 1794 lacks stem ends to the wreath.

In acquiring early cents, the connoisseur seeks not only high technical grades, but, equally important, coins with attractive planchets and pleasing aesthetic appeal. There are numerous VF-30 1793 large cents, for example, with porous or unattractive surfaces, which, while technically VF-30, do not bring as much in the marketplace as Fine-12 coins of pleasing appearance. Perhaps in more than any other series, technical grade is only a part of the story in valuing early copper cents (and half cents as well).

The Draped Bust motif introduced in 1796, was continued through 1807. A rarity within this date range is the 1799, a coin which is highly prized in all states of preservation. Similarly, the 1804 is elusive.

The Classic Head motif was first used in 1808 and was continued through 1814. All are readily collectible, although the 1809 is considered to be slightly scarcer than certain others. Classic Head cents are obtainable in higher grades such as VF-30, EF-40, AU-50, and even occasionally in Mint State. Many of them were struck on dark planchets due to the quality of the copper used.

Later date large cents: A new style of cent design, the Coronet type, was introduced in 1816 and was continued through 1835, at which time it was modified slightly. Several other modifications took placed through 1839, in which year the Braided Hair or Petite Head was introduced, a style continued through the end of the series in 1857.

Among later-date large cents of the 1816-1857 years, the scarcest date is 1823, followed by 1821. Toward the end of the series the 1857 is considered to be elusive, although not necessarily expensive. As might be expected, cents of the later dates are more readily available in higher grades than are earlier ones. Coins from the 1840s onward are regularly seen in Mint State, usually with light to medium brown surfaces. Examples with full fiery original mint red are scarce, especially if they are dated prior to 1850.

Many numismatists have made a specialty of collecting one of each date and major variety from 1816 through 1857. Among the more interesting varieties are the 1817 with 15 (instead of the normal 13) obverse stars, and the curiously-named 1839 *Silly Head* and *Booby Head* pieces. Just why these were so named is not known, but this nomenclature was in use as far back as the early 1860s. There are no impossible rarities among dates and major varieties in the 1816-1857 span, and a set in a grade such as EF-40, if gathered with care, can form a beautiful and very appealing exhibit.

• **Budget Recommendations:** Build a type set or date set with the early issues 1793-1814 in G-4 to VG-8 grade and the later issues 1816-1857 in F-12 to VF-20 preservation. Such rare dates as 1793 and 1799 may be obtained in AG-3 grade, and for the later scarce dates, 1821 and 1823, VG-8 is a possibility. Select coins with attractive surfaces.

• • **Recommendations for the Connoisseur:** Start by building a type set of large cent designs 1793-1857. Cents of 1793 are good values in F-12 to EF-45 grades, pieces dated 1794-1814 are worth buying in VF-20 to EF-45 grades, and dates of the 1816-1857 era are recommended in EF-40 to MS-60. Especially recommended are issues dated from 1821 to 1834 in EF to MS-60; most of these are very undervalued. Once you build a type set, it is an easy matter to expand your interest to include dates and major varieties. In all instances, pick pieces with pleasing surface characteristics.

• • • **Elite Recommendations:** Build a type cent of cents to gain familiarity with the series, then expand to a date and major variety set. Buy early issues 1793-1798 in AU-50 or better grade, as available; 1799 in VF-30 or better grade; 1800-1814 MS-63 or so, as available; 1816-1820, the Randall Hoard years, MS-65; 1821 and 1823 MS-60 (if you can find them; otherwise EF-45 or better; 1821 is somewhat less of a challenge than 1823); other issues 1822-1839, MS-63 or better; 1840-1857 MS-64 or better. Such a high grade collection is recommended, for investors have not significantly skewed the market for early copper coins (with the possible exception of MS-65 red large cents of later dates), and a high-grade collection put together with care will undoubtedly reward its owner well. Among Uncirculated cents I personally prefer glossy brown pieces to those with mottled red and brown surfaces—a nice situation, for they are also less expensive than red and brown ones!

Flying Eagle Cents (1856-1858)

Although large cents were produced in larger than ever quantities in the 1850s, they were becoming expensive to make, and the Mint sought to create a substitute. In that decade experiments were made to create a smaller, more convenient coin, finally culminating in 1856 with the production of the Flying Eagle cent. In that year 600 or more patterns were produced of the new cent, of a much smaller diameter, and struck in copper-nickel alloy, composed of 88 parts copper and 10 parts nickel. The work of James B. Longacre, the 1856 Flying Eagle cent was not an original design in any sense of the term. The obverse motif was taken from Christian Gobrecht's flying eagle first used on silver dollars of 1836, and the reverse, with a wreath composed of corn, cotton, and tobacco, was lifted from that used on Longacre's gold dollars and $3 pieces of 1854.

Patterns of the new design were given to congressmen, newspaper editors, and others of influence. In February 1857 the Flying Eagle cent became a reality when it was officially adopted as the new standard. Coins of this design were made for general circulation in 1857 and 1858. The motif presented difficulties in striking, particularly with regard to the head and tail of the eagle on the obverse. The heavy wreath on the reverse caused metal flow into the recesses of the die, thus taking metal away from that needed to fill up the deeper areas of the eagle motif on the obverse. Weak striking resulted.

The Mint realized that the 1856 Flying Eagle cent was becoming popular with collectors, due to its scarcity, so around 1858-1860, large numbers of them were restruck, perhaps somewhere between 1,200 and 1,800 additional pieces, all with Proof finish.

Mint officials were interested in restriking for two reasons: First, but possibly not foremost, was in connection with the expansion of the Mint Cabinet, the official collection formed at the Mint beginning in 1838. From time to time the Mint would restrike earlier issues, or create special varieties to exchange with collectors in order to acquire pieces desired for the Mint Cabinet. Probably more important was the profit motive. Favored insiders at the Mint sold 1856 Flying Eagle cents, 1804 silver dollars, and other specially made pieces to dealers and collectors. This was done secretly for private profit. Sometimes Mint officials went to great lengths to deny that such things were going on, but the evidence of commercial transactions weighed against them. Historian Don Taxay, in his book *U.S. Mint and Coinage*, called the Mint at that time "a workshop for their gain," a reference to illegal profits made by officials and others who worked at the institution.

Soon after its initial coinage the 1856 Flying Eagle cent became known as a key American rarity. Today, probably about 1,500 pieces are known, primarily Proof restrikes. Most originals were produced with Uncirculated or business strike surfaces and today are considerably scarcer than Proofs. No price differentiation is made between restrikes and originals in the marketplace.

• **Budget Recommendations:** Buy the 1857 and 1858 issues in G-4 to VG-8 grades.

• • **Recommendations for the Connoisseur:** If you want a true American numismatic classic, the 1856 Flying Eagle cent is a good buy in MS-63 and MS-64 grades or in Proof-63 and Proof-64 preservation. Most pieces you will be offered will have dingy surfaces. Take your time and pick a nice one! For 1857-1858 cents I recommend MS-63 and MS-64 as well. MS-65 coins are wonderful, but they cost many multiples of the MS-64 level, and I am not sure they are worth it. However, if money is no object, go ahead.

• • • **Elite Recommendations:** Buy the 1856 Flying Eagle in MS-65 grade (very rare) or Proof-65 (easier to find, but still elusive), picking pieces with excellent aesthetic appeal. MS-65 is a good goal for the 1857 and 1858 varieties. Proofs of the 1857 and 1858 years are extremely rare; fewer than two dozen 1857 Proofs are known and fewer than 50 dated 1858.

Indian Cents (1859-1909)

In 1859 a new cent design made its debut, the Indian type. A laurel wreath was used on the reverse this year, but in 1860 it was replaced with an oak wreath surmounted by a shield. Indian cents minted from 1859 through 1864 were struck in copper-nickel alloy similar to that used for Flying Eagle cents.

In beginning of the summer of 1862, a time when the outcome of the Civil War was uncertain, citizens hoarded coins of all descriptions, and before long copper-nickel Flying Eagle and Indian cents were scarcely to be seen. Filling a need for everyday pocket change, merchants and others distributed millions of cent-size tokens, mostly made in bronze (an alloy of copper, zinc, and tin). Mint officials took note of the popularity of these thin bronze cents and began experiments of their own. In 1864, after a number of copper-nickel cents had been struck bearing that year's date, the official standard was changed to bronze and the authorized weight was lowered. The bronze standard was used until the end of the Indian cents in 1909 and was continued in the Lincoln cent series until 1982.

Among Indian cents of the 1859-1909 era, the most desired date is the 1877, followed by 1872, 1871, and a variety of 1864 with L (the initial of the designer, Longacre) on the headdress ribbon. Toward the end of the series, Indian cents were struck at a branch mint for the first time. 1908-S and 1909-S Indian cents are both prized today, with the 1909-S being considerably scarcer.

Indian cents were high on the list of popular American series until the mid-1960s, when several dealers made a practice of artificially treating Extremely Fine and AU pieces to make them appear to be Uncirculated. Offered at bargain prices to the unwary, such "Uncirculated" coins found a ready market. Later, as collectors discovered the deception, there was much disillusionment. As methods of treating and processing coins became more sophisticated, more and more Indian cents were artificially colored. As a result, since the mid-1960s Indian cents have attracted a much smaller following. Today it takes an experienced buyer to tell original toning from artificial, and as if that were not enough, coins with original surfaces are few and far between.

For the patient, knowledgeable collector the formation of a set of high grade Indian cent can be a fascinating challenge and, when completed, will constitute a beautiful display. However, forming such will require a great amount of work, and no small degree of frustration, for even slabbed MS-63 and finer coins often have poor aesthetic appeal. Forming a nice set of Indian cents does not have to be an expensive undertaking. Not to be overlooked is the pleasure, low cost, and numismatic satisfaction of assembling a set of Indian cents in nicely matched EF-40 or AU-50 grade. This also will require some effort but not a great deal of expense.

Interestingly, prices for high grade Indian cents are not much higher now than they were 15 years ago, an anomalous situation caused by damage done to the market by the cleaning and artificial toning referred to earlier.

• **Budget Recommendations:** Build a nicely-matched circulated set, with the issues 1858-1878 in G-4 to VG-8 grade, and the later issues VF-20. The scarce 1908-S and 1909-S may be acquired in F-12 grade. A "short set" of Philadelphia Mint cents 1879-1909 in EF-40 grade is inexpensive, beautiful, and satisfying to own.

• • **Recommendations for the Connoisseur:** Issues 1859-1878 in EF to MS-60 grades are recommended for the budget-minded collector. MS-63 and MS-64 are suggested for the connoisseur who wants a good value. MS-65 is ideal for the connoisseur as well, for MS-65 coins today are cheaper in many instances than they were 15 years ago! Proof-63 to Proof-65 coins are good buys as well. Among cents 1879-1909 I recommend MS-60 to MS-64 for the budget-minded buyer, and MS-65 for the buyer with more money to spend. Proof-63 to Proof-65 coins are good values as well. Caveat: Be sure to buy coins that have not been cleaned, coins without spots, coins with evenly-toned, aesthetically pleasing surfaces. For my money, I would rather have a nice glossy brown EF-45 1877 Indian cent than a spotty Proof-63! Be fussy!

• • • **Elite Recommendations:** Take your choice of either MS-65 or Proof-65, and of a color objective (such as brown, nicely blended red and brown, or red), and then build a matched set in that category. If you elect to buy Proofs, you may have to acquire the 1864-L in MS-65 grade (for fewer than 20 Proofs are known) and the 1908-S and 1909-S likewise MS-65 (as no Proofs were made of branch mint issues). Observe the caveat mentioned above. Such a set does indeed have excellent investment possibilities, in my opinion, for Indian cents have been overlooked in recent years.

Lincoln Cents (1909 to Date)

In the summer of 1909 the Lincoln cent made its first appearance in circulation. The earliest pieces bore on the reverse the initials V.D.B., for the engraver, Victor David Brenner. A popular rarity was created during the first year of the Lincoln cent, the 1909-S with V.D.B. on the reverse. Just 484,000 were struck.

Copper and Nickel Coins

As time progressed, Lincoln cents were produced at the Denver Mint as well. The series continued more or less regularly, until 1922, when coins were struck only at the Denver Mint. However, some Denver Mint issues had the D mintmark clogged or worn away in the dies, creating a mintmarkless piece which has been designated the 1922 "plain." Choice Uncirculated examples are worth many thousands of dollars, an interesting instance of a high price being paid for a poorly struck, defective coin!

Uncirculated Lincoln cents were set aside in quantity during the first year of issue, 1909, but after that they were generally ignored, except for a small band of collectors who acquired them by date and mintmark varieties. Beginning in the mid-1920s, saving coins in bank wrapped rolls became popular, and from then onward Uncirculated pieces were set aside in larger quantities. Beginning in the early 1930s, roll hoarding became a passion, and from that point in time very large quantities were saved. During the same decade "penny boards," consisting of cardboard sheets with openings for Lincoln cents and other coin varieties, were distributed by several individuals and firms, including the Whitman Publishing Company. The widespread availability of these low cost panels spurred the collecting of Lincoln cents by dates and mintmarks, and certain earlier issues became the object of desire of countless thousands of Americans who dreamed of finding valuable 1909-S V.D.B., 1914-D, and other scarce Lincoln cents in circulation.

Among interesting and significant Lincoln cent varieties produced since 1909 are the scarce 1909-S V.D.B. and 1914-D earlier noted, the curious 1922 plain, the low-mintage 1931-S, and the inexpensive issues of 1943, the latter being struck in zinc-coated steel to alleviate a war time shortage of copper.

In 1955 an obverse die was double punched at the Philadelphia Mint, causing coins struck from that die to have blurred lettering. Known as the 1955 Doubled Die cent, the issue was produced to the extent of about 24,000 pieces, most of which were released into circulation in Upstate New York and Massachusetts. From the outset the variety was recognized as scarce, and today an MS-65 coin is worth several thousand dollars.

In 1959 the reverse of the Lincoln cent was redesigned by mint engraver Frank Gasparro, and a motif featuring the Lincoln Memorial was substituted in place of the former wreath. In 1960 nationwide attention was caused when it was discovered that certain varieties of the year had the date figures in smaller numerals. Today it is believed that only four million 1960 Small Date cents were produced, from a total production of over 586 million coins.

As recently as the early 1960s, Lincoln cents were the most popular series on the American coin collecting scene. However, since that time interest has faded, and today relatively few people aspire to acquire one of each date and mintmark variety from 1909 onward. In Uncirculated grade, especially with attractive mint color, examples of the branch mint (Denver and San Francisco) issues from 1910 through 1924 are fairly difficult to locate, and some are exceedingly scarce, despite modest catalogue valuations. Many branch mint issues 1915-1925 are weakly struck. Dr. Sol Taylor, who has specialized in the study of Lincoln cents for many years, has written extensively on the challenges of collecting early issues.

As is the case with Indian cents, many AU and lower grade Uncirculated Lincoln cents have been cleaned or processed to make them appear in higher grades, so the buyer is cautioned to be wary. Lincoln cents after 1930 are plentiful in Uncirculated grades. Most of them sell for relatively low values, so forming a set of them, especially of selected pieces, will take some time and patience, simply because most dealers do not want to be bothered handling coins which are worth a few dollars each, or less. Later date cents are most conveniently purchased in sets, such as a collection from 1934 to date or a collection of the Memorial reverse from 1959 to date.

• **Budget Recommendations:** Build a set of date and mintmark varieties 1909-1931 in G-4 to VG-8 grade and later dates EF-40 or better. You can find recent issues in pocket change.

• • **Recommendations for the Connoisseur:** Issues from 1909 to 1930, MS-60 to MS-64, are good buys, although MS-65 coins are great, too, and in this series are *not* overpriced. Issues from 1931 onward are best acquired in MS-65 grade. Caveat: Pick only pieces with evenly toned or evenly brilliant surfaces. Avoid spotted, cleaned, and discolored coins (which are plentiful on the market). Among early mintmarks, select sharply struck coins. Most people don't bother checking the strikes, so you can often get a better coin for the same amount of money.

• • • **Elite Recommendations:** Build a set of date and mintmark varieties 1909 onward in MS-65 grade with brilliant, red surfaces, undipped and uncleaned (this will take some doing, and you will have to be picky!). Pick sharp strikes, which are especially hard to find among certain Denver and San Francisco issues circa 1915-1925.

Two-Cent Pieces (1864-1873)

Two-cent pieces first appeared in 1864 and were made as an answer to the lack of government coins in circulation in an era in which the public engaged in widespread hoarding. The outlook for the new denomination was optimistic, and in the first year over 19 million were struck. However, two-cent pieces proved to be unpopular, and in 1865 the production dropped to 13 million, then to three million in 1866, declining steadily until a low of just 65,000 coins was reached in 1872, at which time production for circulation was discontinued. A thousand or more Proofs were made for collectors in 1873, after which two-cent pieces were no more.

There are no great rarities within the two-cent piece series, although a variety of 1864 with IN GOD WE TRUST in slightly smaller letters, known as the Small Motto issue, is elusive, particularly in higher grades, and the Proof-only 1873 is difficult to find. As is the case with Indian and early Lincoln cents, many higher grade two-cent pieces seen on the market today have been cleaned, artificially toned, or otherwise processed. Pristine pieces with full or nearly full original mint color or decidedly difficult to locate, as are pristine Proofs.

Forming a set of high-grade two-cent pieces will require time and patience. The greatest demand for two-cent pieces is on the part of the type collector, who desires but a single example of the 1864-1873 type to illustrate the denomination. For this purpose a relatively common issue such as 1864 Large Motto or 1865 will serve the purpose well, although there is something to be said for acquiring a scarcer issue, such as one dated from 1866 through 1871, for these cost only slightly more than the first two dates in the series.

• **Budget Recommendations:** Build a set 1864-1872 in G-4 to VG-8 grade. The rare 1873 can either be omitted, or you can purchase one in impaired Proof grade.

• • **Recommendations for the Connoisseur:** MS-60 to MS-64 coins are especially good values as are Proof-63 and Proof-64 issues. Caveat: Pick evenly toned or evenly brilliant coins. Avoid spotted, discolored, cleaned, etc. coins. Buying nice two-cent pieces will require some effort, but the reward is worth it.

• • • **Elite Recommendations:** Take your choice of MS-65 or Proof-65 and build a matched set with red surfaces. Pick undipped, uncleaned coins with excellent aesthetic appeal. Get set for a lot of hard work, for such coins are few and far between.

Nickel Three-Cent Pieces (1865-1889)

In the United States series, nickel three-cent pieces, minted from 1865 through 1889, are unusual inasmuch as only one design was produced over a relatively long span of years. Mintage was continuous, although in the years

1877, 1878, and 1886 no specimens were struck for commerce, and examples were limited to Proofs made to be sold at a premium to collectors.

There are no great rarities in the nickel three-cent piece series, although the 1877 and 1878, are elusive. In addition to the regular date sequence, there is a variety which is included in the set, the 1887/6, which is an interesting example of an overdate in Proof grade (most overdates in other series are found among business strikes).

In general, business strikes are apt to show areas of weak striking, particularly on the reverse denomination (which is expressed as the Roman numeral III). The denticles (toothlike border segments) on the obverse and reverse are sometimes indistinct, even on Proofs. Forming a set of MS-65 business strikes from 1865 onward will require years of patience, for some dates are truly elusive. The gap is filled nicely by Proofs which were made in reasonable quantities from beginning to end. The first year of issue, 1865, is the scarcest Proof variety in the series, for the nickel three-cent denomination was not produced until later in the 1865 year, by which time many Proof sets lacking this denomination had been sold to collectors. Relatively few took the time to contact the Mint to acquire the extra piece when it became available.

Proofs of the earlier years, 1865 through 1876, are considerably scarcer than those of the later period. However, the later pieces are in greater demand, for toward the end of the series very few business strikes were minted, and thus overall mintages—a combination of Proofs plus business strikes—tended to be considerably lower. Nothing increases demand more than having a low mintage figure published in the *Guide Book of U.S. Coins*.

The nickel three-cent piece met the same fate as the two-cent piece. At the beginning the outlook was optimistic, and 11 million were produced for circulation. They did not catch on as well as expected, and production declined sharply to fewer than five million the next year, fewer than four million the next year, and so on. Finally, in 1889, the denomination was discontinued.

• **Budget Recommendations:** Build a set of dates 1865-1889, with 1865-1876, 1881, 1888, and 1889 in G-4 to G-8 grade, and the others in the lowest grades (down to G-4) you can find, which will probably be VF-20 to EF-40. For some of the dates of 1877 to 1887 span Proofs are more common than EF-40 coins!

• • **Recommendations for the Connoisseur:** For those who can afford it, the formation of a set of Proofs from 1865 through 1889 offers an interesting challenge. I recommend issues in Proof-63 to Proof-65. Avoid spotted or rubbed pieces.

• • • **Elite Recommendations:** Assemble a set of Proof-65 coins, nicely matched and with pleasing surfaces, from 1865 to 1889.

Shield Nickels (1866-1883)

Like the two-cent piece and nickel three-cent piece, the nickel five-cent piece was introduced during the Civil War era (actually a year after the Civil War in the present instance) to supply coins for circulation in a time when silver pieces continued to be hoarded. Unlike its smaller denomination counterparts, the nickel five-cent piece proved popular, and "nickels" are still produced in large quantities today.

The first nickel five-cent pieces produced were of the Shield type and display on the obverse a motif somewhat similar to that used on the two-cent piece—an ornamented shield. The reverse shows a circle of stars with the inscription UNITED STATES OF AMERICA around, the numeral 5 at the center, and the inscription CENTS below. All issues of 1866 and some of 1867 have rays or bars between the stars. Later 1867 issues and all others of the Shield type through 1883, lack the rays.

Production of Shield nickels was continuous. Business strikes were produced for all years 1866-1883 except in 1877 and 1878, when mintages were limited to Proofs for collectors. Among surviving business strikes today, sharp examples are scarce, particularly of the earlier dates, and especially for the first year of issue, 1866, which is typically poorly defined. The hardness of the nickel alloy caused fast die wear and frequent breakage, and it is not at all unusual to see numerous die breaks on the obverse and reverse of a typical specimen.

Proof Shield nickels were struck with more care than business strikes, and most Proofs have excellent definition of detail, although the fields can be somewhat grainy, especially on pieces produced toward the end of the series.

Interesting varieties among Shield nickels include the scarce 1867 With Rays, which is a major rarity with Proof finish, the 1873 with large over small 3 in date, and the 1879/8 overdate (which exists only in Proof condition and which is two or three times scarcer than a regular date 1879 Proof), and the 1883/2 overdate.

• **Budget Recommendations:** Build a date set 1866-1883 in G-4 to VG-8 grade. If you include the Proof-only 1877 and 1878 years, buy impaired Proofs.

• • **Recommendations for the Connoisseur:** MS-63 and MS-64, Proof-63 and Proof-64 coins are good buys. Select pieces with excellent aesthetic appeal. An attractive Proof-63 Shield nickel can be more pleasing that a stained Proof-65. In MS-63 and MS-64 grades the 1867 With Rays nickel is especially undervalued.

• • • **Elite Recommendations:** Pick either MS-65 or Proof-65 and build a nicely matched date set. The MS-65 set will be quite a challenge, especially if you pick sharply struck coins. The Proof 1867 With Rays is a major rarity in a complete Proof set.

Liberty Head Nickels (1883-1913)

In 1883 the Liberty Head nickel made its appearance. Designed by Charles E. Barber, the first pieces struck had the denomination on the reverse expressed simply by the Roman numeral V. Unscrupulous individuals gold plated them and passed them off as $5 gold pieces of similar diameter. The government realized its mistake, and the design was corrected to add the word CENTS below the V. A popular speculation arose when the design error was publicized, and 1883 without CENTS nickels were hoarded in large quantities, a situation which resulted in their being common to this day.

From late 1883 through 1912, Liberty nickels with CENTS were minted continuously, both as Proofs and business strikes. A rarity was created in 1885, when the business strike mintage dropped to slightly over 1.4 million, a tiny fraction of what it had been in earlier years. The next year, 1886, saw a production of only 3.3 million, thus also creating a scarce issue. In 1912, Liberty nickels were struck at branch mints for the first time. The 1912-D and 1912-S were both produced in relatively low quantities for the period, with the 1912-S registering just 238,000 coins.

As Proofs were made continuously for collectors, numismatists desiring top grade specimens today can obtain Proof examples without difficulty, although Proof-64 and Proof-65 pieces are scarcer than lower grades and may take some time to find, especially if pieces with a high degree of aesthetic appeal are desired. Business strikes are also readily available for most issues, with dates from 1897 through 1912 being the easiest to find. Among earlier issues, the 1885 and 1886 in MS-65 grade are quite rare, much more so than with Proof finish. Veteran dealer Abe Kosoff once told me that he had spent several *years* looking for a nice Uncirculated 1891 nickel, a coin with a relatively high mintage. Whether his experience is indicative of the true scarcity of this variety, or whether he simply didn't look in the right place, I don't know, but the situation does illustrate that putting together a set of top grade business strikes can be a challenge.

Mention is also made of the 1913 Liberty head nickel, a coin produced under undocumented circumstances, probably by Samuel W. Brown, an employee of the Mint in 1913. In 1920 Samuel Brown displayed five 1913 Liberty head nickels at the annual convention of the American Numismatic Association. Prior to this, collectors did not know of the existence of the issue, although Brown sought to cover his tracks by running advertisements to *buy* such pieces in 1919. Whether the production was limited to just five coins, or whether more were made, will never be known. It is believed that just five exist. One of these, valued at the best part of a million dollars, was donated to the American Numismatic Association by Aubrey Bebee. Another coin was donated to the Smithsonian Institution by the Norweb family, in a transaction in which I had a part in the 1970s. A third coin was sold by Superior Galleries in 1985 for $385,000 and was purchased by Reed Hawn, a Texas financier and numismatist, who later proudly displayed it with another rarity in his collection, and 1804 silver dollar. The fourth coin is in the Eliasberg Collection, while the fifth is believed to be owned by the Reynolds family in North Carolina.

The fame of the 1913 Liberty nickel can be laid at the doorstep of Fort Worth, Texas dealer B. Max Mehl, who for many years offered to pay $500 for a specimen. It is reported that transit companies had a big problem when streetcar and trolley conductors slowed down their operations to examine the date on each Liberty nickel offered as a fare! Not a single 1913 Liberty head nickel ever turned up in pocket change, for no pieces were put into circulation to begin with, but the publicity helped B. Max Mehl sell countless thousands of his *Star Rare Coin Encyclopedia* premium guide books.

• **Budget Recommendations:** Build a set 1883-1912 in G-4 to VG-8 grade.

• • **Recommendations for the Connoisseur:** Form a nicely matched collection 1883-1912 in MS-63 to MS-64 or Proof-63 to Proof-64 grade. Select coins with excellent aesthetic appeal. A little secret (which also applies to Proof nickel three-cent pieces): A set of Proof-63 Liberty nickels purchased today will cost you less than half of what a similar set would have cost 10 years ago!

• • • **Elite Recommendations:** Pick either MS-65 or Proof-65 and assemble a nicely matched set.

Buffalo Nickels (1913-1938)

In 1913 the nickel five-cent piece was redesigned, and James E. Fraser's Indian motif took the place of the Liberty issue. The obverse featured the portrait of an American Indian, while the reverse showed a standing bison. In popular parlance the issue became known as the Buffalo nickel.

Two main design types were produced of the Buffalo nickel, the first being limited to early 1913 issues with the buffalo (bison) standing on a raised mound and the second, with the buffalo standing on a plain or a line, employed on all later issues through the end of the series in 1938. It proved difficult for the various mints to strike Buffalo nickels with sharp detail, as the design was in high relief, and many pieces seen today, particularly those struck at the Denver Mint in the mid-1920s, are apt to be poorly defined on the higher spots.

The sculpted appearance of Buffalo nickels and their irregular surfaces combine to make grading difficult, and nowhere else in numismatics are grading opinions apt to differ more widely than in the Buffalo series. Before embarking on a collection of Buffalo nickels I recommend studying many pieces and gaining acquaintance with grading and differences in striking sharpness.

All Buffalo nickels minted from 1913 through 1938 are available, although in high grades a number of the branch mint issues, especially of the decade 1915-1925, are rare. The key issue in the series is an overdate, 1918/7-D, of which only a handful exist in Mint State. Even well worn coins are rare. In sharply struck MS-65 grade the 1926-D is a major rarity, although in weakly struck MS-65 preservation it is common.

Toward the end of the series two curious varieties were produced. The first is the 3 Legged issue, which has the front leg of the buffalo missing, due to the grinding down or resurfacing of a production die. The second is the 1938-D/S, with a D mintmark over a previous S. In the year 1938 it was recognized that the Buffalo nickel would be discontinued, and it was also known that no pieces would be struck that year at the San Francisco Mint. Some reverse dies with S mintmarks had been made earlier at the Philadelphia Mint (where all dies or branch mints are produced), and it was decided not to waste them. D mintmarks were stamped over the previous S mintmarks, and the dies were shipped to Denver to create 1938-D/S nickels. Not until 1961 did collectors notice that such an "overmintmark" had been created, for the undertype S had not been noticed!

• **Budget Recommendations:** Build a set of dates and mintmarks 1913-1931 in G-4 to VG-8 grade, with later dates 1934-1938 in VF-20 preservation.

• • **Recommendations for the Connoisseur:** Form a set 1913-1938 in nicely matched MS-63 to MS-64 grade, selecting *sharply struck* pieces (which will take some doing, as slabbed coins are not marked as to the quality of strike;

you will have to cherrypick). You will find that the mintmarked issues from 1914 to 1926, and especially 1918-1926, are hard to find and that the Denver Mint coins in particular are hard to find sharply struck (it may take a year or two to find a 1926-D that is sharp!). Common in Uncirculated grades are issues 1931-1938, as these were saved in roll quantities. Most common of all is 1938-D.

• • • **Elite Recommendations:** Build a set 1913-1938 in MS-65 grade, sharply struck. The 1918/7-D overdate is virtually unobtainable in Mint State, so any piece MS-60 or finer will be worthwhile; you may not live long enough to find a true MS-65.

Jefferson Nickels (1938 to Date)

In 1938 the government announced a competition to redesign the nickel, and some 390 artists applied. The winner was Felix Schlag, who created an obverse design of Thomas Jefferson, based on a bust sculpted by Jean Antoine Houdon. For the reverse he suggested an angular view of Monticello, Jefferson's home. The Treasury Department rejected the reverse and substituted another design, but the obverse was utilized more or less as submitted.

Jefferson nickels have been produced continuously since 1938. Many people have completed sets of Jefferson nickels, and in Uncirculated grades this can be accomplished with relative ease. However, sharply struck Jefferson nickels are another thing entirely. Numerous business strike issues of otherwise common dates are very rare with all details sharply defined. The specialist uses the steps on the front of Monticello as a guide to sharpness. To qualify as an exceptional coin, all of the steps must be clear.

• **Budget Recommendations:** Build a set in F-12 or better grade. Recent issues can be picked from circulation.

• • **Recommendations for the Connoisseur:** Forming a *sharply struck* (with fully struck steps on Monticello) date and mintmark collection can be a great challenge, although not much money is involved. You might as well go for MS-65.

• • • **Elite Recommendations:** Same as the preceding.

CHAPTER THIRTEEN

Silver Coins

Silver Three-Cent Pieces (1851-1873)

In 1851 the silver three-cent piece made its appearance and became the smallest silver piece ever to be produced by the United States. The denomination, officially called a trime (but few collectors have ever used the term), was intended to facilitate the purchase of three-cent stamps at the post office. Although production quantities were generous during the first several years of production the three-cent piece soon fell out of favor, and after the Civil War few were produced (except Proofs for collectors), although the denomination did not expire until 1873.

Silver three-cent pieces were produced in three varieties. The first, struck from 1851 to 1853, bears on the obverse a plain six-pointed star. The second variety, produced from 1854 through 1858, has three lines bordering the star, while the third type, produced from 1859 through 1873, has two outlines. Pieces made from 1854 onward have an olive branch over the denomination III on the reverse and a bundle of three arrows below it. Trimes of the first type, 1851-1853, are composed of .750 silver and .250 copper, an alloy not used elsewhere in American coinage. Beginning in 1854 the alloy was changed to .900 silver and .100 copper, the standard used on other silver denominations.

In general, silver three-cent pieces of the type I style (1851-1853) are readily available in Mint State, although MS-65 pieces may prove elusive. This type contains the only variety struck at a branch mint: the 1851-O, which in higher grades is elusive. During the period 1851-1853 over 35 million coins were produced, thus accounting for their availability today.

By contrast, the total mintage of the 1854-1858 type II style amounted to less than five million pieces. Most examples of the type II design are lightly struck, especially around the border lettering on the obverse. The Mint had a great deal of difficulty in making the revised motif strike up sharply, and this is why after 1858 the design was again modified. Striking sharpness was not a problem later. Type II pieces are very elusive in high grades, and MS-63, MS-64, and MS-65 coins, especially if well struck, are considered rare. Some Proofs were struck for collectors, but not more than a few dozen each year until

1858, when 80 were produced. Proofs are occasionally seen and may fill the bill for the numismatist looking for high grade examples.

Although fewer than two million business strikes were produced of the type III style (1859-1863) Proof mintages were adequate, and today a minimum of several hundred Proofs exist for each date within that range. Numismatists desiring high grade examples can obtain Proofs without difficulty. Business strikes are readily available for certain early dates of the type, especially 1860-1862, but later business strikes are rare, especially after 1864. As an illustration of this rarity, I point to the 1872, of which 1,000 business strikes and 950 Proofs were minted. All of the Proofs were sold to collectors, who specifically saved them. The business strikes were either melted or released in the channels of commerce, and the survival of high grade pieces is strictly a matter of chance. Probably 500 to 700 of the 950 Proofs struck still exist today, whereas of the business strikes, I doubt if more than a dozen or two Mint State coins could be found, and even this estimate may be on the high side.

Why aren't business strikes priced at many multiples of the Proof price? The answer to this is simple: many collectors consider Proofs to be a *better* grade than Mint State, so they are satisfied with the Proofs. In reality, Proofs represent a *different* (not better, but different) finish than business strikes, and each should be evaluated separately. However, this probably will never happen, and while enlightened specialists may pay a small premium over the Proof price in order to acquire a business strike, I doubt if any business strikes from this era will ever emerge as rarities worth many multiples of the Proof valuations.

  • **Budget Recommendations:** Build a set of the 1851-1858 years, covering types I and II, in G-4 to VG-8 grade. Trimes of the 1859-1873 years are usually available only in higher grades, as later issued did not circulate extensively. Buy the lowest grades you can, down to G-4. However, for the years 1859-1862 most pieces on the market are at least VF-20, and for the issues 1863-1873 you may have to acquire EF-40 or better coins, including impaired Proofs.

  • • **Recommendations for the Connoisseur:** I suggest buying a trio to illustrate the various design types, 1851-1853, 1854-1858, and 1859-1873, in MS-63 to MS-64 grades. If you want to cherrypick some rarities, go for pieces dated 1854-1858, *sharply struck*, and buy all you can (you won't be able to buy many). If you want to form a complete date set, then MS-63 to MS-64 is a good objective for the dates 1851-1858, and Proof-63 to Proof-64 for the issues from 1859 to 1873.

• • • **Elite Recommendations**: Build a set of 1851-1858 coins in MS-65 grade, sharply struck (quite a challenge for the 1854-1858 years), and 1859-1873 coins Proof-65.

The 1792 Half Disme

Half dimes, called half *dismes* at the time, were first minted for circulation in 1792. In that year some 1,500 to 2,000 were produced. The Philadelphia Mint was not ready for commercial coin production, so 1792 half dismes are believed to have been struck in the cellar of John Harper, a Philadelphia saw maker who had connections to the Mint. In his December 4, 1792 presidential message George Washington mentioned that a beginning in United States coinage had been made with such pieces, due to the need for coins in circulation. Today many consider the 1792 half disme to be a pattern coin, but such students of the series as Harold P. Newlin and Daniel W. Valentine each made strong cases for it to be included in the regular series.[1]

The design of the 1792 half disme closely follows certain patterns of the year. The obverse depicts Miss Liberty facing left, a portrait some have credited as that of Martha Washington, although no corroborative evidence has ever been found to support this. Surrounding is the inscription: LIB. PAR. OF SCIENCE & INDUSTRY.[2] The date 1792 is below the neck truncation. Nearly all specimens in existence today show evidence of considerable circulation.

• **Budget Recommendations:** G-4 to VG-8.

• • **Recommendations for the Connoisseur:** Nice VF-20 to EF-45, with smooth surfaces.

• • • **Elite Recommendations:** MS-65 coins do exist, and a couple of years ago dealer Ed Milas had a coin which was at least MS-65, perhaps finer (I don't recall its precise numerical designation), which was one of the most spectacular coins I've ever seen. Any MS-63 or better coin is a numismatic treasure worth owning!

Early Half Dimes (1794-1837)

After the 1792 pieces, half dimes were next struck in quantity bearing the dates 1794 and 1795. These issues are known as the Flowing Hair design and portray Miss Liberty facing right, with tresses streaming out behind her head. The reverse is the Small Eagle type and shows a delicately engraved eagle perched on a rock, enclosed by a wreath. The same general design, believed to have been the work of Robert Scot, was used for other silver coins of the era, namely the half dollar and silver dollar. Curiously, the half dimes of 1794 and 1795, indeed those of the following type was well, bore no indication of denomination. Half dimes of Flowing Hair type are elusive, with the 1794 being rarer than the 1795.

In 1796 the design was modified to what numismatists know as the Draped Bust type with Small Eagle reverse. Miss Liberty's ample bosom is shown, held at the bottom by drapery. The upper part of her hair is tied with a ribbon behind her head. The Small Eagle design employed on the reverse is different from the Small Eagle motif of 1794-5 in that the later version shows a stocky eagle perched on a puffy cloud, within a wreath. In general, half dimes of the 1796-1797 years, produced in several die varieties, are scarcer than the types before or after.[3]

Draped Bust type half dimes with Heraldic Eagle reverse were minted from 1800 to 1805. The reverse displays an eagle holding arrows and an olive branch, with stars and clouds above, an adaptation of the Great Seal of the United States. A rarity within this span is the 1802, a coin to which Newlin devoted considerable space in his 1883 monograph on the series. Only a few dozen examples exist. The other dates of this type are readily available, although in high grades all but the 1800 are rare.

After 1805 no half dimes were struck until 1829, in which year a new design, the Capped Bust style, engraved by John Reich, made its appearance. Earlier, the Capped Bust motif had been used on dimes, quarters, and half dollars. The reverse shows an eagle perched on an olive branch and arrows. The Capped Bust style was minted continuously from 1829 to 1837, with no rarities within the span.

•**Budget Recommendations:** Build a type set or date set in G-4 to VG-8 grade. As always, select coins with nice surfaces.

• •**Recommendations for the Connoisseur:** Early issues 1794-1805 are good values from Fine-12 to EF-40. 1796 and 1797 seem to be undervalued. Consider forming a type set of half dime designs. Only the brave specialist will want to tackle a variety collection of the early dates. Pick sharp strikes, which will be a challenge for the 1801-1805 dates. Issues 1829-1837 AU-50 to MS-60 are cheap. Nicely matched MS-63 coins of the 1829-1837 years would make a nice date set; the easiest way to do this is to look at a lot of slabbed coins and cherrypick those with good strikes and aesthetic appeal.

• • •**Elite Recommendations:** Build a date set or type set AU-50 or better, with MS-60 or better coins as you can find them (which won't be often). Such dates as 1802 (in particular), 1803, and 1803 are prohibitively rare in grades above EF-40. Issues 1829-1837 can be obtained in MS-65 with some patience. As always, cherrypick for quality.

Liberty Seated Half Dimes (1837-1873)

The Liberty Seated design by Mint engraver Christian Gobrecht made its debut in 1837. Philadelphia Mint Liberty Seated half dimes dated 1837 and New Orleans half dimes of 1838 had no stars on the obverse. The reverse design featured the inscription HALF DIME within a wreath.

Beginning in 1838 stars were added to the obverse, and were used through 1859. Part way through the year 1853 and continuing through 1855, arrows were added to the sides of the date to signify a slight reduction in the authorized weight of the denomination. In 1860 the obverse stars were discontinued, and the inscription UNITED STATES OF AMERICA appeared around the border of the Liberty Seated design. The reverse wreath was modified to a heavier and more ornate design. This style was utilized through 1873, when the half dime denomination was abolished.

Liberty Seated half dimes are very collectible, and with the exception of the 1870-S, of which just one is known, all are readily available, although a dozen or more varieties are rarities in Mint State. A pleasant pursuit is the building of a half dime collection in high circulated grades, such as Extremely Fine or AU, with the addition of occasional Uncirculated and Proof pieces. Over the years I have handled a number of important half dime holdings, including the Montgomery and Levine collections and, in the late 1980s, the unique 1870-S, formerly the property of John Abbott, which was purchased by dealer Martin Paul, who added it to his superb set of the denomination.

• **Budget Recommendations**: Build a type set or date and mintmark set in G-4 to VG-8 grade. Even the rarities are inexpensive in these states of preservation.

• • **Recommendations for the Connoisseur**: Forming a basic type set of designs is a good way to start. I suggest EF-40 to MS-60 coins if you want to get a lot of coins for the money. MS-63 and MS-64 specimens offer excellent possibilities. A set of dates and mintmarks is another interesting challenge. A nicely matched EF-40 set is inexpensive, save for a few issues. The specialist with a good bank account may wish to try for MS-63, but several issues of the 1840s will be nearly impossible to find (making it all the more interesting if some of them are found).

• • • **Elite Recommendations**: Build a type set or date and mintmark set with MS-65 as a goal, except for Philadelphia Mint coins 1858-1873 in Proof-

65 finish. However, as noted above, certain issues of the 1840s are not available in MS-65 grade, so lesser pieces will have to be purchased, perhaps under a plan of buying MS-60 or better, as found, and upgrading later as possibilities occur.

Early Dimes (1796-1837)

Dimes or 10-cent pieces were first minted for circulation in 1796. The design used in that year and the following was the Draped Bust type with Small Eagle reverse, as used on half dimes of the same span. Then followed dimes of the Draped Bust obverse type with Small Eagle reverse, minted from 1798 through 1807, again following the half dime motifs of the same era. Like the half dimes, the dimes bore no indication of value.

There are no landmark rarities among early dimes, although several varieties are decidedly scarce, notably the 1798/7 overdate with 13 reverse stars. Of particular interest is the 1804 dime with 14 reverse stars; it was struck from the identical reverse die used to coin $2.50 gold pieces of the same year.

In 1809 the Capped Bust design, by Mint engraver John Reich, was introduced. The motif was the same as that used on half dimes 1829-1837 and certain other silver denominations. Capped Bust dimes were produced intermittently from 1809 through 1837. No date rarities were created within that span, although several specialized die varieties are elusive.

For several generations, dimes were generally ignored by serious scholars. In the 19th century Maris, Crosby, Andrews and others studied minute die varieties of large cents, Newlin contributed a work on half dimes, and Haseltine created his *Type Table of United States Dollars, Half Dollars, and Quarter Dollars*. Overlooked were ten-cent pieces. In 1945 dimes had their due, sort of. In that year F.C.C. Boyd secretly consigned his collection of United States silver coins to the Numismatic Gallery, a New York City coin partnership owned by Abe Kosoff and Abner Kreisberg. Billed as "The World's Greatest Collection," with no mention of Boyd, the auction offering contained gems in all silver series (Boyd's gold coins were sold by the same firm a year later). The separate catalogue featuring dimes was written by Abe Kosoff, and described the die varieties Boyd had been able to acquire. Although the work was hardly definitive, and copies were soon out of print, it was the best effort in the dime series of any professional numismatist up to that point.

In 1984 the John Reich Collectors Society[4] published *Early United States Dimes 1796-1837*, by David Davis and four co-authors, a masterpiece of numismatic scholarship and writing. At long last aficionados of the series had a reference book which could hold its own with the finest in any other series.

• **Budget Recommendations:** Form a type set or date set in G-4 to VG-8 grade.

• • **Recommendations for the Connoisseur:** Form a basic type set or a date set. F-12 to EF-40 grades represent good values. MS-60 to MS-63 coins are rare and are undervalued in comparison to MS-65 pieces, but even lower grade Mint State coins are expensive.

• • • **Elite Recommendations:** Form a type set or date set in AU-55 or better grades for the 1796-1807 years, acquiring Mint State pieces as they become available. Later dimes, 1809-1837, can be acquired in MS-63 or better grades, as available, which is less of a problem toward the end of the date span, in the 1830s.

Liberty Seated Dimes (1837-1891)

In 1837 at the Philadelphia Mint and 1838 and the New Orleans Mint (1838-O) the Liberty Seated design, without obverse stars, was introduced. After these two issues were minted, stars were added to the obverse of subsequent pieces. In 1853-1855 arrows were placed alongside the date to indicate a weight reduction. In 1860 the legend UNITED STATES OF AMERICA replaced the stars on the obverse. In 1873-1874 issues were made with arrows at the date, this time to indicate a slight increase in authorized weight. In general, dime designs followed those of half dimes of the period (up to 1873, at which point the half dime denomination was discontinued). Liberty Seated dimes were produced through 1891.

Liberty Seated dimes 1837-1891 have attracted a wide following, and many collectors aspire to own one of each collectible variety. The only "impossible" rarity in the series is the 1873-CC without arrows, of which just one is known to exist, the specimen in the Eliasberg Collection. A number of other varieties range from scarce to rare.

Perhaps the most publicized rarity in the series is the 1844, which isn't really a rarity at all. Years ago it was realized that only 72,500 dimes were struck in 1844, a low mintage for the era, as compared to 1,370,000 struck the preceding year, 1843, and 1,755,000 struck in the following year, 1845. Fanciful stories were created to explain the supposed rarity of the issue, one tale relating that all of the 1844 dimes had been sent to Mexico to pay troops there, but the entire shipment was stolen by bandits, and most coins were melted.

In actuality the 1844 dime is elusive, but no more so than its mintage suggests. Probably all were put into general circulation, and today the coin is available in proportion to its mintage. A client of mine told me that he once attempted to corner the market on 1844 dimes, having heard that they were very rare, but gave up after he had acquired over 200 pieces, with no end in sight. It is significant to mention that not a single one of these was in Uncirculated grade. In Mint State preservation the 1844 is indeed a rarity, as are the 1845-O, 1846, 1849-O and several other dimes of the decade.

Among later Liberty Seated dimes the 1860-O has attracted attention now and then, in the manner of the 1844 dime, with some believing it to be a great rarity. However, although the 1860-O is scarce, it is not a rarity, except in higher grades. Truly rare are the first two Carson City Mint dimes, the 1871-CC and 1872-CC. Then there is the previously-mentioned unique 1873-CC without arrows at date. Somewhat scarce is the 1873-CC with arrows. For reasons unexplained, this issue is nearly always seen in circulated grades, typically Fine to Extremely Fine, but nearly always with a porous or granular surface. Another rarity is the 1874-CC. Further down the line, the 1879, 1880, and 1881 Philadelphia Mint dimes have always attracted a following because of their low mintage. I once purchased a hoard of dozens of Proof 1879 dimes from H.E. MacIntosh, of the Tatham Stamp & Coin Company, a Springfield, Massachusetts firm that was a prominent advertiser in numismatic periodicals until MacIntosh's death in the late 1950s.[5]

Before leaving the subject of Liberty Seated dimes I should mention Kamal Ahwash, who in 1977 published a book, *Encyclopedia of United States Liberty Seated Dimes 1837-1891*, which described numerous die varieties. Ahwash attracted quite a following, and he bought many coins from me for his customers. He was an accomplished vocalist, and at several numismatic events, including the annual get-together of the Numismatic Literary Society, he sang solo songs, something that Ed Reiter, for years the numismatic columnist for *The New York Times*, did also.

Let me also mention Proofs. Beginning in 1858, Proof coins were sold to collectors and others who applied for them. Prior to that time the distribution of Proof pieces was mainly to politicians, dignitaries, and collectors with connections to the Mint. Proof dimes (and Proof issues of other series) were issued continuously from 1858 onward. In the Liberty Seated dime series Proof mintages after 1858 ranged from a low of 460 pieces in 1863 to a high of 1,355 in 1880.[6] All Proof dimes from 1858 to 1891 are collectible, although some patience is required to track down pieces which have a nice appearance. This commentary concerning Proofs is generally applicable to most other silver series as well.

• **Budget Recommendations:** Build a type set or date set G-4 to VG-8. As always, select pieces with smooth, attractive surfaces.

• • **Recommendations for the Connoisseur:** My advice parallels precisely that given for contemporary half dimes: A basic type set of designs is a good way to start. I suggest EF-40 to MS-60 coins if you want to get a lot of value for the money. MS-63 and MS-64 coins offer excellent possibilities for the connoisseur. A set of dates and mintmarks is another interesting challenge. A nicely matched EF-40 set is inexpensive, save for a few issues. The specialist with a good bank account may wish to try for MS-63, but several issues of the 1840s will be nearly impossible to find. Proof-63 and Proof-64 coins 1858-1891 are undervalued in comparison to Proof-65 pieces, but be sure to cherrypick for aesthetic appeal.

• • • **Elite Recommendations:** Build a set in MS-65 grade, as available, with the Philadelphia Mint coins 1858-1891 in Proof-65 finish. Certain varieties, such as 1844, 1846, New Orleans Mint coins of the 1840s, early San Francisco dimes, and Carson City coins of the early 1870s may not be obtainable MS-65, so aspire for AU-50 or better, adding higher grade coins as you can get them.

Barber Dimes (1892-1916)

In 1892 a new dime design, by Charles E. Barber, made its appearance. Known first as the Liberty Head dime and later (and currently by collectors) as the Barber dime, the motif featured an androgynous depiction of Liberty, not clearly a "Miss" but intended as such. Barber dimes were produced continuously through 1916 with no major changes. All issues are readily collectible, save for the 1894-S of which just 24 were struck.

In the "Trends" column of *Coin World*,[7] Keith M. Zaner commented on Barber coins in general and a collector's enjoyment of Barber dimes in particular:

"The demand for circulated key and semi-key and semi-key date coins is rapidly increasing. Recent activity at major shows has indicated strong demand for 19th and 20th century rare dates. Is it the collector or the investor who is buying? It really doesn't matter, because throughout the history of coin collecting, price appreciation for rare dates more often than not has been better than its common-date counterparts. The more difficult dates are usually last to occupy those spaces in one's album, including the difficult dates and mintmark varieties which aren't readily available to the collector even if he is willing to pay the current prices.

"Significant gains in value have occurred for these key and semi-key date coins. The Barber dime, quarter dollar and half dollar series quickly come to mind. The desire to acquire scarcer date Fine, Extremely Fine and About Uncirculated coins dominates demand. Not only is this a challenging task, but it can also be quite rewarding monetarily. There are many dates and mint varieties which have been moving up in value. A look at recent 'Trends' will bear this out.

"The Barber coins are doing well because there are many semi-key and key dates available. A young collector becoming interested in the Barber series can afford the challenge and at the same time complete the collection in his lifetime. Of course, most would have to exclude the 1894-S Barber dime.

"One new coin collector that I know has chosen Barber dimes. He picked this denomination over the quarter dollar or half dollar because it fits his budget better. Initially, the design interested him enough to want to know more. However, the chance to put together a decent collection in Very Fine or better condition became most attractive. Collecting these Barber dimes offers entertainment value, so there isn't any concern about future price appreciation, although I do think it is in the back of his mind."

• **Budget Recommendations:** Build a set in G-4 to VG-8 grade.

• • **Recommendations for the Connoisseur:** My advice parallels that given for Barber quarters and half dollars. Start with one nice coin for "type." If you want to form a date and mintmark set, EF-40 coins are an economical way to go. While MS-60 through MS-62 specimens are cheap (relatively speaking), most specimens look rather scruffy in these grades. For the connoisseur I recommend a nicely matched set of MS-63 and MS-64 coins, cherrypicked for aesthetic appeal. A good way to go is to look at a large number of slabbed coins and pick out those which are attractive. A set of Proof-63 to Proof-64 coins, again cherrypicked, forms a nice display. MS-65 and Proof-65 coins are gorgeous but are pricey, due to demand by investors, although many scarce branch mint coins in MS-65 are underpriced in relation to the commoner issues.

• • • **Elite Recommendations:** Build a set in MS-65 grade, except for the 1892-1915 Philadelphia Mint coins which can be Proof-65.

Mercury Dimes (1916-1945)

In 1916 a new dime motif appeared. The work of sculptor Adolph A. Weinman, Miss Liberty now had wings on her head. As noted earlier in the present text, although the Mint intended that it be called a Liberty Head dime, the public quickly called it the Mercury dime, illogically so, for Mercury of mythology was a *man* who had wings on his *feet*.

The 1916 Mercury dime joined the Standing Liberty quarter and Walking Liberty half dollar of the same year as a new departure in American silver coinage. For the first time, circulating silver coin designs were prepared by artists not on the Mint staff. Precedents had been established with the 1909 Lincoln cent, 1913 Buffalo nickel, and the gold coins of 1907-1908, all of which had been created by outside talent.

Mercury dimes were immediately appreciated and desired by numismatists. The design was continued through 1945. Examples were coined in all years except 1922, 1932, and 1933. The rarest regular variety in the series is the 1916-D. Two overdates are likewise rare, the 1942/1 and the 1942/1-D.

• **Budget Recommendations:** Build a set of 1916-1931 issues in G-4 to VG-8 grades and the later issues 1934-1945 in F-20 or better grades.

• • **Recommendations for the Connoisseur:** Forming a short set of dimes from 1931 (or 1934) to 1945 is easy to do. MS-65 is a good goal. If you want coins with fully struck bands on the reverse, these will be harder to find for some issues, and the otherwise common 1945 is a major rarity. A date and mintmark set of the earlier issues 1916-1930 can be very attractive in nicely matched MS-63 and MS-64 grades. Cherrypick nice strikes and coins with excellent aesthetic appeal.

• • • **Elite Recommendations:** Form a set in MS-65 grade, sharply struck. If desired, the 1936-1942 Philadelphia Mint issues can be added in Proof-65.

Roosevelt Dimes (1946 to Date)

Following the death of President Franklin Delano Roosevelt in 1945, it was decided to change the design of the dime to feature his portrait. The Roosevelt motif was prepared by John Sinnock, chief engraver at the Mint. The design has been used ever since. After 1964 dimes were made of a clad alloy rather than silver.

In terms of popularity today, dimes of the early years, 1796-1837, are collected by a small group of specialists; Liberty Seated dimes 1837-1891 attract a wider following; Barber dimes 1892-1916 appeal to still a wider circle of friends; Mercury dimes 1916-1945 are desired by thousands of collectors; and Roosevelt dimes are collected by millions.

• **Budget Recommendations:** Build a set in VF-20 or better grade.

Recent issues can be found in pocket change.

• • **Recommendations for the Connoisseur:** Build a set in MS-65 grade, adding Proof-65 coins for certain issues. Bruce Amspacher once conducted a study which revealed that truly fine MS-65 coins were much scarcer, as a complete set, than normally realized.

• • • **Elite Recommendations:** Same as the preceding.

Twenty-Cent Pieces (1875-1878)

While the odd twenty-cent denomination is popular with collectors today, the public could never understand the coins, and from the moment that they were first released into circulation in 1875 they were confused with quarter dollars. And no wonder. The Liberty Seated obverse design was the same as found on the quarter, the eagle design on the reverse if not the same was quite close to the quarter motif, at least as seen by the average citizen's eyes, and the diameter wasn't much different either. With all good intentions the government produced well over a million twenty-cent pieces in 1875. Then, as it was realized that the denomination was a grave mistake, production screeched to a near standstill; fewer than 25,000 were minted for circulation the next year, 1876, after which only Proofs were struck, for collectors, in 1877 and 1878.

This short-lived denomination was produced in only a few varieties: 1875, 1875-CC, 1875-S, 1876, 1876-CC, 1877, and 1878. You would think that such a restricted series would be eagerly collected, but as the 1876-CC is a great rarity—fewer than two dozen are known—this has dampened enthusiasm.[8]

The main sale for twenty-cent pieces is to collectors desiring to build a type set of U.S. coins. Every type set needs one twenty-cent piece, and the coin that most people pick is usually an 1875-S, the commonest variety.

• **Budget Recommendations:** Buy one coin in G-4 to VG-8 grade for type, or collect the available date and mint varieties (1875, 1875-CC, 1875-S, and 1876) in G-4 to VG-8 grade.

• • **Recommendations for the Connoisseur:** Buy one twenty-cent piece for "type." Such issues as 1875, 1875-CC, and 1876 are much rarer than the common 1875-S and yet cost very little more. Choose one of these. I like nice MS-63 and MS-64 coins. I like MS-65 twenty-cent pieces too, but they are a bit pricey in the current market.

• • • **Elite Recommendations:** Form a set of branch mint coins (decide on your own about the 1876-CC!) in MS-65 grade and Philadelphia Mint pieces in Proof-65 finish. Or just buy one MS-65 or Proof-65 coin as a representative of the design type.

Quarter Dollars (1796 to Date)

An overview of quarter dollars: Among numismatists quarter dollars, somewhat like dimes, have "fallen through the cracks" and have not enjoyed a wide following; this is particularly true of quarter dollars of the earlier era 1796-1838.

Liberty Seated quarters of the next era (1838-1891) have been popular in recent years, particularly since a spurt of interest in Liberty Seated coinage in general began in the 1970s. The activities and publications of the Liberty Seated Collectors Club have served to maintain the current enthusiasm.

Barber quarters (1892-1916), once orphans in the coin market, like Barber dimes and Barber halves, have enjoyed renewed popularity in recent times. Standing Liberty quarters (1916-1930) have always been popular and year in and year out have enjoyed a wide market. Washington quarters (1932 to date) are perhaps too recent to attract serious numismatists in large numbers, but there is no doubt that early Washington issues of the 1930s, particularly in higher grades, have been hard to find. I note that highly-regarded newsletter publisher David Hall recently recommended the field of Washington quarters as being an overlooked area for investment purposes.

Silver coins of the late 18th and early 19th centuries exhibit a sameness of design, and it will come as no surprise to the reader to learn that quarter dollars from 1796 through the early 20th century are little different from contemporary dimes and half dollars except for size. It was not until the early part of the present century that designs of various denominations each became distinctive in their own right.

Early Quarters (1796-1838)

The first quarter dollar variety, minted in 1796, is highly important for several reasons. First, it is the initial issue of the denomination, and for this reason alone it has attracted many buyers over the years. More significant, however, is its status as a type coin. The year 1796 represents the only instance in which the Draped Bust obverse was minted in combination with the Small Eagle reverse. Just 6,146 were coined, making 1796 quarters rare in any grade.

Interestingly, at least several hundred 1796 quarters in Mint State were preserved at the time of issue. The late Abe Kosoff told of seeing a hoard of dozens of these which came on the market in the early 1940s through Philadelphia dealer James Macallister, who obtained them from the estate of Col. E.H.R. Green.[9] Each piece was said to have been prooflike and virtually perfect in preservation. Apparently the hoard was sold intact, allegedly to a Wall Street broker. What has happened to it in the meantime is anyone's guess. Perhaps some day that long-forgotten hoard of 1796 quarters will come on the market, and if it does I would like nothing better than to have the chance to offer them for sale! One of the delights of being a professional numismatist is the handling from time to time of surprising hoards of one coin or another—groups which have either been long forgotten or which no one knew existed.

On this subject, I recall fondly the Emery-Nichols Collection which we handled at auction a few years ago. Around the turn of the century S. Benton Emery was a numismatist of renown and was a major client of the Chapman brothers and other dealers of the day. He acquired numerous rarities in virtually all series, including many Proof sets ordered directly from the Philadelphia Mint. The holding stayed in his family and passed to Walter P. Nichols, a professional accountant who at one time was a member of the American Numismatic Association Board of Governors and who also served as official distributor for the York County (Maine) commemorative half dollars.

After Nichols' death in the early 1940s, the holding was relegated to a bank vault and was forgotten. When the Nichols heirs approached my company in the 1980s and contracted to have us catalogue and present the coins for sale, it was like a dream come true. Virtually every piece was in its original wrappings, some bearing notations from 80 years earlier! As the collection had been carefully preserved, nearly all pieces were beautiful gems. When all was said and done and the collection had been catalogued, publicized, and sold to new bidders, the record books had to be rewritten. One thing I have learned as a professional numismatist over the years is this: quality never goes out of style.

After 1796 no quarter dollars were minted until 1804, at which time the Draped Bust obverse was employed in combination with the Heraldic Eagle reverse, to create a type which was used through 1807. Of the dates produced in this span the 1804 is the rarest. Only a few examples can lay claim to being in Mint State, a notable specimen of which was sold at an auction by Lester Merkin in the 1970s for the then-unheard of price of $25,000. Undoubtedly this coin, if auctioned today, would stand a chance of bringing 10 times that sum! Most quarter dollars of the 1804-1807 type are weakly struck. This is particularly true of pieces dated 1806 and 1807. Some 1807 quarters must have been as flat as the proverbial pancake at the moment they left the dies.

After 1807 quarters were not coined again until 1815, at which time the Capped Bust Left style made its debut, a design continued through 1838, although in 1831 the diameter was reduced and other revisions were made. A classic rarity in this span is the 1827, of which 4,000 pieces were said to have been struck, of which only a dozen or so originals are known, all Proofs. It is probably the case that Proofs were made for collectors and dignitaries in 1827, including four Proofs known to have been sold to pioneer collector Joseph J. Mickley for face value, but that the business strike mintage figure of 4,000 coins represented pieces made from earlier dies, perhaps dated 1825. In the early years of the Mint it was the practice to keep dies on hand until they broke or wore out. Little attention was paid to striking coins with dies corresponding to the calendar year. For this reason many early mintage figures must be taken with a grain of salt.

The reader interested in exploring the early series further should to acquire a copy of *The Early Quarter Dollars of the United States 1796-1838*, by A.W. Browning, published in 1925, and revised and updated by Walter Breen in a new edition scheduled for publication by Bowers and Merena Galleries in 1991. Although the 1796 quarter dollar may be expensive to acquire, the 1823/3 is a rarity, and an 1827 original is a coin of which dreams are made, nearly all other varieties in the series are surprisingly affordable. A definitive collection of later date Capped Bust quarters of the small diameter format, 1831-1838, costs very little if assembled in grades such as EF or AU. There is always the chance of discovering a new die variety and paying no more than a "common" price for it; it has been done before.

• **Budget Recommendations:** Form a type set or date set in G-4 to VG-8.

• • **Recommendations for the Connoisseur:** Form a type set or a date set. F-12 to EF-40 coins are recommended for just about everyone, although if you can afford it, there are some good values in higher levels, up to MS-63 and MS-64. Pick sharp strikes, which will be difficult for the 1804-1807 type.

• • • **Elite Recommendations:** Form a type set or date set in MS-63 or better grade. As always, cherrypick for quality. Such a set will take a long time to form. Certain varieties, namely the 1823/2, may not be available in high grades. On the other hand, you will be able to find a prooflike MS-65 1796.

Liberty Seated Quarters (1838-1891)

Of all 19th century series, Liberty Seated quarters are, as a class, one of the most elusive. As a dealer I can say that I always have in stock more Liberty Seated dimes and half dollars than I do quarters.

As a rule of thumb, Uncirculated quarters dated before 1853 are quite scarce, as most were melted when the metallic content of silver coins rose above the face value (the authorized weight was reduced in 1853, solving the problem). This is particularly true of New Orleans pieces, except issues of the early 1840s which were discovered in quantity a few years ago when a hoard was excavated in the downtown section of the city, not far from the old New Orleans Mint. These coins, considerably blackened, had been hidden away for nearly a century and a half. Among later Liberty Seated quarters, Uncirculated specimens of San Francisco issues are rare through the early 1870s. Carson City issues of the 1870-1874 years are rarities in all grades.

Liberty Seated quarters dated after 1874 are for the most part readily available through 1891, the last year in the series. A number of dates from 1879 onward have very low business strike mintages, adding to their popularity with collectors.

Readers interested in Liberty Seated quarters or any other silver coins of the mid-19th century would do well to join the Liberty Seated Collectors Club, publisher of *The Gobrecht Journal*. This informative magazine carries much information about rarity ratings, new discoveries, die characteristics, and other related topics.

• **Budget Recommendations:** Build a date and mintmark set in G-4 to VG-8 grade. Select pieces with attractive surfaces.

• • **Recommendations for the Connoisseur:** Form a type set. EF-40 to AU-55 coins are incredibly cheap in relation to their scarcity; this is especially true of issues before 1853. With relatively few exceptions, MS-63 and finer business strikes are rare. Proof-63 and Proof-64 coins 1858-1891 are undervalued in comparison to Proof-65 pieces, but be sure to cherrypick. Forming a date and mintmark set can be a lifetime challenge, and only a few collectors have ever attempted the task, although if you have the energy and patience, here indeed is an interesting series. Texas numismatist Reed Hawn is notable among those who have specialized in the series in recent times, as is Fred Matthews, whose collection my firm auctioned in 1990, and who assembled a holding of 1838-1891 quarters lacking only two or three varieties.

• • • **Elite Recommendations:** You can aspire to build a set in MS-65 grade, but completion will not be possible. For certain scarce and rare issues, you will have to settle for lesser grades (see above commentary). Perhaps the best way to go is to spend the first two or three years acquiring issues of the 1838-1874 years in MS-60 or better grades and quarters of the 1875-1891 years in MS-64 or better. Then take stock of your holdings, and for issues for which you have not obtained a specimen, lower your objective by a couple of grade points. You can always upgrade here and there, as later opportunities present themselves. Philadelphia Mint dates 1858-1891 can be added in Proof-65 finish.

Barber Quarters (1892-1916)

Barber quarters first saw the light of day in circulation in 1892 and were produced continuously through the year 1916. There are three notably rare issues, pieces which even if worth smooth are worth hundreds of dollars: the 1896-S, 1901-S, and 1913-S. All other issues are readily available in all except the higher Mint State levels.

• **Budget Recommendations:** Form a set of date and mintmark varieties in G-4 to VG-8 grade. See comment above concerning three rare San Francisco Mint issues.

• • **Recommendations for the Connoisseur:** My advice parallels that given for Barber dimes and half dollars: Start with one nice coin for "type." If you want to form a date and mintmark set, EF-40 is an economical way to go. While MS-60 through MS-62 coins are cheap (relatively speaking), most specimens look rather scruffy in these grades. For the connoisseur I recommend a nicely matched set of MS-63 and MS-64 coins, cherrypicked for aesthetic appeal. No matter which grades you choose, the 1896-S, 1901-S, and 1913-S will be expensive. A good way to go is to look at a large number of slabbed coins and pick out those which are attractive. A set of Proof-63 to Proof-64 coins, again cherrypicked, forms a nice display. MS-65 and Proof-65 coins are gorgeous but pricey.

• • • **Elite Recommendations:** Build a set in MS-65 grade, except for the 1892-1915 Philadelphia Mint coins which can be Proof-65.

Standing Liberty Quarters (1916-1930)

Standing Liberty quarters, minted from 1916 through 1930, were designed by Hermon A. MacNeil, a well-known sculptor, and have a timeless, classic beauty. Particularly attractive are the Type I issues bearing the date 1917, which often have matte-like fields and are exceedingly sharply struck. Throughout the life of the design, striking was a problem, and more often than not, pieces of the Type II style (1917-1930) are not fully struck up, particularly on the design details of Miss Liberty's head. Nowhere is this more apparent than among Denver Mint coins. Particularly egregious is the 1926-D.

Probably 99 out of 100 surviving Uncirculated 1926-D quarters lack detail. The 1918/7-D overdate is rare in all grades.

J.H. Cline's book, *Standing Liberty Quarters*, published in 1976 and updated since then, furnishes an effective passport to the series and is recommended for the advanced buyer. Indeed, in general I recommend that you buy books on any series in which you have even a single coin. The price of Cline's book is but a tiny fraction of the price of even the commonest Uncirculated Standing Liberty quarter, and there is no doubt that by reading about the series you will enhance your enjoyment. It has always been amazing to me—and this comment covers all series—that buyers will rush into the coin market and spend thousands of dollars on their first pass through, but will balk at the idea of shelling out $10 or $20 for a reference book!

• **Budget Recommendations:** Build a set in F-12 grade (G-4 to VG-8 coins are apt to be unattractive).

• • **Recommendations for the Connoisseur:** Start by buying one of each of the two types. EF-40 to AU-55 coins are bargains. Attractive, well-struck MS-63 and MS-64 coins are good buys as well, but you will have to cherrypick to avoid stained, mottled, and ugly pieces.

• • • **Elite Recommendations:** Build a set in MS-65 grade with full heads on Miss Liberty. The 1918/7-S will be a toughie.

Washington Quarters (1932 to Date)

Washington quarters, first minted in 1932, were intended to be commemoratives to observe the 200th anniversary of our first president's birth. The obverse portrait was taken from Jean Antoine Houdon's famous bust of Washington. The first year of issue saw the production of two key scarcities, the 1932-D and the 1932-S, both of which were not saved in appreciable quantities at the time of release and are thus decidedly difficult to find in higher echelons of Mint State today.

The 1776-1976 bicentennial quarter design bears on the reverse the motif of a colonial drummer, the design of Jack L. Ahr. The issue is quite attractive, although from a numismatic viewpoint so many millions were minted that our grandchildren will undoubtedly consider them to be common.

In general, Washington quarters represent a fertile field for the collector wanting to get in on the ground floor of a series which eventually will probably have its day in the sun. While certain issues of the 1930s are elusive in higher grades and are not exactly cheap, there are probably a number of pieces dated in 1940s and early 1950s which are rare in higher Mint State levels—although to this point I am not aware of anyone who has studied the series to find out. Eventually this will happen, as it does in all series.

   • **Budget Recommendations:** Form a set with the issues of the 1930s in G-4 to F-12 grade, issues 1940-1963 VF-20 or better, and later issues EF-40 or better. Recent issues can be found in pocket change.

   • • **Recommendations for the Connoisseur:** Go for MS-65 all the way. Add some Proof-65 coins for certain issues, if you wish.

   • • • **Elite Recommendations:** Same as the preceding.

Early Half Dollars (1794-1839)

   Unlike dimes and quarters, half dollars have attracted a large and loyal following of numismatists, almost from the cradle days of the hobby. This is due no doubt to the fact that early 19th century issues were minted in very large quantities, second only to one-cent pieces in terms of production, and are thus readily available for reasonable prices. Nothing stimulates interest in series more than to have an inexpensive and easy entry. This is precisely why Morgan silver dollars, once collected by very few, have been high on the popularity list ever since the Treasury Department released untold millions of them in 1962.

   Back to the subject of half dollars: The denomination was first minted for circulation in 1794. In this and the following year the Flowing Hair motif was used, the same design employed on half dimes and dollars of the same dates. The denomination appeared nowhere on the obverse or reverse but was relegated to the edge, which was lettered 50 CENTS OR HALF A DOLLAR. Today the 1794 half dollar is multiples rarer than the 1795, as might be expected from the relative mintage figures: 23,464 pieces produced dated 1794 and 299,680 with the 1795 date. As noted earlier, such figures must be taken with a grain of salt. Although the numbers seem precise enough, in reality it may have been the case that certain pieces included in the 1795 number were made from leftover 1794 dies.

   One of the most famous of all American coin design types is the 1796-1797 Draped Bust half dollar design with Small Eagle reverse. Just 3,918 were minted for these two years, divided into three distinct varieties: 1796 with 15 stars on the obverse, 1796 with 16 stars, and 1797 (all 1797 pieces have 15 stars). Why the variation in the star counts? This has never been satisfactorily explained, although a likely suggestion is that during this time additional states were being added to the Union, giving a reason to increase the star count from the normal 13. However, in practice those individuals making dies at the Mint seemed to have added stars or to fill out the design in an aesthetic manner, without regard as to how many states were or were not in the Union, although the star count never fell below13 nor did it exceed 16.

Of the 3,918 half dollars minted of the 1796-7 design type, probably fewer than 300 or 400 survive today. In higher grades, these pieces are extreme rarities, although 1796 occurs in AU and Uncirculated preservation more frequently than 1797. When I catalogued the Norweb Collection for sale at auction in 1987 and 1988 I was delighted to encounter a superb gem Uncirculated 1797—a coin which I had never seen in this grade level. It is now owned by a private client on the West Coast, a connoisseur who appreciates it as much as I did when I catalogued it.

After 1797 no half dollars were struck until 1801, when the Draped Bust obverse was employed with the Heraldic Eagle reverse. Half dollars of this new type were minted through 1807. As is the case with quarter dollars, those pieces toward the end of the series are nearly always seen poorly struck; this is especially true of Draped Bust halves dated 1807.

Partway through the latter year a new design was created, the Capped Bust type, said to have been the work of John Reich (who I mentioned earlier under the subjects of half dimes and dimes). Capped Bust half dollars were produced continuously through 1836, with the exception of the year 1816. At the time silver dollars were not being produced for general circulation, so it fell to the half dollar denomination to become the workhorse coin for everyday commerce. Accordingly, production was typically over a million each year, a large quantity for the time. The Capped Bust series contains many interesting variations, especially overdates. Most of these are available in higher circulated grades such as EF and AU for prices in the general range of $100 to $300 or so.

Attributions of early coins in the series can be made to Al C. Overton's book, *Early Half Dollar Die Varieties 1794-1836*, published in 1967 and later revised. Overton was a well-known dealer in his time and conducted many mail bid and public auction sales, most notably the 1963 ANA convention sale. Capped Bust half dollars were his collecting specialty, and he was always ready to share his enthusiasm with others. Earlier students of the series include John W. Haseltine, who described certain varieties in his 1881 work, *Type Table of United States Dollars, Half Dollars and Quarter Dollars*, and, in particular, M.L. Beistle, a Shippensburg, Pennsylvania manufacturer of cardboard boxes and other paper goods (including coin album pages, the patent for which was later licensed to Wayte Raymond), who was an ardent numismatist and who in 1929 published the *Register of United States Half*

Dollar Die Varieties and Sub-Varieties. The Beistle work remained standard until superseded by the Overton tome. A group of aficionados styling themselves as the Bust Half Nut Club meets occasionally at conventions and exchanges a newsletter on the series. An excellent study of rarity ratings was undertaken by the group and published in the pages of *The Numismatist.*

In 1836 the half dollar design was modified to a smaller size with reeded edge, with the denomination expressed on the reverse as 50 CENTS. With a design change in 1838 (the denomination inscription was changed to read HALF DOL.) the general style was used through mid-1839. A major rarity of this era is the 1838 New Orleans issue (1838-O), of which it has been said that just 20 were struck, a statement which may indeed be true, as fewer than that number can be traced today.

• **Budget Recommendations:** Like large cents, early half dollars furnish a fertile field for collecting, and there are many possibilities. Forming a type set is a popular way to go, especially if you want to acquire the early issues. For 1807-1836 issues I highly recommend forming a date set in F-12 grade. You will enjoy having many coins for a relatively small amount of money, and you will delight in owning so many interesting varieties, including numerous overdates.

• • **Recommendations for the Connoisseur:** For the 1794-1795 Flowing Hair halves, I like VF-20 to EF-45. AU-50 to MS-63 coins are good values but are hard to find and are expensive. Half dollars of 1796-1797 are very rare, and I will leave it up to you to consult current prices to determine which grades you want. For 1801-1807 halves I like EF-40 to AU-50; there are many good values here, but be sure to pick sharply struck coins (virtually impossible for the year 1807, however). Forming a date set of 1807-1836 Capped Bust halves is highly recommended as a fascinating numismatic endeavor. Pick a grade range such as EF-40 to AU-50 if you want to get a lot of coins for the money. If you can afford it, collect MS-60 to MS-63, cherrypicking all the way. These coins are very beautiful and are quite undervalued, in my opinion.

• • • **Elite Recommendations:** MS-60 or better is a reasonable goal for the 1794-1807 issues. You can add pieces in even higher grades as they become available, which for some issues will not be often, if at all. For 1807-1836 issues build a set in MS-64 or finer grade, selecting each coin for its aesthetic quality. You may not be able to find the rare 1815 in this grade, however.

Liberty Seated Half Dollars (1839-1891)

Liberty Seated half dollars were first produced for circulation in 1839 and were minted continuously through 1891. Several different design variations were made during this span. In general, Liberty Seated half dollars are inexpensive, particularly in circulated grades, and the formation of a set of these can be a pleasant pastime. As is true of many series from the mid-19th century, there are numerous issues which are virtually impossible to find in higher Mint State levels, a situation which may dissuade the investor who is tuned in to hearing that something must be MS-65 to be worthwhile. However, for the knowledgeable buyer who can go beyond such market puffery, there is great satisfaction in acquiring coins which are rarities in grades such as Extremely Fine and AU. One particular rarity in the series, the 1853-O without arrows, does not exist in grades above Very Fine.

The subject of high condition as a key to coin collecting enjoyment and profits has been vastly overblown in recent years, particularly beginning with the popularity of certified coins. During the past several years great emphasis has been placed on the investment aspect of coins, and it is true to state that for every dollar spent advertising a "collector" series such as Liberty Seated half dollars, $100 or more is spent in advertising investment coins—MS-65 Morgan dollars, 20th century coins, etc. A beginning collector can readily understand that a coin in MS-65 or better grade is in high condition and is desirable. The same person would have a great deal of difficulty comprehending why on earth anyone would want to own a Very Fine 1853-O Without Arrows half dollar! Of course, as a professional numismatist I would travel across the country to buy a worn 1853-O of this type, as would any one of my contemporaries!

While completion is a laudable goal in any series, for the majority of collectors completion of a set of Liberty Seated half dollars is not possible. So far as I know, there are only three 1853-O half dollars known of the Without Arrows type (not to be confused with 1853-O half dollars *with* arrows at date and rays on the reverse, minted later in the year, which are quite common). Thus, only three collectors on the face of the globe can have a truly complete collection. Does this mean that you should not collect Liberty Seated half dollars? Of course not. No art collector can ever have one of each significant painting style, no collector of automobiles can own one of each marque, and so on. Although Louis Eliasberg, the great Baltimore collector, by 1950 had done what no one had ever done before and had acquired one of each date and mintmark issue of United States coins from half cent to double eagles, the fact remains that there are hundreds of thousands of other collectors who have enjoyed coins without absolute completion of all series.

Among Liberty Seated half dollars there are many challenges. The 1842-O

Small Date is rare even when worn nearly smooth, but still a numismatically acceptable piece can be acquired in the $1,000 range. Very hard to find are early Carson City issues, 1870-CC through 1873-CC, but again these are surprisingly affordable. Particularly popular, and widely available, are the low-mintage half dollars dated from 1879 through 1890. Production of these was very restricted, as the Philadelphia Mint was busy at the time turning out unprecedented quantities of Morgan silver dollars under the terms of the Bland-Allison Act. The result was that a whole string of rarities emerged from the Mint. Still, enough exist in collectors' hands that a set can be obtained today without a great deal of difficulty.

The 1886 half dollar is a case in point. Just 5,000 business strikes were minted, plus 886 Proofs. As the Proofs were specifically sold at a premium to collectors who saved them, of the 886 Proofs minted probably 500 or 600 exist today, although numerous pieces show signs of mishandling. Of the 5,000 business strikes, probably only a few hundred survive, most of which show signs of wear. All in all, it is probably correct to state that close to 1,000 half dollars bearing the date 1886 are preserved by the numismatic fraternity. This quantity is sufficient to supply those desiring an example. Numismatists forming a type set of half dollars do not need an 1886, for they can be satisfied with a less expensive date. The only buyer specifically needing an 1886-dated coin is someone putting together a date set. For several hundred dollars a nice VF or EF piece can be obtained, certainly not a high price to pay for a classic Liberty Seated rarity.

• **Budget Recommendations:** Form a date and mintmark set of G-4 to VG-8 coins.

• • **Recommendations for the Connoisseur:** The preceding narrative gives some guidelines, but let me add the following: A basic type set is a good way to start. EF-40 to AU-50 coins are cheap and readily available. Forming a set of dates and mintmarks in the same grade can be a rewarding activity. MS-63 and MS-64 coins are quite undervalued throughout the series, particularly in the general date ranges of 1839-1852 and mintmark issues 1853-1874. An interesting short set can be formed by buying one each of the low mintage dates 1879-1891. Proof-63 and Proof-64 coins 1858-1891 are undervalued in comparison to Proof-65 pieces, but be sure to cherrypick.

• • • **Elite Recommendations:** Aspire to build a set in MS-65 grade, but realize that certain issues may not be available in this grade, especially certain early New Orleans and San Francisco varieties and early Carson City issues (these can be acquired in AU-55 or better grades, upgrading as better pieces become available). Philadelphia Mint coins 1858-1891 can be added in

Proof-65 grade. As always, be fussy about quality.

Barber Half Dollars (1892-1915)

Barber half dollars, produced from 1892 to 1915, have been gaining in popularity in recent years, due to the efforts of David Lange (who has written several articles about them) and the formation of the Barber Coin Collectors Society, among other considerations.

The series of Barber half dollars contains no great rarities, and completion is within the grasp of virtually everyone, although in very high grades there are several varieties which will take a long time to find. When I first began my collecting interest in the 1950s I was attracted to Barber half dollars and put together a set of Proofs. The typical Proof issue dated from 1892 through 1913 was apt to cost in the $10 range, I paid $25 for the scarcer 1913, and, if I recall correctly, the 1914 and 1915 were priced somewhere in the $100 to $200 range. At the time a Virginia collector made a specialty of hoarding pieces of these two latter dates, thus causing a price anomaly. Of course, today these prices sound like something from Never Never Land!

• **Budget Recommendations:** Form a collection of G-4 to VG-8 coins. There are no rarities to contend with.

• • **Recommendations for the Connoisseur:** My advice parallels that given for Barber dimes and quarters: Start with one nice coin for "type." If you want to form a date and mintmark set, EF-40 is an economical way to go. While MS-60 through MS-62 coins are cheap (relatively speaking), most specimens look rather scruffy in these grades. For the connoisseur I recommend a nicely matched set of MS-63 and MS-64 coins, cherrypicked for aesthetic appeal. A good way to go is to look at a large quantity of slabbed coins and pick out those which are attractive. A set of Proof-63 to Proof-64 coins, again cherrypicked, forms a nice display. MS-65 and Proof-65 coins are gorgeous but are pricey, although certain San Francisco and New Orleans varieties of the 1896-1904 years are underpriced.

• • • **Elite Recommendations:** Build a set in MS-65 grade, except for the Philadelphia Mint coins which can be Proof-65.

Liberty Walking Half Dollars (1916-1947)

In 1916 the Liberty Walking half dollar appeared. The work of sculptor Adolph A. Weinman, the design was produced intermittently through 1947. As with the other new 1916 silver designs—the Mercury dime and Standing Liberty quarter—the Walking Liberty half dollar immediately attracted a wide circle of numismatic friends. The popularity continues to the present day. A survey conducted by *Numismatic News* in 1990 found that readers selected this design as their favorite, followed by the Saint-Gaudens $20 and the Standing Liberty quarter.[11]

Certain early issues are elusive, particularly in higher grades, but the building of a "short set" from 1941 through 1947 is a possibility for just about anyone, for Uncirculated coins exist in quantity. Those who are braver or who have better fortified checkbooks can build an expanded short set containing coins dated from 1933 through 1947. Relatively few numismatists desire to collect the entire 1916-1947 series in Uncirculated grade, for major stumbling blocks are provided by the low-mintage issues of 1921, particularly 1921-S, as well as several other key dates.

• **Budget Recommendations:** Form a set of the early varieties 1916-1929 in VG-8 grade, and the later issues in VF-20 preservation.

• • **Recommendations for the Connoisseur:** As noted above, forming a short set 1933-1947 or 1941-1947 is popular and will constitute a very nice collection. MS-63 and MS-64 coins are good buys, but even MS-65 coins are cheap now. Among earlier issues, if you can afford it try for nicely matched MS-63 and MS-64 pieces. In all instances be fussy about what you buy, and select sharply struck pieces with excellent aesthetic appeal.

• • • **Elite Recommendations:** Form a set of sharply struck MS-65 pieces with excellent aesthetic appeal. This will take some doing, especially for certain early Denver and San Francisco issues, which are usually found weakly struck. If desired, 1936-1942 Philadelphia Mint coins can be added in Proof-65 finish; actually such a run of Proofs makes a nice little collection all by itself.

Franklin Half Dollars (1948-1963)

Franklin half dollars, first minted in 1948, were produced through 1963, after which time the design was hurriedly dropped to make way for the Kennedy motif, following the assassination of the president. During their time of issue Franklin halves were not popular in a large way, for many numismatists found the design to be unattractive. Pieces, if subjected to just slight handling, were apt to become scarred, particularly on the higher parts of the portrait on the obverse and on the bell on the reverse. When the series breathed its last in 1963, few lamented its passing.

In recent times there has been a revival of interest. Jack Ehrmantraut, Jr. published a study on Proof Franklin half dollars minted from 1950 through 1963, pointing out that certain issues with cameo or frosted heads were especially attractive and desirable. With the advent of the Professional Coin Grading Service and other certification companies, it has been realized that certain common Franklin half dollars are not necessarily common in MS-65 preservation. It is my guess that within the next few years a number of "condition scarcities" (I hesitate to use the term rarities) will emerge in the series. In basic Uncirculated grade, such as MS-60 to MS-63 (a typical grade for a bank-wrapped roll of coins of the period), a Franklin half dollar set is easily completed.

• **Budget Recommendations:** Form a set in VF-20 grade.

• • **Recommendations for the Connoisseur:** Go for sharply struck MS-65 coins (see above commentary).

• • • **Elite Recommendations:** Same as the preceding.

Kennedy Half Dollars (1964 to Date)

From 1964 to date half dollars have been of the Kennedy design, with the obverse portrait by Gilroy Roberts and the reverse motif by Frank Gasparro. Shortly after producing the Kennedy half dollar, Roberts exited the Mint and became a major factor in the launching of Joseph Segel's General Numismatics Corporation, later renamed the Franklin Mint. This private minting enterprise was certainly one of the greatest numismatic financial success stories of all time. For the Franklin Mint Roberts designed many limited edition medals, achieving a personal wealth which no other former Mint chief engraver had ever enjoyed. A minor mystery is this: While millions of business strike Kennedy half dollars are produced each year, such pieces are hardly ever seen in circulation. What happens to them all?

• **Budget Recommendations:** Form a set in VF-30 or better grades. Recent issues can be found for face value by looking through rolls obtained from banks.

• • **Recommendations for the Connoisseur:** Go for MS-65 all the way, although you might want to add Proof-65 coins as applicable.

• • • **Elite Recommendations:** Same as the preceding.

Early Silver Dollars (1794-1804)

Silver dollars were minted for circulation from 1794 through 1935. Later-dated coins of the dollar denomination (beginning with Eisenhower dollars in 1971) are more aptly called *metal* dollars, for with the exception of certain pieces minted for collectors, they did not contain silver. Since time immemorial, or at least as time is measured in the numismatic hobby, silver dollars have been popular with collectors. Until the 1960s they remained more or less in the background, taking a secondary position to such series as Lincoln cents, Liberty nickels, commemoratives, and the like, but beginning in the 1960s silver dollars came to the forefront, and they have remained before the footlights ever since.

Silver dollars divide themselves into several neatly defined groups. The first, early dollars minted from 1794 through 1803, is comprised of issues which appeal to two collecting disciplines: specialists and type collectors.

The collector of design types has three motifs to choose from. The first, the Flowing Hair motif minted in 1794 and 1795, is a stylistic carbon copy of the contemporary half dime and half dollar. The second, the Draped Bust obverse in combination with the Small Eagle reverse, minted from 1795 through 1798, likewise mirrors the design used in smaller silver denominations. The third, the Draped Bust obverse with Heraldic Eagle reverse, produced from 1798 through 1803, completes the early date range. In addition there is the 1804 silver dollar, which is in a class by itself.

The first United States silver dollars, dated 1794, were produced to the extent of 1,758 pieces according to contemporary Mint records, although some scholars, Robert Hilt prominent among them, have suggested that several thousand pieces included as part of the 160,295 mintage for 1795 were in fact struck from 1794-dated dies. No matter what the original situation was, today the 1794 dollar is a rarity. Approximately 120 different specimens are known, most of which are in grades from Fine to Very Fine. Extremely Fine pieces are very rare, AU coins are major rarities, and in the Uncirculated category the number of surviving specimens can be counted on the fingers of one's hands. The ownership of a 1794 silver dollar in any grade has always been regarded as a source of pride and a mark of distinction.

With relatively few exceptions, 1794 silver dollars are lightly struck at the lower left side of the obverse and on the corresponding part of the reverse, due to the faces of the coining dies not being aligned parallel with each other. Several years ago Jack Collins undertook a study of 1794 silver dollars sponsored by the American Numismatic Society. Using photographs in old auction catalogues and other data he traced the pedigrees of pieces which have appeared on the market during the past century and a half.

The type collector desiring an example of the Flowing Hair style can be satisfied with a 1795-dated piece, of which at least several thousand exist in numismatic circles. Most of these are in worn grades, although an occasional Uncirculated piece is encountered in the marketplace.

Draped Bust half dollars with Small Eagle reverse, first minted in 1795, are readily available today as a type. Within the span of coinage, a number of rare varieties occur, the most famous of which is the 1797 with nine stars to the left of the obverse and seven on the right, and with small letters on the reverse. I have handled only a few of these over the years, and I consider the variety to be extremely undervalued.

The most often seen early dollars are those of the Draped Bust obverse, Heraldic Eagle reverse style, minted 1798-1803, particularly dollars bearing the dates 1798 and 1799. Several hundred dollars will buy an attractive example in one of the lower circulated grades.

The 1804 silver dollar is arguably the most famous United States coin rarity, although some might say that the 1913 Liberty Head nickel edges it out. Unquestionably, a couple generations ago, when Texas dealer B. Max Mehl focused many advertising campaigns around the 1913 Liberty Head nickel, it was king, but in recent times more publicity has been given to the 1804 dollar. In the late 19th and early 20th centuries, many columns of print were devoted to this coin in the pages of *The Numismatist*, the *American Journal of Numismatics*, and other publications of the day. In 1962 a book was written about it, *The Fantastic 1804 Dollar*, by Eric P. Newman and Kenneth E. Bressett. Some 15 dollars dated 1804 are known, divided into three styles, sometimes designated as classes I, II, and III.

While a detailed history of the 1804 dollar could and has occupied a book, as noted, suffice it to say here that Mint reports stated that 19,570 silver dollars were coined in 1804. However, it is virtually certain that none of these pieces was dated 1804 but, rather, represented coinage accomplished in 1804 from earlier-dated dies. In the 1830s Mint officials desired to put together presentation sets illustrating the various United States coin denominations. Checking the official records, and not having great numismatic knowledge, those in charge at the Mint concluded that United States silver dollars were last coined in 1804, and were presumably dated 1804. As no dollars were being minted or were authorized to be minted in the 1830s, to fill out the presentation sets they decided to produce some additional copies of the last official issue—which they presumed had been dated 1804. Searching in the die vaults, no 1804-dated dies were found, so the Mint simply created some, undoubtedly with no intent to deceive. The largest gold coin denomination, the $10 piece, likewise had not been minted since 1804; no 1804-dated $10 dies could be found on hand, so new ones were made up as well. In 1834 the Mint created presentation Proof sets containing one of each denomination currently being minted, from the half cent through the half dollar, plus the

$2.50 and $5, plus back-dated 1804 $1 and $10 pieces, for the latter two denominations were not currently being struck. The King of Siam set earlier mentioned was such a presentation group and was given as a gift to the ruler of that land.

Collectors in the 19th century first learned of the existence of the 1804 dollar through an illustration of a piece in the Mint Cabinet, in a book published in 1842, and desired to own examples. Certain individuals at the Mint complied, producing additional pieces which were sold privately. Before long a controversy arose, and some scholars branded the 1804 dollars as concoctions. The Mint responded with a cover-up operation, issuing false statements that indeed 1804 dollars were without question minted in the year 1804.

The subject was debated, seemingly endlessly, at the same time drawing great attention to the dollar. Just about every leading collector of the late 19th century, and the present century as well, aspired to own an example of what B. Max Mehl called "the King of American Coins." As pieces crossed the auction block, they consistently set record levels for the United States silver series. Today, as in days gone by, the exhibition of an 1804 silver dollar at a convention is apt to draw great attention and a wide circle of admirers. It has been my good fortune to have handled 1804 dollars at auction several times, and in each instance a lot of publicity has been generated.

Business strike silver dollars of the 1794-1803 years were studied by M.H. Bolender, and die varieties were described in his book titled *The United States Early Silver Dollars from 1794 to 1803*. In the 1950s and 1960s I had several dozen clients who were collecting early dollars by Bolender numbers. Today the specialty has faded somewhat, undeservedly so, for nearly all of the issues are relatively inexpensive in circulated grades. In Very Fine preservation most varieties are priced at less than $1,000 each. There are many bargains to be had. For example, dollars dated 1801, 1802 and 1803 are much scarcer than those dated 1798 and 1799, and yet catalogue values do not reflect this.

Die variety collecting is very active in the fields of half cents, large cents, and half dollars in particular, and to a lesser extent with half dimes, dimes, and quarters. Early silver dollars probably finish last in the popularity parade. One of these years someone will start an Early Silver Dollar Collectors Club, the race will be on, and rare die varieties will sell for multiples of the prices of common ones.

• **Budget Recommendations:** Form a type set or variety set in VG-8 to F-12 grade. These are very cheap on the market now.

• • **Recommendations for the Connoisseur:** It is bargain time among early silver dollars, and with the exception of coins in higher Mint State levels, nearly all varieties are cheaper now than they were 10 to 15 years ago! Start with a type set of the three designs. VF-20 to EF-40 are very affordable grades, although higher grades are even nicer to own. There are many die varieties among 1794-1803 dollars. As noted above, if you obtain a copy of M.H. Bolender's book, *The United States Silver Dollars from 1794 to 1803*, you can have a field day, especially with slabbed coins, as most are not marked as to variety, and you don't have to pay a premium for rarities.

• • • **Elite Recommendations:** Aspire to acquire as many major varieties as you can in AU-50 or better grade, acquiring the occasional MS-60 or finer piece as it comes on the market.

Liberty Seated Dollars (1836-1873)

After the pieces dated 1803, no dollars were struck for circulation until 1836, in which year Christian Gobrecht's Liberty Seated design was produced, possibly as a pattern, for all were made with Proof finish, hardly the format to use for business strikes. However, nearly all of the 1,000 pieces struck in 1836, and 600 additional 1836-dated pieces struck on March 31, 1837, were deliberately placed into circulation by the government, so these are de facto business strikes, no argument. Certain varieties of Liberty Seated patterns were also made dated 1836, and additional pieces were produced in 1838 and 1839. In the latter year some 300 pieces were produced for circulation, again with Proof finish. The last word has not been written on this subject, although Robert W. Julian, through essays published in *The Rare Coin Review, Coin World*, and elsewhere, has done much to clarify the status of 1836-1839 Gobrecht dollars.

Beginning in 1840, silver dollars were again struck in large quantities for circulation, during which year 61,005 were minted. The obverse featured the Liberty Seated design with stars, while the reverse depicted a perched eagle similar to that found on quarters and half dollars of the era. Liberty Seated dollars were produced continuously through 1873, with a design modification in 1866 when the motto IN GOD WE TRUST was added to the reverse.

Several prime rarities were produced during that span, including the 1851, of which 1,300 originals were made, and the 1852, struck to the extent of 1,100 pieces.[12] Another famous dollar is the 1858, struck only with Proof finish, quite possibly to the extent of just 80 coins, equal to the number of silver Proof sets believed to have been sold by the Mint that year. No 1858 dollars were made for general circulation.

In 1870 the Carson City Mint opened for general business, and in that year some 12,462 Liberty Seated dollars were struck in addition to coins of other denominations. During the following year 1,376 1871-CC dollars were made, followed by 3,150 1872-CC pieces and, finally, by 2,300 dollars of the 1873-CC issue. Although 1873-CC does not have the lowest mintage, it is the rarest Carson City Liberty Seated dollar. Examples are elusive in any grade, and Mint State coins are fantastic rarities. However, the Liberty Seated specialist need not despair, for in lower circulated grades pieces can be obtained in the four-figure range.

In general, Mint State Liberty Seated dollars are rare, exceptions being 1859-O and 1860-O, many hundreds of which came to light during the Treasury release of silver dollars in 1962. At the same time many thousands of circulated Liberty Seated coins were released. I recall purchasing large quantities of these, shipped to my company unsorted in Treasury Department bags. Jim Ruddy, my business partner at the time, and I were so excited that we worked nonstop for a few days—not even going out for lunch—to arrange these dollars in poker-chip fashion in piles according to date, from 1840 onward. As I recall, we had more 1847-dated dollars than any other issue.

Today the building of a set of Liberty Seated dollars affords an interesting challenge. The 1870-S is a great rarity and is seldom available, and the aforementioned 1851, 1852 and 1858 are seldom seen, but if these four varieties are excluded, the building of a set from 1840 through 1873 is within the grasp of just about everyone. A nice condition to aim for is Extremely Fine to AU. There is something basically nifty about handling a large, heavy Liberty Seated silver dollar from the 1840s and wondering where it has been and what it has seen in the meantime.

• **Budget Recommendations:** Build a date and mintmark set in F-12 grade. This will be a fascinating endeavor, as the varieties are quite interesting. Many issues are sleepers, even in these grades. Such dates as 1862, 1863, 1864, and 1865 are examples.

• • **Recommendations for the Connoisseur:** Start by building a type set. EF-40 is an affordable grade, except for the 1836-1839 Gobrecht design. Forming a set of dates and mintmarks of 1840-1873 dollars is a challenge. EF-40 to AU-50 is a good goal. If you have the time and money, MS-63 coins furnish a stimulating pursuit. I have never seen an MS-63 or finer collection, for many of the issues are extremely rare. Easier to find are Proofs, especially 1859-1873, although these must be selected with care.

• • • **Elite Recommendations:** Aspire to build a set of MS-63 or finer coins *plus* (not instead of) as many Philadelphia Mint Proofs as you can find

(Proofs 1840-1857 can be Proof-63 or finer, except for the restrike 1851 and 1852 in Proof-64 or finer); 1858-1873 can be Proof-65). As your set nears completion, I would love to be able to see it! No one has ever put together such a set before!

Morgan Dollars (1878-1921)

Now we come to Morgan silver dollars, the most active series among older coins in American numismatics. As noted earlier in the present book, Morgan dollars were first minted in 1878, although no one particularly wanted or needed them. By that time silver had fallen to a low point on the world markets, and in silver-mining areas, unemployment was rife and the economic outlook was grim. There simply was no market for the vast quantities of silver being brought up from the Comstock Lode in Nevada and from the hills west of Denver. True to time honored American tradition, politicians stepped into the situation and suggested that Uncle Sam purchase millions of ounces of silver in order to buoy the market.

What to do with this unneeded, unwanted silver? Coining it into dollars was the most expedient plan. George T. Morgan, who had come to the Mint from England in 1876, and who in 1877 had posed Philadelphia school-teacher Anna Williams and had copied her portrait for use on a pattern half dollar, was commissioned to create a new silver dollar design. Early in the year 1878 his 1877 half dollar die ideas were dusted off, expanded into silver dollar form, and what was called the Bland Dollar (after the Bland-Allison Act of 1878, which caused the government to buy silver), became a reality. Later, collectors were to know the coins as Morgan dollars.

The engraver's initial M appears at the truncation of the neck of Miss Liberty on the obverse and at the wreath ribbon on the reverse. In the numismatic field complaints were rife about the Morgan dollar. The eagle resembled a turkey or, worse, a buzzard, and in any event the whole motif was exceedingly inartistic, according to comments printed in the *American Journal of Numismatics* and elsewhere. Morgan dollars were without honor in their own time, and during the early years of their coinage, 1878 through 1904, very few numismatists bothered to collect them. Those who were interested were apt to buy Proofs of the Philadelphia Mint issues. So far as I know, during the 1870s and 1880s not a single collector desired to own Carson City, San Francisco, or New Orleans pieces! Of course, this makes amazing reading today, but that's what the situation was back then.

The various mints continued to produce silver dollars in staggering quantities, bagging them and storing them in vaults. Problems arose, and at one time the huge storage vault in the Philadelphia Mint became damp, the cloth bags which contained 1,000 dollars each rotted, and chaos ensued. Other facilities were pressed into use for storage, including the New Orleans Mint. No one knew what to do with all of these round discs.

To be sure, silver dollars were used in circulation, particularly in the American West, where they were ideal to pass across a bar or use in a poker game. However, in the major cities and centers of civilization, few people cared to jangle a pocket full of heavy dollar-size coins. Most stayed in banks, where they could be obtained on special request.

The Pittman Act of 1918 provided for the wholesale melting of silver dollars, and 270,232,722 dollars were reduced to silver bullion. Unfortunately, or, depending on how you look at it, fortunately, no record was kept of the specific dates and mintmarks melted. Still, silver dollars amounting to the hundreds of millions remained in Treasury and bank vaults. In 1921 it was decided to coin additional silver dollars, and the Morgan design, unused since 1904, was resurrected for further use.

In December 1921 a new design, the Peace dollar, appeared. Peace silver dollars were produced through 1935. Peace dollars suffered their own melting situation; tens of millions were reduced to silver bullion in order to obtain metal for use in the Manhattan Project, which saw the production of the first atomic bomb. Again, no records were kept of the dates and mintmarks destroyed.

Throughout the 1940s there was a relatively minor collecting interest in dollars. In the 1950s the interest grew somewhat, and such dealers as Norman Shultz and Bebee's made a specialty of Morgan and Peace dollars, offering many different varieties for scarcely over face value. Toward the end of the 1950s, Harry Forman, the Philadelphia dealer, developed a lively trade in selling Carson City and other dollars in roll and bag quantities. Investment interest was piqued, and by the early 1960s many issues had shown an attractive rise in price from the levels of a decade earlier.

In particular there was one great rarity in the Morgan silver dollar series, the 1903-O, which catalogued for $1,500 in the standard arbiter of values, *A Guide Book of United States Coins*. Although mintage figures revealed that 4,450,000 1903-O dollars had been struck, it was generally assumed that nearly all were melted in 1918 under the provisions of the Pittman Act. Well worn specimens came on the market occasionally, but Uncirculated pieces appeared in auctions less often than examples of that great American rarity, the 1804 silver dollar!

By 1962 my business was firmly established as one of the leading dealerships in the United States, and yet I do not recall ever handling an Uncirculated 1903-O. B. Max Mehl, when he sold the William Forrester Dunham Collection in 1941 specifically singled out an Uncirculated 1903-O dollar as one of the collection's major rarities—and this was in company with such stellar rarities as an 1804 silver dollar and an 1822 half eagle! Although the 1903-O dollar catalogued $1,500, undoubtedly if I had offered to pay $5,000 for one, none would have been forthcoming. In fact, most dealers in America had never even *seen* an Uncirculated 1903-O, let alone owned one!

The Treasury hoard: In the autumn of 1962 a few Uncirculated 1903-O dollars found their way into the market. A few days later more came on the market, and before long it was realized that the Treasury had distributed several thousand of these erstwhile great rarities. The price dropped precipitously, and general panic ensued among dealers. Would the government be destroying the very structure of the coin market by releasing rarities in quantity?

While some dealers were worried, other people were happy—especially collectors and members of the public who had the good fortune to buy bags of 1903-O, 1898-O (another prime rarity of the time) and 1904-O dollars (still another rarity), and other issues for face value. The idea of acquiring a $1,500 1903-O dollar for just one dollar was like finding gold in the streets. Television, newspapers, and other media picked up the situation, and a treasure hunt was on! People with wheelbarrows stood in line to buy bags of silver dollars from banks.

At first the Treasury was delighted to get rid of the coins, as the government's storage and inventory problem was ended. The public continued to have a good time, and a new market arose—as thousands of people desired to acquire as many different Morgan dollar date and mintmark varieties as possible. Within a year the Treasury vaults were nearly empty, except for three million pieces, primarily Carson City coins, which the government held back and decided to sell at premium prices (this was later done through a series of sales conducted by the General Services Administration, a government agency). In the meantime, millions of other Carson City, New Orleans, San Francisco early dollars reached the hands of eager collectors and investors.

While market levels fell sharply for certain issues, particularly the 1898-O, 1903-O, and 1904-O, in most instances the price drops were short-lived, and within a few years most issues of Morgan dollars were priced substantially higher than they had been before the great Treasury release. Although Morgan dollars were now much more common, the number of collectors and investors interested in them had expanded even more than the supply of coins available, and Morgan dollars became the most desired American coin series.

Earlier, veteran dealer Abe Kosoff conducted a survey among his clients and sought to determine the most popular United States numismatic specialties. Morgan dollars did not finish even in the top 10! The most sought-after series, as I recall, was Buffalo nickels. Beginning after the Treasury release of 1962, Morgan dollars went right into the top 10, right up to number one, and have remained near or at the top of the list ever since. So popular have silver dollars been that a special group, the National Silver Dollar Roundtable, exists to conduct an annual convention specifically treating the field.

In 1976 a book, *The Comprehensive Catalogue and Encyclopedia of U.S. and Morgan Peace Silver Dollars*, by Leroy C. Van Allen and A. George Mallis, was released and sold to the extent of thousands of copies. The authors described in detail minute die varieties of Morgan dollars, and a new generation of specialists was created. Later the book went out of print, and at the same time prices continued to rise, so as these words are being written, in 1990, most collectors desire Morgan dollars not by minute die varieties, but by date and mintmark issues. In other words, just one 1881-S dollar is needed in a collection, not a number of minute die varieties.

Morgan dollars are extremely affordable, and a set consisting of 97 different basic varieties is within the reach of most serious collectors. Scarce and rare issues are several, and include the 1889-CC, 1893-S, and 1895. In higher condition levels, such as MS-65, a number of other rarities emerge, including such issues as 1886-O, 1892-S, 1893-O, 1894-O, 1895-O, and 1896-O, among others. It has been my experience that the average collector of Morgan dollars does not aspire to own a complete set but, rather, endeavors to acquire a basic collection of the more affordable varieties. In September 1990, according to *The Coin Dealer Newsletter*, about 60 different Morgan dollar varieties were valued in MS-63 grade for less than $100 each, and many of these were valued for considerably less than $50 each. Certainly, this low price range was a powerful incentive to begin collecting!

It would be an interesting exercise to study the Morgan silver dollar market for the years since 1962. Endless paragraphs have been devoted to Morgan dollars in the pages of investment newsletters and numismatic periodicals, not to overlook dealer advertisements. The 1881-S Morgan dollar, the most common variety in higher grades, has bounced around like a ping-pong ball. In the 1980s tens of thousands of 1881-S dollars came on the market, as the result of a hoard discovered in a Chicago bank. Dollars of this particular variety became an investment medium in their own right, and for a time a firm listed bid and ask quotations daily in *The Wall Street Journal*. At one time there was a special flurry of investor interest, and I recall hearing that $2,000 was paid for a particularly nice MS-65 coin! Then by mid-1990 the price slipped to the $200 range, or even less. In recent years the market price of the 1881-S has been up, down, and sideways.

Scarce and rare issues are less affected by market conditions and vagaries of investment desire. When I sold the Norweb Collection, a particularly nice 1893-S crossed the auction block at a staggering $357,500—the most ever paid for a Morgan silver dollar before or since! In 1990 I sold at auction in our Sussex Collection sale a very nice 1893-S described as MS-65, but not to equal the Norweb coin, for $154,000.

As I see it, the continued popularity of the Morgan silver dollar is assured. In September 1990 dealer John Highfill informed me that he is planning to publish an encyclopedia-sized book on silver dollars. Anticipated to be over 1,000 pages in length, the volume will contain essays by two dozen or more dealers and specialists. Bowers and Merena Galleries announced that Robert W. Julian and the present author are collaborating on another reference, a book which will detail the history of silver dollars from 1794 onward and which will present much information not hitherto easily available. These two books will probably do much to further interest in what is already America's most popular series.

• **Budget Recommendations:** You will have to consult current price guides such as "Trends" in *Coin World* or "Coin Market" in *Numismatic News* in order to formulate a plan under my guidelines, which are these: Make a list of all the varieties you wish to include. Then use MS-60 to MS-63 for all varieties you can buy for less than $50 each. Then use EF-40 as the objective for all remaining varieties you can buy for less than $50 each. Then use VF-20 in the same manner, then F-12. By this point you will be down to just a few, and you can determine on your own what do do about the 1889-CC, the 1893-S, and the Proof-only 1895.

• • **Recommendations for the Connoisseur:** Morgan dollars lend themselves to building a collection within a collection. Among Carson City issues, a set can be made of the early varieties produced continuously through 1878 through 1885. Although 1879-CC is elusive, thousands of them exist, and a set of 1878-CC to 1885-CC dollars can be assembled without undue difficulty. Carson City dollars of the later range, those minted from 1889 through 1893, are considerably harder to find, but still are very collectible. A set of New Orleans dollars offers another possibility, as does a set of San Francisco dollars. Here is one idea for a specialized collection: Build a set of date and mintmark varieties of 1878-1921 dollars in nicely matched MS-63 and MS-64 grade, except for the half dozen or so rarer issues, for which you can determine your own budget and grade level. Such a collection, containing nearly 100 coins, forms a beautiful exhibit.

• • • **Elite Recommendations:** Build a set in MS-65 grade, sharply struck, each coin selected for lustrous, frosty surfaces (I personally prefer these to prooflike finish coins, but you may differ). For the Philadelphia Mint coins buy Proof-65 examples. Be very fussy all the way, and select coins with superb aesthetic appeal. Over a period of time you should be able to acquire all but two or three varieties (1886-O is a prime rarity and is virtually unobtainable in MS-65, for example), and these can be obtained in MS-63 or MS-64 preservation. A good way to go is to look at many slabbed coins and then cherrypick those which meet your qualifications for striking and aesthetic appeal. For some issues you may have to view a couple dozen or more certified coins before finding one which is just right, but your patience will be rewarded when you acquire a long sought-after variety.

Peace Dollars (1921-1935)

Peace silver dollars have also been popular in recent years, not as popular as Morgan dollars, but still very much in the center of activity. Unlike Morgan dollars, all Peace dollars are readily available in Uncirculated grade, and the building of a set of 24 different varieties minted from 1921 through 1935 is a definite possibility for just about everyone, although the 1934-S is apt to be expensive. A Mint State 1934-S costs several thousand dollars or more, depending upon the degree of quality.[13]

To illustrate how a small difference in grade can make a big difference in price let me mention two sets of Peace dollars which I was offered in 1990. The first was a set of MS-63 dollars, hand-picked, in PCGS slabs for about $12,000, and the second was a set of MS-65 coins, again in PCGS slabs, for $200,000, except that the seller was missing four pieces from the second set, but promised to buy them for me—figuring he could get them somewhere or other. To the untrained eye both sets were about the same quality, and each contained sparkling, lustrous, brilliant coins. Of course, the specialist would recognize that while the MS-63 coins were indeed of excellent quality and very desirable and collectible, the MS-65 pieces, with their pristine surfaces, were measurably nicer.

I have always liked Peace dollars bearing the date 1921, for these are in high relief and are distinctively different than later issues. It is one of the injustices of numismatics that the 1921 dollar is not recognized on a widespread basis as a distinctly different design type. I once asked Harry Forman, who probably has handled as many bags of silver dollars as anyone in the business (including countless thousands of bags after the Treasury release of 1962), if he had ever seen or handled a bag of Uncirculated 1921 Peace dollars, and the answer was in the negative.

Years ago I had the opportunity to talk at length with Mrs. Anthony DeFrancisci, the former Teresa Cafarelli, widow of the designer of the coin. She posed for the Peace dollar, she said, and indeed I am sure she did, although there is no doubt that the face of Miss Liberty on the Peace design bears a very close resemblance to the Miss Liberty used by Augustus Saint-Gaudens for his 1907 $10 piece. More about that Miss Liberty later.

As a rare coin dealer, one of the things I try to encourage people to do—including you as a reader of this book—is to collect with a purpose. It has never ceased to amaze me that the average buyer of silver dollars, whether they be Morgan dollars or Peace dollars, seems to prefer accumulating silver dollars than to collecting them. For every person I have seen trying to complete a basic collection of 24 different Peace silver dollars 1921-1935, I have seen a couple dozen buyers squirreling away hoards of silver dollars, perhaps a quantity of some common date as 1924 or 1925, with no apparent rhyme or reason apart from having read one investment recommendation or another.

One thing to remember about many investment recommendations is this: the recommended items are apt to be what the seller has for sale, rather than what the buyer should buy, and in instances in which recommendations are given by someone engaged in the mass marketing of numismatic items, chances are excellent that common coins, not rare ones, will be recommended—as common coins are easier to stock and are available in virtually unlimited quantities. I have always encouraged investors to think for themselves, and not to rely on the advice of others. The main theme of my book on the subject, *High Profits from Rare Coin Investment*, is that the best investment has traditionally been a fine collection gathered over a period of years. This is true in the field of silver dollars as well as in just about any other numismatic area you can name.

A personal experience: I have always liked Peace silver dollars, for reasons which I cannot fully explain, except to say that they evoke a certain nostalgia, a sense of the 1920s and the romantic era associated with that time—although this era was long before I was born. In the 1950s, when I was a beginning collector, I would go to banks near my home town of Forty Fort, Pennsylvania, and look through their stocks of silver dollars. At the time the typical financial institution had in its vault a few sacks of silver dollars. The

Forty Fort State Bank, located on the corner of Wyoming Avenue and Fort Street, only a couple of blocks from my home, had 500 to 1,000 silver dollars as its typical stock, but would order more on request. A more fertile field was provided by the Kingston National Bank, in an adjacent community, which usually had 5,000 to 10,000 coins on hand. The Second National Bank in Wilkes-Barre, Pennsylvania (in which building my father had his structural engineering office) and the Miners National Bank across the street each had much larger quantities—many bags of dollars. Although now as a business-man many years later, I can't quite figure out why these and other banks would have been so kind as to help a high school kid interested in finding silver dollars, back then these financial institutions didn't mind at all if I plunked down $1,000 (representing a good part of my stake in the coin business) for a bag of silver dollars, removed the bag to a safe deposit room, looked through the pieces, took out the ones I wanted, and replaced them with common issues.

It was my cherished dream to find a Morgan silver dollar with a Flying Eagle reverse, as also used on 1836-1839 Gobrecht dollars, for I thought that such existed. The reason was that by mistake the *Guide Book* illustrated this as the Morgan dollar reverse in one of its early issues. I didn't know that a mistake had been made until George P. Williams, a friendly local collector, set me straight.

I looked through thousands of silver dollars. In Northeastern Pennsylvania in the early 1950s it was a simple matter to find Uncirculated examples of many different Philadelphia issues and occasional Uncirculated specimens of San Francisco pieces. New Orleans and Carson City varieties encountered were nearly always worn. In fact, I don't recall ever seeing an Uncirculated Carson City coin taken from a bank bag. I never found an 1895 Philadelphia Mint Morgan dollar in any grade, for only Proofs and impaired Proofs existed, but I was able to find all of the others, including the rare 1903-O (a couple of well-worn examples). The typical grade encountered was Extremely Fine to AU, except that most Carson City coins were extensively worn, from VG to VF. This made them all the more interesting, for I had dreams of their being used in the Wild West, as indeed they were.

There was no particular premium attached to most varieties of Morgan dollars, and once I had acquired an example for my collection, I was not apt to save duplicates. As time went on, my dealership grew, and I no longer could afford the luxury of spending days in bank vaults looking through sacks of dollars. Instead, I started buying and selling collections which had already been formed. Whenever I bought a Morgan or Peace dollar collection, I would break out the Uncirculated pieces or coins worth, say, $2 each or more, and simply spend the others. My fellow dealers in the profession did likewise, as there was no financial point in stocking common dates. In the early 1960s I recall that the wife of a publisher in Vestal, New York, where I lived at the time, became interested in silver dollars, and I helped her begin her set by giving her many different dates and mintmarks at face value, instead of turning them in to a bank.

I put together a set of Peace dollars lickety-split. In circulated grades, all dates and mintmarks were readily available. One or more of the early issues of the *Guide Book* carried the statement that 1928 Peace dollars were minted only for "cornerstone purposes." When I found my first 1928 Philadelphia Mint dollar in a bank bag, I believed that somehow or other it had escaped from a cornerstone, perhaps from one in an old courthouse or bank that must have been broken open years ago. Then I found another 1928 dollar, then another, and before long many more. So, I stopped saving them. Years later, in 1989 as I was completing research for my book, *The American Numismatic Association Centennial History*, I came across a notation printed in *The Numismatist* in the late 1920s, which stated that the Treasury Department had announced that 1928 silver dollars had been released (not minted) for cornerstone purposes.

Apparently what happened was that 360,649 silver dollars were minted in Philadelphia in 1928, but these were not needed in the channels of commerce, so they were simply stored. However, there was a call for some of them for cornerstone or other presentation purposes, so the Treasury Department decided to let some of them out. Somehow or other this got translated into the notation which appeared in the *Guide Book* and which made the issue seem incredibly romantic! In later years dollars of this date eventually were parceled out into circulation, so that by the 1950s, when I was looking for them, they weren't particularly rare.

• **Budget Recommendations:** Form a set in VF-20 grade.

• • **Recommendations for the Connoisseur:** Build a nicely matched MS-63 or MS-64 set. Select nicely struck coins with good aesthetic appeal.

• • • **Elite Recommendations:** Form a set in nicely matched MS-65 grade, cherrypicking for quality and aesthetic appeal. The easiest way to do this is to look at many MS-65 slabbed coins and pick out the high-end examples that appeal to you.

Eisenhower Dollars

In 1971 a new type of dollar appeared, no longer a *silver* dollar, except for certain issues made for collectors, but a clad metal dollar made of copper-nickel alloy. Bearing the visage of President Dwight D. Eisenhower, these dollars were produced from 1971 through 1978, with the exception of 1975. Surviving business strikes are apt to be rather unattractive in appearance, for like Franklin half dollars, Eisenhower dollars tend to nick and scar easily. However, there is no doubt that selected Uncirculated pieces can be attractive, and that Proofs can be gorgeous, that is if you find the basic design to be appealing (which not everyone does).

• **Budget Recommendations:** Buy MS-63 or better coins. These are unattractive enough as it is (personal opinion here!), and are even less appealing in worn grades.

• • **Recommendations for the Connoisseur:** Acquire MS-65 business strikes and Proof-65 coins, as part of a date and mintmark set.

• • • **Elite Recommendations:** Same as the preceding.

Anthony Dollars

Susan B. Anthony dollars minted from 1979 through 1981 were also produced in clad metal. When the government decided that a small dollar-size coin would be produced in order to save money (it was felt that a metal dollar would remain in circulation much longer than a paper dollar), Frank Gasparro, then chief engraver at the Mint, hoped that he would be allowed to create a classic design. He prepared sketches and models for Miss Liberty with a pole and cap behind her head, reminiscent of the Liberty Cap cent of 1793. However, politics intervened, and he was directed to prepare a design with the portrait of Miss Susan B. Anthony, which he subsequently did.

With great optimism, Anthony dollars were produced to the extent of hundreds of millions in the year 1979. It soon developed that these were a flop in circulation, as the public mistook them for quarters. Not helping matters was the public resentment against the double-digit inflation of the Jimmy Carter administration. As a satire on the diminishing purchasing value of the dollar, Anthony coins were called by some "J.C. (for Jimmy Carter) pennies," a pun on J.C. Penney, the merchandising chain. Frank Gasparro could have told the Treasury Department about the mistaken identity problem, for he related in a conversation with me that he took one of the earliest pieces minted and endeavored to spend it in the employees' cafeteria at the Philadelphia Mint, where the cashier immediately mistook it for a quarter!

The government tried to spur the circulation of Anthony dollars, and put up signs in post offices stating that they would be paid out and received there. Although it was realized that the public did not want the coins, the Treasury gamely produced millions more in 1980, followed by a few million more in 1981, at which time the series was terminated. As these words are being written, hundreds of millions of the things are still stored in Treasury vaults. One of these days the public will catch on to them as collectors' items, and the Treasury will sell out of them quickly—just wait and see! However, the issues of 1979 in particular, each minted to the extent of many millions, will never be rare.

As a frequent visitor to New York City I remember seeing signs printed in black against an orange dayglo background at entrances to the tunnels and bridges leading to Manhattan, stating that Anthony dollars would be accepted at the toll booths. I considered taking a picture of these signs, but never got around to doing it. I wonder if anyone else did? Such a picture would be a nice numismatic memento.

I find the Anthony dollar to be an attractive little coin, cameolike in its appearance, and one which is worthy of more attention than it has received. Perhaps the fact that these issues are common has mitigated against their popularity. My friend, Rick Sundman, whose family operates the Littleton Coin Company, told me that he achieved excellent success in selling these coins to the public in national advertisements in non-numismatic periodicals. Someday someone in numismatics should give Littleton Coin Company an award for helping to spread the word, in an honorable way, about the appeal of coin collecting—as B. Max Mehl did in the 1920s, 1930s, and 1940s. Certainly, the hobby could use more good missionary work of this nature.

Before leaving the subject of Anthony dollars, I admit to having a prejudice in favor of this coin, inasmuch as prior to and during its creation I had a number of conversations and visits with Chief Engraver Frank Gasparro, a selfless, dedicated artist with great ideals. Later, after he retired from the Mint and entered private practice, Ray Merena and I commissioned him to design a series of limited edition silver medals for Bowers and Merena Galleries. One of these designs, the Spirit of Liberty created in 1990, was done after Ray and I asked Frank to come up with a design which in his opinion would represent his ideal image of Miss Liberty for use on a coin, had he been able to have had his own way on the subject.

• **Budget Recommendations:** Buy MS-60 to MS-63 and Proof-63 coins as part of a date and mintmark set. Your local bank may be able to supply some for face value.

• • **Recommendations for the Connoisseur:** Buy MS-65 and Proof-65 coins as part of a date and mintmark set. If you want to hoard a few coins, 1981 and 1981-D business strikes are especially cheap now.

· · · **Elite Recommendations:** Same as the preceding.

Trade Dollars (1873-1885)

Following an extensive coinage of patterns in 1872, trade dollars, at first called commercial dollars, were struck in large quantities in 1873. These silver coins, 420 grains in weight and heavier than a standard United States silver dollar, were intended for use in the Orient to compete with Mexican silver dollars. Merchants in China preferred Mexican coins, which contained more silver than American dollars, and American commerce suffered. The trade dollar would remedy the situation, it was hoped, and the effort ultimately succeeded.

Most business strike trade dollars were produced in the West at the San Francisco and Carson City mints; for two reasons: proximity to China and nearness to sources of silver for coinage. At first, trade dollars were legal tender in the United States, but Congress repealed this provision in the enabling act, and the coins became worth only bullion or melt-down value. For years afterward coin dealers offered common trade dollars for sale retail for less than $1 each!

The formation of a complete set of business strike trade dollars 1873-1878 is a distinct possibility for just about anyone, for there are no major rarities (although the 1878-CC is quite scarce).

Proofs were minted of all dates from 1873 through 1883. Toward the end of the series, the trade dollars from 1878 onward were Proof-only issues, as no related Philadelphia Mint coins of these dates were struck for circulation. A few Proofs were secretly struck in 1884 and 1885, and today these pieces, of which just 10 and five are known respectively, are great rarities.

During the early period of Proof trade dollar issuance, from 1873 to 1877, the coins were not desired by many collectors. As the pieces were sold as part of silver Proof sets (containing silver issues from the half dime to the standard dollar in 1873; and from 1874 to 1877, from the dime to the half dollar), numismatists were forced to buy them. As soon as the sets were unwrapped, many collectors simply spent the Proof trade dollars, with the result that today Proofs of the early dates, especially Proofs in high levels of preservation, are considerably rarer than the mintage figures indicate. On the other hand, the later Proof-only issues (1878-1883) were recognized at the time as having a special value, and most of these were carefully preserved.

• **Budget Recommendations:** Build a set of 1873-1878 coins in VF-20 to VF-30 grade. Certain higher graded coins with chopmarks (punchmarks stamped on the coins by Oriental merchants, to signify that the pieces were of good weight and fineness) are cheap, so sometimes you can acquire AU-50 chopmarked coins for little more than a regular VF-30 would cost. Proofs 1878-1883 can be bought in impaired condition.

· ·**Recommendations for the Connoisseur:** There are several ways to go: 1. Buy a basic coin as a type; I recommend EF-45, MS-63, or Proof-63, depending upon your budget. If you select Proof-63, pick a date in the 1878-1883 range as it is interesting to own a low mintage issue of which only 1,000 coins or so were ever made (although Proofs of earlier issues are rarer, these earlier dates are readily available in business strike form). 2. Build a set of dates and mintmarks. If you are on a budget, use EF-40 to AU-50 as an objective for the issues 1873-1878 and Proof-60 for the later rare Proofs through 1883. If you can afford it, try for a set of MS-63 business strikes of the branch mint issues and Proof-63 coins of the Philadelphia varieties. Of course, MS-64 and Proof-64 would be even nicer, but there is a substantial jump in price from the 63 level. 3. Build a date set of Proofs 1873-1883 in Proof-63 or Proof-64 grade.

· · ·**Elite Recommendations:** Form a set of 1873-1878 branch mint coins in MS-65 grade and 1873-1883 Philadelphia coins in Proof-65 preservation. Certain of the branch mint coins will be quite a challenge.

CHAPTER FOURTEEN

Gold Coins

Gold Dollars (1849-1889)

The gold dollar, the smallest denomination regular issue United States gold coin, first appeared in 1849, when the government introduced two new denominations, the dollar and double eagle, to exploit vast quantities of yellow metal coming to the East from the California Gold Rush. Gold dollars were minted continuously from 1849 through 1889, although mintages were largely restricted after the Civil War.

Today most of the demand for gold dollars comes from type coin collectors, who desire one each of the three different design variations. Type I gold dollars, with Miss Liberty's portrait identical to that used on the $20 double eagle, were made from 1849 through 1854, while Type II dollars, with an Indian princess motif, were struck in 1854 and 1855, plus in 1856 at the San Francisco Mint only. Type III dollars, featuring a modified portrait of an Indian princess, were made from 1856 through 1889.

In the early years, from 1849 through the Civil War, the gold dollar was a workhorse denomination. Those of the Type I design, 13mm in diameter, were used often in everyday change, and most examples seen today show wear. In 1854 the diameter was enlarged slightly to 15mm, to make the coin more convenient to handle. The Indian princess design, introduced in that year, created problems, as it was not possible for the metal in the dies to flow into the deep recesses of Miss Liberty's portrait on the obverse and at the same time into the central date digits on the reverse, with the result that majority of pieces seen today are weakly struck on the central two digits (85 in the date 1854, for example). To correct this, the Type II portrait, with Miss Liberty in shallower relief, was created in 1856.

Among the three design types of gold dollars, by far the scarcest is the Type II. The total mintage of Type II gold dollars amounted to fewer than 2 million pieces. Contrast that to the Type I gold dollar, for which over 4 million coins were struck at the Philadelphia Mint in 1853 alone! Similarly, the Type III gold dollar was minted in quantities far larger than the Type II.

Collecting gold dollars can be an enjoyable pursuit, although a good bank balance is necessary to complete the task. Particularly elusive are certain

Charlotte and Dahlonega mint coins, with 1855-D, 1856-D, 1860-D, and 1861-D being prime rarities. Among Philadelphia Mint coins the prize date is the 1875, of which just 20 Proofs and 400 business strikes were minted. How many of these survive, I don't know, but I doubt if more than 50 coins can be accounted for.

In general, Uncirculated gold dollars are rare for all dates prior to 1879, except that because of the enormous mintages, more Uncirculated pieces were saved by chance for such issues as Philadelphia Mint coins of the early 1850s. After 1878 a popular speculation arose whereby jewelers, numismatists, and members of the public enjoyed hoarding gold dollars (and to a lesser extent $3 pieces). Although gold dollars minted from 1879 through 1889 have generally low mintages, in proportion far more Uncirculated pieces survive than do issues of earlier dates.

Let me give an illustration: There were 7,707 gold dollars minted in 1881, including 87 Proofs. Over the years I have probably handled at least several hundred Uncirculated coins. Years ago I remember selling these in groups of a dozen or two at a time to dealers who wanted them in wholesale quantities. This does not detract from the desirability of the 1881, for today it is a highly prized issue, and although I may have handled a few hundred, and although perhaps a thousand or more Uncirculated pieces exist, far more than that number of collectors desire to own them, and when a single coin crosses the auction block today it is eagerly competed for.[1]

By contrast, the 1858-S dollar was produced to the extent of 10,000 pieces. I have only ever seen a few choice Uncirculated 1858-S dollars, and I doubt if more than a couple dozen exist in all of numismatics. In 1858 not a single collector desired to own a San Francisco Mint gold dollar, as collecting by mintmarks was not in vogue. All pieces slipped unnoticed into circulation. When collecting by dates and mintmarks finally became popular, after the publication in 1893 of Augustus G. Heaton's study, *Mint Marks* (the title used two words instead of one, as we do today), a number of people became interested, but by that time Uncirculated 1858-S gold dollars were no longer to be found. The same analogy can be extended to numerous other early varieties.

Over the years it has been my good fortune to have bought and sold several complete sets of gold dollars, including at least two purchased from Jerry Cohen and Abner Kreisberg, who seemed to have a magnetism for attracting such sets (not to overlook other spectacular sets of gold coins, including at one time a complete set of $4 stellas).

As noted, the most popular way to buy gold dollars is to acquire them as part of a type set. This is as good a place as any to mention that a nice basic gold type set, consisting of major design types from the mid-19th century onward, consists of the following: three types of gold dollars, Liberty Head or Coronet quarter eagle and Indian quarter eagle, $3 gold, Liberty Head half eagle, Indian head half eagle, Liberty Head $10, Indian $10, Liberty Head $20, and Saint-Gaudens $20. Each coin in this set is very affordable. If you want to become more technical, you can expand the set to include additional varieties of $5, $10, and $20 gold coins.

Many clever counterfeits exist of gold dollars (and other gold coins), and if you are not an expert yourself, insist on buying coins from a reputable professional numismatist who guarantees everything sold. Counterfeits, particularly of gold dollars and $3 pieces, seem to proliferate overseas, and if I had a nickel for every tourist who has shown me a "bargain" gold coin he bought in Europe, I'd have enough money to keep me in milk shakes for the next 20 years!

• **Budget Recommendations:** No recommendations here, as low-grade gold coins are apt to be quite unattractive. Consider what I have to say under the following listing.

• • **Recommendations for the Connoisseur:** There are two basic ways to go: 1. Build a basic type set consisting of the three designs. EF-40 to AU-50 coins are quite economical and have most of the sharpness of MS-60 coins. For the collector desiring better quality, MS-63 coins offer many possibilities. In all instances Type II dollars are considerably rarer than the other two designs. 2. Build a date and mintmark set. A good objective would be EF-40 or better for the mintmarks and MS-60 or better for the Philadelphia Mint coins. Certain of the Dahlonega Mint coins will present a challenge, especially 1855-D, 1856-D, 1860-D, and 1861-D. In my opinion, 1855-O is a sleeper (and is a good candidate for a type set as well; this is a toughie, and the main challenge will be in finding one, not paying for it!).

• • • **Elite Recommendations:** Aspire to form a set containing as many MS-63 (or Proof-63) or finer coins as possible, filling in the mintmarked issues in AU-50 or better grades, as available.

Early Quarter Eagles (1796-1839)

Quarter eagles, or $2.50 pieces, have long been a popular series with numismatists, especially among collectors of the present century. The denomination is very appealing, for while it contains some landmark rarities, they are not completely impossible—just difficult. With the exception of a handful of major rarities, the completion of a full set of quarter eagles from

1796 to 1929 is a challenge which can be mounted by nearly any serious collector.[2] Along the way much enjoyment will be derived in tracking down issues which have nominal catalogue value but which in reality are rarities in disguise.

The first quarter eagle design, minted in 1796, is of the Capped Bust to Right design without stars on the obverse. Just 963 pieces were struck, after which someone at the Mint decided to add stars on the obverse motif. The with-stars version was produced from 1796 through 1807. Within that span a number of interesting varieties, including variations in star arrangements, were produced. Mintages were fascinatingly low. In addition to the 963 pieces minted for the 1796 without stars, just 432 were minted of the 1796 with stars, only 427 for the 1797, and the following for the other early years: 1798 (1,094), 1802/1 overdate (3,035), 1804 (3,327), 1805 (1,781), 1806 with 8 stars left and 5 stars right (1,136), 1806 with 7 stars left and 6 stars right (480), and 1807 (6,812).

As noted in my discussion of 1794 half dollars and 1794 silver dollars, mintage figures of this era are not necessarily accurate, and certain dies may have been kept over to later years. There is no assurance, for example, that precisely 1,781 quarter eagles were minted bearing the date 1805. Some produced under that heading could have been dated 1804 or earlier.

Quarter eagles of the 1796-1807 span are typically seen in grades from Extremely Fine to AU. Uncirculated coins are rarities. Conversely, well worn pieces are rarities as well (but not necessarily desirable). Due to their high denomination ($2.50 was apt to represent a week's pay) such coins did not change hands often, with the beneficial result that nearly all surviving pieces are in higher circulated grades.

I have found the 1804 quarter eagle with 13 stars on the reverse to be an elusive rarity, and my firm has never had one in an auction sale. However, noted gold specialist Mike Brownlee reports that over the years he has sold three different specimens to his clients, so they can be found.

In 1808 the design was changed to what we now know as the Capped Bust to Left design. Incidentally, such designations as "Capped Bust to Left" are largely the work of Kenneth E. Bressett, editor of A Guide Book of United States Coins, who a few years ago decided to standardize the nomenclature throughout American numismatics. The 1808 quarter eagle, believed to have been minted to the extent of 2,710 pieces, represents the only year of its design type and thus is in fantastic demand for inclusion in type sets. Needless to say, specimens are highly prized and are eagerly competed for when they cross the auction block or appear in fixed price catalogues.

After 1808 no quarter eagles were minted until 1821, when the Capped Head to Left style made its appearance, a design continued intermittently through 1834. Mintages in this range averaged about 3,000 to 4,000 coins per year, with just 760 registered for 1826 and a high of 6,448 for 1821. Again, it is probably the case that strict die dating was not observed, so the production quantities published in standard references bear only an approximate relationship to present day availability.

Of this design type the following issues were made: 1821, 1824/1 overdate, 1825, 1826, 1827, 1829, 1830, 1831, 1832, 1833, and 1834. By far the rarest is the last issue in the series, 1834, of which 4,000 were stated to have been coined, but of which only a few dozen exist today. The reason is that by 1834 the price of gold had risen on the world markets, and most American gold coins were either melted down for their bullion value or exported. Probably only a couple hundred or so 1834 quarter eagles of this style (with the motto E PLURIBUS UNUM on the reverse, as differentiated from later 1834 issues without motto) ever found their way into circulation, and even this estimate may be on the high side.

To remedy the untenable situation of melting and exporting, Congress passed the Act of June 24, 1834, which reduced the authorized weight of American gold coins. Issues made after August 1, 1834 were of lighter weight and thus stayed in circulation. To differentiate the pieces, the obverse and reverse designs were modified, and the motto E PLURIBUS UNUM was deleted from the reverse. A perusal of old-time financial publications, such as *Niles Register*, an early-day equivalent of *The Wall Street Journal*, reveals that gold coins minted prior to August 1, 1834 (the date in which the change took place) were described as "old tenor" issues and traded above face value by bullion dealers, while later pieces sold at par. During the 1830s, and continuing through the Civil War, bullion traders, securities houses, and bankers did an active business in buying and selling gold and silver coins by weight.

As noted, quarter eagles produced after August 1, 1834 lacked the motto E PLURIBUS UNUM on the reverse to immediately distinguish them from the earlier issues, and were stylistically different in other ways as well. Known as the Classic Head type, another designation I believe to have come from the fertile mind of Kenneth E. Bressett, quarter eagles of this style were produced continuously through 1839. There are no rarities among Classic Head quarter eagles, although the 1838-C, with its low mintage of 7,880 pieces, must be counted as rare, especially as contrasted to the most prolific issue of the era, the 1836 Philadelphia Mint quarter eagle which posted a production of 547,986.

• **Budget Recommendations:** No recommendations here, as low-grade gold coins are apt to be quite unattractive. Besides, all early quarter eagles are rarities. Consider what I have to say under the following listing.

• • **Recommendations for the Connoisseur:** There are two basic ways to go: 1. Build a type set consisting of the basic issues: 1796 without stars, 1796-1807, 1808, 1821-1834, and 1834-1839. I recommend EF or better. MS-60 to MS-63 coins are especially attractive but are expensive and for some issues (specifically 1808) are nearly impossible to find. 2. Build a date and major variety set in EF-40 or better grade. This forms a truly beautiful exhibit and contains no impossible rarities, although some will be very difficult to find (recall what I had to say about the 1804 with 13 stars on the reverse).

• • • **Elite Recommendations:** As preceding, but in higher grades.

Liberty Head Quarter Eagles (1840-1907)

Coronet or Liberty Head quarter eagles, minted nonstop from 1840 through 1907, are remarkable in American coinage as having the longest continuous production of any design without a major change. In essence, a Coronet quarter eagle of 1840 looks just like one of 1907, except for the date numerals. There were several rarities produced within that span, notably the 1841 (believed to have been made only with Proof finish), the 1863 (struck only in Proof finish, to the extent of just 30 coins), and the seldom-seen 1854-S (of which just 246 business strikes were made).

Particularly notable in the quarter eagle series is the 1848 CAL. quarter eagle, of which 1,389 were produced using gold bullion brought to the Philadelphia Mint from California, one of the earliest shipments to the East from the Gold Rush. The distinguishing counterstamp, made at the Mint while the coins were still in the die, served to hallmark the issue and at the same time to specifically create a souvenir for those desiring same. In actuality, the 1848 CAL. quarter eagle is the first official United States commemorative coin, although few people recognize it as such. Probably somewhere between 200 and 300 specimens survive today. In my own business I have probably handled three or four dozen of them over the years.

• **Budget Recommendations:** No specific recommendations here, as low-grade gold coins are apt to be quite unattractive, although Coronet quarter eagles in VF-20 or better, especially among the earlier issues, can be quite desirable. Consider what I have to say under the following listing.

• • **Recommendations for the Connoisseur:** Coronet quarter eagles form a nice set, uniform in appearance, a display which is challenging to

Gold Coins

assemble because of the scarcities and rarities therein. Pieces were produced at various branch mints up through 1879, after which coinage was effected at the Philadelphia Mint only. A collection within a collection can be made of quarter eagles toward the end of the series, from 1880 to 1907. There are no great rarities within this span, although the 1881 and 1885 are very elusive. These two dates are not particularly high priced, as scarce issues within the series are somewhat neglected by numismatists. Coins dated 1840 through the 1870s are most easily collected in higher circulated grades, EF and AU. For most issues Uncirculated examples are decidedly rare. The collecting of Uncirculated coins becomes feasible for pieces dated after about 1880.

• • • **Elite Recommendations:** Aspire to collect the early issues in higher grades such as AU-50 or finer, buying Mint State pieces as they become available. Buy issues after 1880 in MS-65 grade. Proofs are collectible as well; aspire to own Proof-64 or Proof-65 grades.

Indian Quarter Eagles (1908-1929)

In 1908 the quarter eagle motif was changed to feature the portrait of an American Indian, said to have been the first real native American ever shown on a coin. Earlier representations, including the Indian cent, were stylistic and did not represent actual people. Indeed, the Indian cent (minted 1859-1909) represented a woman in a war bonnet, a situation inconsistent with ethnology. Boston sculptor Bela Lyon Pratt, a student of August Saint-Gaudens, was given the task of redesigning the quarter eagle and half eagle, to complete the work of Saint-Gaudens, who had died of cancer the year before.

The same Indian design was used for the half eagle as well. The new Indian quarter eagle and half eagle of 1908 represented an innovation in American coinage. The designs were incuse or inset in the surface, with the field of the coin, normally the lowest part, being in the present instance the highest part. Incuse coins had been made in ancient times, but never before in circulating United States issues. Curiously and inconsistently, Indian quarter eagles and half eagles struck at Denver and San Francisco (half eagles, but not quarter eagles, were struck at New Orleans as well), with mintmarks, bore the mintmark raised on the coin—extending above the field. Apparently it was too much trouble to have the mintmark incuse. This is probably just as well, for one can imagine a proliferation of phony mintmarks made for collectors, by punching D and S letters into the fields of Philadelphia Mint coins!

Indian quarter eagles were produced intermittently from 1908 through 1929. Some 15 different varieties were coined, the scarcest of which by far is the 1911-D, of which just 55,680 were minted, the only issue to be produced in a quantity of fewer than several hundred thousand pieces. Really choice Uncirculated Indian quarter eagles are hard to find, particularly among the earlier dates, for the nature of the design was such that even a small amount of handling tended to emphasize nicks and marks on the surface.

• **Budget Recommendations:** Build a date and mintmark set in VF-30 grade.

• • **Recommendations for the Connoisseur:** A set of 15 varieties in MS-60 or better grade, hand-selected for aesthetic appeal, forms a nice exhibit. The grade MS-63 in particular offers a nice combination of high quality and reasonable price.

• • • **Elite Recommendations:** Build a 1908-1929 set in MS-65. Few people have ever done this. For good measure, you can also form a set of Matte Proofs, which were minted of the Philadelphia issues 1908-1915 only.

$3 Gold Pieces (1854-1889)

One of the most curious of all United States coin denominations is the $3 gold piece, minted continuously from 1854 through 1889. The precise reason for making the $3 value has never been explained to the satisfaction of numismatists. It has been suggested that it offered a convenient way to buy three-cent stamps in sheets of 100. Inasmuch as the $2.50 piece was a well-established denomination at the time, the making of a $3 piece in the same approximate value range seems quite redundant. Three-dollar gold pieces were minted to the extent of 138,618 coins at the Philadelphia Mint in 1854, by far the highest mintage of any variety, after which production quantities fell sharply. The series was never popular, and most later mintages were very small.

Today, the major demand for $3 pieces is by type coin collectors who desire one example for a gold set. Collecting $3 pieces by date and mintmark sequence is also popular, and I have several clients who have made this a specialty. Just one, Harry Bass, the distinguished Texas collector, has a complete set—for he possesses the only known example of the 1870-S, the unique specimen from the Eliasberg Collection, which my firm auctioned for $687,500 in 1982. Other rarities in the $3 series include the famous 1875, of which just 20 are believed to have been coined, and the 1876, of which just 45 were struck. Beyond that, there are numerous issues with mintages in the hundreds or the low thousands.

Just one variety was made at the Dahlonega Mint, 1854-D, and just one at the New Orleans Mint, 1854-O. Of the 1854-D the mintage was 1,120 pieces. Jack Hancock, a specialist in Dahlonega Mint coins, told me that he thought that between 100 and 120 specimens of the 1854-D survive today, a figure which would indicate that perhaps 10% of the original mintage exists.[3] The 1854-O, of which 24,000 were struck, is much more readily available, although like any $3 piece, it is scarce. Norman Stack has written that there is no such thing as a common $3 piece, and this is true. In comparison to many other United States coins, even in the 1854 $3, with its mintage of 138,618, can be classified as either scarce or rare.

The first 1854 $3 piece I purchased in my professional career was obtained for the then princely sum of $35 from a rare coin dealer, whose name I do not recall, who held forth in a shop in the Hotel Redington in Wilkes-Barre, Pennsylvania, not far from my home town of Forty Fort. A lustrous, frosty Uncirculated coin, the same piece would sell for $10,000 or more today. It's too bad I didn't hold on to it! But, then, the function of a dealer is to deal, to buy and sell. Investment profits go to my clients.

As was the case with contemporary gold dollars, $3 pieces formed a popular speculation for investors after 1878, and those pieces dated from 1879 through 1889 exist in Uncirculated grades in proportionally larger quantities than their low mintages would suggest. Still, the absolute population is sufficiently low that examples are and always have been in strong demand. Of particular interest is the 1881, of which just 500 business strikes were produced.

• **Budget Recommendations:** No recommendations here, as low-grade $3 gold coins are apt to be quite unattractive. Besides, as noted, all issues are rare. Consider what I have to say under the following listing.

• • **Recommendations for the Connoisseur:** If you are typical, you will want just one $3 in your collection, to illustrate the design. However, forming a date set can be a fascinating challenge, and if you omit the unique 1870-S and do not include the Proof-only 1875 and 1876 issues, this can be done with some patience. A California client recently put together such a set in EF-40 or better grade for about $75,000. If you want to cherrypick single coins, be aware that Mint State issues of just about everything from 1854 to 1872, but especially 1855 to 1858, are rare (the 1854 Philadelphia Mint issue is an exception; these are readily available).

• • • **Elite Recommendations:** Aspire to build a set in the highest grades possible, up to MS-65 and Proof-65, first consulting David Akers' book on the series in order to determine the availability of certain issues.[4]

$4 Gold Stellas (1879-1880)

Four-dollar gold pieces, or stellas, so-called from the five-pointed star on the reverse, are patterns, not regular coins. Stellas were produced in 1879 and 1880 at the suggestion of Hon. John A. Kasson, U.S. minister to Austria, who felt that a coin of this value would have used by foreign travelers, as it could be readily exchanged for gold coins of approximate equivalent value in France, Germany, and other European countries. Indicative of its intended international nature, the obverse legend of the $4 piece expressed its metallic content as follows: 6G, .3S, .7C, 7 GRAMS.

Two obverse designs were produced, the Flowing Hair type by Charles E. Barber (who was chief engraver of the Mint at the time) and the Coiled Hair type by George T. Morgan (he of 1878 silver dollar fame). On the reverse, instead of IN GOD WE TRUST, the motto appears as DEO EST GLORIA, or "God is Glorious." Mintages of the various issues are not known with certainty, but the *Guide Book* estimates 425 for the 1879 Flowing Hair, the issue most often encountered, just 10 for the 1879 Coiled Hair, 15 for the 1880 Flowing Hair, and 10 for the 1880 Coiled Hair. Actual mintages were probably slightly higher than those figures.

Walter Breen in his *Encyclopedia of U.S. and Colonial Proof Coins* recites the tale that madams in the red light district of Washington, D.C. received numerous 1879 $4 pieces as gifts from congressmen customers, as evidenced by a fair supply of such pieces today which show signs of having been mounted for use in jewelry. Whether this story has a basis in fact is not known, but it is known that many congressmen received 1879 Flowing Hair $4 pieces at the time of issue, to acquaint them with the proposed design. Although $4 stellas are patterns, as noted, they have been incorporated into many regular collections and are extremely popular today.

• **Budget Recommendations:** Gold-plated copper and aluminum $4 patterns can make nice fillers and, mounted in holders, cannot be easily differentiated from gold issues (which prompts me to suggest that if you ever consider buying any $4 in a slab, insist on knowing the weight of the piece. I know of a buyer who was fooled when he purchased a gold plated *copper* coin for a gold coin price!).

•• **Recommendations for the Connoisseur:** Most collectors buy an 1879 Flowing Hair to illustrate the denomination. Forming a complete set of four 1879-1880 varieties is in the dreamland category, but several numismatists have done it in the past.

••• **Elite Recommendations:** Visit dreamland, as just noted!

Early Half Eagles (1795-1838)

Half eagles or $5 pieces, a denomination produced intermittently from 1795 to 1929, include some of the greatest rarities in American coinage. Particularly famous is the 1822 $5, of which just three are known, two of them being in the National Collection at the Smithsonian Institution. The third, the Eliasberg coin, was auctioned by my firm in 1982 for $687,500, the same price realized by the unique 1870-S $3. At the other end of the spectrum, numerous half eagles of the late 19th and early 20th centuries were produced by the millions and were used in quantity for large international transactions and are very common today.

In general, half eagle designs follow those of contemporary quarter eagles. There are, however, numerous differences, one of them being the first half eagle design, with Capped Bust to Right obverse and Small Eagle reverse, which has no equivalent in the quarter eagle series, but which is similar to that used on the contemporary $10 piece. $5 pieces of the Small Eagle reverse type were minted through 1798. Those dated 1798 are extreme rarities, and fewer than a dozen are known to exist.

Capped Bust to Right half eagles with Heraldic Eagle reverse were minted with dates from 1795 through 1807, although it is believed that those struck with dates prior to 1798 were produced in 1798 by using obverse dies on hand from earlier years. Part way through 1807 the motif was replaced by the Capped Draped Bust to Left style (1807-1812) and then the Capped Head to Left design (1813-1834, with a change in diameter in 1829).

While all early half eagles are scarce, the era of the 1820s in particular contains several notable rarities. The aforementioned 1822 is the most famous, but all other issues are elusive as well. Mintage quantities were fairly substantial, amounting to the tens of thousands of pieces, but nearly all were melted or exported.

After August 1, 1834, Classic Head half eagles, of reduced weight and without the motto E PLURIBUS UNUM on the reverse, were produced, a design continued through 1838.

• **Budget Recommendations:** No recommendations here, as low-grade gold coins are apt to be quite unattractive. Besides, all early half eagles are rare. Suggesting that someone collect early $5 on a budget is like suggesting that a driver who wants to pinch pennies should buy a Rolls Royce! Consider what I have to say under the following listing.

• • **Recommendations for the Connoisseur:** Unless your name is Rockefeller or Vanderbilt, you will probably want to limit your purchases to one each of the major design types. EF-40 to MS-60 coins represent good buys, and Mint State coins up to MS-63 are likewise interesting.

• • • **Elite Recommendations:** Endeavor to form a high grade type set MS-63 or finer, or a date set(!) in MS-63 or finer, as available, with the great rarities, as they become available (some never will), in AU-50 or better grades.

Liberty Head Half Eagles (1839-1908)

Coronet or Liberty Head half eagles were made from 1839 through 1908, with the motto IN GOD WE TRUST added beginning in 1865. In this series there are several rarities, the most prominent being the 1854-S, of which just 268 were made, and the 1887, of which only 87 (all Proofs) were struck. There are many Coronet half eagles which are prime rarities in higher grades such as AU and Uncirculated, but which have very low catalogue values, as few specialists collect the series, and there is no widespread demand.

• **Budget Recommendations:** No recommendations here, as low-grade gold coins are apt to be quite unattractive. However, buying an EF-40 piece as part of a type set is a possibility (the same is true for various other late 19th and early 20th century gold coins, but I won't keep repeating it). Consider what I have to say under the following listing.

• • **Recommendations for the Connoisseur:** If you are typical, you will probably want one of each of the two major design types, without motto and with IN GOD WE TRUST. I recommend MS-63 as a good value for the early series and MS-63 or MS-64 for the later. Avoid common dates among the later issues, for semi-scarce dates can be obtained for little more. As one of many examples, I note that in MS-60 grade a 1901-S $5 catalogues for $250 in the *Guidebook of U.S. Coins,* and that a 1904-S similarly preserved catalogues $300. In MS-60 grade the 1904-S is at least *one thousand times rarer* than the 1901-S! If you really want to do some cherrypicking, study the rarity of 1839-1880 issues and you will find that many issues which list for nominal prices in MS-60 grade are *great rarities.* The same is true, by the way, for contemporary $10 pieces.

• • • **Elite Recommendations:** Aspire to form a date and mintmark set, with the early issues AU-50 or finer, the issues 1880-1900 MS-63 or finer, and issues 1901-1908 MS-65 (except that you won't be able to find a 1904-S in a grade much above MS-60).

Indian Half Eagles (1908-1929)

Indian Head half eagles, designed by sculptor Bela Lyon Pratt, were minted from 1908 through 1929, the same span as the quarter eagles of like design. The $5 pieces, like their $2.50 counterparts, have the designs incuse, except for the mintmarks on certain issues. The two rarities in the Indian series are the 1909-O and 1929, with the latter being particularly elusive. Although 662,000 1929 half eagle were struck, fewer than 200 are believed to exist today. Most of the pieces were stored by the Treasury Department after mintage, were never released into circulation, and when gold coins were discontinued in 1933 they went to the melting pot.

Among Indian Head half eagles, with the exception of 1909-D, and to a lesser extent 1908, most varieties are quite rare in Uncirculated grade, and are very rare in MS-64 or better preservation.

• **Budget Recommendations:** Build a date and mintmark set in VF-20 grade.

• • **Recommendations for the Connoisseur:** Build a complete set, if you can afford it, in MS-60 or better grade. I recommend MS-63. The 1909-O will be a stumbling block, and then there is the rare 1929 to be considered.

• • • **Elite Recommendations:** Build a complete set 1908-1929 in MS-64 to MS-65 grade. This will be a real challenge! While you are at it, consider putting together a set of Matte Proofs of the Philadelphia Mint coinages 1908-1915.

Early $10 (1795-1804)

Eagles or $10 pieces represented the largest United States coin denomination when the first pieces were produced in 1795, a status which the $10 piece enjoyed until the advent of the $20 double eagle in 1850. Early $10 pieces were minted from 1795 through 1804 inclusive, after which coinage was suspended until 1838. Eagles of the early type are divided into two designs, the Capped Bust to Right with Small Eagle reverse minted 1795-1797, and the same obverse design, but with Heraldic Eagle reverse, struck from 1797 through 1804. There are no impossible rarities among these early pieces, although several varieties are very elusive. These were workhorse coins, so most of them seen today show evidence of circulation. The same is true of virtually all gold coins of that era.

• **Budget Recommendations:** No recommendations here, as low-grade gold coins are apt to be quite unattractive, and all early $10 issues are rarities. Consider what I have to say under the following listing.

• • **Recommendations for the Connoisseur:** Acquire one each of the two major design types, with the Small Eagle reverse and the Heraldic Eagle reverse. Buy EF-40 or better, with AU-55 representing an especially good value. MS-60 to MS-63 coins are excellent values, but be fussy about quality, for many coins seem to me to be overgraded.

• • • **Elite Recommendations:** As preceding, but aspire to collect MS-60 or better, buying occasional MS-63 pieces as they become available.

Liberty Head $10 (1838-1907)

When $10 coinage recommenced in 1838 a new design, the Coronet or Liberty Head style, was employed. This motif continued through 1907, with a slight change in the portrait in 1839, and with the addition of the motto IN GOD WE TRUST in 1866. As is the case with contemporary half eagles, few people collect Liberty Head eagles by date and mintmark varieties, with the result that there are many rarities, particularly among Uncirculated coins, which have relatively low catalogue values. No one has ever assembled a set of Uncirculated Liberty Head $10 pieces, and no one ever will, for numerous early varieties are virtually impossible to find in this preservation. After the early 1880s, Uncirculated $10 pieces become more available, and issues of the early 20th century are plentiful, particularly 1901-S, the most often seen variety.

• **Budget Recommendations:** No recommendations here, as low-grade gold coins are apt to be quite unattractive. Consider what I have to say under the following listing.

• • **Recommendations for the Connoisseur:** Most buyers will want one each of the basic types. I recommend MS-60 or better for the 1838-1866 type and MS-64 for the later type. Among later eagles, try to pick a rarer date, for it will cost little more than a common one. See my comments above and also my comments under Liberty Head $5 pieces (1839-1908) for more suggestions concerning early issues, a field laden with unrecognized rarities.

• • • **Elite Recommendations:** Aspire to form a date and mintmark set, with the early issues AU-50 or better, the issues 1880-1900 MS-63, and later varieties MS-65.

Indian $10 (1907-1933)

In 1905 President Theodore Roosevelt commissioned noted sculptor Augustus Saint-Gaudens to redesign the entire American coinage spectrum from the cent to the double eagle. Working in his studio in Cornish, New Hampshire (now a National Historic Site), the artist prepared many sketches. In failing health, Saint-Gaudens was able to complete or nearly complete work for just two denominations, the $10 and $20, both of which were first struck in 1907.

His $10 design bore on the obverse a female wearing an Indian war bonnet, said to have been taken from the portrait of his mistress, Davida Clark, with whom he is alleged to have had a child (although biographers have never been able to confirm this). There was an objection in the popular press concerning the portrait, for it was stated that the effigy was of one Mary Cunningham, an Irish-born waitress who worked in a restaurant in Windsor, Vermont, across the river from Cornish, New Hampshire. Some do-gooders said that an immigrant girl should not be depicted on our coins, and that such a design was unfit for use. All of this made interesting reading at the time, but was quickly forgotten.

The reverse of the Indian $10 piece depicted an eagle perched on a branch, the same design used a year later, in modified form, by Bela Lyon Pratt for use on the $2.50 and $5 pieces of 1908.

Eagles of the Saint-Gaudens Indian design were produced continuously from 1907 through 1916, then in 1920 (at the San Francisco Mint only), 1926, 1930 (San Francisco Mint only), 1932, and 1933. Within the 1907-1933 span there are several rare varieties, including the last year of issue, of which just 312,500 were minted, but of which nearly all were melted. Numbered among other rarities are varieties of the 1907 with periods before and after E PLURIBUS UNUM, the 1920-S, and the 1930-S.

The collecting of Indian $10 pieces has formed a popular specialty with many collectors, and the same people who pay no attention to Liberty Head $10 pieces of the 1838-1907 years, collect with fervor the later Saint-Gaudens pieces. As a result, top grade issues have always found a ready market. Most often seen in Uncirculated grades are the 1926 and 1932, which must be rated as common. Apart from these two issues, all high grade Uncirculated pieces are scarce to rare.

• **Budget Recommendations:** To say that a set of 1907-1933 $10 pieces can be acquired if you are watching your pennies may be like saying that Fabergé eggs, Mucha posters, or autograph letters of George Washington can be collected on a budget, so it is best to forget it. However, there is no doubt that a basic set of $10 pieces in VF-20 grade would be cheaper than that recommended in the next paragraph.

• •**Recommendations for the Connoisseur:** Start with one each of the two major types in MS-63 grade. For the 1908-1933 with-motto style pick something besides 1926 or 1932, for these two dates together account for probably 80% or more of the known MS-63 or better $10 pieces of this type.

• • • **Elite Recommendations:** Form a set of 1907-1933 $10 pieces in MS-64 to MS-65 grade. In 1980 Bruce Amspacher, a dealer who has certainly seen his share of coins, noted that an MS-65 1933 $10 which he had for sale was *the* finest rarity he had ever owned. A complete Mint State set of Indian $10 would be a joy to own.

Liberty Head $20 (1850-1907)

Following the discovery of vast quantities of gold in California, the Treasury Department decided to create a new denomination called the double eagle, for it was twice the size of the previous highest denomination, the eagle. First minted for circulation in 1850, production of $20 pieces was continued through the year 1933. Vast quantities were minted of certain dates, as they served as a convenient way to convert gold bullion into coinage form. Double eagles facilitated international transactions of large value in an era in which foreign governments and commercial interests were wary of accepting paper money.

Double eagles of the 1850-1907 years are of the Liberty Head type and are the work of James B. Longacre, who produced many other designs of the mid-19th century. There are actually three varieties of Liberty Head double eagles: the 1850-1866 style with the denomination expressed as TWENTY D, the 1866-1876 style with the denomination expressed the same way but with the addition of IN GOD WE TRUST, and the 1877-1907 type with the denomination expressed as TWENTY DOLLARS.

Among double eagles of the 1850-1907 era, there are a number of scarce and rare issues, notably the 1854-O, 1856-O, 1861-S Paquet reverse, 1870-CC (a particularly elusive variety), and the 1879-O. Among Philadelphia Mint coins, the 1883 and 1884 were minted only in Proof finish, with no related business strikes, to the extent of just 92 and 71 pieces respectively. Several other issues are elusive, and the Philadelphia Mint version of the 1861 Paquet reverse is a landmark rarity.

Notice must be paid to the 1857-S double eagle, not a rare issue, as 970,500 were minted, but a piece which is not particularly easy to find in Uncirculated grade (nor is any other double eagle of the 1850-1866 type plentiful in Mint State). In 1989 the numismatic fraternity—indeed the entire world, consisting of numismatists and everyone else—was surprised and delighted by the news that a team of skilled scientists had discovered the wreck of the S.S. *Central America*, which had sunk in a hurricane off the coast of North Carolina in autumn 1857, with the loss of several hundred lives, one of the greatest disasters of the era, a tragedy which, somehow, had largely been forgotten in popular literature since that time.

Using sophisticated recovery techniques, employing a robot device and a special chemical preservative compound to surround the artifacts discovered, the team brought to the surface a vast treasure of numismatic items, including thousands of 1857-S double eagles in pristine condition, which had been part of a shipment from the San Francisco Mint to the New York Assay Office. As this book is being written, exploration is continuing, and the eventual disposition of this and other numismatic treasures has not been decided. Eventually, numismatists will probably be able to own these items which will combine not only a remarkable degree of quality and preservation, but a fascinating history. If marketed effectively, the treasure from the *Central America* may well serve to significantly increase interest in all United States gold coins, just as the availability of large quantities of Morgan silver dollars following the Treasury release in 1962 served to propel that series to the forefront. The auction house of Christie's, assisted by John Jay Ford, Jr., has served as numismatic advisor to the recovery team.

• **Budget Recommendations:** No recommendations here, as low-grade $20 are apt to be quite unattractive. Consider what I have to say under the following listing.

• • **Recommendations for the Connoisseur:** Start with a type set of the three major designs. AU-50 to MS-60 is a practical objective for the 1850-1866 type, MS-60 to MS-63 for the 1866-1876 style, and MS-64 for the 1877-1907 design. For the last-named try to pick something besides a common issue (the commonest are 1904, in particular, and 1904-S). Believe it or not, many people have endeavored to build a date and mintmark set of Liberty Head double eagles. The challenge is there, and the cost is not as much as you might think. If you can live without the top dozen major rarities, you can form a set with the earlier pieces EF-40 to AU-50 and the later ones AU-55 or better, with the vast majority of the pieces costing less than $700 each. As these words are being written, gold bullion is at a low point, and many double eagles are cheaper now than they have been in many years. Recently, the Blanchard Company ran nationwide advertisements pointing out this very opportunity.

• • • **Elite Recommendations:** Read the preceding, then escalate your grade objectives upward, but before you do so consult David Akers' book on $20, which gives an indication of the availability of issues in higher grades. For example, finding Mint State examples of early New Orleans issues is a practical impossibility.

Saint-Gaudens $20 (1907-1933)

In 1907 Augustus Saint-Gaudens redesigned the $20 piece, employing as the obverse motif the figure of Miss Liberty striding forward. The initial Saint-Gaudens design was struck in high relief, giving the coins an almost sculptured appearance. The date was expressed in Roman numerals, MCMVII. Some 11,250 of these coins were struck, after which the design was modified to a shallow format to permit production on high speed coinage presses. It is a tribute to Saint-Gaudens that when the Mint in 1986 decided to create bullion-type gold coins, it could not improve upon what Saint-Gaudens did in 1907, and it resurrected his design, even using updated Roman numerals.

MCMVII High Relief pieces are scarce today, although probably at least 2,000 or 3,000 exist. The demand for them is such that they have always found a ready market. Nearly anyone who aspires to form a set of gold coins desires to own at least one specimen. Among later Saint-Gaudens double eagles of the modified design there are a number of scarce and rare issues, particularly among mintmark varieties of the 1920s. All issues after 1928 are rarities.

Particularly hard to find is the 1927-D, of which 180,000 were minted, but of which fewer than a dozen can be traced with certainty today. Apparently most were melted and not released. The last year of issue, 1933, saw production of 445,500 pieces, a dozen or so of which found their way into collections during the early 1930s. The vast majority of the mintage went to the melting pot. In the 1940s the government took the position that no 1933 $20 pieces had been officially released (although $10 pieces of the 1933 design were no problem), and that any pieces in the hands of collectors were illegally held. Louis Eliasberg and most other collectors dutifully surrendered their pieces to the Treasury Department, receiving face value for them.[5] Although it could be argued that someone going to the Philadelphia Mint in 1933 and offering to exchange a $20 piece of an earlier date could have received an 1933 legally, the government alleged that no records of such transactions exist, and seized all it could find. An exception was an example which was sold in the collection of King Farouk of Egypt, and which was scheduled to cross the auction block in 1953 after the assets of the deposed king were seized by the Egyptian government. Just before the sale the 1933 $20 piece was withdrawn, but where it went, no one knows. Rumors had it that the piece made its way back to the United States, where it was added to a well-known specialized collection.

In 1989, when William Metcalf of the American Numismatic Society invited me to give a presentation on United States gold coins as part of the Coinage of the Americas Conference held in New York City, I desired to illustrate my talk with illustrations of famous American rarities. Elvira Clain-Stefanelli and Cory Gillilland of the Smithsonian Institution, and their staff, obliged by furnishing color transparencies of the rarest of the rare in the National Collection, including a prize 1933 $20 piece which they can legally hold, even if private collectors can't. Also shown were other treasures, including the unique pattern 1849 $20 and two varieties, each unique, of the famous 1877 gold $50 patterns. At one time it was proposed that coins of the latter denomination be produced for circulation, to be called the "half union," but the idea never progressed beyond pattern form. However, in California 1851 and 1852 $50 pieces were produced under the auspices of the United States government and circulated widely. Years later, in 1915, commemorative $50 pieces were produced in connection with the Panama-Pacific International Exposition.

• **Budget Recommendations:** No recommendations here, as low-grade Saint-Gaudens $20 pieces are apt to be quite unattractive. Consider what I have to say under the following listing.

• • **Recommendations for the Connoisseur:** Start with buying one of each major type, including the MCMVII (if you can afford it, I highly recommend owning a specimen of this gorgeous design), the 1907-1908 Arabic numerals without motto, and the 1908-1933 with motto. I like MS-63 and MS-64 grades. You might want to consider building a date and mintmark set, for most issues are inexpensive. You may never acquire the rarities of the 1920s, but still a very nice basic collection can be formed, and it is easy to complete a set of the early years 1907-1916.

• • • **Elite Recommendations:** Aspire to build a set in MS-64 to MS-65 grade. You will be flying with the eagles, financially and otherwise, for the atmosphere is rarefied, especially when it comes to certain of the later-date issues!

CHAPTER FIFTEEN

Commemoratives

Commemorative Silver Coins

As noted earlier, the first official United States commemorative coin was really the 1848 CAL. gold quarter eagle, of which 1,389 were minted, but standard reference books do not recognize this, and it is "proper" to state that the first commemorative coin was the 1892 Columbian silver half dollar. The spectrum of American commemorative coinage is a broad one. Each design has its own story, and as there are dozens of different designs, a recitation of the background of each would make a book in its own right. Indeed, several authors have written such books, B. Max Mehl, David E. Bullowa, Anthony Swiatek, Don Taxay, and Walter Breen among them. On my own "things to do list" is the writing of a book on the subject (if indeed *another* book is needed!).

I like to divide commemoratives into several series. The first is that of silver coins minted during the earlier years from 1892 to 1954. Within this range we have the 1893 Isabella quarter, the only commemorative of its denomination, the 1900 Lafayette silver dollar, and 48 different designs of commemorative half dollars.

The Lafayette dollar is interesting for several reasons. Some 50,000 pieces were *prestruck* in December 1899, using four different die pairs (although no one I know of collects them by die varieties today). As it was not legal to strike a coin in advance of the date shown on the dies, the Mint circumvented the question by stating that the coin really had no date (which brings up another question: was it legal to mint a coin without a date?). On the reverse of the Lafayette dollar appears the inscription PARIS 1900, which was not the date of the coin, according to Mint officials, but, rather, was the date at which a statue, also depicted on the reverse, was to be erected in Paris.

Another interesting thing about the Lafayette dollar is that only 36,000 were distributed. Most of the rest of the 50,000 mintage went to the melting pot, some of them not until the 1940s. Had collectors of the 1930s and early 1940s known that the Treasury Department had on hand thousands of Uncirculated Lafayette dollars there would have been a great rush to buy them, but no one was aware of this, and only after they were melted was the situation disclosed in a government report! What a numismatic shame.

As noted, from 1892 through 1954 some 48 different commemorative designs were minted. In addition certain issues were produced with slight design differences, or in mintmark varieties, bringing the total number of commemorative half dollar varieties in the span to 142.

Years ago the *Guide Book* and other references used to list commemorative silver coins in chronological order, which to me made sense then and would make more sense today. Beginning the series were the first silver varieties issued, the 1892 and 1893 Columbian half dollars and the 1893 Isabella quarter, after which were found the 1900 Lafayette dollar, the 1915-S Panama-Pacific half dollar, the 1918 Lincoln-Illinois, and others, chronologically down to the last design in the series, the Washington-Carver issues of 1951-1954.

However, apparently the chronological listing was too complicated for numismatists to figure out, particularly those who didn't want to spend any time studying. Where would one look for a Huguenot half dollar, for example, or a 1937 Boone set, or where could one find a Cincinnati? To simplify matters, later editions of the *Guide Book*, and other reference works as well, not to overlook market price guides such as the *Coin Dealer Newsletter*, listed commemoratives alphabetically. Now the pieces were easy to find, but they bore no relationship to their sequence of issue. By way of analogy, can you imagine, for example, studying American history in alphabetical order by subject, rather than by time line? Long after learning about George Bush you would finally encounter George Washington!

The *Guide Book* is inconsistent in its alphabetical listings, for we have the Old Spanish Trail half dollar of 1935, which should be listed under O, now listed under S, for Spanish Trail—the "Old" apparently isn't important, although OLD SPANISH TRAIL is the inscription on the coin. Similarly, we have the Fort Vancouver issue, which according to what I learned in grade school should be listed under F, now listed under V. The California-Pacific International Exposition half dollars are listed under S, for San Diego, where the event was held. On the other hand, the Panama-Pacific International Exposition coins, minted for an event held in San Francisco, are not listed under S for San Francisco, but are found under P for Panama-Pacific. So much for logic! (Could it be that logic doesn't have much of a place with many, possibly even the majority of people in the rare coin business?!)

I have always enjoyed buying and selling commemorative half dollars, for the wealth of history and intrigue they contain. Each coin has its own story. Whenever I see a 1936 Cincinnati half dollar I think of the shenanigans that went on when Thomas G. Melish, a well-known numismatist, decided to turn a quick profit and persuaded Congress to create for him a commemorative half dollar and give him the right to issue it for whatever price he pleased! Melish and his associates posted the selling price at $7.75 for a set of three coins (one each from the Philadelphia, Denver, and San Francisco mints), the highest price of any set up to that time, but sold just a few of the 5,000 sets at that price, preferring instead to send "sold out" notices to many applicants, who were then free to buy Cincinnati sets on the open market for prices far above the $7.75 price, in fact, at the $50 level.

Apparently there was nothing worthwhile to commemorate on the Cincinnati half dollar, so Melish dreamed up the idea of placing the portrait of Stephen Foster on the obverse, although Stephen Foster had very little to do with the city. The reverse noted that Cincinnati was celebrating its 50th anniversary 1886-1936 as "a musical center of America," although to this day no one has ever come up with an explanation of what occurred musically in Cincinnati 50 years earlier in the year 1886!

Other commemorative half dollars had more validity in history, and few would question, for example, that the 1935 commemorative half dollar issued to celebrate the 300th anniversary of the state of Connecticut was worth issuing. Thoroughly confusing was the Delaware half dollar, ostensibly struck to celebrate the 300th anniversary of the landing of Swedes in that state, a coin authorized in 1936, bearing the date 1936 on the obverse, but actually struck in 1937, and on the reverse bearing the date 1938. You figure it out!

In 1936 when sets of Rhode Island commemorative halves were distributed through banks and agents, they were sold out in just six hours after being placed on sale, according to official news reports. However, anyone who missed the opportunity to buy sets at the original issue price could obtain some by paying a premium to—guess to whom?—some of the official distributors who just happened to set aside a few extras.

Some commemorative issues turned into a veritable annuity for their issuers, none more so than the Daniel Boone half dollars sold by C. Frank Dunn, whose office was in an upstairs room in the Hotel Phoenix in Lexington, Kentucky. Dunn distributed Daniel Boone half dollars in 1934, ostensibly to commemorate the bicentennial of the famous explorer's birth. Not satisfied to let it go at that, he decided to keep celebrating the situation, and was able to create not one coin, but a set of three coins from three different mints in 1935. As if that were not enough, still more varieties were made for the year 1935, bearing the small date "1934" on the reverse. Additional Boone sets were minted from 1936 through 1938. All of this poured thousands of dollars into Dunn's pockets, amid outcries from collectors who on one hand complained about the inequities of such profiteering, but on the other hand considered their holdings incomplete if they did not own, for example, a rare 1935-D Boone half dollar with small "1934" on the reverse, not available any longer from Dunn, for these had been "sold out" at an early date, but obtainable only on the open market for multiples of the original issue price.

One old-time dealer in commemoratives told me that he visited Dunn in the Phoenix Hotel, and that Dunn had two offices—one room in which he received mail and sold commemorative half dollars at the issue price—and another room on the same floor, not generally open to visitors, in which he maintained his stock of "sold out" issues and offered them secretly at advanced prices.

The 1936-S half dollar bearing the inscription on the reverse SAN FRANCISCO-OAKLAND BAY BRIDGE, is listed alphabetically in the *Guide Book* where do you suppose? Under—S for San Francisco? No. O for Oakland? Would you believe B for Bay? Yes! This particular issue has the unique distinction of being the first and possibly the only commemorative half dollar available for sale at a drive-up window. Examples were offered for sale to automobilists who visited toll booths at each end of the famous span.

I mentioned the long series of Boone half dollars and the varieties associated therewith, and I mentioned the three varieties of 1936 Cincinnati half dollars, so it's only right that I mention certain other series. The Arkansas centennial was to be celebrated in 1936, but promoters could not wait, so pieces were produced at the Philadelphia, Denver, and San Francisco mints beginning in 1935! Production continued through 1939, thus observing the centennial in a rather extended (and greedy) fashion. Of all commemorative half dollar sets, Arkansas pieces were the most poorly produced, with unsatisfactory finishes, often showing extensive bagmarks and dull lustre. Even pieces taken from original wrappings are apt to look like they have been severely mistreated. For this reason, Arkansas half dollars, although quite rare in many instances, have never been popular with collectors.

Oregon Trail half dollars, first issued in 1926, turned into another scandal, and by the time the last Oregon half dollars were produced in 1939, just about everyone was thoroughly disgusted with them, with the possible exception of Wayte Raymond and J.W. Scott & Co.—distributors of most of the later issues. Raymond, by the way, was a professional numismatist of great reputation, and certainly one of the most influential and most important dealers of our century. It was Raymond who launched the *Standard Catalogue of United States Coins*, thus paving the way to the widespread collecting of dates and mintmark varieties. Raymond sponsored the early research activities of Walter Breen, who later went on to be one of the greatest numismatic scholars ever. Similarly, he acted as a mentor to John J. Ford, Jr., who went on to revolutionize the way auctions were catalogued.[1] However, like nearly all professional numismatists of the 1930s, Raymond had to work hard to make a living, and as long as there were people buying commemorative half dollars, Raymond and others sold them. I imagine that had I been living in the mid-1930s, I would have liked nothing better than to have had a commemorative half dollar distributorship of my own!

Today each of the 48 basic varieties of commemorative half dollars minted during the 1892-1954 span is readily available, although the 1928 Hawaiian, 1935 Hudson, and 1935 Old Spanish Trail are elusive. In MS-60 to MS-63 grades most commemoratives are quite reasonable in price. MS-65 and higher coins have been eagerly sought after by investors, who have driven the market price out of the reach of many collectors. However, a nice MS-63 coin can be nearly as attractive as an MS-65 coin, and as the price can be just a tiny fraction of the MS-65 level, there is no reason not to be satisfied with an MS-63 coin.

In a recent[2] telephone conversation, well-known Rhode Island dealer Steve Innarelli told me that he recommended building a set of MS-63 commemorative half dollars as an excellent way to begin an interest in numismatics, and that his clients who started in this manner, perhaps by buying an Iowa, Long Island, or other inexpensive issue, often became serious collectors. Steve is the type of dealer that numismatics needs more of; a dealer who is interested in popularizing the hobby by helping youngsters, assisting with coin club activities, and otherwise giving of his time and energy to spread the word.

• **Budget Recommendations:** Form a type set containing the Isabella 25c, Lafayette $1, and 48 different half dollar designs of the early period 1892-1954, in grades from EF-40 to MS-60.

• • **Recommendations for the Connoisseur:** Form a type set. I recommend MS-63 and MS-64 grades as being exceptional values. In fact, many MS-63 coins are bargains.

• • • **Elite Recommendations:** Form a type set, or better yet, a complete variety set, in MS-65 grade. The best way to do this is to look through *many* slabs marked MS-65, and pick out the ones which meet your requirements for aesthetic appeal.

Commemorative Gold Coins

Another commemorative category is that of early 20th century gold coins, consisting of 11 different varieties of commemorative gold dollars minted from 1903 through 1922, the 1915-S Panama-Pacific quarter eagle and the 1926 Sesquicentennial quarter eagle, and, not often collected due to the rarity, the immense $50 round and octagonal pieces minted in 1915 for the Panama-Pacific International Exposition. All of these early gold coins are scarce, and some of them, particularly, the 1904 and 1905 Lewis and Clark gold dollars and the 1915-S Panama-Pacific $50 pieces, are rare.

• **Budget Recommendations:** Build a set of 11 gold dollars and two quarter eagles, in EF-40 grade.

• • **Recommendations for the Connoisseur:** Build a set of 11 gold dollars and two quarter eagles. I like the MS-63 grade for its value. As always, cherrypick for quality!

• • • **Elite Recommendations:** Build a set, as preceding, but in MS-65 grade. Acquire the two varieties of 1915-S $50 pieces if you wish (they are truly impressive to own!). Don't forget to cherrypick for quality.

Modern Commemorative Issues

The third major category of commemoratives is that of modern issues, beginning with the beautiful 1982-S Washington half dollar created by Elizabeth Jones in 1982, and continuing through various silver and gold issues to the present time. The Olympic games held in Los Angeles in 1984, the centennial of the Statue of Liberty in 1986, the bicentennial of the Constitution in 1987, and the Olympic games held in 1988 have furnished the occasion for a number of modern commemorative issues, some of which have been exceedingly beautiful and others which are best forgotten.

Without delving into the subject too deeply, as not to offend a number of artists and engravers still living, let me concentrate on the plus side of the ledger and mention that Elizabeth Jones' $5 piece created for the 1988 Olympics was considered by the editor of *Numismatic News* to be an even finer piece of work than anything turned out years earlier by Augustus Saint-Gaudens, a tribute which would be difficult to surpass!

Under the directorship of Donna Pope, the United States Mint has been very enlightened in recent years and has created a fine relationship with collectors. I share the hope of others that as years go by, additional commemorative and other new designs will be produced, to keep numismatics ever-changing, and to carry on the tradition of innovative designs.

• • • • **Recommendations for All Classes of Buyers:** Buy one each of the modern commemoratives in grades as issued.

CHAPTER SIXTEEN

Other Collecting Areas

Pattern Coins

Patterns, it has been said, are what might have been in coinage but weren't. The field covers coins struck in experimental alloys, coins of weight or size different from the standard, coins illustrating designs which were never adopted, and other pieces produced in the course of determining what designs and standards to use for circulating coinage.

Since 1792 over 1,500 different varieties of pattern, trial, and experimental coins have been produced. Some, such as the $4 gold stellas of 1879 and 1880, never advanced beyond the dreams of their proposers. Others, such as the pattern 1872 commercial dollars, which furnished the basis for trade dollars, served to pave the way for designs or denominations which became standard. Still others were produced mainly to sell to collectors; the Standard Silver patterns of the late 1860s, made in an unnecessarily wide variety of metals and edge types, are prime examples.

Some of America's most beautiful designs were made only in pattern form. The 1872 Amazonian silver and gold denominations, the 1882 Shield Earring pattern silver coins, and the 1879 Schoolgirl silver dollar were never made for circulation, although few would argue that any one of these designs would have been an artistic improvement upon the 1878 Morgan silver dollar. Certain other pattern coins were ugly.

Sometimes regular dies for Proof coins were used to strike pieces in non-standard metals, such as an 1885 Liberty Seated half dollar in aluminum instead of silver, an 1868 $20 in aluminum instead of gold, or an 1866 Indian cent in copper-nickel instead of bronze. While the official explanation was that most of these were made to "test the dies," in actuality many were made for private sale to collectors. Nearly all patterns were produced with Proof finish, but there were a few exceptions, the 1859 Indian cent with the reverse design of 1860 (with oak wreath and shield) being one of these.

There are some interesting patterns from our own era. For example, in 1974 the Philadelphia Mint produced several dozen or more Lincoln cents in aluminum, rather than the usual bronze alloy, to test the metal. Mint Director Mary Brooks passed out samples of these aluminum cents to various individuals on Capitol Hill, keeping no particular track of where they went. Then she realized that these might become valuable collectors' items, and an effort was made to get them back, but she found that all but a few had disappeared.

United States Pattern, Experimental and Trial Pieces, by Dr. J. Hewitt Judd, is the standard reference for the series. Andrew W. Pollock III of the Bowers and Merena Galleries staff has been conducting research which will lead to the publication of a new work, incorporating much new data and information.

• **Budget Recommendations:** No recommendations here, as low-grade pattern coins are apt to be quite unattractive. Consider what I have to say under the following listing.

• • **Recommendations for the Connoisseur:** I recommend that you collect patterns in conjunction with a regular series. If you like nickel five-cent pieces, then collect some patterns of this denomination to add to your exhibit of regular Shield and Liberty pieces, etc. Study the field carefully before making any decisions. Patterns should be purchased in higher grades such as Proof-63 or finer, with emphasis on pieces of attractive aesthetic appeal. Some great rarities may not be available in this high grade, so you will have to make your own determination about purchasing a lower grade coin or doing without it entirely.

• • • **Elite Recommendations:** As preceding, but Proof-64 or finer, except in the case of extreme rarities which may not be available in such a high grade, in which instances Proof-63 or so would be fine.

Territorial and Private Gold Coins

During the 19th century numerous assayers, bankers, and others produced gold coins which served as a circulating medium in areas in which federal coins were scarce or non-existent.

Beginning in 1830 Christopher and August Bechtler in North Carolina struck gold coins of $1, $2.50, and $5 denominations. When the Charlotte and Dahlonega mints began operations in the same general area in 1838, the private coinage of the Bechtlers was not interfered with by the government.

In California during the Gold Rush the United States Assay Office of Gold, an agency (but not an official mint) of the government, produced coins valued from $10 up to the large and impressive $50 octagonal gold "slugs." Moffat, Miners Bank, Baldwin, Dubosq, Kellogg, and others struck and distributed a wide variety of types and designs of gold coins with face values from $5 to $50.

The Mormons in Salt Lake City, Utah struck gold coins dated 1849, 1850, and 1860. These are highly desired today. A private partnership in Oregon made $5 and $10 pieces. In Colorado several coiners, the firm of Clark, Gruber & Co. prominent among them, produced pieces of denominations from $2.50 to $20.

Territorial and private gold coins are highly prized today. Most exist in circulated grades from Very Fine to AU. Mint State examples are rare, except for certain issues. Few American series embody as much history and romance as do these numismatic souvenirs from the last century.

• **Budget Recommendations:** No recommendations here, as low-grade territorial and private coins are apt to be quite unattractive and/or damaged. Consider what I have to say under the following listing.

• • **Recommendations for the Connoisseur:** Study the availability of various issues and build a type set of some of the more readily available varieties. I suggest EF-40 or better grades.

• • • **Elite Recommendations:** As preceding, but acquire AU-50 or higher grades, as available. Develop a specialty, such as Bechtler coinage, pieces issued by Clark, Gruber & Co., etc.

Proof Coins and Sets

Beginning in 1817 at the Philadelphia Mint specially prepared coins designated as Proofs were made by imparting a fine polish to the fields of coin dies and carefully striking pieces using specially-finished planchets of excellent quality. The resultant coins typically had mirror fields and had frosted motifs and devices.

In the early years Proofs were distributed to government officials, dignitaries, collectors who had close ties to the Mint, and others, but were not openly sold. Beginning in 1858, Proofs were made available to the public and were sold at a modest premium above face value. In that year an estimated 80 silver sets (containing the three-cent piece, half dime, dime, quarter dollar, half dollar, and silver dollar) were sold, plus approximately 200 Flying Eagle cents. Gold coins were sold individually, and very few were issued.

From 1858 through 1916, minor coins (copper and nickel issues, from the cent through the nickel five-cent piece) were sold in sets, and silver coins were likewise sold in separate sets. Gold coins continued to be sold individually (there were some exceptions, but in general this rule was followed). An example is provided by the year 1881 which saw the production of 3,575 minor Proof sets containing the Indian cent, nickel three-cent piece, and Shield nickel; 975 silver Proof sets (containing the dime, quarter dollar, half dollar, silver dollar, and trade dollar; actually Mint records state that just 960 trade dollars were made), and the following individual quantities of gold Proofs: gold dollars (87), quarter eagles (51), $3 gold pieces (54), half eagles (42), eagles (40), and double eagles (61).

Although most Proofs were of the mirror type earlier described, beginning early in the 20th century the Mint undertook experiments with different finishes, drawing upon technology developed at the Paris Mint and elsewhere. Beginning with Lincoln cents in 1909, Buffalo nickels in 1913, and gold coins in 1908, various matte or "sandblast" surfaces were used on different series. Most collectors did not like these finishes, and orders for Proof coins dropped sharply. After 1916 the production of Proofs for collectors ceased.

In 1936 Proof sets were again issued, of the mirror type, and were continued through 1942, when production was terminated due to the war effort. Proofs could be ordered by the piece or as sets of five coins, from the Lincoln cent to the Walking Liberty half dollar.

Proof set production was resumed in 1950, at which time coins could be ordered only as sets of five pieces. From 1950 through 1964 coinage was continuous, after which time a nationwide coin shortage forced the Mint to stop the service to collectors. In 1968 Proof sets were again issued, breaking tradition, for instead of the Philadelphia Mint, the San Francisco Mint was utilized, and all sets from that time onward have borne the distinctive S mintmark.

Proof coins are eagerly collected today and form a separate area of specialty and study for many numismatists. *Walter Breen's Encyclopedia of Colonial and United States Proof Coins 1722-1989* details the history of federal Proofs as well as various earlier issues and is the standard reference on the subject.

As Proofs were specifically distributed to collectors who paid premiums for them, most of them have survived to the present day. By contrast, business strikes, made for circulation, were saved only as a matter of chance, and the rarity of Uncirculated coins from the original business strike mintages often bears no relation to the quantities originally produced. The Liberty Seated half dollar of 1888 provides an effective illustration of this. Mint records reveal that 833 Proofs and 12,001 business strikes were made. Of the 832 Proofs struck, all were sold to collectors, and nearly all were preserved with care. Over the years numerous pieces have fallen victim to mishandling, cleaning, loss through various misfortunes, and a few were even spent and found their way into circulation. However, of the 832 Proofs made, it is probably reasonable to assume that 500 or 600 survive today. Depending upon how well they have been handled by collectors in the meantime, the grades of most of these pieces currently range from Proof-60 to Proof-65.

On the other hand, the 12,001 business strikes were put into circulation, and no thought was given to saving them. Collectors of the era who desired an example of the current half dollar opted to buy Proofs. The only Uncirculated 1888 half dollars surviving today are from a few stray pieces which were saved as a matter of chance. No more than a few dozen Uncirculated 1888 half dollars exist. In Mint State the 1888 half dollar is far rarer than with Proof finish. Although at one time Mint State pieces, with a mintage of 12,001 coins were, approximately 15 times more plentiful than Proofs, of which 832 were minted, today Proofs are at least 15 times more plentiful than Mint State coins!

• **Budget Recommendations:** No recommendations here, as low-grade Proof coins are apt to be quite unattractive. Consider what I have to say under the following listing.

• • **Recommendations for the Connoisseur:** Proof coins of the 1858-1916 era are, for the most part, good buys in Proof-63 and Proof-64 grades. I do not recommend lesser condition Proofs as they are apt to have too many hairlines, be cloudy, or have other problems. In all instances, Proofs in slabs should be cherrypicked for quality. Proofs from 1936 to date should be purchased in Proof-65 grade, preferably intact as sets, as they are cheaper this way. Avoid paying stiff premiums for high-grade modern sets (1968 to date) for they are very common.

• • • **Elite Recommendations:** Buy Proof-65 issues of hand-selected aesthetic quality. If you are forming a set, match the coins for surface appearance (all brilliant, all lightly toned, or some other objective).

Rolls of Coins

From the first decade of the 20th century, and perhaps even before then, it was a popular practice for banks to distribute coins in paper-wrapped rolls. Typically, a roll of cents contains 50 coins, a roll of nickels 40 coins, a roll of dimes 50 coins, a roll of quarters 40 coins, a roll of half dollars 20 coins, and a roll of silver dollars 20 coins. Although it is certainly possible to *collect* rolls, typically rolls provide a convenient way to invest in or hoard coins. Rolls have always been popular, although in recent years many earlier rolls have been broken up, as emphasis has been on precise grading, and pieces within a roll which grade at high levels are worth significant premiums, making it economically desirable to investigate each individual coin carefully. Rolls offered today often contain culls left over after higher grade pieces, such as MS-64 and MS-65 coins, have been pulled out. For these reason, rolls as a class are much less appealing in the 1990s than they were even a decade ago.

• **Budget Recommendations:** No recommendations here, as there is no point to buying rolls of lower-grade coins. Consider what I have to say under the following listing.

• • **Recommendations for the Connoisseur:** Buy scarcer dates and mintmarks. Examine each coin in each roll carefully. Buy well-struck coins of pleasing appearance, for someday their value will be dependent on the price of each individual coin in the roll. Avoid cull rolls.

• • • **Elite Recommendations:** No recommendations here, as coins in very high grades should not be kept in contact with other coins in rolls.

Bullion Coins

Beginning in the 1970s there was a widespread interest on the part of the American public in gold and silver bullion. To fill this need various refineries, banks, foreign governments, private mints, and others created ingots and discs containing stated quantities of silver or gold. By the mid-1980s a great commerce had arisen in the purchase and resale of gold bullion coins in particular, with the krugerrand (minted in South Africa), the Maple Leaf (minted in Canada), and the 50-peso piece (minted in Mexico) heading the popularity list. Such bullion coins provided a convenient way to hoard gold bullion as a hedge against inflation and as protection in the event of international turmoil and uncertainty.

The United States government recognized a good thing when it saw it, and beginning in 1986 commenced issuing its own bullion coins. Silver pieces, called "eagles," have been minted at Philadelphia and San Francisco since then. Each piece contains one ounce of nearly pure silver. Coins are available in frosty Uncirculated finish as well as mirrorlike Proof format. The Mint utilized for the obverse the Walking Liberty motif created by Adolph A. Weinman in 1916 for the half dollar, and for the reverse Mint engraver John Mercanti created his version of a heraldic eagle.

Gold bullion coins have been produced by the Treasury Department since 1986 and are denominated as $5 (containing 1/10 ounce of pure gold), $10 (1/4 ounce), $25 (1/2 ounce), and $50 (1 ounce). The coins were not made for circulation, as the gold bullion value far exceeds the face value. An earlier effort to sell gold in half-ounce and one-ounce medals, with no stated denomination, was not a success, so the Treasury Department gave each of the new bullion coins a stated denomination, thus increasing the appeal of the pieces to collectors. The obverse of each piece depicts Saint-Gaudens' design of Miss Liberty as originally used on the 1907 double eagle, in combination with a new reverse, featuring a family of eagles, designed by Mrs. Miley Busiek. Dates are expressed in Roman numerals. Coinage has been accomplished at the Philadelphia and West Point mints. Pieces are available in Uncirculated and Proof finishes.

These new bullion coins are very attractive, and I have every reason to expect that as years go by they will become important parts of many collections. The values of the pieces has been dependent on two considerations: the quantities minted and the price of bullion. The gold issues in particular have moved up and down in keeping with the fluctuation of gold bullion on world markets.

• • • • **Recommendations for All Classes of Buyers:** Buy one each of the silver and gold bullion coins produced since 1986, or just buy the one-ounce silver and one-ounce gold pieces. Superb quality coins are easily available now for "regular" prices.

Tokens

Tokens are privately issued "coins" distributed by merchants, individuals, and others for the purpose of advertising themselves or their services. Tokens are a relatively small part of the numismatic hobby and are generally ignored by the typical investor. However, some tokens can be quite valuable, and without doubt most of them carry interesting stories.

The field of tokens and medals, sometimes grouped under the heading of numismatic Americana or exonumia, is a popular one and in recent years has attracted many who have found in the series the possibility to acquire interesting pieces for tiny fractions of the prices of federal coins. The Token and Medal Society, publisher of the TAMS Journal, numbers several thousand members and is very active.

Tokens divide themselves into a number of specialties. Among the most popular are these:

• **Hard Times tokens:** Mostly the size of contemporary large cents, Hard Times tokens were minted circa 1832-1844, and display a wide variety of designs and inscriptions, including political motifs and advertisements of merchants. At the turn of the century Lyman H. Low described 183 different pieces in his book, Hard Times Tokens. In recent years Russell Rulau has vastly expanded the list.

In 1989 and early 1990 Michael Hodder and I had the pleasure of cataloguing the Michael B. Zeddies Collection of Hard Times tokens—pieces, mostly in copper and the size of a large cent, which were issued in and around 1837, a period of political controversy and economic difficulty in the United States. In the course of examining and describing over 100 different varieties, I experienced a feeling that I had been transported to a century and a half earlier, to the presidency of Andrew Jackson, to the time after May 10, 1837 when banks stopped paying out coins and there were virtually none to be found in circulation, to an era when transportation by canals was all the rage, and the railroad was newer then than space travel is today.

One of the lots in the Zeddies Collection consisted of a token issued by the Roxbury Coaches. This piece was described in our auction catalogue as follows:

"Low-129. Roxbury Coaches. Boston. 1837. German silver. VF-35. Planchet defect near rim, as illustrated.

"Tokens such as this are what numismatics is all about. At this sale the present example of L-129 will probably sell for a couple hundred dollars or so, certainly a small amount in the overall scheme of things on today's market, where even a common-date Morgan dollar will bring more than this, in higher grades. We suggest that the collector who desires a generous measure of history and romance with his or her purchases would do well to read the following inscription, extracted from Lyman H. Low's 1899 reference, to contemplate the fact that the token in question was probably handled by a number of riders on the coaches in question, then consider whether such a coin might indeed be interesting to possess:

"The 'Roxbury Coaches' were those which ran through what is now Washington Street, Boston, over 'the Neck,' to the top of the hill in Roxbury where once stood the old church in which the Apostle Eliot preached in the ancient days of New England. The Norfolk House, a famous hostelry on the opposite side of the street, was their stopping place until the line was discontinued. These coaches were long omnibuses, carrying 16 to 20 persons inside, and were drawn by four horses. At first they made hourly trips, and hence were called the 'Roxbury Hourlies.' They were handsomely painted, and on their sides bore a distinguishing name—'Regulator,' 'Conqueror;' and one, the 'Aurora,' with the goddess in her cloud-borne chariot on its yellow sides, made a great impression on the juvenile mind when it first appeared.

"For a long time Mr. King managed the business; later he met with opposition from a line of coaches of more modern style, like the New York 'Stages,' which was started, I believe, by Mr. Hobbs, and made more frequent trips. The Roxbury Coaches continued to run for a short time after the horse-cars were introduced as competitors on the same route, but finally succumbed to the 'march of improvement' about 1856, if memory serves."

At the sale itself the coin sold for $143. To me this little token is incredibly romantic, and I defy anyone to show me any other object from the year 1837—whether it be a painting, statue, or anything else—which has more history than does this inexpensive memento of a long-forgotten stage line.

• **Civil War tokens:** Mostly the size of contemporary Indian cents, Civil War tokens were produced during the war between the states, particularly in the year 1863, and exist to the extent of nearly 10,000 varieties. Many bear political inscriptions, but many more were used as advertisements by merchants. The Civil War Token Society is comprised of devotees of the field. Attributions are to published reference works by George and Melvin Fuld.

• **"Good Fors":** Sometimes tokens have a face value, good only in exchange, such as one cent, five cents, ten cents, or are denominated some other way such as "GOOD FOR ONE DRINK," "GOOD FOR ONE FARE," or, in the case of a token issued by Si Rowe, who maintained a saloon in Grass Valley, California at the turn of the century, good for one tune in an automatic banjo machine. Thousands of varieties of "good fors" exist and most from the early part of the present century are priced from about $1 to $5 each.

• **Counterstamped coins:** Regular issue United States and foreign coins were often counterstamped with advertisements, hallmarks, names, and other identification, to make the pieces useful as advertisements, to promote a political cause, or for some other reason. Dr. Gregory Brunk, Frank Duffield, Maurice M. Gould, Kenneth L. Hallenbeck, Russell Rulau, and others have written extensively on the field of counterstamped coins.

I admit a personal preference for counterstamped large cents of the 1793-1857 era, for I have collected them since 1955. Nearly all of the pieces in my collection are well worn, some of them to the point of virtual smoothness, and each is counterstamped with the imprint of a merchant, jeweler, patent medicine vendor, political slogan, or some other motif. In their day, large cents acted as traveling billboards, and any message, name, or sentiment impressed on them by a punch and a hammer would be carried over hill and dale, through cities and villages, to citizens everywhere. Dr. G.G. Wilkins, a Pittsfield, New Hampshire dentist, advertised by stamping thousands of large cents with his name.

Among my favorite counterstamps are early United States cents of the 1830s and 1840s punched with the bold inscription VOTE THE LAND

FREE. At some time, in some place, someone took a bunch of perfectly nice copper cents, placed a punch over them, and whacked them with a hammer, imprinting each with the VOTE THE LAND FREE motto. As no specimen has been seen bearing a date later than 1848, it has been assumed by various numismatists (see below) that the Free Soil Party, which fielded a presidential candidate in the election of 1848, but lost to Zachary Taylor, used these counterstamped cents as political tokens.

I have quite a collection of these cents, as I have endeavored to acquire the stamp on cents of as many different dates as I can find. In 1955 at the age of 16 I acquired my first specimen, an 1838 cent so marked, paying Maurice M. Gould, who used to operate the Copley Coin Company in upstairs offices on Boston's busy Boylston Street, the princely sum of $2 for it. Now I have over 30 examples, including duplicates, one of the most recent of which, an 1840 cent with the counterstamp, was purchased from the firm of Rossa & Tanenbaum for $40 in October 1988, which might indicate that this obscure speciality has been a good investment over the years! However, few collectors care for such things, and more likely than not the average dealer would consider such a counterstamped coin to be a candidate for the junk box.

In trying to find out more about the VOTE THE LAND FREE counterstamp I consulted the published articles and works of Frank Duffield, Maurice M. Gould, Kenneth L. Hallenbeck, Gregory G. Brunk and others, but I know little more now than I did in 1955. Brunk's magnum opus, *American and Canadian Countermarked Coins*, presents on page 183 an enlarged illustration of an 1841-dated VOTE THE LAND FREE coin from my collection, and on the facing page this notation is printed: "In the 1840s support for the Free Soil and Free Speech Party lay primarily in Massachusetts, New York, and Ohio. Its slogan was 'Free Soil, Free Speech, Free Labor and Free Men.' During the 1848 presidential campaign for Martin Van Buren they circulated coins stamped VOTE THE LAND FREE."

No doubt the Free Soil Party did just that, but I have been nagged by this question: Why didn't they stamp coins with the legend FREE SOIL, which would have fit in with the wording of their slogan? I have perused many books about Martin Van Buren and I have examined Free Soil Party campaign literature and advertisements from the year 1848, but nowhere does the VOTE THE LAND FREE appear, except on the counterstamped cents. Here indeed is a mystery! Perhaps this makes the cents all the more intriguing and interesting. Then there is the curious enterprise of Dr. Shattuck, whose "Water Cure," located in Waterford, Maine, was advertised by counterstamping large cents. Try as I might, I have never located any newspaper or magazine advertisements placed by the doctor, although I imagine that these exist and would serve to tell more about him.

• **Other areas:** Other interesting areas of tokens include early American pieces, late 19th-century issues, transportation tokens, and political campaign tokens. While Hard Times tokens and certain other early issues range in value from several dollars up to thousands of dollars, and Civil War tokens can cost from a couple dollars up to several hundred dollars, most 20th-century pieces are priced from a dollar to $10, providing a truly inexpensive area for numismatists.

• • **Recommendations for the Connoisseur (and everyone else):** Buy some books first, then begin buying, based on what appeals to you the most.

Medals

A medal, usually round, but sometimes square or some other shape, typically was issued by an individual, company, civic authority, government, or other entity to honor a person or event, to observe an anniversary, or for some other commemorative purpose. Medals have no face value and are not redeemable for cash, goods, or services.

The Philadelphia Mint has produced medals nearly since its inception. Subjects covered by Mint medals cover such areas as the War of 1812, presidential terms, lifesaving awards, Indian peace medals, directors of the Mint, and the annual meeting of the Assay Commission, among many other topics. Today, many varieties of medals, including restrikes of early issues, can be ordered from the Mint.

The Medallic Art Company, presently located in Danbury, Connecticut, has been in business since the turn of the century and has produced thousands of medals covering virtually every subject imaginable, from civic awards to space exploration. The firm has the distinction of having produced dies for the U.S. Mint, when the official government facility was too busy to ready certain commemorative issues for production.

Each time a new president is elected, he becomes the subject of an official inaugural medal. Our firm had the honor of being official distributor of the inaugural medals produced by the Medallic Art Company for Ronald Reagan and George Bush. These medals depicted the incoming president on the obverse and an emblem on the reverse, and were sold at a premium to collectors, historians, and others who desired mementos of these events in American history.

In the 1960s and through the 1970s the Franklin Mint, the brainchild of Joseph Segel, sold hundreds of millions of dollars' worth of commemorative medals to the public, at first billing them as an excellent investment, then backing off and describing them as historical mementoes. For a time there were more members in the Franklin Collectors Society, sponsored by the Franklin Mint, than there were members in the American Numismatic Association! The Franklin Mint scored a coup in the 1960s when United States silver dollars were no longer available to Nevada gaming casinos. The private minting company came up with beautifully designed nickel-alloy medals which could be used in slot machines and on the gaming tables, thus solving the problem and at the same time producing substantial revenue.

Many other private mints and distribution agencies have sold interesting and historically significant medals to collectors and the public over the years. Many coin collecting groups, including the American Numismatic Association and the American Numismatic Society, have issued medals as well.

• • **Recommendations for the Connoisseur (and everyone else):** Buy some books first, and then begin buying the pieces that interest you the most. A little bit of money will go a long way when buying medals on today's market.

Paper Money

Currency, or paper money, comes in many forms. Specimens are avidly collected by many numismatists. In America, currency notes have been produced since colonial times. Particularly popular with collectors are paper notes issued at par by banks and others during the early nineteenth century, but now not worth face value. Such pieces were produced in many denominations which seem unusual today, including $4, $6, $7, and even $1.75 and $6.25.

A number of years ago my then business partner, James F. Ruddy, formed a large collection of $3 bills, a denomination which was, believe it or not, one of the most popular values issued by private banks in the era from about 1820 to 1860. I later acquired this holding, added many pieces to it, and presented it to the American Numismatic Association Museum, where it reposes today and is the largest such collection ever assembled, to the best of my knowledge. In the 1860s the federal government considered issuing $3 bills, then decided against the idea. Later, the expression "queer as a three-dollar bill" became a part of the American idiom, and a new generation of citizens never realized that at one time there were such things as real $3 bills.

Paper money issued by the Confederate States of America from 1861 to 1865 forms an important specialty within numismatics. The best known rarities in the series are the $500 and $1,000 notes issued when the capital of the Confederacy was Montgomery, Alabama. Col. Grover C. Criswell, a long-term governor of the American Numismatic Association and one of the best known figures on the collecting scene, has made Confederate paper money his life's specialty. On a nationwide television program he was described as a "Confederate millionaire," for he had $1 million face value in Confederate notes.

Paper money or "greenback" notes produced by the federal government from 1861 to 1928, usually called large-size notes, and the smaller-size notes produced since 1928, are the focus of attention for many numismatists. While today in the 1990s most modern notes look alike, at one time there was a truly wide diversity of designs, some of which, such as the elegant "Educational" $1, $2, and $5 Silver Certificates of 1896, are quite artistic. Five-dollar Silver Certificates of the Series of 1886 depict across the back of the note five Morgan silver dollars bearing that date, and are beautiful specimens of the engraver's art.

Did you know that national banks all across America issued their own currency from the 1860s until 1929? These notes were produced by the Bureau of Engraving and Printing and bore standard designs, but with the imprint of the Wolfeboro National Bank, of Wolfeboro, New Hampshire, or any one of hundreds of other national banks. Backed by the federal government, national bank notes were redeemable anywhere in the United States. Today, collectors often aspire to collect notes from as many different banks as possible from their own states.

• **Budget Recommendations:** Pick a specialty, and acquire nice Fine notes, which are often available for prices far less than New (equivalent to Uncirculated) examples. See below for some ideas.

• • **Recommendations for the Connoisseur:** Form a type set of $1 large size United States notes for starters. This will acquaint you with the discipline of collecting. I like grades of New to Choice New. Later, you can expand your type set. If you live in a state in which many varieties of national bank notes were once issued, you might try to acquire notes from as many different banks as possible. If you like collecting dates and mintmarks of coins, you might like collecting varieties of small $1 notes, by signature combinations and Federal Reserve bank locations, for the philosophy is about the same; opt for Choice New grade. Broken bank notes of the general era 1820-1864 are fun to collect, but seek a specialty before you start buying. Grades generally range from Good to Extremely Fine for notes which actually circulated; these notes are the most interesting. The majority of New notes are what are called "remainder" notes—

leftovers which were never signed or used; many such notes are common.

• • • **Elite Recommendations:** Acquire notes in New to Choice New in your favorite specialty. Be aware that grading standards have not been universally adopted, andone person's New can be as nice as someone else's Choice New or Gem New. Learn about currency grading first!

Numismatic Books

While books are the key to research and learning, no single person can possibly assimilate all of the knowledge that is in print. In fact, you could spend a year in the libraries of the American Numismatic Association in Colorado Springs or the American Numismatic Society in New York City and still not read about everything. Some coins have never been documented, either because no information is available or because no one cares. The VOTE THE LAND FREE counterstamped large cents mentioned earlier are an example of an issue for which no documentation is known..

Contrasting these cents are such issues as the 1909 Lincoln cent with the initials of the designer, Victor David Brenner (V.D.B.), on the reverse and the MCMVII (1907) High Relief gold $20 piece, each of which has been the subject of numerous detailed articles. In fact, I once devoted an entire chapter of one of my books, *U.S. Gold Coins: An Illustrated History*, to the background of the MCMVII issue. The point is that no book, or library for that matter, can cover all aspects of coin collecting.

Reference books in the American series range from general volumes such as *A Guide Book of United States Coins* to specialized books such as *Penny Whimsy*. Those with an inclination will find it fascinating to attribute die varieties to a specialized reference work. Such references exist for most all early United States coins minted during the general period 1792-1836. As a rare die variety can be much more valuable than a common one, die variety attribution is important. An Ohio consignor sent a common-looking large cent to one of our recent sales. He had paid $200 for it, and undoubtedly he would have been pleased had it realized $300. However, Andrew W. Pollock III of our staff attributed it as a rare die variety, and when it crossed the auction block it sold for $12,500!

Excellent books are in print or can be borrowed from libraries,[1] on such subjects as Liberty Seated dimes, Morgan silver dollars, commemoratives, Jefferson nickels, Barber coins, Franklin half dollars, Standing Liberty quarters, gold denominations, Lincoln cents, and most other series. If more than one book is available on a given series, as is the case with Morgan silver dollars, read all of them, as viewpoints and facts often differ. Don't overlook *The Coin World Almanac*, which gives all sorts of good information about numismatic societies, mint engravers and other personnel, coinage laws, and other things (including a chapter on coin investment contributed by the present author and a chapter by Raymond N. Merena on the subject of auctions).

While most numismatists concern themselves with the acquisition of coins, tokens, medals, or paper money, some specialize not in such things but in numismatic literature and books. In 1972 I had the privilege of selling at auction the memorable collection of rare pattern and other coins formed over a long period of years by Armand Champa, a well-known Louisville, Kentucky businessman. Armand's collecting instinct remained after his coins were sold, and he went on to build a truly fantastic collection of reference books, auction catalogues, long-forgotten dealers' price lists, periodicals, and other items. At the 1989 convention of the American Numismatic Association a videotaped tour of his book collection took the best part of an hour to present and was a prime attraction at a meeting of the Numismatic Bibliomania Society (at the 1990 convention, the highlight of the NBS meeting was an address by veteran numismatist John Jay Pittman, who told of his experiences with books and printing).

Catalogues and reference works on out-of-print numismatic literature issued by George F. Kolbe, Function Associates, Remy Bourne, Money Tree, Frank and Laurese Katen, Orville Grady, Charles Davis, Sanford Durst, Cal Wilson, and others have become collectible in their own right.

Modern books are available from many dealers and booksellers, who offer a wide variety of titles which can be ordered by mail. Most books in print are surprisingly inexpensive and are in the $10 to $25 range. Special credit goes to the Numismatic Literary Guild, which encourages the writing and dessemination of numismatic research and information, and to nationally prominent columnists—Roger Boye, Kenneth E. Bressett, Michael R. Fuljenz, Clifford Mishler, Col. William Murray, Robert Obojski, Edwin V. Quagliana, Peter M. Rexford, Ed Rochette, Michael Thorne, and Scott Travers are just a few examples—who recommend that their readers gain education and buy books before making large expenditures on coins.

- Start by building a basic library of books in print on United States coins, then add books on colonial and early American coins, tokens and medals, and paper money. Back-dated numismatic magazines and newspapers are very inexpensive and contain a treasure trove of information.

CHAPTER SEVENTEEN

Maximizing the Rewards

Maximizing the Rewards

What are the rewards of coin collecting? Ask some, and they'll say the rewards are investment, investment, and investment. But as you know by this time in the present text, my view differs. I suggest that you can maximize the rewards of numismatics, *including investment*, if you widen your interest to include history, romance, art, camaraderie, and excitement.[1]

History? Consider the coins shown to visitors in the halls of The Smithsonian Institution, where I was honored to give a talk, which I titled "Maximizing the Rewards," to numismatists who had come from all over the country. Only a few steps away in the same building were the treasures displayed in the National Numismatic Collection. I paused to reflect upon some of the pieces on view, and considered their incredible backgrounds.

Who can doubt that a $5 piece minted in Oregon in 1849 from gold brought north from California, and a $1 Continental Currency note printed in the midst of the American Revolution, are not history you can hold in your hands?

Romance? What about coins of the Spanish Main, the legendary pieces of eight and gold escudos of pirate fame?

Art? Augustus Saint-Gaudens, considered to be the greatest sculptor in America at the time, designed the new American gold $10 and $20 coinage for 1907.

Camaraderie? Gathered there in the lecture hall in the Smithsonian were many old friends of mine, and many new faces as well—all together in the spirit of numismatics, to hear what I and other speakers had to say—all united by the common theme of numismatics. Some had traveled great distances to attend.

Excitement? The thrill of the chase is ever present in numismatics—whether you are collecting and are looking for a key silver dollar to finish a set of Carson City issues, or a scarce Newcomb variety of large cent dated 1824, or are engaged in research—like a number of people are—and are endeavoring to see how many times an Uncirculated 1840 Liberty Seated dollar has crossed the auction block during the past century.

All of the above equates to a final result: having a good time. Let me discuss each aspect in turn.

History

It has been said that coins are the footprints of history. Years ago dealer B. Max Mehl told of the double appeal of numismatics; as a source of pleasure and as a worthwhile investment.[2] His words are still relevant today:

"Coin collecting as a hobby affords more pleasure and greater interest than any other collectible objects. It opens a wide field of study. It develops a taste for art and stimulates research in nearly every branch of learning. It teaches us history and geography, and while a very fascinating and instructive pastime, it has also been the source of much profit, as no one knows better than those who have collected coins in the past, that good coin collections increase in value from year to year, thus providing an excellent investment. Coins are often the only historical records that we have of nations which have long since passed away, and which would have been buried in oblivion but for the coins that bear the names of kings and records of events relating to the countries whose money they once were."

A few years ago I chanced to be in Atlanta, Georgia with Ed Rochette, who at the time was executive director of the American Numismatic Association. A local radio station wanted to do a feature on coin collecting, and Ed and I took a taxi to the studio to be interviewed. The movie *Cleopatra*, with Elizabeth Taylor and Richard Burton, was on the screens across America, and the subject of Cleopatra came up in the interview.

"While Cleopatra may be gorgeous on the movie screen," Ed Rochette related, "in reality she was as ugly as a toad. How do I know? Her portrait on coinage tells us so."

Similarly, the prognathic jaw (as medical experts would call it today) of Leopold the Hogmouth of Austria is there for all to see on his silver thalers, even as the abnormality progresses in its extent. Many faces in history are known to us only through coinage, for no paintings, sculpture, or other delineations survive.

In 1920, Frank Morton Todd wrote a history of the 1915 Panama-Pacific International Exposition, including in his five-volume study an article, "The Coin Outlives the Throne." The subject of the article was Farran Zerbe, who managed the coin and medal exhibit at the Exposition and who displayed his collection, titled Moneys of the World. On view were the engraved images of kings and queens, of schemers and scholars, and others who for one reason or another had their portrait placed on coins, tokens, medals, or paper money over the years. For many individuals little is known except the tangible evidence of their coinage—indeed, for many the coin did outlive the throne, just as B. Max Mehl said (perhaps he was inspired by Todd).

Contrasting the countless famous as well as obscure personalities who were pictured on coinage, there is Columbus, for whom no authenticated (to everyone's satisfaction) portrait exists. Depictions on various coins and medals, including the 1892 World's Columbian Exposition half dollar, are composites. The same is true for Jesus Christ, depicted on countless medals and coins[3]—no one knows what He looked like, but guesses are aplenty.

Paper money from our own country has a rich and rather checkered history. The United States government was not off to a good start with its Continental Currency, issued to finance the Revolution, which was soon repudiated and not worth the paper it was printed on, giving rise to the saying "not worth a Continental" or in its expanded form, "not worth a Continental damn." Of course, all things come to him who waits, and today numerous Continental Currency notes are indeed worth more than face value. However, one wouldn't want to compute the interest the money could have earned in the meantime!

This reminds me of a calculation once done by *Forbes* magazine which revealed that in the $24 trade for the island of Manhattan, the Indians came up with the better part of the deal—for if they had invested their money at 6% compounded interest since the early 17th century, today they would have more money than the assessed valuation of all the real estate in New York City![4]

The so-called Panic of 1837 was one of the most interesting times in American history, and perhaps someday someone will write a dissertation on its numismatic consequences. Best remembered are the so-called "wildcat notes" issued by banks which were organized with a small capital, say $25,000, only a fraction of which was ever paid in, and then went about issuing hundreds of thousands of dollars' worth of currency. Of course, all came to an abrupt halt when such currency was presented for redemption. To counter this, the most profitable technique was to distribute bills as far away from the bank location as possible!

The Panic of 1837 was in what was called the "Hard Times" era, giving rise to a series of tokens of that name, encompassing a span from the early 1830s through the early 1840s. Particularly fascinating are the multitude of pieces, mostly dated 1837, concerning Andrew Jackson, the Bank of the United States, the suspension of specie (coin) payments by the government on May 10, 1837, and related personalities and events. Mostly of large cent size, these pieces circulated for many years.

An American historical event with outstanding numismatic conse-quences was the Civil War. Beginning in the summer of 1862, widespread coin hoarding by the public took place, and soon even Indian cents could not be found. Barbers, coffee houses, horsecars, newspaper vendors, and other merchants found it impossible to do business without coins, so quickly a variety of substitutes arose—including postage stamps pasted to cardboard (inserted loosely in printed envelopes, or encased behind mica) and, in particular, thousands of different varieties of small metallic tokens, mostly bronze and of one-cent size.

The federal government got into the act with its own issue of "greenback" paper money notes, which at one time it refused to redeem for coins at face value! The possessor of a United States $5 bill in 1863 could not take to a bank, or to the United States Treasury, and receive silver dollars, quarter eagles, or any other coins on an even exchange for it! Coins were available on the open market, but only if the notes were discounted.

During the Civil War era the Philadelphia Mint continued to produce Proof coins for collectors, but the Mint would not accept government currency at par in payment! Intending purchasers of Proof coins had to buy gold or silver coins at a premium on the open market and submit them to effect the purchase. Curiously, at the same time, out in Denver the banking firm of Clark, Gruber & Company issued its own bank notes which were indeed redeemable at par, in $2.50, $5, $10, and $20 gold coins minted by the firm in 1860 and 1861. So, during the Civil War, privately printed Clark, Gruber paper currency was worth more than federal currency—an interesting footnote to American financial history.

Among the most interesting of all United States notes are the inexpensive and generally ignored (I don't recall anyone making special mention of them in recent times) Civil War era five-cent fractional currency pieces bearing the portrait of "Clark."[5] Members of Congress, the public, and others who saw these notes when they were circulated thought that the depiction was of that of William Clark, who with Meriwether Lewis mounted the famous Lewis and Clark Expedition to the Northwest in 1804-1806. But they were wrong! The portrait was unauthorized and showed Spencer M. Clark, director of the National Currency Bureau (later renamed Bureau of Engraving and Printing), a very colorful individual who, among other things, arranged the hiring of teenaged girls at the Bureau to include those who didn't mind granting him sexual favors. There was nothing Clark liked to do better than to take a young female employee with him to a hotel for the weekend, or for an overnight romp in his Washington home while his wife was away in the countryside.[6]

Then there is the story of the Confederate States of America, and the story of how Philadelphia engraver George Lovett received an order through Bailey & Company, local jewelers, to produce one-cent pieces for the Confederate States of America. Crafting a head of a goddess on the obverse, and a wreath composed of Southern products on the reverse, he created a copper-nickel cent of distinctive design. Twelve pieces were struck, and he contemplated them with enthusiasm, for they were indeed beautiful. Then he had second thoughts. What if he were branded as a traitor to the Union cause, for aiding the Confederacy? Fearful of the consequences, Lovett hid the pieces and forgot about them, except for one coin which he carried as a pocket piece. As chance would have it, this little Confederate cent was spent over the counter at a bar one day, and soon came into the hands of John Haseltine, a Philadelphia coin dealer, who recognized the portrait on the obverse as being identical to that used by Lovett on an 1860 token bearing his advertisement. He went to Lovett and asked about the Confederate cents, and Lovett denied everything. Later Lovett told truth and produced the remaining 11 pieces as well as the dies. In 1874 some restrikes were made, believed to have amounted to 55 bronze pieces, 12 silver coins, and seven gold. These plus the 12 originals in copper-nickel serve to document this interesting chapter in American numismatics.

The Confederate States of America had grand designs to produce its own silver coins, and in 1861 a distinctive reverse die was made up at the New Orleans Mint, and four coins were struck, in combination with an official United States obverse Liberty Seated die. This idea, too, did not see fruition in regular coinage, and the original pattern coinage of four pieces constituted the entire production.

The World War in Europe was reflected in the new United States silver designs for the 1916 year; the Standing Liberty quarter, with Miss Liberty holding a shield and adopting a defensive mode, and the Liberty Walking half dollar with its perched eagle, prepared to strike if necessary. Perhaps no more beautiful motif in American numismatics can be found than on the obverse of this half dollar, with Miss Liberty striding toward a radiant sun, her features outlined against a star-spangled cape. In 1921 the Peace dollar was created, with the word PEACE at the bottom of the reverse, to signify what was hoped to be an end to worldwide conflict.

And then there is the series of commemorative half dollars, each one of which relates a bit of history, from Columbus' sailing ship on the 1892 half dollar to anniversaries of the Civil War battles of Antietam and Gettysburg, to rather obscure observations such as anniversaries associated with the cities

New Rochelle and Hudson, New York, not to overlook the 100th anniversary of Elgin, Illinois. As noted earlier, a coin observing the 300th anniversary of the landing of the Swedes in Delaware bore three different dates, a somewhat confusing situation. But, the 1930s were noted for their confusion, and commemorative half dollars just added to what everybody else was doing!

The history of other countries is likewise related in their coinage, and typical among the first duties of any dictator, monarch, or other ruler was the creation of coins bearing his or her portrait. Architectural history is reflected in the beautiful city view thalers of Germany and Switzerland. What did Basel look like 200 years ago? Numismatics tells the story. Legends and traditions are likewise related, as on the "Wildman thaler," the Lady Godiva tokens, and the omnipresent British motif of St. George slaying the dragon. A separate chapter could be written on the history of any one of these coins.

Romance

Intertwined with history is romance. I earlier mentioned the Spanish Main, and there is no doubt that among the most interesting news stories in recent years have been those of ships from the Spanish treasure fleet being discovered off the coast of Florida and elsewhere. Gold doubloons, silver 8 real pieces and other coins have come to light, sometimes in large quantities.

Somewhat related is the large series of medals devoted to the exploits of Admiral Vernon. In their day, Admiral Vernon medals were collected with great enthusiasm by armchair dilettantes in England, the same type of individuals who chased after varieties of conder tokens years later. In his book on tokens related to American history, C. Willys Betts devoted an entire chapter to Admiral Vernon medals, pieces which in their day may have been every bit as popular as collecting large cents is right now in the 1990s.

The discovery of gold on the American River in California in 1848 and the consequent Gold Rush is an important part of American history and helped shape the divisions on the map as we know them today. Without this discovery, California might now belong to Mexico, and who knows how the rest of the West would be configured? Stories of the treasures of the gold fields were greeted with skepticism until an official government agent brought with him a quantity of bullion to Washington. Later the metal was sent to Philadelphia and coined into golden quarter eagles, the smallest gold denomination at the time, for use as souvenirs for anyone desiring to obtain a specimen made from California metal. Each piece was officially counterstamped at the Mint with the notation CAL. on the reverse. In actuality, it would be proper to consider this coin our very first United States commemorative issue, as I mentioned earlier in the present text.

Then came a rush of privately issued pieces, including the gorgeous $10 "horseman" or "vaquero" issues of Baldwin & Co., so beautiful to collectors today, but repudiated in their own time, for they were not of full weight. The issues of the Miners Bank, Moffat & Company, Wass, Molitor & Co., Kellogg, and others are a reflection of the economic times of the era.

Romance in the most literal sense has been documented on tokens and medals for a long time. Indeed, within numismatics there is an entire branch called "love tokens," consisting of federal and other coins which have been smoothed down on one side and engraved with different sentimental remembrances, perhaps a gift a departing soldier gave to his sweetheart before going to the Civil War, or perhaps an engagement token. Some of these are fascinating for the stories they don't tell. *I love you forever, Nellie, July 5, 1878, Robert,* engraved in script on the reverse of a Liberty Seated half dollar may have been an engagement token, or perhaps Robert was headed out to sea for a long voyage and intended the coin as a keepsake for his sweetheart. We will never know.

In Europe, marriage thalers and medals were produced on numerous occasions, and some pieces went so far as to show the children of the union. In our own time, the bethrothal of Prince Charles to Diana was greeted by a spate of tokens and medals commemorating the event, as the whole world shared vicariously in the romance of the year.

Before leaving the subject of romance, or romance and history combined, let me touch upon one of my favorite numismatic items: the Washington-Lafayette counterstamp on United States coins. In 1824 Marquis de Lafayette, French hero of the American Revolution, returned to the United States and was given a triumphal welcome. Parties, dances, parades, and other civic events were staged all along the Eastern seaboard. Somewhere along the line a pair of dies was prepared, one die depicting Washington and the other Lafayette. These dies were counterstamped on many United States coins, most notably large cents of the era, and were intended as souvenirs. How they were distributed remains a mystery. Some suggest that they were purchased by the public and thrown in front of Lafayette as he paraded down city streets, but considering that some of the counterstamps were on half dollars, it is difficult to envision anyone throwing away a coin of this value. Indeed, back in 1824 even a cent had significant purchasing power.

Others have suggested that these counterstamps were applied at the Philadelphia Mint. If so, then such pieces would constitute official commemoratives antedating the 1848 CAL. commemorative $2.50 gold coins mentioned earlier, but I doubt if this was the case, and I suspect that the issue was private.

A few years ago I chanced upon a set of *Niles Register*, which in the early 19th century gave its readers information on the financial world as well as the American and international scene in general. This particular run of issues had been in the reference collection of the Bank of the United States and, now unwanted, had passed into the hands of a dealer in old books. After acquiring the set, I looked through it and was impressed by the tremendous amount of news which was related in one way or another to numismatics—what the Mint was doing, different exchange rates, and so on. Beginning with Lafayette's arrival in 1824 and continuing until his departure in 1825, the week-by-week travels of "our nation's guest," as he was was designated by Congress, were given in detail. I spent several evenings reading of what Lafayette did and where he went, but nowhere could I find a mention of counterstamped coins. Hope springs eternal, and more research in this area is on my list of things to do.

Art

President Theodore Roosevelt visited the Smithsonian Institution in 1904 or 1905 and was impressed by the Greek coins on display. They had an almost sculptured appearance, he noticed, and in his mind were far superior to the bland coinage currently produced by the United States. Enlisting the aid of an acquaintance, sculptor Augustus Saint-Gaudens, Roosevelt subsequently commissioned the artist to redesign the entire American coinage from the cent through the double eagle. A stipend of $5,000 got things started.

There were a few problems, but Roosevelt brashly ignored them. Up to this point the preparation of new coinage designs was something done within the walls of the Philadelphia Mint. Although outside artists were aplenty, their talents were not wanted. After all, George T. Morgan, Charles E. Barber, and others in the engraving department of the Mint had spent their lives creating coins and medals. They knew what the public wanted and how to produce such pieces. or at least they thought they did.

Further, Augustus Saint-Gaudens had no experience at all relating to coinage, and although he informed President Roosevelt that in his opinion the most beautiful American coin produced to that date was the 1857 Flying Eagle cent, that was about the limit of his numismatic knowledge. Coins were and still are more than just metallic tokens bearing inscriptions—great care has to be taken in the placement of lettering and design elements, the creation of open spaces and areas in relief, and so on, so that pieces when produced on a high-speed press will strike up properly. About this Roosevelt could care less, and damn the torpedoes, Saint-Gaudens went full speed ahead. By late spring 1907, designs were a reality.

At the same time, the artist was in failing health. A number of sketches and designs were completed, but unfortunately only the $10 and $20 pieces ever saw fruition, for Saint-Gaudens died in the summer of 1907. By that time he had largely completed the motifs for the $10 and $20 pieces, with the $20—the largest coin denomination—occupying the most attention. The motif for this was taken from the figure of the goddess Victory, a part of the Sherman Monument, erected in 1903 at the corner of Fifth Avenue and Central Park South, just across the street from where the Plaza Hotel would be built a few years later in 1907.[7]

Imparting a classical element to the $20 design was the date 1907 expressed in Roman numerals as MCMVII. The entire design—the obverse with "Victory" and the reverse with a flying eagle obviously inspired by Saint-Gaudens' like for the earlier American cent design—was in sculpture-like relief, quite pleasing to Roosevelt as it was somewhat similar to the Greek coinage in this aspect. The staff of engraving department at the Philadelphia Mint reacted with a mixture of horror and dismay. Here was a design that they did not want, period. It was impractical, the relief was too high, it wouldn't strike up properly, no one could read the date, and so on, President Roosevelt was informed.

The President, not one to back down when a good fight was in the offing, stated that he didn't care if only one double eagle could be struck *per day*, that's the way it was going to be, and the Mint was to use the design. Well, it turned out that the engraving department was right, in a way, and that the high-relief double eagle would not strike up properly on regular production presses. Therefore, using medal presses, hand-feeding the planchets, and striking each coin three times, the new MCMVII High Relief double eagles were created, and within the space of a few weeks some 11,250 were struck—a tiny fraction of the number which could have been produced of normal coins on high-speed automatically-fed presses.

Once this many had been made, the President was satisfied, and then the engraving department took the design and changed it to their liking. Gone was the MCMVII, replaced by the date expressed in numerals as 1907. Gone was the sculptured appearance, replaced by shallow relief. The new design, quite flat in appearance in comparison to the old, was produced from late 1907 through 1933.

The door thus opened, other artists participated in coinage designs. Next on the list was Bela Lyon Pratt, a Boston sculptor who had studied under Saint-

Gaudens, and who picked up the traces where Saint-Gaudens had dropped them, creating designs for the $2.50 and the $5 gold issues. Many other artists tried their hand at coinage over the years, including Victor D. Brenner, Laura Gardin Fraser, John Flanagan, Hermon MacNeil, Adolph Weinman, and numerous others. The series of United States commemorative coins in particular is a showcase for the efforts of outside artists, and literally no two designs are alike.

Art is in the eye of the beholder, of course, and often what is beautiful to one will be ugly to another. Take for example the 1878 Morgan silver dollar. When it was introduced, virtually every numismatic publication condemned it as being ugly.[8] Today, the Morgan dollar is the single most popular series in American coinage, and I suspect that the hundreds of thousands of collectors and investors desiring them consider them to be quite beautiful, if not elegant.

Similarly, consider the 1793 Chain large cent, a piece criticized in its time. "Liberty appears to be in a fright," a contemporary newspaper said. Today, virtually any large cent specialist would give the proverbial eyetooth for a high-grade example of this cherished design type. Art is like politics or religion—anyone can have an opinion, and your opinion is apt to be as good as mine, and no one is necessarily right or wrong. Is the Eisenhower dollar attractive? I think not, but you may think it is. On the other hand, many do not like the Susan B. Anthony dollar of 1979-1981, but I find it quite pleasing, somewhat "classic" in its own way.

Then there is the 1984 Olympic commemorative silver dollar with two headless torsos—which earns my vote for the least attractive of all modern American motifs. However, I am sure that there are some readers of these words who think it is beautiful. Perhaps the least attractive coin of all is a pattern three-cent piece made in the 1840s. The obverse (or is it the reverse?) bears simply the numeral 3, and the other side bears simply the designation III. You can't get more simple than that!

Just as it is said that prophets are not heroes in their own countries, new coins are often not acclaimed in their own generation, the Morgan dollar being an outstanding example. And yet, today I believe we have a greater sense of numismatic art than ever before. There has been a great clamor for a change in coinage designs to more artistic motifs. Of course, who determines whether or not such motifs are "artistic" is the question.

Investment
I have discussed grading, slabs, the market, etc. already, so I will not dwell upon it here, except to make a few concluding remarks on the subject.

Maximizing the Rewards

First of all, I am an advocate of coin investment: I have written a number of books on the subject, and I believe that coin investment is a fine thing. However, at the same time I reiterate that the best way—perhaps the only effective way—to invest in coins is to build at the same time a meaningful set or collection. In that way you will acquire scarce coins as well as rare ones over a wide diversity of dates and types, achieving balance in your "portfolio."

Collect first, and investment will follow logically. I am reminded of the 1864-S $5 which the Norweb family bought for $75 in Abe Kosoff's sale of of the Melish Collection 1956. In October 1987 I had the honor of auctioning this coin for $110,000. However, if Ambassador or Mrs. R. Henry Norweb were alive today, and you asked them if they bought the 1864-S as an investment, the answer would be "No." They bought it as part of their collection of half eagles.

In the late 1950s I was called to appraise and make an offer for a collection owned by a widow who lived near Albany, New York. Her home was modest, without any aspect of elegance, and it was clear that her three children, while properly clothed and fed, were not acquainted with the luxuries of life. I was shepherded to a nearby bank vault, where I was shown a collection of coins gathered over a period of years by her late husband. She had no idea what it was worth, but suggested that it might be valued at over $100,000. Whatever the sum was, she needed the money, and she hoped that her husband's hobby would now yield something in the way of tangible results. I don't recall the exact figure the collection sold for—the sum of $120,000 comes to mind—but at the time this was equivalent to a fortune, and the financial success of the family was assured. Had her husband spent an equivalent amount of money—and I imagine that his investment was just a few thousand dollars—in any other field, I doubt if his family would have done as well.

I mentioned earlier that the Harold Bareford Collection, which brought $1.2 million at auction, had cost the owner less than $13,000—another dramatic evidence of a collection being a wonderful investment. Those who knew Harold Bareford knew that he was a collector first and an investor second. He *enjoyed* his coins.

I also mentioned earlier that in 1976 Louis Eliasberg, the Baltimore financier, addressed an audience at Evergreen House at The Johns Hopkins University, and told the gathered group of his interest in coin collecting. He had spent about $300,000 on his collection, he said, and had calculated that this had yielded him a compounded return of about 18% per year. In 1982 I had the honor of selling just the gold portion of his collection and it brought $12.4 million—with untold value in other series still remaining unsold!

I knew Mr. Eliasberg quite well, and I can tell you today that he was a collector. The investment part came as a natural sequence. However, as a collector he did what collectors should do: he desired one of each variety, not two of each, and not a roll of each—one of each. Yes, just one. Even though slabbed certified coins had not been invented, he bought with confidence, made excellent buys, and enjoyed himself thoroughly.

Now in the 1990s the collector who is interested in investment, and who learns about coins before buying, can obtain many truly outstanding values. Recently, Keith Zaner, editor of the "Trends" column in *Coin World*, telephoned to say that he had just finished studying American $5 gold coin prices, and that he had found that many issues were great rarities in relation to their modest catalogue values, and that much of the numismatic community was unaware that such bargains existed.

I am again reminded of a situation I mentioned earlier, that of a French restaurant which priced a rather average quality wine at a high price, and bottles from a select vintage at a lower level. The restaurant owner did a land office business selling bottles of the average wine to *nouveau riche* and other uninformed clients, while the connoisseurs were able to enjoy the finer, rarer wines at reasonable prices. In recent years in numismatics investors have been climbing over themselves in their haste to buy common date Morgan dollars, common late-date Liberty Walking halves, superb gem common modern Proof coins in slabs, etc., leaving rare $5 gold pieces and other delicacies to those who are smart enough to recognize them.

Form a collection, build a basic library, pay attention to what you do, have an eye for quality, don't make any purchase without study, and buy carefully—and chances are good that your rare coin collection will be the best investment you ever make. I have seen it happen many times.

Camaraderie

People are social beings, and it is a rare individual who does not like to share his or her experiences with others. Indeed, one of the nice things about coins is that there are nice "coin people." This brings to mind Joseph J. Mickley, the pioneer collector who started his interest in 1816 when he desired to find a cent of the date of his birth, which, as fate would have it, was 1799—a rare year for large cents! This challenge led to others, and within a few decades he had built one of the finest collections ever. Important to the present discussion, Mickley, whose profession was that of a piano repairer, opened his home in Philadelphia to visitors who would come by and "talk coins" into the wee hours of the night. One can imagine all of the fun times that were had.

Maximizing the Rewards

My late friend Oscar G. Schilke, who collected from the 1930s until his death in the 1960s, was an active member of many coin clubs in the New York, New Jersey, and Connecticut area. In his home he had a library lined with coin books and auction catalogues—and many a restful evening was spent there looking at large cents and comparing them to the Sheldon reference, or checking out die varieties of California gold quarters and half dollars, or reading of the history of national bank notes. Oscar's interests were far ranging, and he had just about everything from "hobo" nickels to Proof gold! However, while Oscar liked coins, he enjoyed people most of all, and the majority of stories he related were of the personalities he knew—Wayte Raymond, Thomas Elder, the Stack brothers, and others with whom he came in contact.

Amon Carter, the Dallas collector, will be remembered by many of my readers. I recall that once when I was a teenager and was at an American Numismatic Association Convention—this must have been in the 1950s—Amon brought over to my table his rare 1804 silver dollar, the prize coin of his collection.[9] He suggested that I put it in my display case, for it would call attention to my exhibit and might bring some business my way.

"But I don't have insurance to cover a coin of this amount," I protested.

"Don't worry about it. If it's lost that's my responsibility," he countered.

Once, while I was visiting Amon's office in Dallas, he received a telephone call from Art McKee, who maintained a museum of buried treasure artifacts in the Florida Keys. The conversation was far ranging, and Amon shooed me off to "explore" his bank vault, adjacent to his office, while he talked on and on. Later he told me that he might indeed invest in an undersea recovery operation proposed by McKee, because he had not done that sort of thing before, and it sounded interesting, and, besides, there would be interesting people to meet.

I have been a guest a number of times at the New York Numismatic Club, and years ago (I imagine that the same is true today) the procedure was that a topic would be selected for the evening—perhaps Hard Times tokens, perhaps silver dollars—and each member would bring to the meeting an example in the category mentioned. There would be a "show and tell" session, and the club members, seated around a long table, would in turn each tell the story about a coin they brought. I don't recall anyone ever telling about how good of an investment a coin was—and many were indeed superb investments. Rather, one heard about background, history, art, and so on—all of the things that make numismatics interesting.

Excitement

The thrill of the chase is an important part of numismatics. It is always nice to desire something. One should always have greater ambitions than one can possibly fulfill, in order to maintain challenges in life. It would not be any fun at all if one could write out a check and in one fell swoop acquire an MS-70 set of large cents from 1793 to 1857. If this were the case, virtually no one would collect them. Dr. Sheldon likened the collecting of large cents to a game of golf. In theory, one can play a round of golf in just 18 strokes, but in practice if it can be done in 75 strokes this is doing very well. So it is with large cents.

In theory, all coins were once MS-70, but today the best grade in which some varieties are known might be just VG-8, F-12, or VF-20, and the acquisition of such an "inferior" coin can be a true joy and delight to the specialist. Time and time again while conducting of auction sales and issuing catalogues I have seen so-called captains of industry become as excited as little kids in the quest for an obscure variety of Liberty Seated quarter, or a scarce Hard Times token, or something else—not necessarily a coin worth thousands or tens of thousands of dollars, but one possessing an element of rarity.

I once had a client travel 2,000 miles to spend $200 for a rare but inexpensive Capped Bust half dollar in one of our sales. Another client has spent three years trying to find an Uncirculated 1945 Mercury dime with a sharply struck reverse. This particular dime is one of the most common in the Mercury series, but a sharply struck piece is another thing entirely. At last word he is still looking. About 20 years ago I featured on the front cover of the *Rare Coin Review* and sold an Uncirculated 1824 half dollar counterstamped with the portraits of Washington and Lafayette. Later, I developed an interest in researching and studying such counterstamps, and since then I have tried to reacquire the coin, so far without success, for its owner likes it as much as I do. Perhaps I never will own it again, but if I do it will satisfy a 20-year search.

The thrill of the chase is an important aspect of coin collecting. When you acquire a long sought after coin to complete a set, it is like filling in the last word in a crossword puzzle. There is a great feeling of satisfaction.

There are always new discoveries to be made in coin collecting. In the past 25 years more numismatic history has reached print and more important varieties have been found than in any previous 25-year period of the hobby. I hope that the next quarter century will see an improvement on the excellent work of the present generation. In my own professional work, scarcely a week goes by without my finding a new tidbit of information—a fact I had not known before or possibly some new appreciation of a coin variety. All of this is a lot of fun and makes professional numismatics, for me, a high cut above any other endeavor I can imagine.

In Conclusion

There are some practical aspects of coin collecting. Investment success often comes to those who collect wisely. In this book I have given what I hope you have found to be valuable guidelines for increasing your success when you buy coins, to get a better value for your money. I wish you the best of success in your numismatic endeavors, not only with your purchases but with your enjoyment of the other aspects of what has been called the world's greatest hobby.

In what other hobby can you have your cake and eat it too? In what other hobby can you enjoy collecting for years, meet many wonderful people, read lots of nice books, and then upon selling find that your investment may have appreciated in value much more than it would have if an equivalent amount had been placed in stocks or in a bank account?

There is also the possibility that you might live longer. No one has ever done a study of longevity of numismatists, but I recall reading in *AB Bookman*, leading periodical of the rare book trade, that booksellers, on balance, far outlived their contemporaries in other professions. The reason was given that books provide a certain comfort and satisfaction with life. Similarly, I read that violinists often live to exceed the national average, because they enjoy what they do and get a feedback from their "hobby"–the violin.

I suspect that dedicated coin collectors also live longer. For sure, the younger generation of numismatists has a better life because of coin collecting. The government spends billions of dollars on welfare and trying to prevent juvenile delinquency. I suggest that government researchers study hobbies. If they do so, they will find that virtually any teenager who has an absorbing interest in a hobby–whether it be coins, computers, chess, or whatever–will be the kind who will not become involved in drugs and crime. What kids need is something interesting, and few things can be more interesting and satisfying than a hobby. At the other end of the age spectrum, the formation of a meaningful collection of large cents, commemorative half dollars, gold coins by types, or some other special collection of interest can be an enjoyable and challenging pursuit for the retiree.

Whether you are 14 years old or 94 years old, coin collecting can contribute to your enjoyment and satisfaction with life.

Coins, it seems, have just about everything to offer–a good investment potential, a possibility for longevity, a possibility for study and enjoyment, the camaraderie of other people, romance and history. In fact, now that I think about it, why doesn't everybody collect coins? Well, I guess it is good that everyone doesn't, for there are simply not enough to go around! But, those of us who do collect coins know that we are on to something quite "special."

Notes

INTRODUCTION

[1] I once devoted my monthly column in *The Numismatist* to the seemingly illogical situation of calling the coin *hobby* an *industry*. To me, the industry term more properly describes a field of manufacturing, not one of buying and selling antique items, collectibles, etc. My opinion was and still is in the minority.

CHAPTER ONE

[1] Writing in the "Trends" section of *Coin World*, April 25, 1990, p. 52, Keith Zaner discussed the romantic aspects of owning certain pieces minted during this era: "Coins struck at the Carson City Mint have always been a popular area for coin collectors. Generally, these coins were struck in limited numbers beginning in 1870 and ending in 1893, while being struck from native silver and gold. Also, these coins remind collectors of the exciting and romantic Wild West."

[2] "Study Still Necessary," *Numismatic News*, May 15, 1990, p. 6.

[3] For example, in the book *The Best of Everything*, Simon and Schuster, 1989.

[4] In *The State Coinages of New England*, by Hillyer C. Ryder and Henry Miller, American Numismatic Society, 1920.

[5] *A Guide Book of U.S. Coins*, produced under the direction of Richard S. Yeoman, was first sold in 1946 (bearing a cover date of 1947). In recent years Kenneth E. Bressett has been editor.

[6] By May 1990 at least nine different individuals or firms had announced their interest in developing computer grading services, Amos Press (working with the Battelle Institute of Columbus, Ohio) and Rick Sundman, of Littleton Coin Company, among them. The PCGS computer-grader was dubbed "The Expert."

[7] Including the unique 1870-S $3 from the Eliasberg Collection.

[8] Letter dated July 28, 1990.

CHAPTER TWO

[1] Richard Lederer, in his book *Crazy English,* pointed out that the term *sight-unseen* is an oxymoron, along with *pretty ugly, inside out, random order, tight slacks, spendthrift,* and *old news,* among others.

[2] Popularized by numismatist Bill Fivaz, the *cherrypick* term is used in numismatics to indicate the process whereby many coins are viewed but only the very best are chosen.

[3] The Pittman Act resulted in the melting of 270,232,722 silver dollars, mostly of the Morgan design. No account was kept of the specific date and mintmark varieties destroyed.

CHAPTER THREE

[1] Of course, accumulators should watch what they accumulate, for it is important to be in step with the market. Yesterday's darlings can be today's ugly ducklings. The *Bruce Amspacher Investment Report,* July 1990, noted: "Watch market trends. Every decade has its own special areas of interest, be it coins by the pound (in the 1960s), rarity with or without condition (the 1970s), condition with or without rarity (the 1980s), or whatever it turns out to be in the 1990s."

[2] The statement that the collector is the ultimate consumer of a coin has been reiterated many times by observers of the numismatic scene, particularly those who have been involved in the field for a long time. Examples include remarks given in an address to the ANA Board of Governors by veteran dealer (and president of the Professional Numismatists Guild) Harvey Stack in August 1989 at the annual ANA convention; Keith Zaner in the "Trends" section of *Coin World,* July 25, 1990, p. 48; and an article, "Is the Collector Still King?" by Julian Leidman and Mark Mendelson, in "The Monthly Summary," *The Coin Dealer Newsletter,* July 1990, portions of which are quoted in the present work.

[3] May 9, 1990, p. 4.

[4] A reference to the coin market in the 1860s, when tokens and medals portraying George Washington were among the most popular series in numismatics, an interest spurred by the Mint Cabinet collection which featured Washington pieces in its public display.

[5] This is an interesting point. There are numerous instances in which

hobbies have faded due to what seem to have been excesses of promotion. Examples include modern collectors' limited-edition plates, figural Jim Beam whiskey bottles, and modern medals.

[6] July 1990. Quoted with permission of the publisher.

[7] QDB note: The concept of building a trusting relationship with a dealer is foreign to many coin buyers, who prefer to take an adversary stance. Building a good rapport with one or more dealers is essential, as I discuss later in the present text.

[8] QDB note: In the 1930s at a Rotary meeting in Fort Worth, Texas, dealer B. Max Mehl gave fellow Rotarian Amon G. Carter an 1879 $2.50 gold piece as a memento of Carter's birth date. His interest piqued, Carter went on to acquire a fabulous cabinet of rarities and, along the way, became Mehl's best customer!

[9] The PNG is America's leading professional group. Presumably had the survey been taken among dealers in general, rather than at a meeting of members of this highly-respected guild, the show of hands would have been even fewer.

[10] "Old Money & Loose Change," by Mike Steere, August 12, 1990. *Dallas Life Magazine* is published by *The Dallas Morning News*.

[11] I am reminded of a dealer who stated that he had sold his clients tens of millions of dollars' worth of coins in recent years, and that a typical profit in a client's portfolio was 22% to 24% per year. His guaranteed buy-back program seemingly promised the moon with gold trimmings. It sounded good, but there was a slight problem: in 1990 he told his clients that he was no longer buying coins under this program. He discontinued his high bid prices, and, apparently, terrific losses were sustained. One of my clients, an industrialist who should have known better, told me that he had invested $12,000 (lucky for him; it could have been more) in the scheme and figured that he had lost $8,000.

CHAPTER FOUR

[1] Professional numismatists Robert Medlar, Julian Leidman, and Harvey Stack also assisted the Federal Trade Commission in this case.

[2] *The Investor's Guide to Coin Trading*, pp. 36-37.

[3] *The Investor's Guide to Coin Trading*, p. 35.

[4] *The Investor's Guide to Coin Trading*, pp. 16-17.

[5] Volume VII, No. 2, Summer 1990. Used with permission of the author.

[6] July 11, 1990, p. 5.

[7] While the BBB can provide valuable information in some instances, in some situations it may not be aware of problems. As an example, the New England Rare Coin Co. of Boston, which was closed down in the 1980s following an action by the FTC, was reported on favorably by the BBB until nearly the time of its closing.

[8] For example, no one in the rare coin industry did anything to protect the interests of consumers in what was later alleged to be a pyramid scheme involving Hans Tulving, and investors were said to have sustained losses of millions of dollars. His advertisements continued to be accepted by various publications, including in *The Numismatist*, official journal of the American Numismatic Association, until near the very end.

[9] The "Trends" feature in *Coin World* was originated by James Kelly in the early 1960s. Later, it was conducted by Raymond N. Merena and others.

[10] *A Guide Book of U.S. Coins*, 1991 edition, page 6. Western Publishing Co., Racine, Wisconsin.

CHAPTER FIVE

[1] *Coin World*, July 18, 1990, p. 91.

[2] "Gem" refers to coins at the MS-65 level, "Choice" to coins at the MS-63 level, per the official ANA grading standards.

[3] In *Consumer Alert: Investing in Rare Coins*.

[4] QDB comment: Certain legitimate dealers who sell common coins have used the Salomon Brothers index to help sell such pieces.

[5] July 3, 1990, p. 4.

[6] The index is composed entirely of coins which in Mint State are scarce to rare. The following are among the key issues in their respective series (listed in order as given above): 1873 With Arrows 25c (a key type coin), 1884-S $1 (very rare in higher Mint State grades), 1916 Standing Liberty 25c (the key date in the 1916-1930 series), 1873 2c (rarest date of the denomination), 1866 10c (low mintage issue, as noted), 1886 25c (lowest mintage issue of its era), 1815 50c (extremely rare in Mint State; the rarest date of the 1807-1836 Capped Bust type), 1921 50c (a key date in the 1916-1947 series), 1881 trade dollar (rare Proof-only issue, as noted), 1928 Hawaiian 50c (rarest commemorative 50c type).

[7] January 24, 1990, p. 5.

[8] Adapted from the inscription found on the reverse of 1951-1954 Washington-Carver commemorative half dollars.

[9] January 3, 1990, p. 52.

[10] In 1990 David Hall was named Orange County (California) "Entrepreneur of the Year." An article in *Numismatic News*, July 31, 1990, p. 4, quoted this comment in connection with the honor: "'Few entrepreneurs have a chance to revolutionize an industry, but David Hall has done that to coin dealing by developing a consistent system to rate the condition of collectible coins,' said Jan Norman of the *Orange County Register* newpaper."

[11] This statement is at odds with a survey conducted by *Numismatic News* in 1990, which revealed that the vast majority of collectors, at least as reflected by the readership of that publication, were primarily interested in collecting, with just a small percentage primarily interested in investing.

[12] This echoes the sentiment of Wayte Raymond, who in 1912 advertised as follows: "We feel, however, that the average American collector, while he greatly enjoys his coins, also feels very pleased if on disposing of his collection he realizes a profit." (Quoted in my book, *Coins and Collectors*, page 212.)

[13] August 17, 1990, page C1, continued on page C12. Article by William Power and Michael Sindolfi.

[14] QDB note: No prior FTC approval is needed (per correspondence to the author, QDB, from Phoebe Morse of the FTC, September 26, 1990).

[15] Does this imply that the Numismatic Guaranty Corporation, chief competitor of PCGS, runs a "dirty ship"? The *Wall Street Journal* article noted that "the action against [PCGS] could be a boost for its chief rival, Numismatic Guaranty Corporation of America."

[16] August 16, 1990; article by staff writer Gregory Crouch, "FTC Accuses Big Coin Dealer, Appraiser." The article treated two unrelated situations: the charge by the FTC that a "Newport Beach based Hannes Tulving Rare Coin Investment [was] running a Ponzi scheme that defrauded investors out of more than $40 million" (a claim denied by Tulving, who was quoted in the same article as saying, "We charged a fair value for our product and we have the documentation to prove it."); and the FTC case against PCGS.

[17] August 24, 1990, Seattle, Washington. The forum featured Barry J. Cutler (representing the FTC), Luis Vigdor (representing the Industry Council for Tangible Assets), Phoebe Morse (FTC), and Harvey G. Stack (rare coin dealer). Mr. Cutler's remarks are taken from a printed transcript distributed at the forum, titled "Remarks of Barry J. Cutler."

[18] [Director of Education for the ANA.]

[19] The views expressed in this presentation, and in answers to questions to follow, are my own and do not necessarily reflect the view of the Federal Trade Commission or any individual commissioner.

[20] Although the Federal Trade Commission Act requires that the Commissioners have 'reason to believe' that the allegations of a complaint are true and correct and supported by evidence, the PCGS consent agreement, like other settlements, does not involve adjudication of any issue by the court, or any admission of liability by the defendant for the offenses alleged in the complaint.

[21] [QDB note: There is disagreement on this point within the hobby-industry. The Professional Numismatists Guild, for one, has pointed out that its self-regulation practices among its own dealer membership have been very satisfactory and in fact have been more effective than government regulation would have been. See following commentary by Harvey G. Stack.]

[22] Transcript from "Opening Comments for ANA Forum," furnished to the author by Harvey G. Stack.

[23] GSA Form T-588-B, May 1972. Copy furnished to the author by Harvey G. Stack.

[24] U.S. Treasury/Mint news release, September 19, 1990, "American Eagle Bullion Coin Sales Soar in August," page 1.

[25] In a letter to the author dated September 12, 1990.

[26] July 10, 1990.

[27] In January 1990.

[28] This is not intended as an endorsement of this or any other fund but is included as a personal experience in the field. Before investing in any fund, perform the investigations I have suggested and, of course, read the prospectus.

[29] Letter dated August 28, 1990. Asset values month by month were: March 1989 $995.00, April 1989 $1,048.56, May 1989 $1,112.01, June 1989 $1,041.48, July 1989 $1,050.80, August 1989 $1,068.11, September 1989 $1,042.83, October 1989 $1,082.44, November 1989 $1,073.29, December 1989 $$1,070.01, January 1990 $1,095.63, February 1990 $1,195.87, March 1990 $1,138.05, April 1990 $1,149.22, May 1990 $1,136.71, June 1990 $1,161.70, July 1990 $1,168.15.

CHAPTER SIX

[1] Except for certain coins which may have reserve or starting prices which are not met.

[2] November 1985, Lot 504.

[3] There may be other considerations which influence an opening bid, such as a consignor's reserve, or, an instance in which there are few if any mail bids on a given lot, an auctioneer's starting bid. However, for the vast majority of lots the opening bid is set by the top two highest mail bids.

[4] Gerald Bauman and MTB made the news in July 1990 (front page of *Coin World*, July 25, 1990, for example) when it was announced that the firm had sold an MCMVII Extremely High Relief pattern Proof $20 gold coin, one of fewer than two dozen known to exist, for an undisclosed price estimated to be in the $1.5 to $2 million range.

[5] Of The Johns Hopkins University. The Tripps were also of great assistance with the research I did concerning the Garrett family of collectors, leading to the publication of the book, *The History of U.S. Coinage as Illustrated by the Garrett Collection*.

[6] Mehl, born in Lithuania in 1884, came to the United States in 1893, entered the trade of a shoe clerk, and became a rare coin dealer in 1903. From then until his death in 1957 he conducted dozens of mail bid sales in addition to selling coins through catalogues and want lists.

[7] As an example, when the American Numismatic Association offered a mail bid listing of items to its membership in the Spring 1990 (Vol. 4, No. 2, p. 6) issue of *The ANA Communique*, May 1990, it offered the pieces with terms which included this statement: "All sales are final. Lots are sold 'as is.' "

CHAPTER SEVEN

[1] For some dates in certain series, $3 gold pieces provide an example, a three-digit logotype, such as 187, was used, and the final digit was punched in by hand.

[2] The Massachusetts mint was hastily closed after an audit revealed that it cost the state government two cents to make each one-cent piece!

[3] Contenders for the "first official coins" honor are the 1776-dated Continental Currency issues, usually seen in pewter, but no official documentation linking these with the federal government has ever been found (the

designs are similar to those used on official paper money of the era, however).

CHAPTER EIGHT
---

[1] The Pearlman study will appear in a book, *Best Rare Coin Buys.*

[2] As these words are being written in the summer of 1990, the 1881-S at $190 is selling for about half of its level a year earlier. While the 1881-S in MS-65 continues to be popular, it is not as much in demand as it was a year ago.

[3] Happily for the descendants of those individuals who obtained trade dollars for face value in 1873, but who could not get face value for them later, even a worn trade dollar is apt to be worth $50 to $100 on the numismatic market today, and a superb MS-65 coin would bring a price of several thousand dollars or more! Time makes all things better.

CHAPTER NINE
---

[1] Dr. Sheldon intended the system to apply only to large cents. He proposed that different varieties would be assigned basal values, such as $1, $5, etc., depending upon how rare they were. To determine market value, the basal value, such as $5, was multiplied by the grade, such as VF-30, and the result would be a coin worth $150. The system worked more or less well from about 1949 to 1953, after which it fell apart. Many of the intermediate numbers used today were not used by Dr. Sheldon. VF-25, VF-35, EF-45, AU-53, AU-55, AU-58, MS-61, MS-62, MS-63, MS-64, MS-66, MS-67, MS-68, and MS-69 were not in the Sheldon book.

[2] Letter dated February 11, 1990.

[3] July 31, 1990, "Slab Marketing Lessons," p. 8.

[4] Analyzed in the issue of March 20, 1990 in a long article. See especially p. 54.

[5] Letters to the editor page, issue of June 27, 1990.

[6] *Numismatic News*, February 27, 1990, p. 22.

[7] February 28, 1990, p. 4.

[8] March 28, 1990, p. 4.

[9] In the 1976 I worked with David Hall, Joseph Battaglia, Joel Rettew, and others in the formation of a consortium to bid on the LeVere Redfield silver

dollar hoard. We were the underbidders, it turned out, to A-Mark Coin Company, which secured the treasure trove for $7.3 million in a Nevada courtroom on January 27th of that year.

[10] The American Numismatic Association sold the coin grading service of ANACS to Amos Press (publishers of *Coin World*) in 1990, and the grading facilities were relocated from Colorado Springs to Columbus, Ohio; the statement was given that no mention of the earlier connection with the American Numismatic Association would be given in the name of the service after six months following the transition period. In autumn 1990 Amos Press was conducting the service under the acronym ANACS, without specific further reference to the ANA. In the meantime, the authentication (not grading) business of the ANA was conducted by the ANA in Colorado Springs under the name American Numismatic Association Authentication Bureau (ANAAB), per a display at the August 1990 ANA convention in Seattle. The International Numismatic Service does not encapsulate coins and is best known for its expertise in numismatic authentication. As of autumn 1990, NCI slabbed coins trade from a sharp discount from PCGS price levels. At one time NCI was the subject of an FTC suit (per correspondence from Phoebe Morse of the FTC, the author, September 26, 1990). The present writer is a stockholder in the Hallmark Grading Service but has never participated in the grading of any coins submitted to that service.

[11] Hallmark is an exception; coins of special merit are designated PQ, for Premium Quality.

[12] February 2, 1990

[13] January 5, 1990.

[14] January 19, 1990.

[15] February 2, 1990. Italic emphasis ours.

[16] February 9, 1990. Emphases are those of the newsletter publisher.

[17] This word inserted by the present writer.

[18] April 6, 1990. This paragraph should be worth its weight in gold to any uninformed investor who believes that coins should be purchased sight-unseen.

[19] June 8, 1990.

[20] Published by the Ivy Press, Inc., Dallas, 1990, p. 3. Used with permission. With Steve Ivy, James L. Halperin is a principal of Heritage Rare Coin Galleries.

[21] The present writer (Q. David Bowers) questions whether PCGS and

NGC both employ precisely the same standards, as, for example, the June 29, 1990 issue of the *Certified Coin Dealer Newsletter* indicated that at the time, in the majority of instances, PCGS-certified coins traded above NGC levels, and in many instances the differences involved significant amounts. For example, an 1896-O $1 in MS-65 grade was bid at $46,000 PCGS and $36,500 NGC. I suppose it could be argued that if both do employ the same standards, the differences are due to the PCGS product being more popular than NGC.

[22] Page 10. Parenthetical note by the present writer, Q. David Bowers.

[23] Upon reading this commentary Chris Karstedt of the Bowers and Merena staff made the following suggestion, which seems to have merit: If you do not have time to learn broad-based grading techniques, learn just the grading standards and techniques for those specific coins which you are interested in acquiring. Learning to grade Morgan dollars, for example, is easier than learning to grade everything in the American series from half cents to double eagles. Such knowledge, even if limited in scope, will definitely give you an edge.

[24] Premium Quality (PQ) refers to a coin which is a particularly outstanding example of its grade level, particularly if the coin is MS-65 (or Proof-65) or finer. The Hallmark Grading Service, Lee J. Bellisario, president, is the only certification service as of this writing to note PQ on slabs of applicable coins.

[25] Page 12. Italics added for emphasis by the present writer, Q. David Bowers.

[26] Page 157. Italics added for emphasis by the present writer, Q. David Bowers.

[27] As of the summer of 1990 the two leading electronic quotation systems for sight-unseen trading in slabbed coins are the American Numismatic Exchange (ANE) and the American Teleprocessing Corporation (ATC), the former specializing in PCGS coins and the latter in NGC slabs.

[28] August 29, 1990, p. 4.

[29] Peter A. Barone to Q. David Bowers, July 5, 1990.

[30] April 4, 1990, p. 5.

[31] May 16, 1990, p. 5.

[32] June 13, 1990, p. 5.

[33] February 21, 1990, p. 4.

[34] March 7, 1990, p. 5.

[35] August 1990 issue. Donn Pearlman, a well-known radio broadcaster for CBS, is also the author of several books and the aforementioned monthly column in *The Numismatist*.

CHAPTER TEN

[1] The *Coin Dealer Newsletter* issue of July 6, 1990 and the *Certified Coin Dealer Newsletter* issue of June 29, 1990. "Ask" prices in both publications were used, for the first covers lower grade coins as well as coins graded up to MS-65 (and Proof-65), whereas the second emphasizes Mint State and Proof coins and has grades higher than 65. The second covers slabbed coins only.

[2] Note that the raw coin price for MS-63 and MS-64 is higher than the PCGS price (see following paragraph). This is explained in two ways: 1. Prices are not always consistent. 2. Raw coins sometimes sell for more, for these are often bids for sight-seen coins which can be accepted or rejected, whereas slabbed coin prices are sight-unseen bids. Note the same situation, for example, under the 1923-S Monroe half dollar prices.

[3] Here is a point to ponder: At the same time the bid prices for PCGS 1923-S Monroe halves were $20,000 MS-66 and $30,000 MS-67. Little ever appears in print about such wide variations among the prices listed for leading grading services.

[4] Sometimes a given rarity will appear to be more common than it actually is, because of the frequency of its auction appearances. The writer recalls a specimen of a particularly rare Liberty Seated quarter dollar of the Carson City Mint which appeared in several auction sales within the space of a few years, and an 1876-CC twenty-cent piece also made the rounds of at least four sales.

[5] I have known Ron Downing, publisher of the *Certified Coin Dealer Newsletter* and the *Coin Dealer Newsletter*, for many years, and if there is anyone in the rare coin field with greater integrity, I have yet to meet that other person.

[6] *Coin World*, April 11, 1990, p. 44.

[7] July 12, 1990.

[8] Issue dates used: *Certified Coin Dealer Newsletter* July 6, 1990, *Coin Dealer Newsletter* July 6, 1990 and June 1990 *Monthly Summary*, *Coin World* July 4 and 11, 1990, *A Guide Book of U.S. Coins*, 1991 edition released in July 1990, *Numismatic News* July 3, 1990.

[9] Grading standards used by NCI are acknowledged to be more liberal

than those employed by ANA, NGC, or ANA, hence the lower price levels.

[10] Not generally known is the fact that each time the administration of the Treasury Department changed, the hundreds of millions of silver dollars in government storage had to be counted. This was done by means of a machine which grabbed each coin with a toothed metal cogwheel and fed it through a device which could count 2,000 coins per minute. Imagine the marks each coin sustained by this process.

[11] Prooflike is the term used by the Royal Canadian Mint for its specially prepared pieces, similar to United States Proofs.

[12] March 27, 1990.

[13] Cleaning coins can be harmful to the cleaner, as vividly demonstrated by the sudden end to the life of J. Sanford Saltus, who in the earlier part of this century was a leading member of the American Numismatic Society. One evening in his home he was using a solution of potassium cyanide to clean coins and at the same time was sipping from a glass of ginger ale. In a moment of inadvertence he mistook one container for another, drank some of the coin cleaner, and died moments later.

[14] February 20, 1990, p. 4.

[15] Bruce Amspacher, a founder of PCGS, has produced much excellent information over the years in his *Bruce Amspacher Investment Report*, the publication of which, unfortunately, was discontinued in 1990.

[16] In *How to Grade U.S. Coins*, Ivy Press, Inc., Dallas, 1990, p. 45. Used with permission. I probably shouldn't have mentioned this isolated example of dipping success, for it is not my intention to encourage such. However, the coin was "hideous," and the procedure seems to have been justified.

[17] "Numismatics" column, July 29, 1990.

CHAPTER ELEVEN

[1] Changes in preferences do indeed occur in the marketplace, and in 1974 when I wrote the first edition of my *High Profits From Rare Coin Investments* book I recommended MS-65 coins in many series, for they cost relatively little more than lower Mint State grades. In *Common Sense Coin Investment*, written shortly thereafter for the Whitman Coin Products division of Western Publishing Company, I stated the same philosophy. The extreme differential between, for example, MS-64 and MS-65, began to be seen in the late 1970s and dominated the market in the 1980s.

[2] January 2, 1990, p. 6.

[3] Al Doyle is a *Numismatic News* staff writer, and in the December 12, 1989 issue wrote an article about coin prices and grades.

[4] July 25, 1990, p. 48.

[5] [Usually taken to mean MS-65 and other high grade examples of common coins, an MS-65 1881-S dollar being a typical example.]

[6] As mentioned earlier in the present text, the sale of this coin was memorable in that the consignor, a prominent Cleveland attorney, had paid $200 for the coin and had consigned it, unattributed, as an ordinary 1800 cent!

CHAPTER TWELVE

[1] Mark Borckardt advised the author that he is currently (September 1990) aware of 311 varieties, including 265 numbered varieties plus 1793 Non-Collectible 1 through 6; 1794 NC 1-3, 5, 6, 8, and 9 (NC 4 is a subvariety of S-17 and NC 7 has been disproven); 1795 NC 1, 2; 1796 NC 1-6; 1797 NC 1-8; 1798 NC 1, 2; 1799 NC 1; 1800 NC 1-6; 1801 NC 1-5 1802 NC 1, 2; and 1803 NC 1, for a total of 311.

CHAPTER THIRTEEN

[1] Harold P. Newlin's *The Early Half-Dimes of the United States*, published in 1883, was the first serious study of the denomination. In 1931 it was superseded by Daniel W. Valentine's *The United States Half Dimes*, published by the American Numismatic Society.

[2] The 1792 silver center cent pattern, larger in diameter than the silver half disme, permitted a slight expansion of the same legend, to LIBERTY PARENT OF SCIENCE & INDUST. The large-diameter 1792 Birch cent pattern displayed it in full: LIBERTY PARENT OF SCIENCE & INDUSTRY.

[3] In the late 1960s when James F. Ruddy was gathering photographs for his *Photograde* grading guide he found half dimes of this design to be the most difficult of all silver coin types to locate. Although half dollars of 1796-1797 are far rarer, for some reason photographs were easier to find.

[4] Named for John Reich, the mint engraver who is believed to have created

the Capped Bust coinage. Die varieties described in the book were assigned "John Reich numbers," such as JR-1, a departure from the usual procedure of using the author's initial, as S-1 for the first variety in Dr. William H. Sheldon's *Penny Whimsy* book on large cents. Presumably, as there were five authors to the book, the use of the JR initials was deemed more expedient.

⁵ One day MacIntosh telephoned me to say that he wanted to sell his entire coin inventory, "worth at least a million dollars," for $200,000, if he could be paid immediately. I was skeptical that a leading dealer would make such an offer, and I declined to visit Springfield and check it out. A week or so later, MacIntosh committed suicide, despondent over a real estate deal that had turned sour. His coins were eventually sold by the New Netherlands Coin Co., among others, and did indeed bring over a million dollars.

⁶ In 1863, in the depths of the Civil War, the U.S. Mint would not accept checks or, for that matter, United States paper money at par for Proof coins! In order to buy Proofs, collectors had to remit like for like, and pay in coins. However, due to the uncertainty of the outcome of the conflict, coins were hoarded and could be purchased only at a premium in terms of paper money. Because of this complication in ordering, Proof mintages of the 1863-1865 years were low. The high mintage of 1880 is explained by the fact that beginning in 1879 there was a popular speculation in low-mintage rare coins, primarily gold dollars and $3 pieces, but also in Liberty Seated dimes. As these issues had low business strike mintages, the public and collectors, too, rushed to order Proofs. The Mint was happy to oblige by coining additional pieces.

⁷ March 28, 1990.

⁸ Years ago a hoard of at least eight superb Uncirculated 1876-CC 20-cent pieces came to light in Baltimore, Maryland and was marketed by dealer Tom Warfield, who sold four pieces to John Jay Ford, Jr. of the New Netherlands Coin Company and another four to the present writer. The price was about $2,000 each.

⁹ Green, son of eccentric millionaire Hetty Green (who was known as "the Witch of Wall Street"; her life was chronicled in the book, *The Day They Shook the Plum Tree*), was a hoarder of coins and stamps and accumulated vast quantities of certain issues. At one time he owned all of the five known 1913 Liberty Head nickels (in this connection, a brief biographical sketch of the colonel appears in the present writer's book, *Adventures With Rare Coins*).

¹⁰ The 1828 12-stars half cents and 1832 12-stars $5 pieces were the result of diemaking errors.

¹¹ Issue of March 20, 1990, p. 54.

[12] Proof restrikes were made of 1851 and 1852 dollars. The 1851 restrikes are distinguished by having the date centered between the base of Liberty and the border, unlike the high date on the originals.

[13] Years later, under legislation of August 3, 1964, some 316,076 Peace silver dollars of the 1921-1935 design, bearing the 1964 date, were struck at the Denver Mint. At the time the price of silver was rising rapidly on world markets, and it was determined that the coins, if released, would be seized by speculators. Shortly thereafter, the Denver Mint melted the pieces.

CHAPTER FOURTEEN

[1] T. Harrison Garrett, the Baltimore collector, took a fancy to gold dollars of the dates 1879, 1880, and 1881, and hoarded two thousand or more at the time of issue. Many of these were dispersed in numismatic channels in the 1960s.

[2] In one week early in 1990 I was offered from various sources the three key varieties in the $2.50 series: 1841, 1854-S, and 1863, a very unusual situation, as each of these is a major rarity! Not long after that, a Proof-65 (PCGS) 1877, one of just 20 struck, was consigned to our Robert W. Rusbar Collection auction sale. Around the same time, Heritage offered for sale the Proof 1834 old-style quarter eagle sold a decade earlier in our Garrett Collection offering. Anyone aspiring to put together a complete set of $2.50 pieces could have had a head start at this time in the market.

[3] Genuine 1854-D $3 pieces have an area of the edge reeding which is nearly smooth, as made (due to indistinctly impressed reeding in the original collar). Unaware of this, a few years ago a client of a major coin firm examined an 1854-D which he had purchased a few years earlier, and came to the conclusion that he had been sold a damaged piece. Seeking redress, he threatened legal action, and the matter went to arbitration. At the last minute someone thought to consult David Akers' book on $3 pieces, where it was plainly stated that all genuine 1854-D pieces have this feature.

[4] David Akers' books cover the various gold series from $1 to $20 and use auction data from the 1940s through the 1970s, before Mint State coins were divided into numerical categories. Nevertheless, the books are exceedingly valuable for their indications of what exists within the general Mint State level. These books are out of print but may be borrowed from the ANA Library.

[5] One holdout was a Mr. Barnard, who determined to retain his 1933. In a lawsuit with the government he lost. (Per correspondence from David L. Ganz to the author, July 23, 1990.)

CHAPTER FIFTEEN

[1] Beginning with the 1952 ANA convention sale, Ford, who was affiliated with the New Netherlands Coin Company, produced auction catalogues with detailed, authoritative descriptions, in sharp contrast to the bare-bones listings used by other firms at the time.

[2] July 12, 1990.

CHAPTER SIXTEEN

[1] The ANA Library, located at ANA Headquarters in Colorado Springs, is under the capable direction of Nancy Green, and offers members the opportunity to borrow free of charge (except for round trip postage) nearly all standard reference books.

CHAPTER SEVENTEEN

[1] This chapter is an adaptation of a speech I gave at the Smithsonian Institution in 1988. A slightly different version of "Maximizing the Rewards" appeared in our *Rare Coin Review* No. 73.

[2] In *The Star Rare Coin Encyclopedia*, 1944 edition, inside back cover.

[3] Especially Byzantine coinage.

[4] In correspondence with the author, July 23, 1990, David L. Ganz stated that he had calculated that the value of $24 had increased during the 1624-1989 year span to $74,115,785,543.61.

[5] In the 11th edition of Robert Friedberg's *The Paper Money of the United States* there are four Clark-portrait notes listed, Friedberg Nos. 1236 through 1239. In Uncirculated preservation the notes list from $70 to $150.

[6] Lurid details may be found in *History of the United States Secret Service*, by General Lafayette C. Baker, Philadelphia, 1867, pp. 293-307 (and elsewhere in the same volume). Spencer Morton Clark served as director from August 22, 1862 until November 17, 1868. The official view of the Treasury

Department, as reflected in *History of the Bureau of Engraving and Printing* (Treasury Department, Washington, D.C., 1962, esp. pp. 16-17), was (and perhaps still is) that Clark was a great man, a capable administrator, etc., etc.

[7] This monument stands today. For years it was covered with green copper patination plus the inevitable traces of pigeons. In 1990 Victory was gilded.

[8] See contemporary issues of the *American Journal of Numismatics*, for example. Also see my earlier comment under Morgan silver dollars in the present text.

[9] He also had an 1822 half eagle, an even rarer coin, but was not as attached to it. In the 1960s he sold it privately for $60,000, and it went into the collection of Josiah K. Lilly. The coin is now in the Smithsonian Institution.

Glossary

About Good. Grading term, abbreviated as AG-3, describing a well-worn coin better than Fair but less than Good. Capitalized.

About Uncirculated. Grading term, abbreviated as AU-50, AU-53, AU-55, or AU-58, describing a coin which is very close to Uncirculated or Mint State but which exhibits slight wear or friction. Most of the original mint lustre is present. Capitalized.

abrasions. Scuff marks or light rubbing seen on a coin, from contact with other coins or hard surfaces.

aesthetic appeal. Describes a coin which is very pleasing in appearance to the knowledgeable viewer.

adjectival grading; adjectival grading system. The traditional system employed until superseded by the popularity of the *numerical grading system.* Coins in grades from the most worn (Poor) were described adjectivally through the highest grade, Uncirculated, in these steps: Poor, Fair, Good, Very Good, Fine, Very Fine, Extremely Fine, About Uncirculated, and Uncirculated. Modifiers such as choice and gem are sometimes used to indicate an especially nice specimen within a grade level, such as Choice Extremely Fine or Gem Uncirculated.

adjustment marks. Recessed parallel lines on the fields, lettering, and motifs of early coins, especially silver and gold coins circa 1794-1836, resulting from excess metal being filed from overweight planchets prior to striking.

aesthetic appeal. Term descriptive of the artistic or visual desirability of a coin, in addition to its numerical or technical grade.

akcidefect marks. Archaic and incorrect term used by M.L. Beistle in 1928 to describe *clash marks,* to which refer.

alloy. A metal composed of two or more other metals. Example: copper-nickel alloy used to coin 1856-1858 Flying eagle cents is composed of .88 copper and .12 nickel (88 parts copper, 12 parts nickel).

Almost Uncirculated. See *About Uncirculated,* a grading term.

alteration; altered date. Describes a coin which has been altered after striking to appear to be another variety of coin, typically one more valuable. Examples: 1798 large cent altered to "1799" by removing metal from the last digit of the date; 1916 Philadelphia Mint Mercury dime altered to "1916-D" by soldering or otherwise affixing a mintmark to the reverse.

American eagle. Gold and silver bullion coins, which are available in one-ounce and fractional sizes, first minted by the government in 1986 and sold for investment purposes.

American Numismatic Association (ANA). Non-profit organization of coin collectors founded in 1891 and chartered by Congress in 1912, to promote the educational and other advantages of coin collecting. Publishers of the monthly magazine, *The Numismatist.* Membership information: ANA, 818 North Cascade Avenue, Colorado Springs, CO 80901.

American Numismatic Association Authentication Bureau (ANAAB). Authentication service performed by the American Numismatic Association. New name given to the service in August 1990, following the sale of the grading part of the American Numismatic Association Certification Service to Amos Press (see following listing). Address: ANAAB, 818 North Cascade Avenue, Colorado Springs, CO 80901.

American Numismatic Association Certification Service (ANACS). Authentication service founded in the 1970s through the efforts of Abe Kosoff, John Jay Pittman, Virgil Hancock and others. At first ANACS performed only authentications for a fee. Later, it graded coins and issued accompanying certificates. In 1989 a sonically sealed slab, the ANA Cache, was introduced. Ownership of the *grading service* part of ANACS was transferred on August 1, 1990 to the Amos Press, with facilities in Columbus, Ohio. The statement was made that after a transition period of six months the American Numismatic Association affiliation with ANACS would no longer be mentioned by Amos Press.

American Numismatic Exchange (ANE). Electronic trading network with bid and ask prices for certain coins, especially slabbed pieces. Abbreviated as ANE (pronounced "Annie").

American Numismatic Society. Established in 1858, the ANS maintains a museum, library, and research facility at 155th Street and Broadway, New York City. The organization is devoted to furthering numismatic research and numbers over 2,000 members.

American Teleprocessing Corporation (ATC). A leading electronic coin trading network for slabbed coins.

arrows at date. Arrowheads placed to each side of the date of certain silver 5c, 10c, 25c, and 50c 1853-1855 to indicate a reduction in authorized weight, and on certain 10c, 25c, and 50c 1873-1874 to indicate an increase in authorized weight. Arrowheads used as decorations on certain Connecticut copper coins circa 1787.

artificial toning. Tarnish, coloration, or oxidation effects applied quickly to a coin's surface by means of heat, chemicals, or other treatment, in an effort to simulate attractive natural toning and to increase a coin's value.

ask; ask price. A selling price posted by a dealer on the Teletype or other trading network. Such prices are compiled by *The Coin Dealer Newsletter*, *The Certified Coin Dealer Newsletter*, and others.

auction. A method of buying and selling coins by which multiple bidders compete to acquire coins described in a catalogue, with the highest bidder being the winner. Auctions can be by in-person bidding or bidding by telephone or mail. Also see *mail bid sale.*

bagmark. (Usually written as one word.) A nick or indentation on a coin caused by contact with another coin in a mint bag. The larger and heavier a coin is, the more prone it is to acquiring bagmarks.

Barber coinage. Dimes 1892-1916, quarter dollars 1892-1916, and half dollars 1892-1915 bearing the Liberty Head motif created by Charles E. Barber.

Basal Value. Grading term devised by Dr. William H. Sheldon in 1949, sometimes designated as Poor or Poor-1. Term representing the lowest division on the grading scale. Capitalized.

bicentennial coinage. 25c, 50c, and $1 pieces produced with the date 1776-1976, and employing special designs, to commemorate the nation's bicentennial of independence.

bid; bid price. An offering price posted by a dealer on the American Numismatic Exchange or other trading network. Such prices are compiled by *The Coin Dealer Newsletter*, *The Certified Coin Dealer Newsletter*, and others.

Birch cent. Any one of several pattern one-cent pieces dated 1792 and engraved by Birch.

Bland dollar. Archaic term, primarily used c.1878-1930, for the silver dollar design created by George T. Morgan, and coined under the provisions of the 1878 Bland-Allison Act. Dollars of this style were produced 1878-1921. Also see *dollar, silver, Morgan.*

Blue Sheet. Nickname for *The Certified Coin Dealer Newsletter*, a weekly newsletter giving bid and ask prices for sonically-sealed coins.

Booby Head. Cent variety of the year 1839. This term, in use since the 1860s, is of unknown origin.

brilliant. Bright, without toning. Adjective used in connection with grading.

Brilliant Proof. A Proof coin with mirrorlike surfaces. Also, a Proof coin which is bright or brilliant, rather than toned.

brockage. A mint error coin caused by the failure to eject a struck coin from the dies, after which a blank planchet is inserted into the dies, receiving on one side the correct image of a die and on the other side an incuse impression made from the already-struck coin in the dies. The result is a coin which has one side in relief and the other side with an incuse mirror image of the same die. A brockage can be of a reverse or an obverse. Obverse brockages are more frequently seen.

bronze. An alloy composed of copper, zinc, and tin.

brushing. A series of minute parallel lines caused by rubbing a light abrasive across the surface of a coin.

Buffalo nickel. Popular name for the Indian Head five-cent piece of the type of 1913-1938, designed by James Earle Fraser.

bullion coin. A coin, such as an American eagle gold coin (produced 1986 to date), made for investors and valued at its bullion or melt-down value, plus or minus a handling fee.

business strike. A coin produced for use in everyday circulation in the channels of commerce (as opposed to Proofs made especially for collectors). The grade of a freshly-minted business strike is referred to as Uncirculated or Mint State. The term *business strike* was first popularized by John Jay Ford, Jr. and Walter Breen in the 1950s and has since come into popular use.

California fractional gold. Descriptive of 25c and 50c pieces (also incorrectly extended to describe $1) minted privately in California from the 1850s through the 1880s, and described in literature by Lee, Burnie, Gillio, and Breen.

cameo. Descriptive of a prooflike or Proof coin with exceptionally frosty designs and motifs set against a deeply mirrored field.

Capped Bust coinage. Refers to coins bearing the portrait of Miss Liberty wearing a cloth cap, especially certain silver and gold designs, attributed to mint engraver John Reich, produced beginning in 1807. Term devised by Kenneth E. Bressett for use in *A Guide Book of U.S. Coins*.

Care. A commercial liquid product designated for application to the surface of a copper coin to protect it and give it a glossy appearance.

cast. A counterfeit coin made by casting metal in a mold.

cent, 1793-1796. Liberty Cap type. Designers: Robert Scot and John Gardner.

cent, 1793. Chain type. Designer: Henry Voigt.

cent, 1796-1807. Draped Bust type. Designer: Robert Scot.

cent, 1808-1814. Classic Head type. Designer: John Reich.

cent, 1816-1835. Coronet type, Matron Head. Designer: Robert Scot.

cent, 1835-1839. Coronet type, Young Head. Designer: Christian Gobrecht.

cent, 1839-1857. Coronet type, Braided Hair. Designer: Christian Gobrecht.

cent, 1839. Coronet type, Booby Head. Designer: Christian Gobrecht. The origin of the Booby Head term is unknown, but it was in use as early as the 1860s.

cent, 1839. Coronet type, Silly Head. Designer: Christian Gobrecht. The origin of the Silly Head term is unknown, but it was in use as early as the 1860s.

cent, 1857-1858. Flying Eagle type. Also made in pattern form in 1856. Design by James B. Longacre.

cent, 1859-1909. Indian type. Design by James B. Longacre.

cent, 1909 to date. Lincoln type. Design by Victor David Brenner. Memorial reverse design by Frank Gasparro used since 1959.

certified coin. A coin which is accompanied by a certificate or sealed in a holder which indicates that its authenticity, grade, or both have been certified by an independent service, especially by ANACS, Hallmark, the Numismatic Guaranty Corporation, or the Professional Coin Grading Service.

Certified Coin Dealer Newsletter, The. A weekly newsletter giving bid and ask prices for sonically-sealed coins. Nickname: Blue Sheet. Information: CCDN, Box 11099, Torrance, CA 90510.

Chain cent. 1793 cent bearing on the reverse a linked chain motif.

cherrypick. To review a large number of coins and hand-select those of special merit, such as those of unrecognized rarity or in especially choice condition from an aesthetic viewpoint. The term has been in use for many years, but in recent times it has been popularized by Bill Fivaz and others.

Choice. An adjective, capitalized in grading terminology, used to describe an especially nice example of a coin within a given grade. Thus, in the original numerical scale for grading coins, 20 represented Very Fine while 30 represented Choice Very Fine.

Civil War token; Civil War cent. A metallic token, typically the size of a contemporary Indian cent, privately issued circa 1861-1865, the Civil War period, but usually dated 1863. Such tokens bear commercial as well as political inscriptions and have been described in literature by Hetrich-Guttag, Melvin Fuld, and Dr. George F. Fuld. Many thousands of different varieties were produced.

clad metal; clad coinage. Describes planchets and coins made from two or more metals sandwiched together.

clash marks. Marks seen in the fields of a coin; evidence that two dies once came together without an intervening planchet, with the result that certain parts of the obverse die were impressed on the reverse die, or vice-versa. All coins struck from dies so injured show the same clash marks.

Classic Head. Term descriptive of a style of Liberty Head used on certain coins. Examples: half cents 1809-1836; quarter eagles 1834-1839. Term devised by Kenneth E. Bressett for use in *A Guide Book of U.S. Coins.*

cleaning; cleaned coin. Refers to removing dirt, tarnish, oxidation, or other substances or coloration from the surface of a coin by dipping, treating with chemicals, applying abrasives, or otherwise artificially treating it. Some cleaning, such as judicious dipping of certain coins in a solvent such as acetone or ammonia, may justifiably improve a coin, while the application of abrasives nearly always has a damaging effect. Cleaning should not be done unless the subject is carefully studied first, for many more coins are damaged than are improved by the various processes.

coin. In general, a coin is a minted piece of metal, usually round in shape, bearing designs on the obverse (front) and reverse (back), a date, and the name of the issuing authority. The typical coin is issued by a state, regional, or national government and has a face value which can be expressed in terms of a basic unit, such as one cent, five cents, 10 cents, half dollar, dollar, or in other countries, peso, guilder, ruble, shilling, florin, etc. Coins usually serve as a medium of exchange for the purchase and sale of goods and services and are issued with the intention of being redeemed later by the issuing government. This does not always work out as planned, and in American history we learn that the silver trade dollar, minted for circulation from 1873 to 1878, was later repudiated by the government, and holders of such coins could only receive melt-down or bullion value for them, not the face value of $1.

Coin Dealer Newsletter, The. A weekly newsletter, founded in 1963, giving bid and ask prices for coins, but not those in sonically-sealed holders (those are given in a separate publication, *The Certified Coin Dealer Newsletter*). Nickname: Gray Sheet. Information: CDN, Box 11099, Torrance, CA 90510.

Coin World. Weekly newspaper, founded in 1960, giving current news, research articles, market information, and dealer advertisements; the largest-circulation numismatic periodical. Information: CW, Box 150, Sidney, Ohio 45365.

coin dealer. An individual who earns money by buying and selling coins. There are no accreditations or professional standards, and anyone wishing to call himself a coin dealer may do so.

coining press. A mechanical device which holds an obverse and reverse die and which by means of a hand-turned screw or steam or electric power enables the dies to come together, compress a planchet, and create a coin. Coining presses may also have attachments such as a collar, automatic planchet-feeding device, etc. Today certain coining presses can accommodate four, six, or some other number of multiple die pairs, for high-speed, quantity production. During the 18th and 19th century, U.S. coining presses used just a single pair of dies. At the Philadelphia Mint power was provided by horses until 1836, at which time steam power was introduced. In the 20th century electric motors were adapted to drive the earlier steam-powered presses. Modern presses are electrically driven.

collar. The restraining device, made of steel with a circular opening at the center, which is fitted to a coining press at the point at which the obverse and reverse dies come together during the coining process. The edge of the planchet is forced into the collar when the pressure of the obverse and reverse die causes the planchet to distend. The inside of the collar may be plain, lettered, or ornamented, thus imparting the same characteristic to the coins struck using that collar. The typical early coining collar was made of one piece of steel. Certain later collars were segmented; for example, the collar used to produce the E PLURIBUS UNUM lettered edges of 1907-1933 Saint-Gaudens $20 pieces was made in three segments, which opened up to release each coin after striking.

colonial coins. General term used to describe coins produced in America or produced elsewhere specifically for circulation in America, prior to the establishment of the Philadelphia Mint in 1792. Certain issues are from the true colonial period (before the American Revolution) and others, such as state coinages of 1785-1788, are later. Certain Washington tokens coins dated 1783-1795 are also sometimes included in the category of colonial coins.

commemorative coin. Coin issued to observe an anniversary, accomplishment, or event and typically sold at a premium above face value.

commercial grade. Informal grading term indicating a coin which would not pass as a given grade if examined by a knowing buyer but which may pass as such if sold to an unwary or uneducated customer.

commercial Uncirculated. Informal grading term indicating a coin which would not pass as Uncirculated if examined by a knowing buyer but which pass as such if sold to an unwary or unknowledgeable buyer. Educated buyers would probably call such a piece AU.

computer grading. Grading coins by means of computers became a reality in early 1990 when Rick Sundman and the Professional Coin Grading Service each demonstrated units capable of grading Morgan dollars. A number of others announced their interest in and accomplishments in the field.

condition rarity. Descriptive of a coin which is rare in a particular high grade but which may be common in lower grades. Example: the 1892-S $1 is common in worn grades but is a condition rarity in MS-65.

Coronet type. Descriptive of certain styles of Liberty Head motifs used on coinage. Examples: half cents 1840-1857; quarter eagles 1840-1907. Term devised by Kenneth E. Bressett for use in *A Guide Book of U.S. Coins.* Term devised by Kenneth E. Bressett for use in *A Guide Book of U.S. Coins.*

Deep Mirror Prooflike (DMPL). A grading term, usually capitalized, indicating a business strike coin with deeply mirrorlike fields. Also, Deep Prooflike (DPL).

denticles. A border of toothlike projections or serrations extending from the rim of a coin toward the field.

designer. The person who conceives the motif or image used for a coin, often the *engraver* but not necessarily so.

diagonally reeded edge. The edge of a coin with diagonal indentations or "reeds," made by forcing the edge of a planchet into a collar having finely-spaced grooves. Example: 1795 Washington Grate cents have diagonally reeded edges.

die state. The condition of a die as it experiences wear and damage during its career of striking coins. An early die state refers to a coin struck from new or nearly new dies. An intermediate die state refers to a coin which is struck from a die showing some wear. A late die state refers to a coin struck from a die which shows the effects of extensive wear or cracks.

die variety. A slight variation in the placement of a letter, numeral, or other feature within the coinage of a certain date. Example: among 1794 large cents there are several dozen die varieties and die combinations. Die varieties are often attributed to reference works on a particular series.

die. A piece of steel (usually) which has been engraved or punched with lettering and designs so that when the die is impressed into a blank piece of metal (planchet) the design will be reproduced. Two dies, obverse and reverse, are required to produce a coin.

diebreak; die break. A raised line, often irregular, on a coin caused by metal being forced into a crack or break which developed on the coining die.

die scratch; die striation. A raised line on a coin, usually seen as a group of parallel die scratches, caused by rubbing the die with a file or an abrasive during the die making or die resurfacing process.

dime, 1946 to date. Roosevelt type. Designed by James R. Sinnock.

dime. 1796-1797 Draped bust obverse, Small Eagle reverse. Designed by Robert Scot.

dime. 1798-1807 Draped bust obverse, Heraldic Eagle reverse. Designed by Robert Scot.

dime. 1809-1837. Capped Bust type. Designed by John Reich. Modified in 1828 by William Kneass.

dime. 1837-1891. Liberty Seated type. Designed by Christian Gobrecht.

dime. 1892-1916. Barber or Liberty Head type. Designed by Charles E. Barber.

dime. 1916-1945. Mercury type. Popular term for the Liberty Head dime designed by Adolph A. Weinman and produced 1916-1945. Actually, the name is a misnomer, for the messenger Mercury of mythology had wings on his feet, while the Liberty Head dime shows wings on a woman's head.

dipping. The process of immersing a coin in a silver cleaner, chemical solution, or other liquid in order to remove toning.

disme. Early term for dime, or 10-cent piece, used at the Philadelphia Mint in connection with pattern coins dated 1792.

Dissolve. A commercial solvent used to remove polyvinyl chloride residue.

dollar, gold. Gold coins of the $1 denomination, designed by James B. Longacre, were minted from 1849 to 1889.

dollar, silver. 1794-1795 Flowing Hair type. Designed by Robert Scot.

dollar, silver. 1795-1798 Draped bust obverse, Small Eagle reverse. Designed by Robert Scot.

dollar, silver. 1798-1804 Draped bust obverse, Heraldic Eagle reverse. Designed by Robert Scot.

dollar, silver. 1836-1839. Liberty Seated type with flying eagle reverse. Designed by Christian Gobrecht.

dollar, silver. 1840-1873. Liberty Seated type with perched eagle reverse. Designed by Christian Gobrecht.

dollar, silver. 1878-1921. Morgan type. The silver dollar design created by George T. Morgan; adapted from Morgan's pattern half dollar design of 1877.

dollar, silver. 1921-1964. Peace type. The silver dollar design created by Anthony de Francisci and produced 1921-1935 and again in 1964 (1964 Peace dollars were never released). The Peace dollar was created as the result of a resolution passed at the American Numismatic Association's annual convention in 1920.

dollar, trade. See *trade dollar.*

dollar. 1976 bicentennial design. Dated 1776-1976. Obverse by Frank Gasparro; reverse by Dennis Williams.

dollar. The dollar denomination in U.S. coinage includes silver dollars 1794-1935 and later silver commemoratives; clad alloy dollars 1971 and later; trade dollars 1873-1885; and gold dollars 1849-1889.

double eagle. $20 gold piece minted 1850-1933.

doubled die. A coining die which has received two impressions from the hub or master die, thus causing a doubling of certain features struck from the die. Example: 1955 Doubled Die cent.

Draped Bust coinage. Coins utilizing the Draped Bust design by Robert Scot. Examples: 1800-1808 half cents; 1795-1798 silver dollars.

eagle. $10 gold piece minted 1795-1933; also American eagle silver and gold bullion coins minted from 1986 onward.

Eisenhower dollar. Dollar of the type minted 1971-1978, designed by Frank Gasparro.

electrotype. A counterfeit coin made by the electrodepositation of metal.

engrailed edge. The edge of a coin decorated by a recessed cord-like design made by passing the planchet through a Castaing machine.

engraver. The skilled artisan who takes a coin design and models it in clay or another substance for transferral to a die, or who by means of special tools directly creates a hub, master die, or die, or who otherwise transfers a design to a die.

exergue. Otherwise blank space on a coin, sometimes raised or recessed, where the date is located.

experimental piece. A type of *pattern* (to which refer) coin made to test an experimental concept, such as having raised ridges on the edge of a nickel to aid blind people (made in 1882), to increase the diameter of the $5 gold piece in order to make in thinner (in 1860) so that they could not be hollowed out and filled with less valuable metal, etc.

Extra Fine. Slang for *Extremely Fine,* a grading term, to which refer.

Extremely Fine. Grading term, abbreviated as EF-40 or EF-45 (also sometimes as XF), describing a worn coin with all inscriptions and details sharply defined, but with little or no mint lustre; better than Very Fine but less than About Uncirculated. Capitalized.

eye appeal. Term descriptive of the aesthetic appeal or visual desirability of a coin, in addition to its numerical or technical grade.

face value. The value of a coin as stated on the coin, such as five cents, twenty dollars, etc.

Fair. Grading term indicating a coin which is well worn, sometimes designated as Fair-2; between Poor-1 and About Good-3. Capitalized.

fantasy coin. A coin created for sale to collectors, and struck from dies made later than the date on the dies, and of a variety of which no originals were produced.

fatal flaw. A die crack or break which eventually serves to render the die unfit for use. Term popularized in numismatics by Michael Hodder.

field. The flat (usually) surface of a coin not used for a design or inscription.

Fine. Grading term, abbreviated as F-12 or F-15, describing a worn coin with all or nearly all of the lettering and inscriptions visible; better than Very Good but less than Very Fine. Capitalized.

fineness. The purity of a metal, typically gold or silver, expressed in thousandths. Example: certain $50 gold pieces made in California in the early 1850s were .880 fine.

first strike. Descriptive of a coin struck from an early state of the dies, earlier (in common numismatic usage prior to about 1970) often used to describe a coin with a prooflike surface. However, as many prooflike coins were struck from later die states, in which the dies became polished from use or from resurfacing, the *first strike* term is rarely used.

five cents, nickel. 1866-1883 Shield type. Designed by James B. Longacre.

five cents, nickel. 1883-1913. Liberty Head type. Designed by Charles E. Barber.

five cents, nickel. 1913-1938. Buffalo or Indian Head type. Designed by James Earle Fraser.

five cents, nickel. 1938 to date. Jefferson type. Designed by Felix O. Schlag.

five cents, silver. See *half dime.*

flan. European term for planchet.

flip. Clear plastic or Mylar envelope used to store a coin and permit it to be viewed without touching its surfaces.

Flying Eagle cent. Cent of the type of 1857-1858, designed by James B. Longacre.

flyspeck. A tiny oxidation spot on a coin, particularly on a high grade copper or nickel alloy coin, caused by moisture.

Franklin half dollar. 50c piece of the type minted from 1948 to 1953, designed by John R. Sinnock.

freak. Obsolete term for *mint error* (to which refer), in general use prior to about 1960.

generic coin. A typical or common coin of its type, in average or below average grade. The type of coin for which sight-unseen bid prices are often given.

Gobrecht dollar. The silver dollar type of 1836-1839, with Liberty Seated obverse and flying eagle reverse, designed by Christian Gobrecht.

gold $2 1/2. Quarter eagle. Denomination minted 1796-1929.

gold $3. Denomination minted 1854-1889.

gold $4. Stella. Pattern denomination minted in 1879 and 1880.

gold $5. Half eagle. Denomination minted 1795-1929.

gold $10. Eagle. Denomination minted 1795-1933. Also the American eagle, a gold bullion coin denominated at $50, minted from 1986 to date.

gold $20. Double eagle. Denomination minted 1850-1933 and in pattern form in 1849.

gold $50. Denomination minted as a commemorative for the Panama-Pacific International Exposition in 1915; also the American eagle, a gold bullion coin denominated at $50, minted from 1986 onward.

gold coins. Issues of the denominations $1, $2 1/2, $3, $4 (patterns), $5, $10, $20, and $50 (commemoratives) produced 1795-1933; also American eagle gold bullion coinage produced from 1986 onward.

gold dollar. $1 piece made of gold produced 1849-1889.

Good. Grading term, abbreviated as G-4 or G-6, describing a well-worn coin with the date and most major features visible; better than About Good but less than Very Good. Capitalized.

grade. A designation which refers to the amount of wear or handling a coin has received.

grading systems. See *adjectival grading system, Sheldon Scale, Photograde grading system,* and *numerical grading system.*

Gray Sheet. Nickname for *The Coin Dealer Newsletter,* weekly newsletter giving bid and ask prices for coins, but not those in sonically-sealed holders (those are given in a separate publication, *The Certified Coin Dealer Newsletter*).

Guide Book of U.S. Coins, A. A guide to coin mintages, types, and prices, created by Richard S. Yeoman and published annually since 1946; now edited by Kenneth E. Bressett. Also known as the *Red Book*.

hairlines. Microscopic recessed parallel lines on the mirrorlike fields of a Proof or other coin indicating that it was once cleaned by an abrasive process.

half cent, 1793. Liberty Cap type, head facing left. Designer: Adam Eckfeldt(?)

half cent, 1794-1796. Liberty Cap type, head facing right. Designers: Robert Scot and John Gardner.

half cent, 1800-1808. Draped Bust type. Designed by Robert Scot.

half cent, 1809-1836. Classic Head type. Designed by John Reich.

half cent, 1840-1857. Coronet or Braided Hair type. Designed by Christian Gobrecht.

half dime. 1794-1795 Flowing Hair type. Designed by Robert Scot.

half dime. 1796-1797 Draped bust obverse, Small Eagle reverse. Designed by Robert Scot.

half dime. 1800-1805 Draped bust obverse, Heraldic Eagle reverse. Designed by Robert Scot.

half dime. 1829-1837. Capped Bust type. Designed by William Kneass after a motif by John Reich.

half dime. 1837-1873. Liberty Seated type. Designed by Christian Gobrecht.

half dollar. 1794-1795 Flowing Hair type. Designed by Robert Scot.

half dollar. 1796-1797 Draped Bust obverse, Small Eagle reverse. Designed by Robert Scot.

half dollar. 1801-1807 Draped Bust obverse, Heraldic Eagle reverse. Designed by Robert Scot.

half dollar. 1807-1836. Capped Bust type. Designed by John Reich.

half dollar. 1836-1839. Capped Bust type with reeded edge. Designed by Christian Gobrecht from motifs by John Reich.

half dollar. 1839-1891. Liberty Seated type. Designed by Christian Gobrecht.

half dollar. 1892-1915. Barber or Liberty Head type. Designed by Charles E. Barber.

half dollar. 1916-1947. Liberty Walking type. Design by Adolph A. Weinman.

half dollar. 1948-1963. Franklin type. Design by John R. Sinnock.

half dollar. 1964 to date. Obverse design by Gilroy Roberts; reverse design by Frank Gasparro.

half dollar. 1976 bicentennial design. Dated 1776-1976. Obverse by Gilroy Roberts; reverse by Seth G. Huntington.

half eagle. $5 gold piece minted 1795-1929.

Hallmark Grading Service. Grading service founded in 1988 and launched in 1989 by Lee J. Bellisario and several associates, which for a fee gives impartial third-party grading opinions and sonically seals coins in holders (slabs). Located in Woburn, MA.

Hard Times token. A merchant's store card, political token, or other privately issued token, typically the size of a large cent, produced circa 1832-1844, the span designated as the Hard Times era by Lyman H. Low, who described such tokens in his 1899 work (with a 1906 addendum), *Hard Times Tokens*; later supplemented by Thomas L. Elder and, especially, Russell Rulau. In American history the Hard Times period is that period of economic difficulty which began with the nationwide collapse of banks and unfavorable commercial conditions in the year 1837.

haymarks. Obsolete term, popular pre-1970, to describe *hairlines* (to which refer).

impaired. Damaged or showing wear, as an impaired Proof.

incuse. Refers to a design which is impressed into a coin's surface and is lower than the surrounding field; the opposite of being in relief.

Indian cent. Cent of the type of 1859-1909, designed by James B. Longacre.

Indian Head nickel. Proper name for the five-cent piece of 1913-1938, popularly called the Buffalo nickel, designed by James Earle Fraser.

inscription. Lettering on a coin, such as IN GOD WE TRUST or UNITED STATES OF AMERICA. Same as *legend*.

International Association of Professional Numismatists (IAPN). International group of leading rare coin dealers, each of whom has passed strict admission requirements and pledged to honor a code of ethics.

International Numismatic Society (INS). Authentication and grading service founded by Charles Hoskins.

intrinsic value. The bullion or melt-down value of a coin.

Jefferson Head cent. Cent variety of the year 1795, believed by some to be a counterfeit and others to be a pattern.

Jefferson nickel. Five-cent piece of the type minted from 1938 to date, designed by Felix O. Schlag.

Kennedy half dollar. 50c piece of the type minted from 1964 to date. Obverse design by Gilroy Roberts; reverse design by Frank Gasparro.

key coin. A coin which is among the scarcer varieties of its design type. Term popularized beginning in the 1950s by dealer Jerry Cohen and widely adopted since then. Examples: 1916-D 10c, 1932-D 25c, 1887 $5 gold.

King of American Coins. Designation applied by dealer B. Max Mehl, and adopted by others, to the 1804 silver dollar.

Kointain. Coin holder made of two pieces of inert plastic, thin and round, which snap together to cover and protect a coin. Made by E & T Kointainer Company.

lamination. A flake, strip, or small piece of metal which has become partially or fully separated from a coin's surface, due to improper bonding of the metal strip from which the planchet was cut.

large cent. One cent piece of large diameter of the type made by the Philadelphia Mint 1793-1857 for circulation.

legend. An inscription on a coin, such as LIBERTY, UNITED STATES OF AMERICA, etc.

legend. An inscription or lettering on a coin, such as IN GOD WE TRUST or UNITED STATES OF AMERICA. Same as *inscription.*

lettered edge. The edge of a coin with an inscription, made by forcing the edge of a planchet into a collar having lettering or by passing the planchet through a Castaing edge-lettering machine before or after striking. Examples: U.S. cents dated 1794 have edges lettered ONE HUNDRED FOR A DOLLAR; such lettering was produced by a Castaing machine prior to striking. U.S. $20 pieces of the 1907-1933 Saint-Gaudens design have edges lettered E PLURIBUS UNUM; such lettering was produced at the time of striking by forcing the edge of the planchet into a lettered collar.

Liberty Cap design. Certain half cents 1793-1797 and cents 1793-1796 bearing the portrait of Miss Liberty with a liberty cap and pole. The motif was adapted from the French Libertas Americana medal.

Liberty Head nickel. Five-cent piece of the type minted from 1883 to 1913, designed by Charles E. Barber.

Liberty Seated coinage. Refers to coins bearing the portrait of Miss Liberty, seated, holding a liberty cap and pole. Examples: half dimes 1838-1873, dimes, 1838-1891, 20-cent pieces 1875-1878, quarter dollars 1838-1891, half dollars 1839-1891, silver dollars 1836-1839 (mostly patterns) and 1840-1873. The design was created by mint engraver Christian Gobrecht.

Liberty Walking half dollar. 50c piece of the type minted from 1916 to 1947, designed by Adolph A. Weinman.

Lincoln cent. Cent of the type of 1909 onward, designed by Victor David Brenner; Memorial reverse, designed by Frank Gasparro, used from 1959 onward.

lintmark. An incuse or recessed line, curlicue, or other mark on a coin caused by hair, thread, or other debris on the surface of a die being impressed into the surface of a coin struck from that die. Lintmarks are especially common on Proofs struck at the Philadelphia Mint in the late 1850s and early 1860s.

Little Princess. Designation applied by dealer Abe Kosoff to the 1841 quarter eagle.

lustre. Mint frost or bloom seen on a Mint State coin. Also called *mint lustre.*

mail bid sale. A method of buying and selling coins by which multiple bidders compete by mail or telephone to acquire coins descirbed in a catalogue, with the highest bidder being the winner. Also see *auction.*

Matron Head type. Descriptive of the Liberty Head motif used on certain large cents 1816-1835.

Matte Proof. A coin or medal struck on a slow-speed press from specially prepared dies which have been lightly etched, thus giving the the piece a matte (instead of a frosty, as in a business strike, or mirrorlike, as in a brilliant Proof) surface. Matte Proofs were made of Lincoln cents 1909-1916, Buffalo nickels 1913-1916 (some say 1917), Mint medals since about the turn of the century, and certain other issues.

merchant's token. A metallic (usually) token issued by a merchant or other commercial entity to advertise goods or services. Same as *store card.* Example: the token issued during the Hard Times era by J. Cochran, a Batavia, New York bellfounder.

Mercury dime. Popular name for the 10-cent piece of the type of 1916-1945 designed by Adolph A. Weinman.

milling; milled edge (or milled rim). The raised rim on a planchet or coin caused by passing a planchet through an upsetting or milling machine, which passes the planchet between a roller and a stationary metal matrix, reducing its diameter and at the same time raising the rims. The purpose is to aid the metal flow when the planchet is subsequently made into a coin with raised rims. Also see *upset rim*.

Mint State. Grading term, abbreviated as MS and on the numerical scale as MS-60, MS-61, etc. increasing in quality to MS-70, describing a coin which may show marks and abrasions but which has never circulated in the channels of commerce. Uncirculated. Capitalized.

mint error. A coin which was carelessly or incorrectly manufactured from normal dies and which is double struck, off-center, or which displays some other evidence of improper striking.

mint lustre. Mint frost or bloom seen on a Mint State coin.

mint set. Group of Uncirculated coins, all of the same date and/or mint, sold at the same time by the mint.

mintmark. Letter such as C, CC, D, O, P, S, or W indicating the mint where the coin was struck.

Morgan dollar. Silver dollar of the type minted 1878-1921, designed by George T. Morgan.

motto. In U.S. federal coinage, inscriptions such as IN GOD WE TRUST and E PLURIBUS UNUM.

mule; muling. A coin produced by combining two dies never intended for each other. Example: a coin made by combining a die for a 5-cent nickel coin with a die for a $5 gold piece.

nickel five cents. See *five cents, nickel.*

nickel three cents. See *three cents, nickel.*

numerical grading system. Grading system employing numbers from 1 to 70, adapted from the system devised by Dr. William H. Sheldon in 1949 for use with large cents 1793-1857, and described in the book *Early American Cents* (revised editions titled *Penny Whimsy*). By the 1970s it was in widespread use. In 1978 the American Numismatic Association adapted and expanded it for use in the official A.N.A. grading system. Examples of grades: G-4, VG-8, VF-30, EF-45, MS-65. The system is also used for Proofs, as Proof-60, Proof-61, etc.

Numismatic Certification Institute (NCI). Grading service founded by Steve Ivy and James L. Halperin and operated in Dallas, Texas.

Numismatic Guaranty Corporation of America (NGC). Grading service founded by John Albanese, which for a fee gives impartial third-party grading opinions and sonically seals coins in holders (slabs). Located in Parsippany, New Jersey.

Numismatic News. Weekly newspaper, founded in 1952, giving current news, research articles, market information, and dealer advertisements. Information: NN, Krause Publications, 700 East State Street, Iola, WI 54990.

numismatist. A coin collector, especially one who studies the history and technical details of coins in addition to acquiring them.

obverse. The front or face side of a coin, usually the side with the date and main design.

original. 1. A coin struck in the year dated (as opposed to a restrike struck later than the indicated date). 2. In condition as made or assembled, as an original mint bag of coins, an original bank-wrapped roll, a Proof set in its original box, etc. 3. Natural, as in original toning (toning not applied artificially).

ornamented edge. The edge of a coin decorated with a design, made by forcing the edge of a planchet into a collar having ornamentation or by passing the planchet through a Castaing machine. Examples: The 1792 Washington silver "half dollar" has an edge ornamented with circles and squares. Certain 1793 Wreath cents have edges ornamented with a vine and bars motif.

Orphan Annie dime. Designation applied to the 1844 dime, for reasons unknown today.

overdate. Term indicating one date punched or cut over another in a die, usually as an economy measure at the mint, so that dies of an earlier year can be used for current coinage. Examples: 1942/1-D 10c, 1802/1 $1, 1803/2 $5.

overgraded. Term used to indicate that the grade of a coin offered by one person is given at a higher level than another person thinks it should be

overmintmark. Term indicating one mintmark punched over another in a die. Examples: 1938-D over S overmintmark Buffalo nickel; 1944-D/S Lincoln cent. Term coined in 1961 by Q. David Bowers, when the first overmintmark, the 1938-D/S 5c, was discovered and publicized in *Coin World*. Later, various overmintmarks were discovered among other coin issues.

overstrike; overstruck coin. A coin struck over another previously struck coin, sometimes of a different variety or type, used instead of a blank planchet.

patina. Toning or oxidation on the surface of a coin.

pattern. A coin made to test a proposal, design, denomination, format, alloy, etc. before such design, format, etc. is officially adopted for regular coinage. Examples: pattern $4 pieces made in 1879 to illustrate this proposed denomination; pattern 1879 dollars made in goloid alloy; pattern 1856 Flying eagle cents made a year before the design was adopted for regular circulation. Also see *experimental piece* and *trial piece*.

Peace dollar. Silver dollar of the type minted 1921-1935 and again in 1964 (but not for circulation; 1964 dollars were destroyed), designed by Anthony de Francisci.

Photograde grading system. Photographic grading system devised by James F. Ruddy in 1970 and described in the book *Photograde*.

pioneer gold coin. A gold coin minted by a banker, assayer, or other entity, except a standard U.S. government mint, in a territory (strict definition) or state, especially California 1849-1855, Oregon 1849, Utah 1849-1860, or Colorado 1860-1861. Same as *territorial gold coin*.

plain edge. The edge of a coin which is not reeded or ornamented. Examples: current U.S. cents and nickels have plain edges.

planchet. A blank disc, circular in shape, which after being stamped by dies becomes a coin, token, medal, etc. Planchets can be simple discs punched from a strip of metal, or they can be second process (or type 2) planchets with raised rims, caused by passing a plain disc through an upsetting or milling machine.

political token. A metallic (usually) token issued in connection with a local, state, national, or other political candidate or in connection with a political movement or situation. Example: tokens dated 1837 satirizing President Andrew Jackson.

polyvinyl chloride (PVC). Substance used in the manufacture of clear, flexible coin envelopes or "flips." Coins stored for a period of time in such envelopes are apt to acquire PVC residue, a sticky, greenish substance which can etch or corrode a coin's surface, particularly in the case of copper or nickel alloy coins.

Poor. Grading term indicating a coin worn to virtual smoothness, sometimes designated as Poor-1 or Basal State (per Dr. William H. Sheldon's *Penny Whimsy* book). Term representing the lowest division on the grading scale. Capitalized.

premium quality. Term devised by Q. David Bowers in November 1985 to designate a coin which not only is of the proper numerical grade but which is also sharply struck, well centered, etc., and which also has exceptional aesthetic appeal. This term is usually employed in connection with coins grading MS-65 (or Proof-65) or better. Sometimes capitalized. Abbreviated as PQ.

prestrike. A rare term. Applies to a coin struck earlier than the date indicated. Examples: 1900-dated Lafayette dollars were prestruck in December 1899; many 1976 bicentennial coins were prestruck in 1975.

private gold coin. A gold coin minted by a banker, assayer, or other entity, except a standard U.S. government mint, especially North Carolina (Reid coinage 1830; Bechtler coinage 1830-1852), California 1849-1855, Oregon 1849, Utah 1849-1860, or Colorado 1860-1861.

processing. Refers to wire brushing or burnishing a worn coin to give it the appearance of being Mint State.

Professional Coin Grading Service (PCGS). Grading service founded in February 1986 by David Hall and several associates, which for a fee gives impartial third-party grading opinions and sonically seals coins in holders (slabs). PCGS revolutionized the rare coin business. Located in Newport Beach, CA.

Professional Numismatists Guild (PNG). Association of rare coin dealers founded in 1955 by Abe Kosoff. Dealers must meet strict membership requirements and pledge to adhere to the PNG Code of Ethics in order to belong. Most members live in the United States.

professional numismatist. An individual who earns money by buying and selling coins. There are no accreditations or professional standards, and anyone wishing to call himself a professional numismatist may do so.

Proof (usually capitalized). A coin struck on a slow-speed press from specially prepared, highly polished dies, using a specially prepared planchet. The resultant coin has mirrorlike fields. Also known as a *brilliant Proof*. Other types of Proofs, to which refer, are of the *Roman finish, matte,* or *sandblast* types. In the *numerical grading system* various qualities of Proofs are described as Proof-60, Proof-61, etc. to Proof-70.

Proof set. Group of Proof coins, all of the same date, sold at the same time by the mint.

prooflike. Describes the surface of a business strike (not Proof) coin which has been struck on a high-speed press, using a normal planchet, but from dies which have been polished. This polishing was not intended to create mirrorlike coins for collectors but, rather, was done to remove rust, die clash marks, or to resurface a business strike die for further use.

quarter dollar. 1796 Draped Bust obverse, Small Eagle reverse. Designed by Robert Scot.

quarter dollar. 1804-1807 Draped Bust obverse, Heraldic Eagle reverse. Designed by Robert Scot.

quarter dollar. 1815-1838. Capped Bust type. Designed by John Reich. Modified in 1831 by William Kneass.

quarter dollar. 1838-1891. Liberty Seated type. Designed by Christian Gobrecht.

quarter dollar. 1892-1916. Barber or Liberty Head type. Designed by Charles E. Barber.

quarter dollar. 1916-1930. Standing Liberty type. Design by Hermon A. MacNeil.

quarter dollar. 1932 to date. Washington type. Design by John Flanagan.

quarter dollar. 1976 bicentennial design. Dated 1776-1976. Obverse by John Flanagan. Reverse by Jack L. Ahr.

quarter eagle. $2 1/2 gold piece minted 1796-1929.

raw coin. A coin which has not been slabbed.

recut date; recut letter, etc. Term, largely obsolete, for a *repunched* date, letter, or other device on a coin.

red. Refers to the original brilliant color of a copper or bronze coin, as in MS-65 red.

red and brown. Refers to the original color of a copper or bronze coin in combination with some areas of natural brown toning.

Red Book, The. Name for *A Guide Book of U.S. Coins*, a guide to coin mintages, types, and prices, created by Richard S. Yeoman and published annually since 1946; now edited by Kenneth E. Bressett.

reeded edge. The edge of a coin with vertical indentations or "reeds," made by forcing the edge of a planchet into a collar having finely-spaced grooves. Examples: current U.S. dimes and quarters have reeded edges. Also see *diagonally reeded edge*.

relief. A raised design or portion thereof.

reminting. A term devised by the American Numismatic Association in connection with producing additional examples of the 1989 ANA convention medal in 1990; presumably a gentler term than *restriking*.

repunched date; repunched letter, etc. A date, letter, or other device which has been double punched, as a die preparation error, or to strengthen a feature, etc. Examples: 1867 Shield nickel with triple-punched date; 1869 Indian cent with final digit double punched.

restrike. A coin struck from original dies later than the date on the dies. Examples: In 1858-1860 the Mint restruck 1856 Flying Eagle cents; in the 1960s the various mints struck Lincoln cents from dies dated a year or two earlier.

reverse. The back or tails side of a coin.

Roman finish Proof. A gold coin circa 1909-1911 which had its surface treated by a process, the details of which are not known today, giving it a bright, satiny surface.

Roosevelt dime. 10c piece of the type minted from 1946 to date, designed by John R. Sinnock.

rubbing. Evidence of friction seen on the surface of a coin.

Saint-Gaudens coinage. $10 and $20 pieces minted 1907-1933, designed by noted sculptor August Saint-Gaudens.

Saints. Slang term for $20 pieces of the 1907-1933 type, designed by noted sculptor August Saint-Gaudens.

Salomon Brothers survey. An annual survey conducted by a well-known Wall Street firm, in conjunction with Stack's, whereby the price changes in 20 selected United States coins (not including gold) are monitored. As of 1989. rare coins ranked as the best of all investments for a 20-year long term span and high on the list of 5-year and 10-year investments.

Sandblast Proof. A coin or medal which has had its surface treated, after striking, with a fine air-propelled stream of sand particles, thus imparting a matte surface. This process was used to produce certain gold Proofs circa 1908-1915.

Satin Proof. A coin, such as certain cents and nickels of 1936, made from incompletely polished dies, resulting in a coin which has a combination of satiny and mirrorlike surfaces.

semi-prooflike. Refers to a coin with a partially prooflike surface.

series. A date run or group of coins having the same design. Examples: the Mercury dime series 1916-1945; the Lincoln cent series 1909 to date.

sharp strike. Refers to a coin with all of its minute design details sharply defined.

Sheldon Scale. Numerical grading system employing numbers from 1 to 70, devised by Dr. William H. Sheldon in 1949 for use with large cents 1793-1857, and described in the book *Early American Cents* (revised editions titled *Penny Whimsy*). Later, others extended the Sheldon Scale to other coins. By the 1970s it was in widespread use. In 1978 the American Numismatic Association adapted and expanded it for use in the official A.N.A. grading system. Examples of grades: G-4, VG-8, VF-30, EF-45, MS-65.

Shield nickel. Five-cent piece of the type of 1866-1883, designed by James B. Longacre.

sight seen bid. A bid price posted by a dealer on the Teletype or other trading network, with the proviso that the offer is not valid until the particular coin desired has been examined and approved by the bidder. Sight seen bids are often higher than sight unseen bids. The term is mainly used in conjunction with coins encased by grading services such as the Professional Coin Grading Service, Hallmark, ANACS, and Numismatic Guaranty Corporation.

sight unseen bid. A bid price posted by a dealer on the Teletype or other trading network, with assurance that the bid will be honored regardless of the appearance or quality of the coin. Sight unseen bids are often lower than sight seen bids. The term is mainly used in conjunction with coins encased by grading services such as the Professional Coin Grading Service, Hallmark, ANACS, and Numismatic Guaranty Corporation.

Silly Head. Cent variety of the year 1839. This term, in use since the 1860s, is of unknown origin.

Silver center cent. A variety of 1792 pattern one-cent piece.

silver dollar. See *dollar, silver.*

silver five cents. See *half dime.*

silver three cents. See *three cents, silver.*

slab. Popular term for a sonically sealed plastic holder used to encase a coin, particularly those encased by grading services such as the Professional Coin Grading Service, Hallmark, ANACS, and Numismatic Guaranty Corporation.

slider. Grading term indicating a coin that because of friction or rubbing is not quite Uncirculated.

slug. Slang term for a $50 gold piece, derived from the 19th century tale which stated that a group of these large, heavy coins, if wrapped in a handkerchief, would make a good weapon to "slug" someone; alternatively, the heavy coin can be likened to an ingot or slug of metal.

small cent. One cent pieces of small diameter of the type made from 1857 to date for circulation.

small denomination gold. Gold coins of the 25c, 50c, and $1 denominations minted privately in California from the 1850s through the 1880s, and described in literature by Lee, Burnie, Gillio, and Breen.

spark erosion process. Refers to a method of creating dies for counterfeiting coins by a pantagraph, one end of which electrically etches away at the die.

split grade. Refers to a coin graded differently on the obverse and reverse. A silver dollar graded as MS-60/63 has an MS-60 obverse and MS-63 reverse.

Standard Silver. A series of pattern coins made in the late 1860s as a proposal for a coinage intended to aid in the retirement of paper fractional currency notes from circulation.

standard dollar. The United States silver dollar, especially circa the 1870s, as contrasted to the trade dollar and the gold dollar.

Standing Liberty quarter. 25c piece of the type minted from 1916 to 1930, designed by Hermon A. MacNeil.

Starred Reverse. Cent variety of the year 1794, listed as Sheldon-48, with 94 tiny five-pointed stars around the reverse border, for reasons unknown today.

state coins. Refers to copper coins produced under the auspices of or with inscriptions referring to certain states, specifically Connecticut 1785-1788, Massachusetts 1787-1788, New Jersey 1786-1788, New York 1786-1787, and Vermont 1785-1788.

stella. Pattern $4 issue produced in gold, aluminum, copper, and white metal 1879-1880. So called because of the star (stella) on the reverse.

store card. A metallic (usually) token issued by a merchant or other commercial entity to advertise goods or services. Same as *merchan's token*. Example: the tokens issued in 1837 by Smith's Clock Establishment, New York City.

striations. Light parallel lines raised on the surface of a coin, caused by striking from a die which had file or polishing marks.

strike. Refers to the degree of sharpness, or lack thereof, manifest on a coin, as in sharp strike or weak strike.

striking. The process by which coins are struck in a coin press.

suction marks. Archaic and incorrect term for *clash marks*, to which refer.

Susan B. Anthony dollar. Dollar of the type minted 1979-1891, designed by Frank Gasparro.

technical grade. The numerical grade of a coin, without regard to other factors such as sharpness of strike, aesthetic appeal, etc.

territorial gold coin. A gold coin minted by a banker, assayer, or other entity, except a standard U.S. government mint, in a territory (strict definition) or state, especially California 1849-1855, Oregon 1849, Utah 1849-1860, or Colorado 1860-1861. Same as *pioneer gold coin*.

three cents, nickel. Denomination produced for circulation 1865-1889. Design by James B. Longacre.

three cents, silver. Denomination produced at the Philadelphia Mint 1851-1873 and at New Orleans in 1851. Officially known as a *trime*, a term seldom used by collectors today.

toning. Natural tarnish or oxidation on the surface of a coin. Unsightly, corrosive, or heavily mottled toning can lower a coin's value. Attractive toning can increase a coin's value, sometimes substantially.

trade dollar. A special type of silver dollar of 420 grains weight made from 1873 to 1878 as an export item for trade in the Orient, where they were intended to replace Mexican silver coins. Trade dollars were legal tender in the United States until 1876, after which time the government repudiated them, and they became worth only bullion or melt-down value. Proofs for open sale to collectors were made through 1883, and pieces dated 1884 and 1884 were produced clandestinely in limited numbers.

Trends price; Trends. The market price of a coin as derived from the "Trends" column in the weekly publication *Coin World.*

trial piece. A type of coin generally classified under the *pattern* (to which refer) category, but made in a less valuable metal than usual for the denomination, in order to test the dies. In practice, gold coin denominations struck in aluminum (as in the year 1885, for example), silver denominations struck in copper (1869, for example), etc. were usually produced for the Mint or Mint officials to sell or trade at a profit to coin collectors.

trime. Official but seldom-used term descriptive of the silver three cent piece made 1851-1873.

twenty-cent piece. 1875-1878. Liberty Seated type. Designed by William Barber; obverse adopted from Christian Gobrecht's design.

two-cent piece. Denomination produced for circulation 1864-1872 and in the form of Proofs for collectors in 1873. Design by James B. Longacre.

type. The basic design of a coin.

Uncirculated. Grading term, abbreviated as Unc. or, on the numerical scale, MS (for Mint State), as MS-60, MS-61, etc. to MS-70, describing a coin which may show marks and abrasions but which has never circulated in the channels of commerce. Mint State. Capitalized.

undergraded. Rare term used to indicate that the grade of a coin offered by one person is given at a lower level than another thinks it should be.

unsealed. Term indicating a coin which has been rejected by a certification service because the coin has PVC contamination, artificial toning, or another problem which prevents it from being assigned a standard grade.

upset rim. The raised rim on a coin or blank planchet caused by passing a planchet through an upsetting or milling machine, which passes the planchet between a roller and a stationary metal matrix, reducing its diameter and at the same time raising the rims. The purpose is to aid the metal flow when the planchet is subsequently made into a coin with raised rims. Also see *milling.*

variety. A minor change within a coin design or type.

Very Fine. Grading term, abbreviated as VF-20, VF-25, VF-30, or VF-35, describing a worn coin with all inscriptions visible and clearly defined; better than Fine but less than Extremely Fine. Capitalized.

Very Good. Grading term, abbreviated as VG-8 or VG-10, describing a well-worn coin better than Good but less than Fine. Capitalized.

Washington quarter. 25c piece of the type minted from 1932 to date, designed by John Flanagan.

weak strike. Describes a coin struck with poorly defined details, particularly on the higher parts of the design; usually caused by the dies being spaced too widely apart.

wear. Removal of metal from a coin's surface due to handling or circulation.

whizzing. Refers to the wire brushing or burnishing of a worn coin to make it appear Mint State.

wire rim. A high rim on a coin, usually a Proof, made from excess metal being squeezed between the dies and the collar.

Wreath cent. 1793 cent bearing on the reverse a wreath motif.

Index

A

AB Bookman, 309
Abbott, John, 213
Adams, John Weston, 21, 23
Ahwash, Kamal, 216
Ahr, Jack L., 226
Akers, David, 27, 105, 261, 269
Albanese, John, 23, 77-80
A-Mark Coin Company, 44
American and Canadian Counter-marked Coins, 288
American Half Cents–The "Little Half Sisters", 189
American Journal of Numismatics, 240
American Numismatic Association, 8, 50, 52, 70, 74, 78, 81, 82, 89, 99, 101, 205, 292, 293, 296, 307
American Numismatic Association Centennial History, The, 52, 248
American Numismatic Association Certification Service (ANACS), 57, 77, 90, 108, 132, 134, 136, 142, 144, 146, 156
American Numismatic Exchange (ANE), 138, 152
American Numismatic Society, 14, 27, 50, 103, 270, 290, 292
American Rare Coin Fund Limited Partnership, 44, 73, 78, 93
American Teleprocessing Corporation, 152
Amherst Sale, 108

Amos Press, 36
Amspacher, Bruce, 220
ANA Grading Guide, 84
ANA Grading Service, 136
ANA Summer Seminar, 51
Anderson, Barbara, 108, 109
Anderson, Secretary, 88
Anthony dollars, 249
Anthony, Susan B., 249
Arlin, Liz, 67
artificial toning, 174
Assay Commission, 289
Asylum, The, 60
auction prices realized, 152
Auctions by Bowers and Merena, Inc., 9, 59, 95, 111, 181
authenticity, 70

B

Bagg, Dr. Richard A., 59, 103, 104
Bailey & Company, 299
Baker, W.S., 186
Baldwin & Co., 280, 301
Bank of the United States, 302
Barber, Charles E., 32, 204, 217, 262, 302
Barber Coin Collectors Society, 232
Barber dimes (1892-1916), 217
Barber half dollars (1892-1915), 232
Barber quarters (1892-1916), 225
Bareford, Harold, 43, 305

Barone, Peter A., 141, 142
Barrington Sale, 109
Bass, Harry, 27, 260
Bauman, Gerald, 103
Bebee, Aubrey, 205
Bebee's, 241
Bechtler, August, 280
Bechtler, Christopher, 280
Beistle, M.L., 228
Bentley, Anne, 23
Better Business Bureau, 61
Betts, C. Willys, 300
Bland-Allison Act, 240
Blaylock, Aloma, 240
Blaylock, Richard, 240
Bolender, M.H., 237, 238
Boone half dollars, 275
Borckardt, Mark, 155
Bourne, Remy, 293
Bowers, Q. David, 4, 51, 136
Bowers and Merena Galleries, Inc., 9, 36, 43, 67, 152, 154, 155, 174, 223, 244, 250
Boyd, F.C.C., 214
Boye, Roger, 293
Brand, Virgil, 28, 96, 105
Breen, Walter, 139, 141, 189, 223, 262, 273
Brenner, Victor David, 20, 32, 198, 292, 304
Bressett, Kenneth E., 44, 71, 123, 236, 256, 157, 293
brilliant vs. toned, 170

Brooks, Mary, 279
Brown, Martin R., 123
Brown, Samuel W., 205
Browning, A.W., 223
Brownlee, Mike, 256
Brunk, Dr. Gregory, 287, 288
budget recommendations, 179
Buffalo nickels (1913-1938), 205
bullion coins, 284
Bullowa, David E., 273
Bureau of Engraving and Printing, 291, 298
Burton, Richard, 296
Bush, George, 289
Busiek, Miley, 285
Bust Half Nut Club, 229

—— C ——

Cafarelli, Teresa, 246
California Gold Rush, 253
camaraderie, 306
Capital lucite holders, 177
Carlson, Carl W., 176
Carson City Mint, 19, 116, 239
Carson City, Nevada, 11
Carter, Amon, 307
Caswell, George, 143
Centinel, The, 126
Central States Numismatic Society, 126
Certified Coin Dealer Newsletter, 7, 15, 54, 61, 64, 83, 130, 132, 134, 135, 149, 152, 156, 165, 170

Index

Champa, Armand, 293

Chapman brothers, 222

characteristics of dies, 157

characteristics of the planchet, 159

Charlotte Mint, 115

Christie's, 13

Cincinnati half dollar, 274

circulated grades, 166

Civil War, 203, 209, 257, 298, 301

Civil War tokens, 287

Civil War Token Society, 287

Clain-Stefanelli, Elvira, 271

Clark, Gruber & Co., 281, 198

Clark, Spencer, 298

Clark, William, 298

Cleopatra, 296

Cline, J.H., 226

Cohen, Jerry, 254

Cohen, Roger S., Jr., 139, 141, 189

CoinAge, 58, 151

Coinage of the Americas Conference, 27, 270

Coin Dealer Newsletter, 15, 39, 49, 54, 61, 108, 111, 146, 149, 150, 152, 243

Coin Galleries, 107

Coins magazine, 58

coin storage and distribution, 161

Coin World, 7, 8, 12, 15, 22, 46, 54, 58, 61, 66, 76, 85, 100, 103, 108, 111, 120, 128, 129, 141-148, 153, 156, 162, 181, 217, 238, 306

Coin World Almanac, The, 293

Collection Portfolio Program, 67

collections vs. accumulations, 37

Collins, Jack, 189, 235

colonial and early American coins, 185

Colonial Newsletter, The, 186

Colonial Newsletter Foundation, 186

commemoratives, 273, 304

commemorative silver coins, 273

commemorative gold coins, 277

common coins: advantages and disadvantages, 41

Comprehensive Catalogue and Encyclopedia of U.S. and Morgan Peace Dollars, 243

computer grading, 22

Comstock Lode, 11, 20, 53, 240

condition rarities, 26

Confederate States of America, 290, 298

connoisseurship, 16

Consumer Alert: Investing in Rare Coins, 70

Continental currency, 297

Continental currency "dollar," 185

Copley Coin Company, 288

copper and nickel coins, 185

Cosgarea, Andrew J., 163

counterstamped coins, 287

Criswell, Grover C., 291

Crosby, Sylvester S., 186

Cutler, Barry J., 81, 87, 91, 133

—— **D** ——

Dahlonega Mint, 20, 116

Dallas Life Magazine, 51

dampness, 176

dates of coins, 18

Davis, Charles, 293

Davis, David, 214

dealers' fixed prices, 154

dealing with dealers, 57

DeFrancisci, Mrs. Anthony, 246

Deisher, Beth, 22

denomination, 17

Denver Mint, 19, 116

design type, 20

determinants of value, 119

DiGenova, Silvano, 63

dimes (1796-1837), 214

direct purchases, 57

Dodson, Admiral Oscar H., 104

Douglass, Jennifer, 108

Dubosq, 280

Duffield, Frank, 287

Dumont, Cathy, 24

Dunham Collection, 110

Dunn, C. Frank, 275, 276

Dunn, John W., 123

Durst, Sanford, 36, 293

Dutch tulip bulb mania, 48

—— **E** ——

eagles (1795-1804), 265

Early American Cents, 125

Early American Coppers Club, 127, 189, 190

Early Coins of America, The, 186

Early Half Dollar Varieties 1794-1836, 228

Early Quarter Dollars of the United States 1796-1838, 223

Early U.S. Dimes 1796-1837, 214

Ehrmantraut, Jack Jr., 162, 233

Eisenhower dollars, 248

Eisenhower, Dwight D., 249

Elder, Thomas, 307

Eliasberg Collection, 43, 67, 101, 102, 205, 215, 260

Eliasberg, Louis, 28, 101, 102, 230, 270, 305, 306

elite recommendations, 182

Ellesmere Numismatics, 91

Emery-Nichols Collection, 222

Emery, S. Benton, 222

Encyclopedia of Liberty Seated Dimes 1837-1891, 216

experience, the value of, 154

—— **F** ——

face or metallic value, 121

Fantastic 1804 Dollar, The, 236

Fazzari, F. Michael, 127, 128

Federal Coin Exchange, 44

Federal Reserve, 161, 291

Federal Trade Commission, 59, 61, 70, 74, 80, 83-89, 93, 133

Flanagan, John, 304

Flying Eagle cents (1856-1858), 195

Foley, Kevin, 126, 132
Forbes Magazine, 297
Ford, John J., Jr., 23
Forman, Harry, 241, 246
Forty-Fort State Bank, 247
Foster, Stephen, 275
Franklin Collectors Society, 290
Franklin half dollars (1948-1963), 233
Franklin Mint, 121, 234, 289, 290
Fraser, James Earle, 20, 205
Fraser, Laura Gardin, 304
Free Soil Party, 288
Fugio Cents, The, 186
Fugio copper cents, 185
Fuld, George, 287
Fuld, Melvin, 287
Fuljenz, Michael, 293
Function Associates, 293

——— G ———

Ganz, David L. 73, 74, 100
Garrett Collection, 29, 99-102
Garrett, John Work, 28, 101
Garrett, T. Harrison, 23, 44, 100
Gasparro, Frank, 234, 249, 250
General Numismatics Corporation, 234
General Services Administration, 91, 161
generic coins, 131
Gilkes, Paul, 76
Gillilland, Cory, 271

Gobrecht, Christian, 213, 238
gold bullion coins, 284
gold coins, 253
Gold Coins of the World, 88
gold dollars (1849-1889), 253
Goldman, Kenneth, 65
Gold Rush, 258, 280, 300
"good fors," 287
Gould, Maurice, 287, 288
grade, 120
grade vs. price, 149
grading, 22, 123
grading services, 130
grading systems, 123, 125
Grady, Orville, 293
"greater fool theory," 45
Green, Col. E.H.R., 222
Guide Book of United States Coins, A, 15, 31, 44, 71, 111, 114, 154, 179, 202, 241, 247, 248, 256, 262, 274, 292
Guide to the Grading of United States Coins, A, 123, 156, 188
Gumpel, Mike, 151

——— H ———

half cents (1793-1857), 187
half dimes (1794-1837), 211
half disme (1792), 211
half dollars (1794-1839), 227
half eagles (1795-1838), 263
Hall, David, 76, 79, 80, 130, 221
Hallenbeck, Kenneth L., 287, 288

Hallmark Grading Service, 57, 58, 90, 108, 130, 132, 134

Halperin, James L., 82, 135, 136, 172

Hancock, Jack, 261

Hard Times tokens, 285, 286

Haseltine, John, 214, 228, 299

Hatie, George, 104

Hawn, Reed, 205

Hayes, Jimmy, 65

Hayes, Richard A., Ph.D., 139

Healey, Kelly, 75

Heaton, Augustus G., 254

Helfenstein, Louis, collection, 193

Herbert, Alan, 128

Heritage, 105

Herst, Herman, Jr., 64

Heath, George F., 52

Highfill, John, 244

High Profits from Rare Coin Investment, 43, 246

Higley, John, 19

Higley, Dr. Samuel, 185

Historic Sketch of the Coins of New Jersey, A, 186

history of grading, the, 123

History of U.S. Coinage as Illustrated by the Garrett Collection, 100

Hodder, Michael, 26, 27, 108, 130, 286

Holden, Albert Fairchild, 102

Holloway, Greg, 73

Houdon, Jean Antoine, 226

how coins are made, 113

how to buy at auction, 105

how to buy in mail bid sales, 110

How to Grade U.S. Coins, 135

Humpty Dumpty, 48

—— I ——

Indian cents (1859-1909), 197

Indian eagles (1907-1933), 266

Indian half eagles (1908-1929), 264

Indian quarter eagles (1908-1929), 259

International Numismatic Service (INS), 130

investment, 183, 304, 305

Investor's Guide to Coin Trading, The, 59

Ivy, Steve, 172

—— J ——

Jackson, Andrew, 286

Jefferson nickels (1938 to date), 207

Jefferson, Thomas, 207

Jesus Christ, 297

John Reich Collectors Society, 214

Johns Hopkins University, The, 99, 100, 305

Johnson, Toivo, 139

Jones, Elizabeth, 278

Judd, Dr. J. Hewitt, 280

Julian, Robert W., 238, 244

J.W. Scott & Company, 276

—— **K** ——

Kagin, Art, 99

Kagin, Don, 99

Karstedt, Chris, 108, 109

Kasson, Hon. John A., 262

Katen, Frank, 293

Katen, Laurese, 293

Kaufmann, Dr. Abraham, 37

Kellogg, 280, 301

Kennedy half dollars (1964 to date), 234

Kennedy, John F., 88

Kessler, Alan, 186

Kidder, Peabody & Co., 44, 46, 73, 78, 85, 93

King Farouk Collection, 189, 270

King of Siam, 164, 237

Kingston National Bank, 247

Kingswood Galleries, 9, 107, 109, 111

KoinTains, 177

Kolbe, George F., 293

Kolman, Michael Jr., 44

Kosoff, Abe, 96, 120, 123, 204, 214, 221, 243, 305

Krause Publications, 36

Kreisberg, Abner, 214, 254

krugerrand, 284

Kruzell, Russell, 129

—— **L** ——

Lady Godiva, 300

Lafayette dollar, 273

large cents (1793-1857)

Lassiter, Cynthia, 109

Lee, Ed, 129

Lee Certified Coins, Ltd., 129

Lehmann, Robert, 147

Leidman, Julian, 49, 51

Leopold the Hogmouth, 296

Liberty Head double eagles (1850-1907), 268

Liberty Head eagles (1838-1907), 266

Liberty Head half eagles (1839-1908), 264

Liberty Head nickels (1883-1913), 204

Liberty Head quarter eagles (1840-1907), 258

Liberty Seated Collectors Club, 221, 224

Liberty Seated dimes (1837-1891), 215

Liberty Seated dollars (1836-1873), 238

Liberty Seated half dimes (1837-1873), 213

Liberty Seated half dollars (1839-1891), 229

Liberty Seated quarters (1838-1891), 223

Liberty Walking half dollars (1916-1947), 232

Lilljedahl, Lee, 97

Lincoln cents (1909 to date), 198

Littleton Coin Company, 51, 250

Lipton, Kevin, 44, 93

Long, Dennis Irving, 65

Longacre, James B., 21, 32, 195, 268

Los Angeles Times, The, 81

Lovett, George, 299

Low, Lyman H., 285

Lowell, James Russell, 145

Lutzky, Hal, 61

—— **M** ——————————

Macallister, James, 222

MacArthur, Diane, 108

MacIntosh, H.E., 216

MacNeil, Hermon A., 20, 33, 225, 304

mail bid sales, 107

Maine Antique Digest, The, 7

Mallis, A. George, 243

Maple Leaf, 284

Marion, John, 13

"market grade," 169

marks acquired after a coin is struck, 160

Marner, Silas, 37

Maris, Dr. Edward, 21, 186

Massachusetts Historical Society, 24

Massachusetts silver, 185

McKee, Art, 307

Medallic Art Company, 289

Medallic Portraits of Washington, 186

medals, 289

Mehl, B. Max, 104, 109, 205, 236,

237, 242, 250, 273, 295, 297

Melish Collection, 305

Melish, Thomas G., 274

Melnick, Herbert, 13, 98, 99

Mendelson, Mark, 49, 51

Mercanti, John, 284

Mercury dimes (1916-1945), 218

Merena, Raymond, 65, 108, 293

Merkin, Lester, 193, 222

Merrill Lynch, 46, 85

Metcalf, William, 270

Mickley, Joseph J., 223

Mid-American Rare Coin Galleries, 105, 107

Miller, Henry C., 14, 86

Miner's Bank, 280, 301

Miner's National Bank, 247

mint, 19

Mint Cabinet, 196, 237

Mint Marks, 254

mints and minting, 113

Mint State coins, 162

Mishler, Clifford, 293

modern commemorative issues, 278

Moffat & Company, 180, 301

Money Tree, 293

Morgan dollars (1878-1921), 240

Morgan, George T., 15, 32, 40, 240, 262, 302

Morgan Guaranty Trust Company, 96

Morgan, J.P., 24

Mormons, 281

Morris, Gouverneur, 186

Morse, Phoebe, 59, 80, 93

motivation, 29

MTB Banking Corporation, 103

Murray, Col. William, 293

—— N ——

National Coin Collection, 173

National Collection, 263

National Currency Bureau, 298

National Numismatic Collection, 102, 295

National Silver Dollar Roundtable, 121, 243

Newcomb, Howard R., 190

New England Rare Coin Galleries, 82

Newman, Eric P., 186, 236

New Orleans Mint, 19, 115, 299

New York City Public Library, 104

New York Numismatic Club, 307

New York Times, The, 103, 173, 216

Nevada State Museum, 116

Nichols, Walter P., 222

nickel three-cent pieces (1865-1889), 201

Niles Register, 257, 302

Nixon, Richard, 91

Noe, Sydney P., 186

North, Dr. Gary, 76

Norweb, Ambassador, 102, 103

Norweb, Mrs. R. Henry (Emery Mae), 28, 102, 103, 305

Norweb, R. Henry, Jr., 103

Norweb, Libby, 103

Norweb Collection, 175, 228, 244

Norweb family, 305

Norweb, Mrs. Henry (Libby), 28, 102, 103, 305

Numismatic Bibliomania Society, 60, 293

numismatic books, 292

Numismatic Certification Institute (NCI), 85, 130, 136

Numismatic Gallery, 214

Numismatic Guaranty Corporation (NGC), 23, 57, 77, 79, 90, 108, 130, 132, 134, 136, 137, 139, 145-147, 155, 156, 164, 165

Numismatic Literary Guild, 97, 293

Numismatic Literary Society, 216

Numismatic News, 7, 8, 13, 15, 54, 58, 61, 66, 75, 103, 108, 111, 127, 128, 148, 154, 156, 163, 164, 233, 244

Numismatic Scrapbook Magazine, The, 15, 171

Numismatist, The, 15, 52, 71, 123, 125, 148, 171, 173, 236, 248

—— O ——

Obojski, Robert 293

Office of Gold and Silver Operations, 88

Official ANA Grading Standards for U.S. Coins, 123, 151, 157, 169

Olympic Games, 278

opportunities for the collector-investor, 35

Oregon Trail half dollars, 276

Orosz, Dr. Joel, 60

Overton, Al C., 21, 139, 228

——— P ———

Pacific Coast Auction Galleries, 105

Panama-Pacific International Exposition, 296

Panic of 1837, 188, 297

paper money, 290

Parker, Dorothy, 16

pattern coins, 279

Paul, Martin, 213

PCI, 134

Peace dollars (1921-1935), 245

Pearlman, Donn, 28, 120, 147

pedigree, 25

Pennington, Samuel C., 7

Penny Whimsy, 174, 190, 292

Penny-Wise, 127

Philadelphia Mint, 21, 114, 173, 211, 289, 298, 303

Photo-Certified Coin Institute, 130

Photograde, 123, 169, 172, 174

Pittman Act, 39, 241

Pittman, John Jay, 99, 293

Plaza Hotel, 303

Pollock, Andrew W. III, 108, 292

polyvinyl chloride (PVC), 176

Pope, Donna, 91, 278

popularity, 119

population reports, 155

Pratt, Bela Lyon, 259, 303

"premium quality," 58, 137

price, 24

Professional Coin Grading Service (PCGS), 22, 57, 76, 77, 80, 84-86, 90, 108, 121, 130, 132, 134, 136, 137, 139, 145-147, 155, 156, 164, 165

Professional Numismatists Guild (PNG), 8, 51, 61, 87, 89, 90

Proof coins, 162, 281, 282, 283, 298

prooflike coins, 165

public auctions, 95

publicity and promotion, 121

purchase recommendations, 179

——— Q ———

Quagliana, Edwin V., 293

quantity and quality, 43

quarters (1796-1838), 221

quarter dollars (1796 to date), 221

quarter eagles (1796-1839), 255

——— R ———

Rare Coin Galleries of America (RARCOA), 59, 60, 105

Rare Coin Review, 141, 238, 308

Rare Coins of Georgia, 84

rare coins: advantages and disadvantages, 41

rarity, 25

Raymond, Wayte, 188, 228, 276, 307

Reagan, Ronald, 289

recommendations for the connoisseur, 180

Redfield, LaVere, 44

Register of United States Half Dollar Varieties and Sub-Varieties, 228-229

Reich, John, 212

Reiter, Ed, 216

Rexford, Peter M., 293

Roberts, Gilroy, 234

Robinson, Frank S., 46

Rochette, Ed, 293, 296

Rogak, Lawrence N., 129

rolls of coins, 283

Romano, Don Corrado, 44

Rome, Bernard, 107

Roosevelt dimes (1946 to date), 219

Roosevelt, Franklin Delano, 33, 219

Roosevelt, Theodore, 53, 266, 302, 303

Rosa Americana issues, 185

Rosen, Maurice, 77, 145

Rosen Numismatic Advisory, 7, 145

Rossa & Tanenbaum, 288

Rothert, Matt, 104

Rowe, Si, 287

Roxbury Coaches, 286, 287

Royal Canadian Mint, 163

Ruddy, James F., 102, 123, 172, 239, 290

Ruggles, L., 144

Rulau, Russell, 285, 287

Ryder, Hillyer C., 14, 186

—— S ——

Saint-Gaudens, Augustus, 20, 32, 246, 259, 266, 270, 302, 303, 304

Saint-Gaudens double eagles (1907-1933), 270

Salomon Brothers, 73-75, 82, 85

Salyards, Harry E., M.D., 127

San Francisco Mint, 19, 116

Schilke, Oscar G., 307

Schlag, Felix, 207

Schoen, Nat, 44

Schultz, Norman, 241

Schulyler, Philip, 91, 144

Sconyers, Hugh, 44, 78, 79, 93

Scott, J.W., 105

Scrooge McDuck, 37

Second National Bank, 247

Securities and Exchange Commission (SEC), 86-88

Security Rare Coin, 81, 83, 84

Segel, Joseph, 234, 290

selecting a fund or partnership, 92

Sewall, Judge Samuel, 53

sharpness or weakness of strike, 167

Shattuck, Dr. William P., 288

Sheldon, M. Vernon, 104

Sheldon, Dr. William H., 125, 139,

174, 190, 308

Sheldon grading system, 81

Sherman Monument, 303

Shield nickels, 203

silver coins, 209

silver dollars (1794-1804), 234

silver three-cent coins (1851-1873), 209

Sinnock, John, 219

Sipe, Arthur, 104

slabbed coins, 12, 36, 69, 80, 91, 130

Smithsonian Institution, 103, 263, 271, 295, 302

Society of Lincoln cent collectors, 128

Sotheby's, 13

sources of pricing information, 151

Specialty Books, 36

Sphinx, 17

Spirit of Liberty, 250

S.S. Central America, 268, 269

St. George, 300

Stack, Harvey, 87, 307

Stack, Norman, 261, 307

Stack's, 43, 51, 65, 105

Standard Catalogue of U.S. Coins, 123

Standing Liberty Quarters, 226

Standing Liberty quarters (1916-1930), 225

Star Rare Coin Encyclopedia, 205

State Coinages of New England, The, 14, 186

Stellas (1879-1880), 262

Stevenson, Jed, 173

Steve's Coney Island, 119

storage, display, and handling, 175

Sundman, Rick, 250

Superior Galleries, 105, 205

surface characteristics, 157

Sussex Collection, 97, 244

Swiatek, Anthony, 273

—— T ——

TAMS Journal, 285

Tangible Investments of America, 63

Tatham Stamp & Coin Company, 216

Taxay, Don, 196, 273

Taylor, Elizabeth, 296

Taylor, Frederick W., 16

Taylor, Jim, 81

Taylor, Sol, 128

Taylor, Zachary, 288

Teletrade, 107

Thorne, Michael, 293

three-dollar gold pieces (1854-1889), 260

Todd, Frank Morton, 296

Token and Medal Society, 285

tokens, 285

Trade dollars (1873-1885), 251

Travers, Scott, 59, 78, 79, 293

Treasury Department, 32, 34, 91, 207, 227, 239, 242, 248, 249,

268, 270, 273, 284

Tripp, David, 105

Tripp, Susan, 105

Trotter, P.B. Jr., 44

Tulving, Hannes, 83

Twain, Mark, 11

twenty-cent pieces (1875-1878), 220

two-cent pieces (1864-1873), 200

Type Table of United States Dollars, Half Dollars, and Quarter Dollars, 214, 228

—— U ——

ultimate consumer, 45

United States Assay Office of Gold, 280

United States Copper Coins 1816-1857, 190

United States Silver Dollars from 1794 to 1803, The, 237, 238

United States Pattern, Experimental and Trial Pieces, 280

U.S. Gold Coin Collection, The, 102

U.S. Gold Coins: An Illustrated History, 292

U.S. Mint, 163

U.S. Mint and Coinage, 196

—— V ——

Van Allen, Leroy C., 243

Van Buren, Martin, 288

Vandervort, Dan, 141

variety, 20

Vernon, Admiral, 300

VOTE THE LAND FREE, 287, 288, 292

—— W ——

Wall Street, 46, 73, 74, 76-78, 80, 81, 83, 85, 86, 90-93

Wall Street Journal, The, 80, 85, 257

Wallace, R.E., 51

Walter Breen's Encyclopedia of United States Half Cents 1793-1857, 27, 189

Walter Breen's Encyclopedia of Colonial and United States Proof Coins 1722-1989, 262, 282

Washington, George, 105, 114, 185, 186, 192, 211

Washington and Columbia medal, 23, 24

Washington-Lafayette counterstamp, 301

Washington quarters (1932 to date), 226

Wass, Molitor & Co., 301

Watson, Gail, 67

ways to buy, 57

Weinman, Adolph A., 20, 33-34, 218, 232, 284, 304

West Point Mint, 117

Whitman Publishing Company, 199

Wilhite, Bob, 62, 154

Wilkins, Dr. G.G., 287

Whitman Coin Products, 36

William Forrester Dunham Collection, 242

Williams, Anna, 15, 240

Williams, George P., 247

Wilson, Cal, 293

Winning Edge, The, 91

Wolfeboro National Bank, 291

Wood, William, 185

Woodruff, Andrew, 146

"World's Greatest Collection, The," 214

Worthy Coin Company, 44

— Z —

Zaner, Keith, 62, 76, 153, 181, 217, 306

Zeddies Collection, Michael B., 286

Zerbe, Farran, 173, 296